A BOOK IN THE SERIES
Latin America Otherwise:
Languages, Empires, Nations

SERIES EDITORS:
Walter D. Mignolo, Duke University
Irene Silverblatt, Duke University
Sonia Saldívar-Hull, University of Texas,
San Antonio

AGAINST WAR

VIEWS
FROM THE
UNDERSIDE
OF MODERNITY

NELSON MALDONADO-TORRES

DUKE UNIVERSITY PRESS • DURHAM & LONDON 2008

© 2008
Duke University Press
All rights reserved

Designed by Katy Clove
Typeset in Scala by Tseng Information Systems, Inc.
Library of Congress Cataloging-in-Publication
Data appear on the last
printed page of this book.

To recognize with philosophy—or to recognize philosophically—that the real is the rational and the rational is alone real, and not to be able to smother or cover over the cry of those who, the morrow after this recognition, mean to transform the world is already to move in a domain of meaning which the inclusion cannot comprehend and among reasons that "reason" does not know, and which have not begun in philosophy. . . .
—EMMANUEL LEVINAS, "GOD AND PHILOSOPHY"

The tragedy faced by anyone seriously engaged in struggle against the institutional encouragement of dehumanization is that institutionalized dehumanization is fundamentally a state of war. . . . To see colonialism and racism clearly is to see that where such conceptions of reality reign, there is a shift in the presuppositions of justice and fairness that may have operated within traditional mores and folkways.
—LEWIS R. GORDON, *FANON AND THE CRISIS OF EUROPEAN MAN*

CONTENTS

About the Series • ix
Preface • xi
Abbreviations of Frequently Cited Titles • xvii
Introduction: Western Modernity and the Paradigm of War • 1

PART I   **SEARCHING FOR ETHICS IN A VIOLENT WORLD:**
         A JEWISH RESPONSE TO THE PARADIGM OF WAR
   1. From Liberalism to Hitlerism: Tracing the Origins
      of Violence and War • 23
   2. From Fraternity to Altericity, or Reason
      in the Service of Love • 51

PART II **OF MASTERS AND SLAVES, OR FRANTZ FANON AND THE ETHICO-POLITICAL**
         STRUGGLE FOR NON-SEXIST HUMAN FRATERNITY
   3. God and the Other in the Self-Recognition
      of Imperial Man • 93
   4. Recognition from Below: The Meaning of the Cry
      and the Gift of the Self in the Struggle for Recognition • 122

PART III **FROM THE ETHICAL TO THE GEOPOLITICAL: A LATIN AMERICAN**
         RESPONSE TO COLONIALITY, NEOLIBERAL GLOBALIZATION, AND WAR
   5. Enrique Dussel's Ethics and Philosophy of Liberation • 163
   6. Enrique Dussel's Contribution to the De-colonial Turn:
      From the Critique of Modernity to Transmodernity • 187
      Conclusion: Beyond the Paradigm of War • 237
      Notes • 255
      Bibliography • 313
      Index • 335

ABOUT THE SERIES

Latin America Otherwise: Languages, Empires, Nations is a critical series. It aims to explore the emergence and consequences of concepts used to define "Latin America" while at the same time exploring the broad interplay of political, economic, and cultural practices that have shaped Latin American worlds. Latin America, at the crossroads of competing imperial designs and local responses, has been construed as a geocultural and geopolitical entity since the nineteenth century. This series provides a starting point to redefine Latin America as a configuration of political, linguistic, cultural, and economic intersections that demands a continuous reappraisal of the role of the Americas in history and of the ongoing process of globalization and the relocation of people and cultures that have characterized Latin America's experience. *Latin America Otherwise: Languages, Empires, Nations* is a forum that confronts established geocultural constructions, rethinks area studies and disciplinary boundaries, assesses convictions of the academy and of public policy, and correspondingly demands that the practices through which we produce knowledge and understanding about and from Latin America be subject to rigorous and critical scrutiny.

Against War argues that European modernity has become inextricably linked with the experience of the warrior and conqueror, and that contemporary civilization, racism, and other forms of social and geopolitical dynamics in the modern world can best be understood in terms of the idea that war, as Nietzsche affirmed, is the natural state of things. This paradigm of war, Maldonado-Torres shows, conceives humanity, knowledge, and social relations in such a way so as to privilege conflict as a means to create order. Against this paradigm and to offer an alternative to it, Maldonado-Torres asserts the viability of subaltern perspectives and secular/religious thought that he gathers from Jewish, black, and Latin American voices epitomized in the work of three philosophers: Emmanuel Levinas, Frantz Fanon, and Enrique Dussel.

Certainly many thinkers have addressed the challenges to Western philosophy and political theory posed by two world wars and the Jewish Holocaust, but *Against War* shifts the terrain of this critique by exploring connections among colonialism, racism, war, and genocide in the long history of European modernity. The book is divided into three parts. The first focuses on elucidating a "master morality" of dominion and control at the heart of racial policies, imperial projects, and wars of invasion—a perspective centered on Levinas's notion of the self in Judaic ethics within the context of French liberalism and Nazi racial politics. In the second part, Maldonado-Torres turns to Fanon, first to refine the diagnosis of modernity's war paradigm via Fanon's phenomenology of the colonized and racial self, and second through a Levinasian interpretation of Fanon and a Fanonian critique of Levinas, which leads Maldonado-Torres to formulate an ethical conception of subjectivity and de-colonial praxis as consistent responses to the perversities of European modernity. Finally, in the third section, Maldonado-Torres uses Dussel to provide a genealogy of the modern imperial and warring self, and he ultimately offers a theorization of race as a naturalization of the death ethic of war.

Against War constitutes an important intervention in critical theory, critical race theory, area studies, and postcolonial thought. Its analysis of the unfinished projects of de-colonialization and deracialization contributes concepts intended to help undo the legacy of colonialism, racism, and war in the contemporary world.

PREFACE

Even though this book was first conceived several years ago, its publication might be more timely now than at any time in the recent past. Humanity witnesses today the utter failure of the most recent military adventure of the world's most powerful nation, and U.S. Americans among others are more prone to reflect now on the way in which discourses of liberty and freedom often go hand in hand with deception and murder. This tie is not only one manipulated by politicians, but it sometimes seems to strike a chord in the public at large as well, particularly when the connection passes as if it were inevitable, natural, or even just. The link between the apparent defense of liberty and freedom, on the one hand, and annihilation, on the other, sometimes even seems like the "stuff" out of which media pundits fuel their diatribes, which cover not only the topic of "Islamic terrorism" but also that of the supposed challenges and menaces that normative identities, allegedly constituted by the highest principles of Christianity, liberalism, and modern republicanism, face today. All of this takes place while traditional victims of modern nation-states' projects and global economics (the indigenous, the black, and nature itself, along with all "deviant," "abnormal," and "suspicious" subjectivities and "empty" or "insignificant" geopolitical spaces) continue suffering in disproportionate form from their "negative effects" and from what often appear as their necessary consequences.

This book is a theoretical analysis of what could be considered as the darkest side of Western modernity, which is found in the naturalization of war.[1] The naturalization of war refers to the radical suspension or displacement of ethical and political relationships in favor of the propagation of a peculiar death ethic that renders massacre and different forms of genocide as natural. Steve Martinot has used the term "death ethic of war" to denote a characteristic feature of U.S. society that is tied not only to war, but to a set of practices and values that extend across war, including the prison industry and the death penalty.[2] The meaning that I give to the concept is related, but it is somewhat different in that I refer with it to the constitutive character of coloniality and the naturalization of human difference that is tied to it in the emergence and unfolding of Western modernity. I also relate it to massacre, instead of solely to sacrifice, following Tzvetan Todorov's discussion of this topic in *The Conquest of America*, to the production of "hell," and the zone of non-being of which Frantz Fanon speaks about in *Black Skin, White Masks*[3] and to "man-made mass death" or death-world that Edith Wyschograd theorizes. In this book I alternate the use of "death ethic of war" with the idea of "non-ethics of war," which refers to the suspension of what usually goes by ethics not only in war, but in civilization. It is this suspension that allows the production of premature death to become normative, at least for well-selected sectors in society and in the globe.

In this sense, the naturalization of war does not simply refer to the continuous exercise of war. As I employ the term here, the naturalization of war involves a qualitative change that makes even ordinary life take the form of a selective suspension, or even a reversal of ethics as normally understood. This suspension is premised on ideas of natural difference that render some subjects or populations not only dispensable but excessive and necessarily *eliminable*. The naturalization of war is, thus, intimately linked with what Sylvia Wynter has called the denial of "co-humanness" (and not simply the "denial of coevalness" as the anthropologist Johannes Fabian has it in his influential formulation), which refers to discourses and practices of racialization and their many combinations with other forms of difference.[4] The naturalization of war, as the darkest side of Western modernity, and the death ethic that is part of it find their most radical expressions in the relations between those who appear to be naturally selected to survive and flourish and others who appear to be, according to the dominant narratives of modernity, either biologically or culturally decrepit.

Even though this book is theoretical, and therefore abstract, the problems that it seeks to diagnose are very much concrete and real. The arguments in the book are articulated in conversation with the work of intellectuals trained in Western thought, but whose exposure to grave historical circumstances and tragedies led them to become skeptic of the West's promises of equality and freedom. I build on the works of a Jewish philosopher, a black theorist, and a Latin American intellectual to exploit the potential of "subaltern" views that provide important diagnoses of our contemporary reality and that help to provide solutions to them. So-called subaltern views are not the only ones that provide useful approaches to understanding reality, but contrary to what most books and curricula in our universities make appear, they are truly indispensable. It should be clear, though, that by a subaltern view (or better a subalter view) I do not have in mind purely a situation or context, but memories and projects that do not belong solely or essentially to any one ethnic group and that can be shared. Subalter memories are memories of suffering and displacement, but also of happiness and hope in the midst of challenges to human existence by repressive and inhumane social orders. Subalter projects of decolonization and liberation refer to forms of resistance and transformation that seek to undo dehumanizing practices and the suffering that ensues from them. I hope that this book contributes to a better understanding of the depth, reach, and significance of these memories and projects.

To be sure, a book of this nature, which combines a wide variety of academic disciplines, cannot by any means pretend to provide a response to every problem linked to the influence of warring ideals in Western civilization or provide a recipe of how to overcome them. No book can provide all of the answers, or even necessarily provide the answers that it offers in an idiom or language in which all of the people affected by the problem treated can immediately understand. This is less of a problem once one recognizes that the fabric of common sense was not completely designed using common-sense terms and ideas. Thus, a radical confrontation with the fundamental presuppositions of common sense as well as the fabrication of new forms of conceiving ourselves and others require technical vocabularies. But technical vocabularies alone will not do anything, even less if they purposely disconnect from social and political struggles or from voices of critique and transformation that emerge in popular culture and other cultural spheres. While this book is mainly theoretical it is rooted in history and inspired by voices of protest and creation that have shaken the entire world and given new hope to those whom Frantz Fanon called *les damnés de la terre*. I seek to connect and build on ideas that are usually separated in established intellectual genealogies with the hope of contributing to the opening of new avenues of thought that further promote alternatives to a pervasive, because naturalized, paradigm of war. The reader should not lose track of this aspect of the book.

The final shape of this book is the outcome of necessity and contingency. It is the outcome of necessity insofar as it expresses a profound and long-lasting interest of mine in questions regarding the *malaise* of Western modernity, radical philosophies, religious thought, ethics, and the politics of liberation. It is the result of contingency in that it would not have come into being without a number of at least partly fortuitous coincidences that involve a number of people and events. It is those coincidences that make me particularly grateful inasmuch as they occurred or were sustained partly through choice and effort, but to a great extent also by the generosity of others. My first expression of thanks goes to Lewis R. Gordon, whose friendship and support have been invaluable in the last decade. I owe to him a great deal of my understanding of Frantz Fanon, the significance of the problem of the color line in modernity, and knowledge of the contribution of thinkers from the West and the African Diaspora to the project of decolonizing epistemologies and forging new sciences of the human. I also owe deep gratitude to Enrique D. Dussel for his utmost generosity, openness, and kindness from the very first day that we met, to my first days in Mexico City, where I went to study with him, to today. I am also thankful for my teachers at the University of Puerto Rico and at Brown University for their dedication and serious work. The department of philosophy at the University of Puerto Rico provided me with a strong foundation in philosophy that parallels that of anyone whom I have met in the United States wherever I have moved. The department of religious studies at Brown, where I studied modern and contemporary philosophy and religious thought, provided a unique environment to explore questions at the intersection of philosophy and religion. I am particularly thankful to Wendell S. Dietrich, with whom I studied Levinas, and to John P. Reeder and Sumner B. Twiss for their valuable insights on religious ethics, hermeneutics, and Kierkegaard.

While at Brown, I received Ford Foundation grants that allowed me to take courses in philosophy and Africana studies at Brown and in philosophy at Harvard University, do research in New York City and Mexico, and collect materials in libraries in Europe, particularly Belgium, France, and Spain. The experience and knowledge obtained contributed in many ways to the arguments in this book. I am grateful to the Ford Foundation for that. I would also like to express gratitude for the help of librarians at the Centre d'Études Phénoménologiques at the Catholic University of Louvain-la-Neuve in Belgium, the Universidad Complutense in Madrid, and the Colegio de México and the Universidad Nacional Autónoma de México in Mexico City. Among the countless list of persons who contributed to the ideas that appear in this book or who inspired me in the process of writing it, I would have to highlight Barbara Sproul from Hunter College (CUNY) for her support during my brief stay there and for her strong commitment to education in general and to my education in particular even after I was no longer in New York. Many others should be named as well, including former colleagues in the religion department at Duke University, particularly those in the area of religion and modernity when I was there, namely, Richard Jaffe, Wesley Kort, Bruce Lawrence, and Ebrahim Moosa. I also benefited greatly from discussions with every single one of the fellow members in the Dialogical Ethics and Critical Cosmopolitanism collective, led by the very generous and vibrant scholars Walter D. Mignolo and Romand Coles under the auspices of the Center for Global Studies in the Humanities at Duke's John Hope Franklin Center. Thanks are also due to the discussion group in theology and politics for inviting me to share in so many intimate and fascinating conversations. They were Richenel Ansano, Teresa Berger, William Hart, Mary McClintock-Fulkerson, Kathy Rudy, Susan Thorne, and Maurice Wallace.[5] At Duke, I must express thanks to Amy Laura Hall, Stanley Hauerwas, Janice Radway, and Antonio Viego with whom I had several pleasant conversations about common interests that relate to this book.

While *Against War* is unthinkable without my preparation in philosophy and religious thought, the real inspiration and its most fundamental locus is the set of approaches that emerged in the heat of political, symbolic, and epistemological struggles at the end of the 1960s and the early 1970s. In most parts today these epistemic sites go by the names of Africana Studies, Ethnic Studies, and Women's Studies. While fields such as sociology, history, and literary and cultural studies have been dominant in these departments, there is also ample work in theory, philosophy, and religious thought that is guided by the same basic epistemic and political coordinates. This book is decidedly one of them. To that extent, I feel fortunate to teach in an ethnic studies department and to interact with colleagues and students who share so many of the same questions and concerns. I thank all of them for their support and comradeship, including various colleagues in other departments, especially African American studies and Spanish and Portuguese. I also thank all of the participants in the Critical Theory Initiative at the University of California, Berkeley, which was led by Judith Butler and Martin Jay. The weekly discussions with them proved important for some of the arguments in this book.

There are two other organizations or collectives that have informed this book tremendously. They are the Caribbean Philosophical Association and the Modernity/Coloniality Collective. They represent two different but related epistemological projects focused on the primordial ethico-political imperative of de-colonization. I thank all of the members and participants, particularly those with whom I have had the pleasure to talk about my work or who have given me feedback. There is one scholar who is connected in different ways with these two collectives and who has been of great inspiration to many of us. I thank Sylvia Wynter for her generosity with her work and for opening up an exciting path of thinking to which this work is very much related.

Finally, I wish to thank all of my family, especially my mother, Carmen, and my grandmother, Filomena, as well as my extended family in the last fifteen years—my in-laws—for their support. Above all, I thank my wife, Celinés, for her continued love and motivation through so many adventures, as well as for valuable input to a wide variety of my intellectual projects. I dedicate this book to her.

ABBREVIATIONS OF FREQUENTLY CITED TITLES

EMMANUEL LEVINAS

DF   *Difficult Freedom: Essays in Judaism.* Translated by Seán Hand. Baltimore: Johns Hopkins University Press, 1990.
OB   *Otherwise Than Being or, Beyond Essence.* Translated by Alphonso Lingis. Pittsburgh: Duquesne University Press, 1998.
RPH "Reflections on the Philosophy of Hitlerism." Translated by Seán Hand. *Critical Inquiry* 17 (1990): 63–71.
TI   *Totality and Infinity: An Essay on Exteriority.* Translated by Alphonso Lingis. Pittsburgh: Duquesne University Press, 1969.

FRANTZ FANON

BSWM *Black Skin, White Masks.* Translated by Charles Lam Markmann. New York: Grove Press, 1968.
WE   *The Wretched of the Earth.* Translated by Constance Farrington. New York: Grove Press, 1991.

ENRIQUE DUSSEL

PL   *Philosophy of Liberation.* Translated by Aquilina Martinez and Christine Morkovsky. Maryknoll, N.Y.: Orbis Books, 1985.

INTRODUCTION
WESTERN MODERNITY
AND THE PARADIGM OF WAR

There were seventy of us in a forestry commando unit for Jewish prisoners of war in Nazi Germany. An extraordinary coincidence was the fact that the camp bore the number 1492, the year of the expulsion of the Jews from Spain under the Catholic Ferdinand V. The French uniform still protected us from Hitlerian violence. But the other men, called free, who had dealings with us or gave us work or orders or even a smile—and the children and women who passed by and sometimes raised their eyes—stripped us of our human skin. We were subhuman, a gang of apes. A small inner murmur, the strength and wretchedness of persecuted people, reminded us of our essence as thinking creatures, but we were no longer part of the world. . . . We were beings entrapped in their species; despite all their vocabulary, beings without language. —EMMANUEL LEVINAS[1]

"Dirty nigger!" Or simply, "Look, a Negro!"
 I came into the world imbued with the will to find a meaning in things, my spirit filled with the desire to attain to the source of the world, and then I found that I was an object in the midst of other objects.
 Sealed into that crushing objecthood, I turned beseechingly to others. Their attention was a liberation, running over my body suddenly abraded into nonbeing, endowing me once more with an agility that I had thought lost, and by taking me out of the world, restoring me to it. But just as I reached the other side, I stumbled, and the movements, the attitudes, the glances of the other fixed me there, in the sense in which a chemical solution is fixed by a dye. I was indignant; I demanded an explanation. Nothing happened. I burst apart. Now the fragments have been put together again by another self. —FRANTZ FANON[2]

The German philosopher Friedrich Nietzsche once asserted that "the normal state of things is *war*" and that "man is by nature destined to only want peace rarely and for brief periods."[3] The history of the twentieth century and already the beginning of the twenty-first would no doubt seem to provide evidence to Nietzsche's dictum. In less than one hundred years we have seen two world wars, the Jewish Holocaust, wars of decolonization throughout the globe, a sinister cold war with dark tensions and perverse repercussions in the emerging postcolonial world, guerrilla wars in Latin America and elsewhere, ethnic cleansing, and the current war against terror, among other terrifying conflicts in the world. Are these isolated phenomena or exceptions from our glorious modernity? The figures whose work I examine here do not believe that, but they do not accept the idea that war is a normal state of humanity either. On the contrary, their work helps us to determine first the roots of violence in the modern world, and second, whether or not human beings could reasonably aspire to peaceful modes of coexistence. *Against War* is a critical intervention in this context that seeks to illustrate the contributions of subaltern perspectives and religious thought to the overcoming of a widespread and influential Western paradigm of war.

This book focuses on responses to Western modernity from the perspective of subjects who inhabit its underside, particularly Jewish, black, and Latin American voices. I take as a point of departure the works of the Lithuanian-born French-Jewish philosopher and religious thinker Emmanuel Levinas, the Martiniquean psychiatrist and political thinker Frantz Fanon, and the Catholic Argentinean-Mexican philosopher, historian, and theologian Enrique Dussel. The diagnosis of modernity and the responses to it offered in this book are elaborated through the critical analysis of the thought of these figures and through the creative construction of ideas at the intersection of their work. I approach Levinas's, Fanon's, and Dussel's contributions to critical theorizing in terms of a de-colonial hermeneutics of suspicion that also involves a constructive and unapologetic effort to articulate a new humanism. Their work complements as it also provides alternatives to the ideas and approaches of the celebrated Western masters of suspicions: Marx, Nietzsche, and Freud. Different from them, Levinas, Fanon, and Dussel respond to Western ideals of the human from the critical perspective of racialized and colonized peoples. Imperial violence and racism become for them the loci where ideals of war more persistently endure. These ideals are embedded in what I refer to in this work as a master morality of dominion and control that can be found at the core of racial policies, imperial projects, and wars of invasion. It is this master morality, and not particularly a slave morality, class struggle, or repressed desires, that becomes the main object of critique for the critical theory that emerges at the intersection of Levinas's, Fanon's, and Dussel's work. This change of focus does not render Marx's, Nietzsche's, or Freud's contributions to the critical analysis of modern society necessarily invalid, but offers a unique horizon for their critical evaluation and possible appropriation.

In modernity, geopolitical space, intersubjective relations, economic activity, and the production of knowledge form a nexus of power oriented by imperatives of domination and control that mirror the logic of a division between masters and slaves. The result is a colonial order of the world, which is arguably seeing today its most radical global expression. The present configuration of power began to take a global form more than five hundred years ago. For 1492 is not only the number of the camp in which Levinas and others were imprisoned by the Nazis, or the year in which Jews and Muslims were expelled from Spain; 1492 is also the year in which the conquest and colonization of the Americas began and the moment to which one can trace the emergence of a firm imperial Europe conceiving itself as the center of the whole world and as the telos of civilization. Modern anti-Semitism, modern anti-black racism, and modern colonialism find a common historical referent in the end of the Spanish *reconquista* and the beginnings of a new form of conquest in the Americas. The year 1492 is a crucial point for understanding the constitution of the episteme and social order that I define here as a paradigm of war.

By a paradigm of war I mean a way of conceiving humanity, knowledge, and social relations that privileges conflict or *polemos*. Enrique Dussel puts it in a most explicit and dramatic form:

> From Heraclitus to Karl von Clausewitz and Henry Kissinger, "war is the origin of everything," if by "everything" one understands the order or system that world dominators control by their power and armies. We are at war—a cold war for those who wage it, a hot war for those who suffer it. . . . Space as a battlefield, as a geography studied to destroy an enemy, as a territory with fixed frontiers, is very different from the abstract idealization of empty space of Newton's physics or the existential space of phenomenology. (PL 1)

The paradigm of war can be characterized in terms of the privilege of conflict or the celebration of the reduction of the singularity of individual entities and subjects to the generality of the concept, to Being, to an ethnos, or to a totality in philosophical reflections. For some, as for

Dussel in the passage above, which is highly inspired by Rosenzweig and Levinas, the fixation with ideas or experiences of conflict and war goes as far back as Greek philosophy and through it to Western thought.[4] In this book I take a different approach to the analysis of this problem. I aim to discern a particularly modern expression of the paradigm of war. That is the reason why the discovery and conquest of the Americas plays a central role in these reflections. I do not pursue here a transcultural theory of the origin of violence and war in civilization, nor do I deny that warring ideals have shaped in one way or another ancient and non-Western ideals of civilization. My argument is rather that European modernity became inextricably linked with the experience of the warrior and conqueror and that modern colonization, racism, and other forms of social and geopolitical dynamics in the modern world can be understood in terms of the naturalization of the paradigm of war. This is a problem for *us* who continue to struggle with the many faces of modernity and its legacies today.

My approach in this book is phenomenological and historical. I base my reflections on the critical analysis of modern Western thought by figures who are acquainted with it but at the same time focus on experiences of war, racism, and colonialism. The analyses that they provide give credence to the idea that the paradigm of war is deeply connected with the production of race and colonialism as well as by the perpetuation, expansion, and transformation of patriarchy. In the modern world, space is mapped as a battlefield principally through colonialism, race, and dehumanizing ways of differentiating genders. War, in turn, is no longer solely found in extraordinary moments of conflict, but rather becomes a central feature of modern life-worlds.

While conflict and war could have served as a paradigm of cosmology and social relations in premodern and non-European civilizations, my argument here is that one of the characteristic features of European modernity is the naturalization of the death ethic of war through colonialism, race, and particular modalities of gender differentiation. Following Tzvetan Todorov, it could be said that this form of naturalization makes massacre, more than sacrifice, a characteristic feature of modern societies, a distinction that he makes in the context of studying the conquest of the Americas.[5] I aim to provide here a philosophical and historical account of modernity as a paradigm of war, as well as a counterparadigm based on the reflections of three twentieth-century philosophers who critically engage Western thought, particularly phenomenology, from three different but related experiences and geopolitical sites. Despite their cultural, ethnic, and religious differences, the French-Lithuanian-Jew Emmanuel Levinas, the Afro-Caribbean Frantz Fanon, and the Christian Latin American Enrique Dussel are, in respect to dominant Western conceptions, racialized subjects belonging to groups that have been typical depositories or distinct objects of the violent tendencies of dominant Western ideals of the human. Violence and war appear to them not as contingent results of particular historical projects, but as constitutive dimensions of dominant conceptions of civilization and civilizing processes. This suspicion is motivated by a tragic twentieth century and by a long modernity whose constitutive features include the conquest of the Americas. Levinas, Fanon, and Dussel share, for different sociopolitical and historical reasons, and in different ways, the legacy of European empires. What makes their work useful for the project of articulating a postimperial way of thinking is both their acute sense of the problems of Western master morality and their ingenious alternatives to its philosophical bases.

Levinas, Fanon, and Dussel, the times in which they lived, and the critical perspectives that they developed were similar to what Paul Gilroy claims of mid-twentieth century figures whose "confrontations with Nazism were tied to the possibility of armed anticolonial resistance and to some powerful commitments to civil- and human-rights struggles." "These events and themes," Gilroy comments further, "combined to produce a philosophically grounded analysis of racism and its political dimensions in several different places, not all of which are obviously or immediately colonial in character."[6] Gilroy cites W. E. B. Du Bois, Hannah Arendt, Levinas, Fanon, Malcolm X, and other intellectuals as examples of such figures. These figures may be connected with what Chela Sandoval has referred to as a "theory uprising" that emerges in response to the internal crisis of Europe and anti-colonial resistance in the twentieth-century. This uprising generates the elements that Sandoval uses to conceive of a "methodology of the oppressed."[7] This book aims to contribute to the understanding, critical appraisal, and creative elaboration of some theories that are part of this theory uprising and of methodologies of the oppressed. I seek to make explicit the connections between Levinas, Fanon, and Dussel, as well as their respective limits in relation to Eurocentrism, male privilege, misguided identity politics, and other related themes. I also aim to build on the possibilities of their thinking beyond such limitations.

Levinas, Fanon, and Dussel respond critically to the realities of war as they encounter them in the context of Nazism, French imperialism, intolerable Eurocentrism, and the menace of U.S. Americanism and its salvific mission of freedom, all of which are preceded if not tied to each other by a long history of racialization and colonization that goes back to at least 1492. By focusing on responses to these different challenges in Western history I seek to provide more effective and informed responses to the darker expressions of Western modernity than other perspectives that more exclusively focus on the first two world wars and more recent wars in Europe. These include influential responses from dominant voices in critical theory (Horkheimer and Adorno), poststructuralism (Vattimo and Derrida), and recent ethical and political theory (Apel and Habermas). These interventions tend to take less seriously than the work of Levinas, Fanon, and Dussel the ways in which racism and (in the case of Fanon and Dussel) colonization are also expressions of conceptions that promote or are complicit with dehumanization, violence, and war. I attempt to respond to these challenges by articulating a diagnosis of modernity and a critical response to its perverse effects that combines ethics, political theory, and ideas that can be traced back to certain forms of religious thought, particularly Christian and Judaic. Levinas, Fanon, and Dussel subvert dominant ideas in Western thought by elevating ethics and the self-Other relation to the status of first philosophy. Levinas connects the notion of the primacy of ethics to Judaism, but he also sees it, along with Fanon and Dussel, as a consistent response to the experience of subalterity in modernity. Levinas encountered the dynamics of subalterity in a radical way in the midst of the Jewish Holocaust, particularly when he was imprisoned by the Germans in the Second World War. His descriptions of dehumanization relate to what was occurring in the concentration camps, but they can also be related, as Fanon's descriptions of anti-black racism suggest, to the slave ship, the plantation, the colony, and wherever the readily visible racially marked body appears. That Levinas did not fully articulate the implications of his phenomenology of the racial encounter and the connections of his critical response to it with wider struggles against racism and colonization does not mean that his work cannot be interpreted and evaluated in that light. I interpret Levinas's efforts to articulate a "humanism of the Other" as, at least partially, a de-colonial project. Indeed, as I approach them here, the works of Levinas, Fanon, and Dussel advance what could be rendered as a de-colonizing ethico-political turn, or de-colonial turn, to which this work aims to contribute.[8]

What I am calling here the de-colonial turn was announced by W. E. B. Du Bois in the early twentieth century. Later on, it was made more explicit by an array of thinkers that stretch from Aimé Césaire and Frantz Fanon in the middle of the twentieth century to Gloria Anzaldúa, Lewis Gordon, Emma Perez, Chela Sandoval, Linda Tuhiwai Smith, Boaventura de Sousa Santos and others at the end of the twentieth century and the beginning of the twenty-first. The de-colonial turn can be understood as an expression or a particular manifestation of the skepticism toward Western theodicy (a form of theodicy in which Western civilization itself takes the place of God and must be thus defended in face of any evil) that, as Levinas points out, became difficult to sustain in the twentieth century.[9] It finds its roots in critical responses to racism and colonialism articulated by colonial and racial subjects since the beginnings of the modern colonial experience more than five hundred years ago. The de-colonial turn is a simultaneous response to the crisis of Europe and the condition of racialized and colonized subjects in modernity. It posits the primacy of ethics as an antidote to problems with Western conceptions of freedom, autonomy, and equality, as well as the necessity of politics to forge a world where ethical relations become the norm rather than the exception. The de-colonial turn highlights the epistemic relevance of the enslaved and colonized search for humanity. It seeks to open up the sources for thinking and to break up the apartheid of theoretical domains through renewed forms of critique and epistemic creolization.[10]

The de-colonial turn began to take definitive form after the end of the Second World War and the beginnings of the wars for liberation of many colonized countries soon after. But it was preceded by early responses to Hitlerism, such as those by Levinas, and by earlier interventions such as those of the great African American intellectual W. E. B. Du Bois and others. Du Bois is a very significant figure because he announced in 1903 that the problem of the twentieth-century was going to be the problem of the color line (*The Souls of Black Folk*, 17), by which he pointed both to the increment of racism and to the radical opposition to it as sources of conflict in the twentieth century. The works of Levinas, Fanon, and Dussel, among others, are a testimony to how right Du Bois was. Du Bois's prophetic warning was based on the problems that emancipated peoples of the African Diaspora confronted at the end of the nineteenth century and the beginning of the twentieth, particularly, but not solely, in the United States. People considered non-people (not the modern "people" of the nation-state nor the multitude of empire, but the condemned of the earth), even after the formal recognition of their humanity, were going to struggle with all their might against others in power who resisted their full recognition as humans.[11] And Du Bois knew that this struggle was global. The color line was not only white and black for him: it included the black and the Jew, as well as peoples from the South, colonies, and former colonies.

A fundamental contribution of Du Bois is that he examined the pathology of the world from the position of those regarded as most pathological and non-human. His work expresses an epistemic shift that involves making visible the invisible and analyzing the mechanisms that produce such invisibility or distorted visibility in light of a large stock of ideas that must necessarily include the critical reflections of the "invisible" people themselves. This means that the very enunciation of the "problem of the color line" was predicated on at least a partial solution, which involved a shift in the theoretical attitude of the knower. While the theoretical attitude requires detachment and wonder, the *de-colonial attitude*, which Du Bois advances, demands responsibility and the willingness to take many perspectives, particularly the perspectives and points of view of those whose very existence is questioned and produced as dispensable and insignificant.[12] If the problem of the twentieth century, and indeed the problem of modernity, is the problem of the color line, the solution for the twentieth and twenty-first centuries is, at least in part, the de-colonial turn. The de-colonial turn includes the definitive entry of enslaved and colonized subjectivities into the realm of thought at previously unknown institutional levels. It introduces questions about the effects of colonization in modern subjectivities and modern forms of life as well as contributions of racialized and colonized subjectivities to the production of knowledge and critical thinking. This work seeks to contribute to those explorations by interpreting, critically evaluating, expanding, and complementing the works of Levinas, Fanon, and Dussel in light of the de-colonial turn.

In this work I argue that while Levinas's main achievement is to provide an ethical interpretation of the constitution of subjectivity and human experience at a transcendental genetic-phenomenological level, Fanon and Dussel contribute to the understanding of the existential and geopolitical implications of understanding subjectivity in ethical terms. Their contributions are not limited to these levels of investigation. My claim is that their respective contributions to each of these different levels provide the bases to articulate a consistent philosophical position that is in line with their general ideas, while it cannot be identified completely with the ideas of any one of them alone. Consistency does not mean finality. The ideas that I present here are indeed open to revision, expansion, correction, and enrichment in light of their implications or in light of the ideas of other thinkers, including Levinas, Fanon, and Dussel themselves. In respect to these three, I also aim to provide fresh interpretations as well as critiques. In this sense, I aim to contribute at least to some extent to the critical literature on these thinkers. At the same time I readily admit that my engagement with these authors is partial inasmuch as I highlight the aspects of their work that are more useful for the enterprise of articulating a response to the paradigm of war as twenty-first-century humanity still confronts it today. But I think that my reflections are consonant with the work of Levinas, Fanon, and Dussel as a whole. I also believe that those reflections connect in important ways with the work of other figures, including indigenous intellectuals, philosophers of the African Diaspora, Asian American scholars, and Chicana feminists, among others. I have explored and continue exploring these connections in other writings.[13]

Levinas, Fanon, and Dussel are different in respect to location, ethnicity, race, and religious affiliation. More than any of the others perhaps, the question of religion engenders anxiety across the secular academic board, from West to East, and from North to South. In order to better understand my approach to these thinkers as well as their own intellectual production, it becomes necessary to consider, if only in passing here in the introduction, the relation between philosophy and religious thought as I approach it in this book. Both Levinas and Dussel are philosophers and religious thinkers. They both have philosophical and confessional or theological writings. Although both insist on the separation between these two activities, they both agree in that religious ideas serve as a source for philosophical thought. Levinas is not afraid to maintain religious terminology intact, even when he has allegedly properly translated it into a philosophical context. God, religion, and expiation along with Judaic conceptions of the female, the family, and the law keep appearing in his texts unabashedly. While Dussel is less intrepid in the articulation of his philosophical thought, it is clear that, for instance, much of his difference with Levinas can be traced to his belief in the incarnation vis-à-vis Levinas's Judaic conception of the wholly transcendent and disembodied G-d.[14] At the same time, the absence of religious terminology in Dussel's philosophical oeuvre may be linked to his explicit critical posture in respect to dominant Christianity. Like many other theologians of liberation, Dussel conceived liberation not only as overcoming dependency but also as liberation from traditional theology. While Levinas tried to rescue and show the philosophical relevance of Judaic spirituality for the West, Dussel was concerned with criticizing

Western Christendom and was thus not particularly interested in using Christian terminology in a particularly positive and constructive way — at least in his philosophical writings. Moreover, while the philosophical community would be open, particularly after the Holocaust, to entertain the idea of Judaic wisdom, any appeals to Christian wisdom would rather be immediately translated as Christian apologetics or dogmatic theology. Levinas and Dussel wrote in moments when the imperative of returning to Judaic sources felt as strong as the need to criticize Christianity's complicity with the Jewish Holocaust and with poverty in Latin America.[15] This tendency may be changing today as open criticisms of the turn to Judaism begin to emerge and complicities with new forms of Christian orthodoxies become fashionable. The work of Slavoj Žižek provides perhaps the best example here.[16]

There is another reason why Dussel may have been less inclined than Levinas to introduce religious terminology in his philosophical work. Dussel's project has been from its inception more cosmopolitan than that of Levinas. This is partly explained by Dussel's concerns with his Latin American identity and his intellectual itinerary. These concerns originated in his first sojourn to Europe. Dussel traveled by boat and had to stop in many ports in South America and Africa before getting to Spain. Dussel recounts how much his vision of the world and his concerns had changed by the time his trip was over. He became aware of the racial and cultural complexity of the Americas and of the cultural links across the Atlantic Ocean. He also realized that Latin Americans were not simply transplanted Europeans and that the Latin American ethos could not be understood solely in reference to Christian Western culture. The problem of identity explains why while Levinas was primarily concerned with reactivating the Judaic sources of the West (in a context of deep European anti-Semitism), Dussel engaged in a physical and intellectual sojourn that took him to different parts of Europe, Africa, and Israel. His trilogy of works on the Greek, the Christian, and the Semitic ethos in the 1960s is the product of Dussel's consuming passion for the question of cultural identity. Where Dussel's efforts clearly fall short is in the absence of references to African culture and to problems confronted by black populations in Latin America. His cosmopolitan consciousness also finds limits at the points in which he portrays Latin America as the most formidable locus of critical rationality and seems to enact a logic of exclusion or segregation. His best side resides elsewhere, precisely at the points where his renunciation of the inflation of the particular leads him to a transmodern perspective and to a critical cosmopolitanism.¹⁷ His work also becomes exemplar, and this is something with much pertinence in our days, at the points in which he pays more attention to the victims of Christianity than to Christianity's claims for embodying everything that is good and true about humanity. I pursue a more ample analysis and critical appraisal of these elements of Dussel's work in chapter 6.

For varied reasons then, Dussel has been less prone than Levinas to universalize his own particular religious experience. He is more unambiguously concerned with the articulation of a critical philosophy that responds to the experience of exclusion and domination, which includes epistemic subalterity. Dussel would argue that this impetus gives testimony to his Christianity. At the same time, however, and this is the crucial issue here, he recognizes the need for the critical reactivation of subaltern knowledges, including those subalternized by the secular discourse of the imperial West and modern nation-states in the periphery. This is precisely one of the meanings of transmodernity. If early modernity is to a great extent dominated by Christianity, and Enlightened modernity is secular, transmodernity is neither Christian nor secular. It rather opens the space for the articulation of different forms of knowledge and conceptions of reality. It goes in line with other efforts to take religious thought seriously beyond the secular prejudices of Enlightened modernity and in a different way from strict confessional adherence to religious creeds.¹⁸ In this line, Dussel has not only attempted to articulate the epistemic value of the Aztecs' rationality, but he has also shown how the most radical Christian ethical view at the time of the conquest was limited in comparison to the Aztecs' point of view.

Critical reactivation is truly not so far from what Levinas himself attempted to do in regard to Judaic religiosity. The basic difference is that Levinas hardly looked beyond the perspectives provided by Greek and Hebrew lenses. Levinas was a great translator and a great inclusivist. He translated Hebrew notions into Greek and saw Judaic components in everything good that he observed. Since he defines the Jew as being aware of responsibility beyond measure, he identifies the traces of Judaism wherever he finds the upsurge of donation and goodness—I will return to this point in the conclusion. In this sense, as much as Levinas tried to escape the insurmountable limits of language by breaking with linguistic conventions and thinking against the grain, he remained committed to modern notions of abstract universality. Transmodernity, in contrast, is neither exclusivist nor inclusivist and is not committed to abstract universality either.¹⁹ It is rather trans-pluri-versal, by which I mean that it transcends and transgresses the impositions of abstract universals while it opens up the path for dialogue among different epistemes. These elements of transmodernity can be observed in varied postcolonial theories that advocate diversality (Mignolo), polycentrism (Majid), conviviality (Gilroy), and epistemic diversity at large (King).[20]

As trans-pluri-versal, transmodernity does not privilege religion over secularity, or secularity over religion. It is in this respect both post-secular and post-religious. Both the secular and the religious have specific meanings in modernity. By post-secularity and post-religiosity I mean that transmodernity questions both the meaning and the logic inaugurated by the secular/religion divide. Transmodernity also aims to interrupt the impetus for modernization, the enchantment with technique, the dominion of instrumental rationality, and the identification of modernity with secularity and premodernity with religion. Transmodernity refers to the activity of thinking about Being and its limits without Eurocentric, theological, or secularistic prejudices. The primary axis of reflection is the question of responding responsibly to subjects in positions of subordination.[21] In this sense transmodernity is first and foremost an ethics and a politics of liberation. Yet, this does not mean that confessional discourse is illegitimate. As Levinas's and Dussel's works clearly evince, there are no religions as such, but rather interpretations of doctrines and ideas that may be mobilized in different directions, given different meanings, and may inspire different projects. Critical reactivation is precisely critical of views and interpretations that are complicit with master or imperial morality. This critique aims both ways, to the secular and to the religious, suspending at the same time the idea of a dichotomous relation between the two. In this sense, as Levinas and Dussel show in different degrees, transmodernity leads to a double critique of the religious and the secular as well as to a suspension of the power of the binary between the religious and the secular.[22]

In this work, I pursue a similar suspension of the religious/secular divide. Insofar as it is Dussel, more than Levinas, who more intrepidly pursues this adventure this work is more Dusselian than Levinasian. And, it is in fact Dussel who also combines insights from Fanon and Levinas. But I try to provide here a different interpretation of both of these figures and the link between Levinas's genetic- phenomenological exploration and the question of the political. It is Fanon's existential phenomenology that serves me to establish a link between these spheres. Not surprisingly, or perhaps too surprisingly for some, I also identify a "religious" vein in Fanon's thought. To some extent at least Fanon, the atheist, appears here as a post-secular and transmodern liberation thinker. It becomes clear in this way that while I strongly object to some of Dussel's interpretations of Levinas's and Fanon's works, it is Dussel's cosmopolitanism that most approaches the kind of work that I try to do here.

Now that the logic of this work is more clear, let us take a look in more detail at its contents and structure. Part I offers an interpretation and critical analysis of Levinas's work in light of the problems posed by paradigms of thought that privilege experiences akin to war, violence, and death. The first chapter focuses on one of Levinas's earliest essays, "Reflections on the Philosophy of Hitlerism." Levinas accomplishes two tasks in this essay: first, he offers valuable suggestions about the interrelation of dominant anthropological and epistemological ideals in the West; second, he provides a sketch of how Western conceptions of freedom and truth are subtly connected with philosophical accounts that legitimate or are complicit in one way or another with sociopolitical expressions of violence. These conceptions are so pervasive that they keep appearing in seemingly alternative philosophical articulations of freedom and truth. I focus in this chapter on two positions alluded to by Levinas in his short essay: those of Friedrich Nietzsche and Edmund Husserl. As opposed to each other as they might seem at first, Levinas suggests that the philosophical positions of these thinkers are clearly connected by their implicit or explicit endorsement of Western society as a "community of masters." These positions are not well equipped to exorcize the terror of Hitlerism, which expresses for him a radical version of the idea of society as a "community of masters." Hitlerism, which advocates the superiority of the Aryan race, defends the condition in which mastery is to be achieved concretely at all costs and in which this can only be assured by actually eliminating the slaves. Levinas suggests that a critical appropriation of the Judaic sources of Western thought offers the possibility of articulating truly alternative anthropological and epistemological views. The second chapter in part I turns to an examination of this more constructive part of his project.

The second chapter provides an interpretation of major themes in Levinas's work in terms of his attempt to provide a philosophical account that evades the limitations and perverse effects of Western master morality. The chapter begins with a critical reflection on the work of Martin Heidegger, who represents for Levinas the most exemplary, if not most dangerous, figure of those whose response to the limits of Western thought ends up reproducing some of its worst dimensions. Instead of repeating the myopic gesture of simply reducing Heidegger's work to his biography, I will try to show here that the problems of Heidegger's thought are not exclusively determined by his temporary allegiance to Nazism. His thought reflects a more general problematic insistence on legitimating anthropological and epistemological concepts that sustain the conception of Europeans, and more particularly Germans, as a community of masters. I will trace the presence of a subtle legitimation of a master morality in some main themes of Heidegger's work and then focus particularly on his conceptions of ontology, human authenticity, and death.

The discussion of dominant Heideggerian themes provides a background to understand the articulation of Levinas's own philosophy and his critical take on Western conceptions of the human. I aim to make evident here why Levinas invests much of his time elaborating on an account that links what he called ethics and metaphysics with a renewed articulation of human fraternity and social life. Then I will assess the virtues and limits of this project. In order to do this, I first consider selected essays of Levinas's intellectual production up to the publication of *Totality and Infinity*, his first major work. This period is characterized by the attempt to ground human fraternity not in terms of abstract equality, a typical strategy of classical liberalism ("liberty, equality, fraternity"), but in terms of sexual difference, thereby rescuing important aspects of the corporality of the subject without collapsing into a racial discourse akin to National Socialism. Clarifying how the idea of fraternity, and not eros or fecundity, is the overarching theme of the early period of Levinas's work serves as an antidote to postmodern reactions, allegedly inspired by Levinas himself, that tend to dismiss hastily the tradition of modern political theory, particularly that of the Enlightenment.

The conceptual horizon offered by the Enlightenment and by the French tradition of political theory is complicated by new articulations of ethics and justice after the end of the Second World War. The reemergence of a discourse on the Rights of Man after 1948 and a more acute perception of the philosophical bases of the genocidal politics of Nazism initiated a shift in Levinas's discourse. The events of May 1968 in France also marked Levinas's work in important ways. *Otherwise Than Being or Beyond Essence*, Levinas's second major work, published in 1974, is clearly in tune with the critical thought that emerged in the wake of the events of 1968 in France. I find in this period a turn from fraternity to a more radical ethical conception that I term *altericity*. Altericity refers to a radical act of giving that is driven by an unequaled concern for the death of the other person. The path from fraternity to altericity sees an intensification of Levinas's discourse on responsibility, on the difference between Being and the Other, and on the biblical theme of "giving to the stranger." Levinas discusses the themes of giving and the gift in terms of a transcendental account of the conditions of possibility for the emergence of subjectivity and signification. Coming back firmly to the work of his teacher Edmund Husserl, Levinas provides the basis for a new conception of philosophy that is tied to the concept of "reduction."[23] The reduction is defined by Levinas in terms of a critical discourse that unveils the ways in which the constitutive event of *giving* to the Other is betrayed by human endeavors that often make justice collapse into an invitation to indifference. The task of reduction appears thus to be animated for Levinas more by love than by wonder, and it expresses a fundamental concern, not so much for one's own death, but for the death of the other person. In this sense, it is possible to say, as I will argue, that the reduction represents a paradigmatic act of altericity.

The Levinasian account of subjectivity, of philosophy as ethical critique, and of the meaning of wisdom contrasts sharply with the anthropological and epistemological bases of the paradigm of violence and war. Yet, while Levinas clearly demonstrates the underlying ethical presuppositions of our ordinary existence, he does not equally consider the many ways in which this very ordinary existence is often vitiated by relations that violate the ethical meaning of human reality. This other dimension of the drama of Being is the privileged focus of Frantz Fanon, to whom I dedicate the second part of this work. In the third chapter I introduce Fanon as a philosopher of reduction in the Levinasian sense of the term. Yet, I argue that Fanon's critical discourse and praxis give expression to a peculiar form of the reduction. I refer to this as the "de-colonial reduction." The de-colonial reduction is a critical discourse that provides a diagnosis of the meaning of institutions and the aspirations behind civilizing, imperial, or de-colonizing projects. It operates by firmly introducing coloniality and the relation between master and slave as axes of reflection in the evaluation of the meaning behind certain expressions of human reality. The discussion of the de-colonial reduction is followed by an exercise in this critical venture. I attempt to offer an answer to the question of how is it that the master, who, according to Fanon, is not even interested in achieving recognition through the slave, confirms his identity as master. I submit that only an imperial God can offer such recognition. The rest of the chapter substantiates and develops this argument. This discussion aims to clarify, in direct opposition to some of his interpreters, that Fanon's thought can hardly be integrated into the premises of neo-Hegelianism.[24]

While the third chapter is dedicated to the articulation and analysis of the intricate ways in which imperial modes of recognition are sustained, the fourth chapter focuses on the search for ways to consistently overcome imperial and colonial modes of recognition. Here we will look for the conditions of possibility for the emergence of love in the slave's struggle for recognition. This discussion represents a most important step in the attempt to articulate a philosophical conception that counteracts the dominance of the paradigm of violence and war. The recognition of the ways in which the relation between master and slave penetrates and shapes ordinary human existence clearly indicates that consistent opposition to the paradigm of violence and war requires an explicit form of political activity. In this way, the reduction takes on not only theoretical and ethical connotations, but practical and political ones as well. The link between the ethical and the political is clearly established by Fanon, or so I will argue, in his account of the struggle for recognition as a struggle for liberation and for non-sexist human fraternity. The articulation of this point is preceded by a phenomenological exploration of the meaning of the "cry" of the slave in Fanon's work, which shows that Fanon clearly sustains a conception of the self as a gift. This conception puts him at odds with classical and more recent formulations of the struggle for recognition. It also distances him from certain aspects of the politics of identity. This interpretation dispels a common view, mainly propagated by hasty judgments about the theme of violence in Fanon's works, that his work represents a simple repetition of what he was attacking so fiercely, the normative force of the ideal of war in ethics and politics.[25] It also contributes to the most important task of shaking the foundations of the comfortable quarters of apolitical ethics (both postmodern and neoliberal), and of promoting an active and progressive effort at advancing decolonization, which means, for Fanon, nothing less than the post-imperial act of *restoring the human being to her and his place.*

Among today's most vibrant, systematic, original, and profound thinkers there is arguably only one whose work has been strongly shaped both by the liberation discourse greatly indebted to Fanon and by the thought of Emmanuel Levinas. Although Levinas interpreters in the United States and Europe are only rarely acquainted with his work, he, along with a group of scholars, was responsible for making Argentina one of the earliest places where the study of Levinas's work found a home.[26] I refer to Enrique Dussel. In part 3 I assess critically Dussel's work in light of the analyses offered in the previous chapters. In the fifth chapter, I focus on the Dusselian argument that a consistent post-imperial philosophy ("filosofía real post-imperial contemporánea") must overcome phenomenology and develop a discourse of liberation through an ethics grounded on the distinction between the self and the Other. Dussel appropriates Levinas's ethical metaphysics to achieve this purpose. For this reason, I come back again in this chapter to phenomenology and to the Levinasian critique of Husserl and Heidegger. This time I focus exclusively on Levinas's account of the self-Other relation in order to assess the adequacy of Dussel's appropriation. I argue that Levinas's reflections on the genesis of the self can be directly applied to historical and sociopolitical issues, but only at the price of confusion and at the risk of falling into a sort of dogmatism or into a problematic foundationalism. Dussel's hasty rejection of phenomenology, and of existential phenomenology in particular, lead him to rely on Levinasian categories at points in which he should have rather learned from Fanon. I will argue that Fanon's examination of the lived experience of the colonized, along with his reflections on the slave's desire for recognition, provide more subtle and progressive accounts of the relation between master and slave in colonial and neocolonial times than Dussel's direct application of Levinas's ethics to concrete experience.

The critique of Dussel's early work from a Levinasian and a Fanonian point of view respectively does not hide, however, the extent to which his work contributes to the critical work of "reduction" that I attempt to formulate through the works of Levinas and Fanon as well as to the decolonial turn that I described previously. It is possible to say, at least in general terms, that where Levinas introduces ethical metaphysics, and where Fanon pursues an existential phenomenological exploration of the lived experience of the black, Dussel provides a systematic exploration into the epistemological pertinence of history and geopolitics. In the sixth chapter I present Dussel's *The Invention of the Americas* as a decolonial reduction of Eurocentric conceptions of world history.[27] Dussel offers in this text a transgressive post-imperial exploration of the history that Husserl recounted in Eurocentric terms. In this text Dussel overcomes the false split between phenomenology and liberation, while he also leaves behind some problematic ideas in his use of the Levinasian conception of the Other.

I conclude with a reflection on the new venues for thinking opened up by the analyses I have pursued. To the difference between Being and beings, or ontological difference, I add here, following Levinas and Dussel, the difference between Being and what is beyond Being on the one hand (trans-ontological difference), and, following Fanon, the difference between Being and what lies below Being, or the "damned," on the other (sub-ontological difference). With the first I intend to spell out the metaphysical character of goodness. The second points to the production of evil. If damnation refers to the status of colonized and dehumanized subjects, goodness is partly defined as de-colonization and humanization, which entails, in this account, a radical expression of love. Evil is understood, in contrast, as a fundamental resistance against generous and receptive interhuman contact. Evil, the negation of the gift through violence, war, or indifference, reaches its climax in genocidal activities and in the unfolding of empire. Opposing racism and imperialism as projects fundamentally involves manifold acts of "reduction" aimed to bring about the overcoming of this sinister sociopolitical and historical force.

The history of ideas is sad and its narration largely driven by Eurocentric prejudices. The sources for doing intellectual work are limited as most of us in the academy tend to identify the contours of rationality with the figures drawn in imperial cartographies. It is necessary to demystify our perceptions on the location of authentically critical discourses. I close this work with a "call" for the transgression of the authority of the bastions of Eurocentrism in the academy through the exploration of new ways of thinking about the relation between knowledge and geographical location. As Dussel has done in his effort to locate the position of Latin America in world history, we should all attempt, attentive to the many "cries" that we have ignored for so long, to respond responsibly to the ones who are "below" and to fight with them in the struggle for their liberation. We need to *hear* and to *learn* from the wisdom of those whose confrontation with evil has turned into the horror of evil and to the fight against it. The consistent opposition to the paradigm of war includes the exploration of an alternative geography of reason, one that allows us to think about human and natural reality without Eurocentric or nationalist prejudices. Writing on Levinas, Fanon, and Dussel (a Jew born in Lithuania, a black Martiniquean, and a Latin American), may be qualified, in this sense, intrinsically as an act of transgression. But it is certainly more than that. It is a tribute to three Quixotic figures whose pain turned paradoxically into love. It is, in addition, a serious attempt to clarify, assess, and develop their more radical humanistic insights. It also represents an effort to think from the limits of Being and to increase our sensibility to the "cries" of ethical revolt that resound all over the world.

SEARCHING FOR ETHICS
IN A VIOLENT WORLD
A JEWISH RESPONSE
TO THE PARADIGM OF WAR

1

FROM LIBERALISM TO HITLERISM
TRACING THE ORIGINS OF VIOLENCE AND WAR

> *Perhaps the most revolutionary fact of our twentieth-century consciousness . . . is that of the destruction of all balance between Western thought's explicit and implicit theodicy and the forms that suffering and its evil are taking on in the very unfolding of this century. This is the century that in thirty years has known two world wars, the totalitarianisms of right and left, Hitlerism and Stalinism, Hiroshima, the Gulag, and the genocides of Auschwitz and Cambodia. This is the century that is drawing to a close in the obsessive fear of the return of everything these barbaric names stood for: suffering and evil inflicted deliberately, but in a manner no reason set limits to, in the exasperation of a reason become political and detached from all ethics.* —EMMANUEL LEVINAS[1]

In a brief autobiographical essay entitled "Signature" Emmanuel Levinas comments that all his life has been marked by the "presentiment and the memory of the Nazi horror."[2] It is most revealing that he uses the notion of "presentiment" and not only of "memory." The word "presentiment" indicates that the "Nazi horror" hardly took Levinas by surprise. Quite the opposite, it is almost as if he was expecting it. Nazism appeared to be for him a lived possibility of a culture, rather than a radical unexpected departure from a moral destiny. The opening lines of the preface to his profound first major work, *Totality and Infinity*, give an indication of the sources for this Levinasian suspicion:

> Everyone will readily agree that it is of the highest importance to know whether we are not duped by morality.
>
> Does not lucidity, the mind's openness upon the true consist in catching sight of the permanent possibility of war? That state of war suspends morality; it divests the eternal institutions and obligations of their eternity and rescinds ad interim the unconditional imperatives. . . . The art of foresee-

ing war and of winning it by every means—politics—is henceforth enjoined as the very exercise of reason. Politics is opposed to morality, as philosophy to naiveté. (TI 21)

Lucidity (clarity and distinctiveness), Levinas points out here, is interrupted by the intervention of morals. If true philosophical knowledge is knowledge *without presuppositions,* then it is clear that morality should be either parenthesized or simply ignored as a significant epistemological factor.[3] The search for the truth thus requires the methodic exclusion of morals. And among the many experiences that bring this clarity war stands at the very top. "In war reality rends the words and images that dissimulate it, to obtrude in its nudity and its harshness" (TI 21). If true knowledge is obtained through a gentle indifference toward ethics, the radical suspension of morality in war accomplishes the most radical and effective means to reach true knowledge and to serve rationality. For Levinas, the Nazi horror was a radical expression of this ideal. It represents the moment where rationality fully joins politics through the achievement of a complete detachment from morals. From this point on rationality and politics unfold as systematic and calculated murder.[4]

Let us examine the Levinasian suspicion that violence and war are not foreign elements of Western culture but logical results of dominant paradigms of thinking. I would like to highlight the idea that Levinas could only have a "presentiment" of the Nazi horror because the possibility of a drama of war and systematic violence was already present in the culture in which he lived. This chapter offers a close reading of Levinas's first explicit exploration into the sources of violence in the West, "Reflections on the Philosophy of Hitlerism." In this essay, Levinas traces the initial sources of violence to the limitations and the ambiguities of a dominant paradigm of thinking inscribed in modern political philosophy—primarily in French liberalism. I expand on Levinas's reflections to show the links not only between liberalism and Hitlerism, but also between these two and two other apparently alternative accounts offered by Friedrich Nietzsche and by Edmund Husserl. Through this exploration it will become clear how the exercise of "war and conquest" may be ultimately traced back to conceptions of subjectivity and human community that reproduce the logic of a division between master and slaves. Hitlerism along with Eurocentrism emerge as two ideals of subjectivity and human community mounted on the privilege of imperial experience. While this first chapter endeavors to clarify the basis of the Levinasian diagnosis of the Western civilizing project, the second chapter will aim to articulate Levinas's alternative accounts of subjectivity and of human interaction.

REFLECTIONS ON THE PHILOSOPHY OF HITLERISM

> *As for the question of knowing, in the context of the violence that fills us all with dread, whether we can incriminate philosophy, in which the concept of man can be comprehended—I think, indeed, that it is in the world of violence that philosophy has been established as Reason and has been explicated as such. Philosophy is one of the essential adventures of reason, without which the philosophy of the absolutely dissimilar I would also present dangers, but which if left to itself would intensify the violence that it wants to combat, wherever it arises.* —EMMANUEL LEVINAS[5]

> *Philosophy's itinerary remains that of Ulysses, whose adventure in the world was only a return to his native island—a complacency in the Same, an unrecognition of the other.* —EMMANUEL LEVINAS[6]

It was 1934, four years after Levinas had completed his doctoral dissertation in Germany, and a year after Hitler had emerged as the new leader of the country and Martin Heidegger had offered several discourses in favor of Hitler's regime, that Levinas wrote his brief essay "Reflections on the Philosophy of Hitlerism."[7] As Manuel Reyes Mate points out, Heidegger had used his philosophical artillery, particularly phenomenology, to explain and defend the emergence of National Socialism in Germany. With his short essay on the philosophy of Hitlerism, "Levinas wishes to make the point that . . . it is possible to make a critical interpretation of Hitlerism using the same philosophical tools."[8] However, while it is true that Levinas draws heavily from phenomenology, his essay offers a different path of thinking that is highly informed by "Jewish wisdom" and the experience of being a Jew in France, particularly after the Dreyfus Affair. His essay is also critical of two of the most significant intellectual sources of Heidegger's work: Nietzsche and the father of phenomenology itself, Edmund Husserl—who, like Levinas, was also a Jew but who did not consider Judaism as a relevant epistemic source. Thus, Levinas's article can be read not only as a critique of Heidegger, but also as a critical response to the Nietzschean and the Husserlian philosophical responses to the crisis of Europe. I will elaborate this point in this first chapter and turn to the Levinasian critique of Heidegger in the second.

Levinas's "Reflections on the Philosophy of Hitlerism" attempts to elucidate the extent of the challenge that Hitlerism poses to Western philosophical and political thought. In a way that is reminiscent of Nietzschean reflections on the sources and motivations of Western thought and morals, Levinas provides the sketch of a genealogical account of dominant Western anthropological and epistemological conceptions.[9] In his essay, he portrays Hitlerism simultaneously as the excessive expression of a logic inaugurated by Western ideals and as the return of what has been repressed in Western culture. Hitlerism does not appear to be a necessary outcome of Western culture, but it is not merely an accidental effect either. It takes Western thought by surprise because it is simultaneously completely strange and uncannily familiar. A close reading of this essay will clarify the fundamental intuition behind the Levinasian diagnosis of modernity and the sources of the alleged violent tendencies in Western civilization.

For Levinas, the most basic anthropological principle expressed in the dominant religious and philosophical ideas of Western civilization is the notion of renovation or freedom from fate or material necessities (RPH 64–65). Although Levinas traces this notion to the Judaic conception of "remorse and pardon," he notes that it also appears in the Christian revolt against the Greek notion of tragedy and temporality (RPH 65). In Christianity, this freedom refers ultimately to the liberty of the soul in respect to everything else to which it might be submitted—for example, to the past or to nature. With modern philosophical and political thought this freedom is transformed into the superiority of humans with respect to the material world, and, ultimately, into the idealism of reason according to which only the spiritual exists. Gradually the Christian notion of "liberation through grace," which indicates regained freedom over causal determination, gives way to the notion of the autonomy of the subject in modern philosophy (RPH 66). This conception of an autonomous human being who escapes physical, psychological, and social determinations is inscribed in the French liberal Declaration of the Rights of Man. Even Marxism, with the ideal of gaining awareness of one's social situation, expresses, according to Levinas, this notion of freedom (RPH 66–67).

The philosophy of Hitlerism is not merely a spurious reaction against liberalism. It takes on and reveals a fundamental experience to which liberalism does not do full justice. Ultimately, the philosophy of Hitlerism makes reference to the unique ties between the self and the body, something that hardly finds adequate expression in the anthropology of liberalism. While for Christianity and liberalism the body is taken as "eternally foreign," Hitlerism takes on the biological bondage of the self. As Levinas points out,

> From this point on, every social structure that announces an emancipation with respect to the body, without being committed to it [*qui ne l'engage pas*], is suspected of being a repudiation and betrayal. The forms of a modern society founded on the harmony established between free wills will seem not only fragile and inconsistent but false and deceitful. The assimilation of spirits loses the grandeur of the spirit's triumph over the body. Instead, it becomes the work of forgers. A society based on consanguinity immediately ensues from this concretization of the spirit. And then, if race does not exist, one has to invent it! (RPH 69)

The anthropological and the social ideas that find place in the philosophy of Hitlerism are matched by parallel conceptions of truth and thinking. Here, again, the philosophy of Hitlerism performs an ingenious but perverse subversion of the dominant ideals in Western civilization. Western epistemology is intrinsically related to dominant Western anthropological conceptions. The free human being, detached from the world, searches for and chooses his truth. "He is free and alone in the face of the world" (RPH 69). This ideal opens the possibility of not choosing or adhering to any truth, that is, of skepticism. The free human being enjoys his freedom and lack of commitment to the point where he suspends all judgment. The lack and the impossibility of conviction are appraised, and the search for truth becomes a foolish hope. The resolute search for the truth becomes only the illusory hope of a heroic age. As Levinas points out, "Sincerity becomes impossible and puts an end to all heroism. Civilization is invaded by everything that is not authentic, by a substitute that is put at the service of fashion and of various interests" (RPH 70). The possibilities of reaching the truth through freedom vanish; the Nazi idea of glory tied to racial determinism becomes a lived possibility for a culture (RPH 70).

The intricate, and at times ambivalent, relations between Hitlerism and liberalism make it difficult to reach a conclusion about Levinas's aims in the essay on the philosophy of Hitlerism. Ultimately, it is not entirely clear if for Levinas the philosophy of Hitlerism represents either a consistent expression of dominant ideals in Western civilization or a dishonest betrayal of whatever is good in French liberalism. Liberalism is grounded on a modern anthropology and epistemology according to which certainty and truth can only be achieved through extreme doubt or skepticism. Cartesianism as well as what often goes as the "philosophy of the Enlightenment" are good examples of this. Both premise the search for truth and epistemic foundations on radical critique. The liberal conception of self as free and autonomous is grounded on the "evidence" of the *cogito* or autonomous self, who is conceived as the indispensable agent of knowledge and critique. The liberal Rights of Man, for instance, are the rights of this ultimate foundation. But the irony is that the idea of the full autonomy and freedom of the subject opens the possibility of a renewed skepticism, based on the notion of a radical freedom beyond absolute norms and values. This new and more radical form of skepticism of transcendental values and concepts, which include the notions of "rights" and Man themselves, opens the door for relativism and natural determinism. The Levinasian lesson is clear: excessively abstract concepts of freedom and subjectivity that promote relativism ultimately lead to decadent forms of nihilism, to racial conceptions of human determinism, or both. The question here is whether such abstract conceptions of freedom and subjectivity and their concomitant outcomes (including Hitlerism) are a consistent expression of the Western search for truth through critique or if they rather represent misguided steps in the veritable search for truth and freedom. If the former, then, the very ideal of searching for truth is at stake. In that case, an alternative response to it would have to demonstrate that attaining the truth is neither possible nor desirable in itself. It would also be necessary to show how a consistent abandonment of the ideal of searching for the truth at all costs represents an authentic liberation, and not an enslavement into the captivity of the body. If, on the contrary, one considered liberalism's excessive abstraction and its results as a betrayal of the search for freedom, which initiated the process of the search for truth and critique in the first place, then the appropriate answer would involve a reaffirmation of the search for the truth on a new basis—which avoids excessive abstraction and relativism. In this case it would be necessary to show that the attainment of truth is not only possible but also desirable (in that it is the best remedy against decadent nihilism and racial determinism). These two possible interpretations of and responses to the predicament of the philosophical anthropology of liberalism point to two influential responses to what is known as the "crisis of modernity." One of them is Nietzschean, the other Husserlian. Levinas was largely acquainted with the two responses. I will attempt to clarify the distinctiveness of the Levinasian response through a discussion of and comparison with these two responses to the "crisis." I first turn to Nietzsche, and then to Levinas's beloved teacher, Edmund Husserl.

THE NIETZSCHEAN RESPONSE

Nietzsche probably went further than anyone else in the history of modern philosophy in sustaining a war against the ideal of the unconditional search for the truth.[10] He took nihilism as an opportunity to advance the cause for the loss of faith in the possibility and desirability of aspiring to attain the truth. Nihilism represented for him in some way a deprivation, in other ways an authentic liberation from ideals that ultimately led to decadence. Like Levinas after him, Nietzsche traces nihilism to the anthropology and epistemology that emanate from Christianity. But while Levinas highlights the Christian conception of freedom, Nietzsche focuses on the Christian ideal of sincerity at all costs.[11] This ideal promotes servitude since it enchains the subject to the truth. Before it appeared in Christianity this bondage and enchantment with the truth was found, as Nietzsche observes, in Greece. As is well known, Nietzsche referred to Christianity as a sort of Platonism for the masses. Both contain the metaphysical idea of a world split in two: a world of mere appearance with relatively little or no authentic value, and the other a permanent world to which we truly belong and to which we should all aspire. The search for the truth becomes in this context the privileged practice of those who desire (as we should all desire) to return to the permanent and real world. The search for the truth takes the form of an ascetic practice that helps us to abandon the world in the correct way.

For Nietzsche the search for truth represents the effort of weak human beings to enact a leveling process whereby individual distinctiveness is deemed as immoral. The liberal idea of equality represented for him an important part of the effort to assimilate the individual into the collective, to favor the weak, and to limit the will of the strong. Nietzsche traced this subversion of values back to what he called a Jewish revolt in morality. The Jews are for Nietzsche the paradigmatic expression of a priestly mode of self-consciousness:[12]

> It was the Jews who, with awe inspiring consistency, dared to invert the aristocratic value-equation (good=noble=powerful=happy=beloved of God) and to hang on to this inversion with their teeth, the teeth of the most abysmal hatred (the hatred of impotence), saying "the wretched alone are the good; the poor, impotent, lowly alone are the good . . . , and you, the powerful and noble are on the contrary the evil, the cruel, the lustful. . . . One knows *who*

inherited this Jewish revaluation. . . . With the Jews there begins *the slave revolt in morality*: that revolt which has a history of two thousand years behind it and which we no longer see because it—has been victorious."[13]

For Nietzsche, these Jews, along with "the descendants of every kind of European and non-European slavery, and especially of the entire pre-Aryan populace—they represent the *regression* of mankind!"[14] Their regressive revolt begins, according to Nietzsche, when their *ressentiment* finally "becomes creative and gives birth to values."[15] Morality in Europe becomes thus the morality of slaves.

It is not entirely impossible that when Nietzsche was writing these lines he was not only following a Christian interpretation of Judaism that depicts Judaism as a vile form of legalism. Perhaps he was also thinking of the ways in which many Jews appreciated so much and identified with the Trinitarian slogan of the French Revolution (liberty, equality, and fraternity) and with the Rights of Man. Levinas, a French-Lithuanian-Jew himself, recalls that since the Revolution of 1789 and the Declaration of the Rights of Man, France represented for many Jews no less than the "apogee of humanity [*forme achevée de l'humanité*]" (DF 261). As the moral and philosophical slogan of the revolution (freedom, equality, and fraternity) became the principle of a nation, France came to be for many the true representative of universality and morals. Becoming French was seen as a sort of "metaphysical act" whereby humanity finds an accomplishment of its true vocation (DF 260). The Jews then seemed to find a permanent home in the liberal France, to the point where, Levinas notes, they could afford to forget or ignore the "religious source of their love" (DF 261). The Jewish perception and appraisal of French liberalism surely may have given the impression to Nietzschean eyes that there was a profound compatibility between the French credo of submission to the rule of equality and the allegedly Jewish appraisal of subordination to the law. In France, the Jews seemed to find a place where they could finally feel at home because they were supposedly seen as free and equal subjects under the law.

The Levinasian description of the enthusiasm of the Jews for French liberalism could legitimately add evidence to the link between the slave morality of the Jews and the slave morality of liberalism if it were not for the fact that, among other considerations, the harmony between the Jews and French liberalism was not going to last for long. Levinas describes a "psychological turn" in the Jewish perception of French liberalism. The event that precipitated this turn was none other than the (in)famous Dreyfus Affair. Alfred Dreyfus was a French army officer who was convicted of treason in 1894, but he was later acquitted when the evidence against him was shown to have been forged by anti-Semites. Levinas notes how, while it is true that when the cases ended justice had prevailed—and thus politics joined morality once more—the event represented the loss of innocence and the enthusiasm to which the Jews attached the promises of French liberalism and the best accomplishments of Western civilization. The disclosure of a strong anti-Semitism in liberal France made evident the "fragility of Reason" and the "power of nihilism" (DF 261). Anti-Semitism represented much more than a certain prejudice against the Jews. Some saw in it "the presence of every racial hatred, persecution of the weak, and of all the exploitations in the world" (DF 261–62, translation modified). A new sensibility emerged in the emancipated Jews. "It did not alter patriotic feeling but created a new vigilance, a new attention paid to the world, a new way of being stirred and tense in one's existence, a reunion with an old religious experience" (DF 262).

There is no doubt that when Levinas described the Jewish perception of French liberalism he was in great part describing his own suspicion about what many consider one of the more revolutionary and profound expressions of Western civilization. Levinas thus shared with Nietzsche a certain mistrust of liberalism. His critique of liberalism, grounded on the experience of disillusion in the Dreyfus Affair, however, reproaches liberalism not for being too ethical (as in Nietzsche's critique), but simply for not being ethical enough. To French Jews liberalism failed not because it betrayed whatever is strong and noble in human beings, but because it was not totally effective in furthering a way of life wherein desire for power and control ceased to be dominant features of the self-identity of its adherents. This Levinasian suspicion ultimately indicates that the "sickness" of Western civilization does not reside so much in the repression of an aristocratic consciousness (through an ascetic morality) but in the violation of ethics and in the exercise of violence over other human beings—by a consciousness of lordship. Nihilism itself would be the result of a radical absence of an ethics and of the evisceration of authentic interhuman contact.[16] Nihilism, in this perspective, would emerge when the freedom of the liberal subject turns into the solitude of a collectivity that can only see hate as a proper motivation for movement and dynamism. Thus, while for Nietzsche liberalism ultimately indicates the failure of humans to express their will to power, for Levinas, liberalism appears to be in contrast one of the most consistent and successful efforts to sustain a position of power or lordship—particularly of abstract individuals over racialized others.

Although Nietzsche did not see the emergence of National Socialism in Germany he was acutely aware of the prospects for violence in a nihilistic age. For him, violence and destruction would become the final outcome of decadence and the will to death that finds expression in nihilism.[17] In this view, submission to the universal ultimately leads to a preference for the logic of submission over the claims of universality. Violence is thus a possible, if not expected, aftereffect of the asceticism of the search for truth and universality. Against the slave morality of asceticism Nietzsche proposed an amoral praxis of self-assertion. To the will to death he opposed the will to power. The affirmation of the will to power liberates a centuries-old repressed aristocratic consciousness. In short, to the passive and inactive nihilism of the slave Nietzsche opposes the Overman. Since Nietzsche can only see in the search for the truth and universality the expression of a slave consciousness, he can only offer a master consciousness for its cure. In truth, however, as Albert Camus points out, Nietzsche aimed to do justice to both, the master and the slave consciousnesses. This is what seems to be at stake in Nietzsche's clamor for a "Roman Caesar with the soul of Christ."[18] But, as Camus notes, "In the last analysis to say yes to both was to give one's blessing to the stronger of the two—namely, the master."[19] Going *beyond good and evil* ultimately means also going beyond the prohibition to commit murder. As Nietzsche puts it, "When the ends are great humanity employs other standards and no longer judges crime as such even if it resorts to the most frightful means."[20] Nietzsche preferred conflict, *polemos*, and the fight of wills to ascetic tranquility. His advocacy of power, however, ignored the extent to which nihilism was the consistent expression, and not the failure, of a grandiloquent project to sustain a logic of power and control.

Nietzsche's philosophical reflections seem to give expression to the perspective of an aristocratic consciousness that finds itself in a stage of decay and stasis. In his effort to advocate the need for dynamic movement and growth, he went as far as to naturalize the realities of violence and war. Morality appeared to him to be counternature. Peace, in this light, represents a futile ideal, since "the normal state of things is war."[21] Peace is to be desired, as Nietzsche's Zarathustra proclaimed, but only as a means to war: "Warriors, my brothers, I love you from the depth of my heart. . . . Desire peace as a means for new wars, and let the peace be short rather than long. War and courage accomplish many more great things than love of the neighbour."[22]

The privileging of warrior ideals in Nietzsche's writings, his vitalism, and his celebration of the will to power, along with the opposition to the liberal conception of universality explain why the Nazis felt so compelled to adopt Nietzsche's rhetoric for their own purposes. Nietzsche's response to nihilism relates to Hitlerism in a way similar to the way in which liberalism stood, for him, in relation to skepticism and nihilism. They both inaugurate a logic that paves the way for apparent contraries. Hitlerism may indeed be called, mimicking Nietzsche's sentence on Christianity, a sort of Nietzscheanism for the masses. That is, Hitler seems to have done for Nietzsche what Nietzsche argued that Christianity did for Platonism. But it was precisely against the dominance of the masses that Nietzsche fought so fiercely. He would have surely opposed the vulgar racism of Aryan superiority. Yet Nietzsche's fixation on power and, particularly, the legitimation of the expression of vital energies at the expense of doing violence to other people is not completely foreign to the Nazi logic. The privileging of energy, force, and power, along with the reduction of sociality to an a posteriori event of authentic human existence—indeed, as the very risk of unfreedom—paves the way for a philosophical and political conception that privileges power and subordination over everything else. The notion of a heroic freedom gained in solitude and in independence from others opens the path to the expression of a power measured in terms of the submission, if not in terms of the very annihilation, of others. Hitler took Nietzsche's logic one step further, for him the will to power was best expressed not in the affirmation of a single human subject but in the will of a people united by elemental ties.

The emphasis on power in Nietzsche's work puts him in line, not only with Hitlerism, but with liberalism as well. Nietzscheanism and liberalism come close at one point: the conception of freedom as an achievement of a lonely subject. The power of an individual subject marks the beginning of the two philosophical approaches. In its conception of freedom, the asceticism of liberalism appears to be, as much as the Nietzschean will to power, an expression of a master consciousness. The enchantment with power is something that the Dreyfus Affair hinted at: the presence of a subject who affirms himself in isolation and hates the Other even while it is simultaneously committed to obeying universal norms. War and the suspension of morals, Levinas suggests, are, therefore, not entirely opposed to the ideals of liberalism. The notion of freedom as absolute independence of the subject distorts other elements of the liberal ideal, for example, the practice of equality and the ideal of human fraternity.

Levinas argues that the liberal concept of freedom is linked to the idea of liberation from fate that undergirds Judaism and to some extent also Christianity. But liberalism accentuates only certain aspects of the idea and ends up making freedom appear more like a heroic individualism or egoism. In contrast, the Judaic conception of freedom (from fate) is based on the recognition of the intrinsic limitations of the human subject and the search for pardon. Since pardon is given by another person, this concept of freedom makes immediate reference to an intersubjective realm—from which pardon can be obtained. It therefore stands in contrast to both the liberal conception of freedom and the privileging of an abstract universality that renders the originality of intersubjectivity an illusion or a deterrence and distortion of the unconditional search for the truth.

Levinas mentions how the realization of the "fragility of Reason" by Jews in France led to a renovation of Judaic religiosity. His piece on the philosophy of Hitlerism makes clear, as does the intellectual work that followed the essay, that this return to Judaism did not represent simply a reactionary movement. The return to the Judaic sources and to Judaic spirituality represented for him the possibility of living the promises of freedom and universality without falling into violence, and of providing a different basis and a different logic for the ideas that became so prominent in the West. This path put Levinas in direct contrast with Nietzsche: instead of embracing fate to the point of saying "*Yes*" to everything—even to murder—Levinas draws on the Jewish notion of forgiveness and pardon through which the subject escapes fate. Levinas finds enslavement in the lonely freedom that dominates, and not in obedience to the law. In this way he began to turn upside down the Nietzschean and the liberal tables. He attempted to do exactly the same with Husserlian philosophy.

Levinas did not take the Nietzschean solution to nihilism, but neither did he take the Husserlian attempt to overcome decadent skepticism by restoring faith in intellectualistic conceptions of truth. Indeed, what he revealed in his work, and what the piece on Hitlerism already suggested, is that the Husserlian conception of freedom and the search for truth was as prone to legitimate warrior and heroic ideals as liberalism or Nietzscheanism. This confirms what Levinas suggested in respect to liberalism, that its conception of freedom reflects more a master morality than a slave consciousness. With this in mind I turn to explore the contrast between the Levinasian and the Husserlian responses to the crisis of modernity.

THE HUSSERLIAN RESPONSE

The Phenomenological Reduction Husserl attempted to exorcize the ghost of naturalism and skepticism from philosophy and from Western culture by giving a new basis to the ideal of the search for the truth. But Husserl was more a revolutionary than a reactionary. He attempted to overcome skepticism by changing the terms according to which truth is found. Husserl observed that the possibility of skepticism is introduced by positing a distance between the knower and the known. But this, for Husserl, is a prejudice. What is given to us, and what we can only be certain of is the phenomenon of a thing. Phenomenology marks a radical turn away from the anthropology of liberalism. If, as Levinas points out, liberalism introduces the possibility of skepticism by relying on the dichotomy between subject and object, or between knower and the known, then phenomenology is a way of giving a new philosophical basis to the idea of freedom as the search for the truth. It offers what modern philosophy could not, the possibility of philosophy as rigorous science.[23]

Phenomenology offers the possibility of gaining access to a field of inquiry where skepticism's thorn cannot sting. It gains access to this field by the phenomenological reduction. It involves the suspension of the belief in the factical existence of the world. In other words, it is a way of *parenthesizing* the thesis about its external reality. The most basic significance of the reduction is that it uncovers a new field of philosophical reflection, a *"new region of being never before delimited in its own peculiarity."*[24] This new field is transcendental consciousness.[25] Transcendentally pure consciousness, Husserl argues, is what remains as a residuum after the *epoché*.[26] The phenomenologist is now left with the task of describing the structure of consciousness, and with establishing the essential modalities that are at work in every individual conscious act. Husserl describes this task as follows:

> We consider mental processes of consciousness *in the entire fullness of the concreteness* within which they present themselves in their concrete context—*the stream of mental processes*—and which, by virtue of their own essence, they combine to make up. It then becomes evident that every mental process belonging to the stream which can be reached by our reflective regard has

an *essence of its own* which can be seized upon intuitively, a "content" which allows of being considered *by itself in its ownness*. Our concern is to seize upon and to universally characterize this own content of the cogitation in its *pure* ownness by excluding everything which does not lie in the cogitation with respect to what the cogitation is in itself. It is equally our concern to characterize the *unity of consciousness* required, and therefore necessarily required, *purely by what belongs to the cogitationes as their own* such that they could not exist without that unity.[27]

Many are the different tasks awaiting the phenomenologist with the opening of this new transcendental sphere. What is most central to this move, at least in Husserl's conception, is that through the phenomenological reduction philosophy finally finds its way to becoming a *strict science*. As a response to the skepticism of the age phenomenology presents itself as the promise of the expectations of all philosophical reflections. This conception is central to Husserl's project.

The following arguments are based on the conviction that the highest interests of human culture demand the development of a rigorously scientific philosophy; consequently, if a philosophical revolution in our times is justified, it must be animated by the purpose of laying a new foundation for philosophy in the sense of strict science. This purpose is by no means foreign to the present age, which is arguably still dominated by "skeptical negativism" of the positivist or postmodern kind, particularly when it comes to questions of liberation and the agency and epistemological contributions of racialized selves. Husserl had a different but related point of view.[28] For him:

> our age is called an age of decadence. I cannot consider this complaint justified. . . . I mean, our age is according to its vocation a great age—only it suffers from the skepticism that has disintegrated the old, unclarified ideals. And for that very reason it suffers from the too negligible development and force of philosophy, which has not yet progressed enough, is not scientific enough to overcome skeptical negativism (which calls itself positivism) by means of true positivism. Our age wants to believe only in "realities." Now, its strongest reality is science, and thus what our age most needs is philosophical science.[29]

Phenomenology enters simultaneously in the drama of the interactions between thought and value, and between the search for knowledge and the pathos of an epoch. Its emergence promises a resolution to the internal and interrelational tensions of these two fields. Phenomenology aspires to accomplish the most central of the philosophical aspirations by becoming a strict science. At the same time phenomenological investigation aims at establishing itself in a more primordial place than scientific research or naturalist philosophy. In this way, and only in this way, it is argued, the age will be liberated from naturalism and historicist skepticism. This is because phenomenology, in contrast to these, is science without presuppositions. It directs its reflection to consciousness, an indubitable sphere that alone is the locus and origin of all sense and meaning. Since the givenness of the world (what is merely presupposed by all natural science and naturalistic philosophy) can only be spelled out in relation to consciousness, the very development of the sciences, their basis, delimitation, and definition will come to depend on investigations of a phenomenological character. As authentic rigorous science phenomenology becomes then the surest way to satisfy the aspirations of humanity of reaching the heights of a true knowledge that escapes the traps of skepticism (because, among other things, it already *parenthesizes* the thesis about the existence of the world) and founds scientific knowledge.

As important as the overcoming of skepticism is for Husserl, Husserlian phenomenology would not have been so influential if it only promised the possibility of achieving rigorous science. More significant and influential was the way in which Husserl offered a different basis to understand and to pursue the achievement of freedom in relation to the search for knowledge and the attainment of truth. Consider that the phenomenological reduction leads the phenomenologist to a sphere of *ownness* where only the phenomenon can be found. Consciousness appears in this way to be primarily a consciousness with a content, and not an ego that confronts an object. In short, consciousness is for Husserl always intentional, it is "consciousness of. . . ." With the thesis about the intentionality of consciousness Husserl not only provides the basis for rejecting naturalism and combating the reification of mechanism; he also offers the possibility to refer to the subject in all its density, recognizing the primordial role of its complex intuitive structure in the revelation of the world. With phenomenology there is then the possibility of overcoming the limitations of the reification of a theory of knowledge according to which the subject's relation to the world is only understood in cognitive terms between two different and forever unreachable substances. So, for instance, Emmanuel Levinas understood it and made it explicit in his influential doctoral dissertation:

We can perceive how, with such an attitude, one can go beyond any philosophy which thinks it must start from the theory of knowledge, as a study of our faculty of knowing, in order to see whether and how a subject can reach being. Any theory of knowledge presupposes, indeed, the existence of an object and of a subject that must come in contact with each other. Knowledge is then defined as this contact, and this always leaves the problem of determining whether knowledge does not falsify the being which it presents to the subject. But this problem is exposed as fictitious once we understand that the origin of the very idea of "an object" is to be found in the *concrete life of a subject; that a subject is not a substance in need of a bridge, namely, knowledge, in order to reach an object, but that the secret of its subjectivity is its being present in front of objects.* The modes of appearing of things are not, therefore, characters which are superimposed on existing things by the process of consciousness; they make up the very existence of things.[30]

For the early Levinas, phenomenology has to do with the rescue of concrete existence and concrete experience.[31] This implies the irreducibility of both the real world and the subject. "Toward the concrete," states Levinas as he describes Husserlian phenomenology by appropriating the terms of Jean Wahl.[32] The phenomenological reduction became not so much the key to accessing a sphere of abstraction and indubitability, but a way of fully recognizing the relevance of concrete life. For Levinas, "The reduction does not attempt to perform a mere abstraction . . . which imagines consciousness without a world. On the contrary, it discovers our truly concrete life. . . ."[33] The reduction was also for Levinas a way for the subject to conceive itself according to its vocation of giving sense. In Levinas's description the reduction becomes "an inner revolution rather than a search for certainties, a way for the mind to exist in conformity with its vocation, and, in sum, to be free vis-à-vis the world. Consciousness of everything . . . is what remains after everything is excluded."[34] In short, for Levinas "the phenomenological reduction becomes a method of spiritual life."[35]

Phenomenology almost acquires soteriological dimensions for the early Levinas. Phenomenology becomes for him (and for others) a way to rescue the concreteness of a subject as well as a way to overcome the "alienating distantiation" (to use Paul Ricoeur's term) between subject and object justified by philosophy and the sciences. Phenomenology also appears to provide the means of linking the subject to the "world of experience" without thereby depending on any notion of the absolute or reflective Spirit.[36] Yet this "return" to experience and the idea of the relation and intentional correlation of subject and world does not lead Husserlian phenomenology to ignore the basic intuition that Kantian philosophy defended: the relative primacy of this subject over the totality of experience. The phenomenological reduction gives back to the subject that very sense of freedom and distance. It is for this reason that Levinas calls it a method of spiritual life, and why he sees the vocation of the human tied to the idea of "being free in relation to the world." It is Sartre who has made perhaps the most vivid remarks on these points:

> Husserl has restored to things their horror and their charm. He has restored to us the world of artists and prophets: frightening, hostile, dangerous, with its havens of mercy and love. He has cleared the way for a new treatise of the passions. We are delivered from Proust. We are likewise delivered from the "internal life": in vain would we seek the caresses and fondlings of our intimate selves, like Amiel or like a child who kisses his own shoulder, since everything is finally outside, even ourselves. Outside, in the world, among others. It is not in some hiding-place that we will discover ourselves; it is on the road, in the town, in the midst of the crowd, a thing among things, a man among men.[37]

Husserl uncovers a new sense of freedom in the search for the truth. The sense of a strong divide between subject and world that offers mastery and independence to the subject, but only at the expense of the always threatening possibility of an alienating detachment from the world, seems to be finally vanquished. The phenomenological reduction simultaneously introduces a new conception of the search for the truth and an innovative conception of freedom *in the world*—the world, of course, not so much as the material pole of intentionality as the totality of meaning that emerges in the lived experiences of the subject. Husserl aims to re-enchant the world once more with the prospects of an existence committed to the search for a forever possible attainment of truth. Levinas was very enthusiastic about these ideas. His enthusiasm, however, was not going to last for long. Early in his philosophical work he pointed out an exacerbated intellectualism in Husserl's work. At the end, Levinas argued, the demands of *theoria* restrict or limit the movement toward the concrete in Husserlian phenomenology. As Levinas puts it in his *Theory of Intuition*:

> We have said that intentionality is not the mere representation of an object. Husserl calls states of consciousness *Erlebnisse*—what is "lived" in the sense of what is experienced—and this very expression connects the notion of con-

sciousness to that of life, i.e., it leads us to consider consciousness under the rich and multiform aspects characteristic of our concrete existence. The practical and aesthetic categories are . . . part of the very constitution of being, in the same way as the purely theoretical categories. However, it would be twisting Husserl's thought somewhat to speak here of equivalence. In Husserl's philosophy . . . , knowledge and representation are not on the same level as other modes of life, and they are not secondary modes. Theory and representation play a dominant role in life, serving as a basis for the whole of conscious life; they are the forms of intentionality that give a foundation to all others. The role played by representation in consciousness affects the meaning of intuition. This is what causes the intellectualistic character proper to Husserlian intuitionism.[38]

The marriage between the search for the truth and a renewed conception of lived freedom proved to be not entirely effective for Levinas since the concreteness of the world and the richness of phenomena appeared to be betrayed by the privileging of a theoretical lens. And, since for Husserl, consciousness is only made manifest in relation to a content, the skewed conception of experience ultimately leads to a distorted conception of subjectivity—that is, the transcendental ego. The theoretical prejudice in Husserl's reduction of consciousness and experience, and the correlation between intellectualist conceptions of ego and world, are tailored to the measure of an equally intellectualist conception of the vocation of humanity, which is, for Husserl, none other than the search for the truth. In this sense, subject, world, and the activity of the subject in the world are all parasitic to the ideal of the search for the truth. Levinas, like Husserl, is committed to the project of searching for the truth.[39] But searching for the truth entails for Levinas ultimately avoiding the collapse of subjectivity and world into categories that do not entirely fit them. Levinas would reject the Husserlian infatuation with the theoretical paradigm in the name of the truth.

Levinas preferred a truth that coincides with peace. The betrayal of concreteness in Husserlian philosophy reintroduces the posture of detachment and mastery of the world so central to Christianity and French liberalism. The betrayal of subjectivity and world by the intellectualist prejudice can only be sustained at the expense of maintaining the possibility of its reversal by a philosophy akin to Hitlerism. That is to say, the persistence of an intellectualist prejudice only makes it easier for dangerous vitalisms to appear. However, if the Husserlian promise of returning faith in the possibility of philosophy as rigorous science were to become a reality, then skepticism and the resultant nihilism would seem to be dispelled or avoided. Western societies may thus be well prepared to avoid the temptation of adopting the Germanic ideal of blood and earth. But, where skepticism and nihilism fail to appear, the elitism of having found the way to the truth would easily begin to emerge. This elitism is clearly found in the way in which concrete ordinary experience is rendered secondary in relation to cognitive acts and to theoretical modes of intuition. From this idea we obtain (1) the privileging of vision as the organ of contact with the real, (2) the privileging of either contemplation or a praxis of apprehension that leads to indifference or to violence, and (3) the idea of the philosopher (vis-à-vis the aesthete, the judge, or the ordinary human being) as the true representative of the humanity of the human. If the consistent expression of the ideal of searching for the truth introduces a sort of elitism, the related idea of universality borders on a dangerous conception of expansionism. This suspicion marks an unexpected direction in Levinas's engagement with liberalism and Hitlerism. Levinas explores the connections between the logic of racism and the universality of the truth. In a universalistic conception of an idea, Levinas observes that

> the idea propagated detaches itself essentially from its point of departure. In spite of the unique accent communicated to it by its creator, it becomes a common heritage. It is fundamentally anonymous. The person who accepts it becomes its master, as does the person who proposes it. The propagation of an idea thus creates a community of "masters"; it is a process of equalization. To convert or persuade is to create peers. The universality of an order in Western society always reflects this universality of truth. (RPH 70)

Universality, as Nietzsche insisted so strongly, involves a leveling process or process of equalizing. Levinas, like Nietzsche, recognizes that universality entails a leveling process. Yet, he notices that the impetus toward equality is only one side of a simultaneous impulse for obtaining privilege. The leveling process introduced by the ideal of universality works more as a way to create a "community of 'masters'" than as a way of restricting the expression of individuality. The idea is that universality works not only as a limitation on individual exceptionality, but as an expansion of the exceptional marvel of attaining the truth. Even Zarathustra, Levinas remarks, "was not content with his transfiguration; instead he came down from his mountain, bringing a gospel with him" (RPH 70). The limits of the use of universality in Western civilization can be traced back not to a slave morality of submission to the truth, but to a master immorality of expansionism. This is the link that ties the philosophical idea of universality with the philosophy of Hitlerism. As Levinas puts it,

> . . . Force is characterized by another type of propagation. The person who exerts force does not abandon it. Force does not disappear among those who submit to it. It is attached to the personality or society exerting it, enlarging that person or society while subordinating the rest. Here the universal order is not established as a consequence of ideological expansion; it is that very expansion that constitutes the unity of a world of masters and slaves. Nietzsche's will to power, which modern Germany is rediscovering and glorifying, is not only a new ideal; it is an ideal that simultaneously brings with it its own form of universalization: war and conquest. (RPH 70–71)

Hitlerism exploits the links between universality and expansionism. It takes on the idea of force that is implicit in the practice of "conversion" and "persuasion" that brings about a "community of 'masters.'" Ironically, the project of the search for truth comes closest to Hitlerism both when it fails and brings about nihilism and when it succeeds and leads to the formation of a community of masters. Hitlerism stands at both ends of the mode in which the grandiloquent project of searching and attaining the truth takes in the West.

Hitlerism is the expected result of projects that privilege force and power. It is the expression of an ideal that values force and power for their own sakes. It takes modern Western civilization by surprise only because it radicalizes values that have been central to it. The Nietzschean and the Husserlian responses to the consequences of liberalism and modern philosophy hardly represent challenges to Hitlerism because they still rely on or justify ideals of force and power that are at odds with the primacy of responsibility and the care for the other person.

I discussed how the Nietzschean idea of the will to power can be read as complicit with Hitlerism. I also suggested that the phenomenological reduction introduces a sort of elitism that is reminiscent of the idea of expansionism that later finds a place in Hitlerism. The Husserlian community of philosophers/masters, however, is not formed by violent expansionism. If anything, Husserl would advocate persuasion and conversion. Levinas mentions that "to convert or persuade is to create peers." Yet, for a community of masters to be formed and persist it is clear that *somewhere* there must be slaves. The community of masters must be exclusive at the same time that it is inclusive. At its best it must reject while it admits. Again, the Nazis gave the most consistent expression of this logic: membership is gained and confirmed by irrefutable facts (by race, not by efforts) and whoever is not a member should simply cease to exist. Master immorality is exclusive at best and homicidal at worst. Exclusion, however, marks the permanent possibility of selected murder. A second look at Husserl's conception of the philosophical task shows how the search for the truth also entailed for him a combined effort of inclusion and exclusion.

Exclusion and Inclusion in Husserl's Philosophy It was 1934, the same year in which Levinas published his reflections on Hitlerism, that Husserl began to reflect more intensely and seriously than ever before on the relation of phenomenology and the "crisis of European humanity."[40] The crisis in question is mainly for Husserl a crisis of rationality with a threefold expression in the crisis of the sciences, both natural and human, the crisis of philosophy, and the crisis of European culture.[41] Naturalism, skepticism, objectivism, and psychologism were Husserl's main enemies. For him, they all gave expression to a stage of decay in Western civilization and posed a risk to humanity at large. This risk was none other than the regression of humankind to barbarism, myth, and irrationality. Europeans like Husserl were particularly concerned about this, not only because Europe was the alleged site of the crisis, but also because it alone represented for them the veritable habitat and the true representative of human rationality. Thus we find Husserl, with an urgency that is not completely strange to our days, complaining somewhat in *despair*:

> Scientific, objective truth is exclusively a matter of establishing what the world, the physical as well as the spiritual world, is in fact. But can the world, and human existence in it, truthfully have a meaning if the sciences recognize as true only what is objectively established in this fashion, and if history has nothing more to teach us than that all the shapes of the spiritual world ... form and dissolve themselves like fleeting waves ... ? Can *we* console ourselves with that? Can *we* live in this world, where historical occurrence is nothing but an unending concatenation of illusory progress and bitter disappointment?[42]

The crisis, the urgency of this call, is to be clearly understood by a "we" who apparently are losing their very identity in the dominion of a scientific perspective that foments different sorts of relativism and undermines the spirit of a philosophical inquiry into the fundamental meaning of human reality. As Husserl does not cease to remind his readers, this "we" is none other than "European Man" who must strive to elaborate a "rigorous philosophy" and vanquish the shadows of relativism and skepticism.[43] Husserl's life-long intellectual project consisted mainly and for the most part in nothing else but the attempt to articulate this "rigorous philosophy."[44]

For Husserl, philosophy must take seriously two challenges: first, the recognition of the significance of non-objectivistic dimensions of human life; and second, having recovered European Man in his concreteness, that is, beyond positivistic reductions, to show that his life is not merely the result of a contingent historical process. If Husserl was so fearful of relativism, it was not only because it challenges the basis of logic and universal reason, but also because it problematizes the idea of progress and universality that sustains the self-understanding of the European, in particular, as it relates to the conception of Europe as the climax of civilization. Husserl must then prove the uniqueness, the historical depth, and the universality embodied in European humanity. For this he will rely, like nineteenth-century social sciences, on particular ideas about the nation and about the relation between space and time. This becomes transparent in a rather long passage that I quote in full.

> Every spiritual image has its place essentially in a universal historical space or in a particular unity of historical time in terms of coexistence or succession—it has its history. If, then, we follow historical connections, beginning as we must with ourselves and our own nation, historical continuity leads us ever further away from our own nation to neighboring nations, and so from nation to nation, from age to age. Ultimately we come to ancient times and go from the Romans to the Greeks, to the Egyptians, the Persians, etc.; in this there is clearly no end. . . . In this process consistent, penetrating observation reveals new, characteristic compositions and distinctions. No matter how inimical the European nations may be toward each other, still they have a special inner affinity of spirit that permeates all of them and transcends their national differences. It is a sort of *fraternal relationship* that gives us the consciousness of being at home in this circle. This becomes immediately evident as soon as, for example, we penetrate sympathetically into the historical process of India, with its many peoples and cultural forms. In this circle there is again the unity of a family-like relationship, but one that is strange to us. On the other hand, Indians find us strangers and find only in each other their fellows. Still, this essential distinction between fellowship and strangeness . . . cannot suffice. Historical humanity does not always divide itself in the same way according to this category. We get a hint of that right in our

> own Europe. Therein lies something unique, which all other human groups, too, feel with regard to us, something that, apart from all considerations of expediency, becomes a motivation for them—despite their determination to retain their spiritual autonomy—constantly to Europeanize themselves, whereas we, if we understand ourselves properly, will never, for example, Indianize ourselves. I mean we feel (and with all its vagueness this feeling is correct) that in our European humanity there is an innate entelechy that thoroughly controls the changes in the European image and gives to it the sense of a development in the direction of an ideal image of life and of being, as moving toward an eternal pole.[45]

For Husserl, Europe can only overcome its crisis if it follows and gives full expression to an immanent telos to which its history and the history of others bear witness. That non-European peoples are "motivated" to Europeanize themselves indicates that the European telos reveals not only the finality and destiny of Europeans, but ultimately the very essence of humanity. The crisis of Europe thus represents in this account the crisis of the human. This preliminary diagnosis and reinterpretation of the crisis of Europe already points to its cure, since the identification of the crisis of Europe with the crisis of humanity renews the idea of the centrality of Europe and rules out the radical relativism that made European history and European Man look insignificant.

For Husserl, the history that reveals the essence of humanity, that is, the history of the European nations, begins with the Greeks and makes itself particularly evident in the Renaissance.[46] While ancient Greece inaugurates the urge for universal and disinterested knowledge, the Renaissance introduces in Europe a properly modern spirit.

> In the Renaissance, as is well known, European humanity brings about a revolutionary change. It turns against its previous way of existing—the medieval—and disowns it, seeking to shape itself anew in freedom. Its admired model is ancient humanity. This mode of existence is what it wishes to reproduce in itself.[47]

For Husserl, among the different disciplines and doctrines, philosophy becomes the best representative of the new "mode of existence" embraced by Europe, since it is precisely through its "new philosophy" that the humanistic renovation primarily takes place.[48] Consequently, the deviation of philosophy from its truly scientific task through its enchantment with extreme forms of positivism and relativism comes to represent for him a menace to the very essence of humanity. The cure for the crisis is to be found, accordingly, in the restatement of the European telos in a *philosophical* project that makes possible the achievement of truth and certainty. As we have seen, Husserl introduces his own phenomenology as the most plausible candidate for this mission.[49]

Husserl's critique of psychologism and the articulation of his own philosophical project reproduce a logic that has accompanied philosophy from its beginnings. This logic combines an urge for the universal with a simultaneous reification of the particular. The move from the particular to the universal, which, according to Husserl, was initiated by the Greeks, gives rise to a regime of power in which the *particular* is now subdued and subordinated to the *universal*. To be sure, what we find is one particular now invested with the power of the universal by considering all others as mere particulars. Thus, as the Greeks become the representatives of the universal, others are certified as barbarians.[50] Husserl mirrors the Greek gesture only too well by salvaging European particularity through a link with the *universal* and an epistemic subordination of particular others. As the crisis of the European sciences questions any actual link between Europe and the universal, the relation can only be interpreted in temporal terms—as if Europe possessed a telos and a destiny only to be unfolded historically. The crisis of Europe is then interpreted as if it were only a betrayal of its telos. While temporality provides the means to reassert the intrinsic link between Europe and the universal, spatiality takes the role of demarcating difference. That is, if time constitutes identity in relation to internal features that mimic mythic ties with the fundamental, space becomes the means to assert identity and protect the *intrinsic* and *fundamental* through difference. The European nations represent the privileged space for the unfolding of the telos of humanity. Once the fragility of European *history* (in its relation to the universal) is made evident, spatiality is (re)introduced as a significant factor in the subalternation of non-European peoples.[51] Husserl's reference to the Indians becomes a necessary step in a perverse logic that aims to establish European greatness through the differentiation and epistemic subordination of others.

Husserl's attempt to confront what he considered to be the crisis of Europe demonstrates that his "unprejudiced" phenomenological description was oriented more by the challenges posed by the barbarism of irrationality than by the barbarism of missionary Eurocentric rationality. As Joan-Charles Mèlich puts it, "Obsessed with denouncing the barbarism of unilateral rationalism, the old Husserl forgets the totalitarianism of philosophical reason. If philosophy is not susceptible to the 'thorn' of strangeness, the strange ends up being swallowed by the subject, by the *ego*."[52] Husserl's main goal is to see an unfinished modernity properly realized in the achievement of a rigorous philosophy. "Only then," Husserl points out, "could it be decided whether European humanity bears within itself an absolute idea, rather than being merely an empirical anthropological type like 'China' or 'India'; it could be decided whether the spectacle of the Europeanization of all other civilizations bears witness to the rule of an absolute meaning, one which is proper to the sense, rather than to a historical non-sense, of the world."[53] To all those who "live for the truth," Husserl preaches then "the faith in the possibility of philosophy as a task." Philosophers are *"called* to this task as serious philosophers." The vocation of the philosopher, quite distinct from the vocation of the politician or the scientist (Weber), has to do with the universality inherent in the human. As Husserl notes, "Human philosophizing and its results in the whole of man's existence mean anything but merely private or otherwise limited cultural goals." From this Husserl cannot but conclude,

> In *our* philosophizing, then—how can we avoid it?—we are *functionaries of mankind*. The quite personal responsibility of our own true being as philosophers, our inner personal vocation, bears within itself at the same time the responsibility for the true being of mankind; the latter is, necessarily, being toward a *telos* and can only come to realization, *if at all*, through philosophy—through *us*, *if* we are philosophers in all seriousness.[54]

In his seriousness the philosopher embodies the idea of an authentic saint, that is, "of someone who does good and knows *why* he or she does that good."[55] The (Western) philosopher is a functionary with the task of vanquishing the shadows of skepticism, relativism, unreflectivity, and non-sense. The expansion of truth and meaning over non-sense provide a motif or aspiration for the expansion of Europe and the Europeanization of non-Europeans. At the end, the imperialism of sense appears to provide the ultimate sense of imperialism itself.

As Levinas points out in his essay on Hitlerism, the community in charge of managing the economy of truth and universality is a "community of masters." At best, it uses persuasion and conversion to achieve its goals. It insists on giving or imposing, but not on receiving. Persuasion and conversion are not necessarily violent means. They may be ways in which subjects and cultures grow and change. In order for this to occur (in a non-pathological manner), however, the subjects or cultures that undergo change must be in a position to exchange ideas at a similar level of influence. They also should be open to expanding their horizons through intersubjective or intercultural exchange. In contrast, the Husserlian conception of the vocation of the philosopher indicates that the process is unidirectional. The idea of the propagation of truth works more as a movement of expansionism than as a dynamic interaction of authentic communication. Philosophers thus appear as organic intellectuals, to use Antonio Gramsci's felicitous terms, of a "community of masters." They are central for the imperial reproduction of the "European species."

The idea of the search for the truth collapses, in influential Western expressions of the ideal, in the creation of a world divided between master and slaves. Eurocentrism had been playing the effective role of creating a reality marked by the imperatives of imperial control long before the emergence of Hitlerism.[56] Hitlerism represents, in a sense, the forces of Eurocentrism going wild—to the point where European territories were humiliated in the process by the Nazis.[57] In Hitlerism, violence does not have to be mediated or softened by "persuasion" and "conversion"; it finds direct and unmediated expression in systematic murder. If Eurocentrism, the trademark of the community of (European) masters, is the establishment of a universal order through "ideological expansion," in Hitlerism, as Levinas well puts it, "it is that very expansion that constitutes the unity of a world of masters and slaves" (RPH 70–71). In Hitlerism, thus, the Eurocentric logic of the relation between the universal and the particulars unambiguously translates itself into the direct and unmediated violent assertion of one (superior) particular (Aryan race) over other (inferior) particulars (weaker races). This does not mean that Eurocentrism is not also backed up by force or supported by racial prejudice. Unlike Hitlerism, however, Eurocentrism can keep its most aggressive tendencies at bay for a considerable amount of time. It can also function well in a context where the slave is maintained alive. For Eurocentrism, the important thing is that the masters keep occupying the "center" and that the slaves stay put in their place. Eurocentrism can, therefore, easily flourish in a condition where everyone more or less knows, or should know, their respective roles in a context where it is evident who the master is. For this reason, when it does not resort to murder, Eurocentrism is satisfied with maintaining colonial and racist legacies with ambiguous codes for inclusion and exclusion into European humanity. I will discuss more in depth the nature of Eurocentrism in chapter 6. My point here is that, from a Levinasian point of view, Eurocentrism appears as a peculiar form of ethnocentrism based on the value of universality—understood as the subsumption of the particular in the general.[58] It is also informed by or even mounted upon colonial and racial perspectives and experiences, which give a particular shape to the dichotomies that it forms.

Levinas gradually came to make more explicit his critique of Western civilization in terms of a philosophical conception that gave primacy to Being over beings, the general over the particular, and essence over singularity. Following Franz Rosenzweig he came to conceive dominant forms of Western ontology, epistemology, and philosophical anthropology as expressions of an "ideology of war."[59] But already in his early essay on Hitlerism he hints at the links between certain conceptions of the universal and the formation of a "community of masters." I have been arguing that his account provides a good description of Eurocentrism—not necessarily Western civilization as a whole. Hitlerism, in turn, is the paroxysm of that community of masters—Europe's violent universalism is displaced by more direct forms of exercising violence, elimination, and control. In both cases, Eurocentrism and Hitlerism, we are dealing with postures that inhibit the idea of human fraternity, which calls for the critique of notions that create "communities of masters." Levinas's own alternative to Hitlerism will draw precisely on this ideal (human fraternity), which is often neglected or subordinated by political visions, including liberal and Marxist, that focus more prominently on freedom or equality. We will have to determine the extent to which Levinas's vision offers a viable alternative to Hitlerism and Eurocentrism (interpreted as the formation of a community of European masters based on the idea of the universal). We are going to determine this in the next chapter.

CONCLUSION

The advent of Hitlerism led both Husserl and Levinas to reflect more seriously on the crisis of the modern West. As we have seen, the Husserlian response to the crisis may be very well interpreted as a call to abandon the radically destructive Hitlerism by returning to the more typical and traditional though not much less problematic and perverse Eurocentrism. In his reflections on Hitlerism Levinas makes clear how the value of universality in the West translates itself into the formation of a community of masters. This idea introduces something unsuspected by Husserl, that the problem of liberal anthropology far surpasses the limitations introduced by the subject-object split. Its fundamental perversion lies in its complicity with forms of human interaction that follow the logic of a division between master and slaves. This is what the Dreyfus Affair hinted at. In his response to the crisis Husserl, in contrast, was bound to repeat what he did not see. Ultimately, his proposal reproduced the tendency to privilege the form of life achieved in a "community of masters."

Levinas's early essay on Hitlerism opens an unsuspected path of reflection. He shows similarities between apparent contraries. First, he provides the basis for understanding the common elements in Hitlerism and Nietzscheanism. Then, he suggests ways in which Husserl repeats patterns of thinking found in liberalism. But, ultimately, Levinas shows how all of them (Hitlerism, Nietzscheanism, Husserlianism, and liberalism) are related. They give expression to a conception of freedom as power. They also lead to skewed forms of human community that perpetuate the logics between master and slave and that privilege experiences akin to acts of war and conquest.

The exposure to Hitlerism and the Holocaust marks Levinas's work in a definitive way. Basically all of his work will reflect the attempt to provide alternative conceptions to paradigms of thought that justify or are complicit with acts of war and conquest. I will elaborate Levinas's response to these paradigms in the following chapter. I will attempt to show its virtues as well as its limitations. As I will try to make clear, Levinas's thought moves toward a conception of ethics and critical thinking that emerges from conditions wherein the experience of evil and the possibility of injustice emerge in the very heart of a seemingly found peace. In this respect, Levinas's reflections will prove pertinent to the challenges found by subjects who live in contexts wherein domination operates behind the alleged tranquility of ordinary life.

2

FROM FRATERNITY TO ALTERICITY,
OR REASON IN THE SERVICE OF LOVE

In the first chapter of *Humanity: A Moral History of the Twentieth Century* Jonathan Glover writes,

> In Europe at the start of the twentieth century most people accepted the authority of morality. They thought there was a moral law, which was self-evidently to be obeyed. At the start of the twentieth century, *reflective Europeans* were also able to believe in moral progress, and to see human viciousness and barbarism as in retreat. At the end of the century, it is hard to be confident either about the moral law or about moral progress.[1]

If anything, the last chapter has made clear that Levinas, a *reflective Lithuanian Jew*, did not have to wait until the end of the century to experience the European mistrust of morals.[2] Indeed, as his critiques of Nietzsche and Husserl show, Levinas noted that there was a high degree of comfort with the effective neutralization of morals in the first half of the twentieth century and even earlier. Consider that when Levinas states in *Totality and Infinity* that "everyone will readily agree that it is of the highest importance to know whether we are not duped by morality [sic]," he does not make explicit the reasons why "everyone" will so readily agree (TI 21). He knows that while some people may be concerned with the future of ethics, others may be more interested in the achievement of lucidity. He is aware that there are many who are fully prepared to abandon ethics at the expense of even small advances in the search for knowledge. A civilization with this sense of priorities commits violence with good conscience. But the terror of violence eventually leads even the skeptic to be concerned with morals.

As we have seen in the previous chapter, the possibility of lucidity or truth is intrinsically connected in Western civilization with the "permanent possibility of war." We have seen that war also emerges as a positive value in dominant, alternative ideals. From the Husserlian concept of the reduction and his idea of philosophers as functionaries of mankind to the Nietzschean advocacy of the will to power and his conception of the Overman, conflict and struggle keep appearing as dominant traits of authentic philosophical inquiry. These themes find a particularly accentuated expression in the work of Martin Heidegger, for whom authenticity is interpreted in terms of stoic resoluteness. A proper exploration of Levinas's response to the ideal of war demands an examination of Heidegger's work. This examination will dramatize the deep implications between the conceptual and the concrete, or between philosophy and politics. The problems in Heidegger's work make even more clear the challenge facing Levinas: to provide an alternative to the paradigm of violence and war not only at the conceptual level but also at the concrete. Levinasian thought can only claim success if it provides the basis for a different way of thinking and for a different way of being in the world.

The critical evaluation of Levinas's thought, however, has more often than not remained almost exclusively at the conceptual level.[3] But conceptual transformations in his intellectual production can hardly be accounted for by referring only to conceptual problems. Indeed, conceptual problems in great part appear as problems in the light of their implications for concrete human existence. At least this is the way in which Levinas proceeded in his criticism of other philosophers, and the way in which I will approach his work here. The trajectory of Levinas's thought can be accounted for in relation to the attempt to overcome the paradigm of violence and war and its implications for concrete historical reality.[4]

As we have seen, the themes of "war and conquest" that appear in his "Reflections on the Philosophy of Hitlerism" occupy a central place in Levinas's first major work, *Totality and Infinity*. The main goal of this work is indeed none other than an attempt to articulate an alternative to the ideal of war. Levinas's general strategy principally involves the effort to redeem ordinary social life. He attempts to do this by combining two approaches that define his work from his essay on Hitlerism up to *Totality and Infinity*: the elaboration of a renewed conception of human fraternity and an account of the origins of human communication in terms of ethics and responsibility. As sophisticated and provocative as the attempted synthesis undoubtedly is, the project of redeeming ordinary life does not offer, or so I will argue, the necessary conceptual bases to confront the problem of violence in its diverse manifestations. Levinas will thus have to turn to the idea of philosophy as critique, which puts him close to philosophical conceptions that foment the kind of philosophical elitism that has been instrumental to the promotion of a predominant Western master morality. Aware of his proximity to this conception, Levinas will adopt the Husserlian concept of *reduction*, but he will alter its meaning in a radical manner. In the final section of this chapter I will explain the renewed conception of reduction and attempt to clarify its significance for the project of a consistent evasion of the paradigm of war and of Western master morality.

HEIDEGGER, MASTER MORALITY, AND THE IDEOLOGY OF WAR

> *It is impossible to be stinting in our admiration for the intellectual vigor of* Sein und Zeit, *particularly in the light of the immense output this extraordinary book of 1927 inspired. Its supreme steadfastness will mark it forever. Can we be assured, however, that there was never any echo of evil in it? The diabolical is not limited to the wickedness popular wisdom ascribes to it and whose malice, based on guile, is familiar and predictable in an adult culture. The diabolical is endowed with intelligence and enters where it will. To reject it, it is first necessary to refute it. Intellectual effort is needed to recognize it. Who can boast of having done so? Say what you will, the diabolical gives food for thought.* —EMMANUEL LEVINAS[5]

In the last chapter I demonstrated that there is a link between the seemingly opposite projects of Nietzsche and Husserl. Both of them share egocentric conceptions of subjectivity that end up promoting a skewed conception of communal life: the community of masters. The community of masters values an ethics of power needed to maintain alive a pathos of domination and self-control. This master morality has been part and parcel of the European project since its inception at a geopolitical level in the sixteenth century.[6] Nietzsche's and Husserl's projects are ingenious ways of reasserting and reinventing the philosophical bases of European master morality after its stagnation in bourgeois nineteenth-century European society. The virtues and limitations of these projects appear once again in the influential work of Martin Heidegger, whose fundamental ontology is arguably complicit with the paradigm of violence and war.

In Heidegger, the ties between philosophy and politics, which according to Levinas have been central to Western philosophy since its inception, become particularly obvious. Heidegger, the philosopher, became a bureaucrat in the Nazi administration.[7] Levinas knew early on about Heidegger's association with Nazism.[8] Years later Levinas recalled,

> I could not doubt the news, but took it with stupor and disappointment, and also with the faint hope that it expressed only the temporary lapse of a great speculative mind into practical banality. It cast a shadow over my firm confidence that an unbridgeable distance forever separated the delirious and criminal hatred voiced by Evil on the pages of *Mein Kampf* from the intellectual vigor and extreme analytical virtuosity displayed in *Sein und Zeit*, which had opened the field to a new type of philosophical inquiry.[9]

The new type of philosophical inquiry to which Levinas refers is fundamental ontology. Levinas strongly believed at one moment that Heidegger's fundamental ontology represented the most promising and viable form of philosophical reflection.[10] Indeed, in his doctoral dissertation Levinas portrays Husserlian phenomenology as an incomplete fundamental ontology.[11] Later on Levinas will judge Heidegger's own efforts as limited, since they allegedly reflect a sociology and an anthropology rather than a consistent ontological conception.[12] By the time in which *Totality and Infinity* appeared Levinas had already condemned ontology and described it as a philosophical category adequate to the concept and the exercise of power.[13] Levinas's project is defined by this increasing suspicion of ontology and by the attempt to refute it. Initially, Levinas thought that ontology represented the culmination of the move toward the concrete that he saw in Husserlian phenomenology.[14] But gradually he noted that the Heideggerian ontological turn concealed a fundamental impetus to maintain master morality. In Domenico Losurdo's terms Levinas realized the extent to which Heideggerian ontology was complicit with an "ideology of war."[15] An anthropology and an epistemology that privilege themes related to war and conquest are found behind the ontological curtain.

The "ideology of war" refers to an ideal that emerges in reaction to the ideas of the French Revolution and their outcome in European societies. It is an ideal of an organic community tied, not by the abstract bonds of equality, but by the solid connection provided by experiences lived in the battlefield.[16] Citizenship, according to this notion, is insufficient as a means of obtaining significant intersubjective connection and individual self-worth. Authentic individuality and community emerge in the pathos of conflict and struggle, which appears when one nation engages against another in war. Heroic and violent patriotism takes the place of courteous civility. The nation becomes the source of an unusual feeling of power and not the climax of respect for the person. Sacrifice, resoluteness, the encounter with death, and the conception of a people united by a destiny are four of the main features of the "ideology of war." These four ideals appear in one way or another in Heidegger's work.

Sacrifice, resoluteness, and struggle (*Kampf*), John Caputo comments, were fundamental concepts in Heidegger's thinking early on in his work. "From the start revolutionary renewal was conceived in terms of 'difficulty' and 'struggle' (*Kampf*). Life, existence, history can never be great if they let themselves be lulled to sleep. . . ."[17] Philosophy is conceived by Heidegger as a battle. But philosophy is a battle for him only because life itself is a battle.[18] Life, for Heidegger, "is an unending concern with our daily bread."[19] This idea is clearly behind the Heideggerian conception of *Sorge*, or care. Care takes the place of intentionality in Heidegger's description of the basic comportment of *Dasein*, or human being. Building on Husserl's distinction between the natural and the phenomenological attitude, Heidegger argues that *Dasein* can adopt two different modes of existence. *Dasein* can be authentic or inauthentic. While authenticity refers to the resolute projection of one's ownmost possibilities, inauthenticity suggests the loss of subjectivity. This loss is brought about by the collapse of one's own possibilities into the dominant patterns of action legitimized by society. Here, Heidegger posits a divide between ordinary, intersubjective life and the achievement of authenticity. Authenticity is obtained in solitude, and more particularly in the confrontation of the subject with death. In Heidegger's formula the difference between the natural and the phenomenological attitude almost takes the form of a Nietzschean critique of herd morality and of an appraisal of the Overman.[20]

The Nietzschean turn in Heidegger's work is more definitive after *Being and Time*. Until then, his *Kampf* philosophy took Aristotle and the New Testament as sources for articulating a philosophical vision grounded in the notion of struggle.[21] Yet, even then, in the early 1920s it is possible to detect the malicious influential force of the experience of war. As Caputo puts it,

> In retrospect, a good deal of what is contained in the lectures of the early 1920's was undoubtedly disturbing, full of bravado and phallic aggressiveness. As Kisiel has shown, Heidegger had a long-standing militaristic streak which led him to use military examples to illustrate phenomenological points, to exaggerate his own military experience, and to favor students like Löwith who had recently returned from the war. Heidegger's first "turning," which shows up in the 1919 "Emergency War Semester" (held for returning war veterans), is immediately consequent upon his own war experience,

which appears in retrospect to have a lot to do with the profound upheaval in his thought between 1916 and 1919. Kierkegaard said it would take an earthquake to shake some scholars out of their academic sleep, but the "force" of "factical life" seems to have been visited upon Heidegger by the sound of gunfire.[22]

Just a year after Levinas concluded his sojourn in Freiburg, Heidegger offered a course in which he reflected seriously on the work of conservative revolutionary thinkers such as Oswald Spengler, Ludwig Klages, and Ernst Jünger.[23] Indeed, the lectures during this period treat themes that are familiar both with the analyses of *Being and Time* and with the shameful *Rektorasrede* of 1933, when Heidegger accepted his appointment as rector of the University of Freiburg and pleaded allegiance to the Nazi agenda.[24] From here on the path was clear. Heidegger began to apply categories of *Being and Time* to the collectivity of the German nation.[25] The turn toward National Socialism was seen as "nothing else than an 'authentic decision' based on Germany's *ownmost potentiality-for-Being a nation or Volk*. Just as in *Being and Time* Heidegger sought to justify the inherent particularity of each individual Dasein, now it is the existential particularity of Germany's Dasein as a Volk that he seeks to underwrite."[26] The *Volk* can only become authentic by making a radical decision that leads to a transformation of its factical life through the election of a *Führer*.[27] For Heidegger, "The Führer alone *is* the present and future of German reality and its law."[28] He is, indeed, the only one who can awaken the will in the entire *Volk* and bring it together in a single decision.[29] As Philip Buckley puts it, "The Führer is the one who has the strength to be open to Being; and as Heidegger states in the *Introduction to Metaphysics*, this strength is found only among the few. The Führer is the special chosen one, who by the active fulfillment of personal destiny becomes the destiny of the community he or she leads."[30]

It could be argued that the application of the main ideas and concepts in *Being and Time* to the question of the nation represents an inadequate formulation of the implications of Heidegger's thought. Yet it is also difficult to see how the rhetoric of authenticity in *Being and Time* could lead to a way of thinking about society that is not consigned simply to showing how authenticity is betrayed in ordinary, everyday life. In a sense, Heidegger's reflections on the *Volk* represent the positive side of the implications of his thought to the social realm. Ordinary life can also be redeemed, Heidegger seems to say, if it takes hold of itself and projects its ownmost possibilities. The search for authenticity would indeed be limited in scope if it ended in the achievement of individual authenticity. Individual authenticity, on the contrary, would seem to find its highest expression in the achievement of communal authenticity. Here the possible idealization of war emerges again. War facilitates both *Dasein*'s confrontation with death and the regeneration of the *Volk*. The realization of these ideas is arguably connected with the experiences of the First World War. Consider Peter Fritzsche's description of the overall effects of the war in Germany:

> World War I occupies such a prominent place in modern history because it created new social formations organized around a national identity that was defined in increasingly populist and racial terms. Over the course of the war the massive mobilization of the population challenged older hierarchies of subordination and protocols of deference. At the same time, war reworked traditional gender roles, overruled long-standing class allegiances, and legitimized exclusive ethnic feelings of being German—to produce a fierce new community premised on the struggle for survival in which a whole people stood to win or lose.[31]

Hitler was well aware of the regenerative powers of war.

> the declaration of war produced a sense of Germanness that filled him with ecstasy. For the rest of his life Hitler struggled to retrieve the unshakable union based on ethnic-based nationalism and public self-sacrifice. In his eyes the summer of 1914 was truly historic because it had created a new historical subject in world history—the German Volk—one unencumbered by past history and past inequities and finally unified to claim its imperial destiny.[32]

It is typically thought that Heidegger abandoned the concern with individual authenticity and his alleged anthropological focus after *Being and Time*. The above considerations indicate that Heidegger's supposed "turn" (*Kehre*) may be accounted for not only in relation to an effort to articulate a more consistent "ontology"—focused more on the question of Being than on the question of Man—but in relation to the need to formulate a nationalistic conception of authenticity. Heidegger's later reflections on technology are accompanied by an emphasis on language—sometimes conceived as the house of Being. Heidegger does not refer to the language used in ordinary communication. He has in mind more particularly poetic language. But not all cultist or artistic language is apt, according to him, to serve as a vehicle for the unconcealedness of Being. Heidegger argues that only Greek and German represent adequate vehicles of philosophical reflection. Consider Heidegger's illuminating answers to questions posed to him in the infamous *Der Spiegel* interview of 1966:

> SPIEGEL: It is exactly at the same place where the technological world originated, that it must, as you think . . .
> HEIDEGGER: . . . be transcended [*aufgehoben*] in the Hegelian sense, not pushed aside, but transcended, but not through man alone.
> S: You assign in particular a special task to the Germans?
> H: Yes, in the sense of the dialogue with Hölderlin.
> S: Do you believe that the Germans have a special qualification for this reversal?
> H: I have in mind especially the inner relationship of the German language with the language of the Greeks and with their thought. This has been confirmed for me today again by the French. When they begin to think, they speak German, being sure that they could not make it with their own language.
> S: Are you trying to tell us that that is why you have had such a strong influence on the Romance countries, in particular the French?
> H: Because they see that they can no longer get by in the contemporary world with all their great rationality when it comes right down to understanding the world in the origin of its being.[33]

In order to understand the significance of these remarks it is important to recall that with the Napoleonic conquest and with the propagation of French liberal thought, France was typically identified by the Germans as the locus of *Zivilization* and with the "merely outward trappings of social refinement." In contrast, Germans used the notion of *Kultur* to refer to "the profound spiritual superiority of German *Innerlichkeit* or inwardness."[34] Heidegger's cultist nationalism may be thus understood as a reaction against the values of civilization. The idea of civilization makes reference in this view to the liberal ideal of the public sphere and of democracy on the one hand, and to the "idolatry" of technology on the other.[35] What Heidegger makes clear in his interview of 1966 is that he found a way to sustain his nationalism and his ideas of collective authenticity without necessarily advocating a Führer principle—we should not forget, though, that there is evidence that indicates that he pledged allegiance to basic Nazi ideas up to at least 1944.[36] In this way, Heidegger followed a path similar to Husserl, who rejected Nazism by advocating Eurocentrism. Heidegger, once a Nazi himself, could have rejected the Führer principle, but he decidedly remained dedicated to his dreams of nationalism.³⁷ Rather than Eurocentric, Heidegger remained Germanocentric. He continued doing at a cultural and intellectual level what Hitler set out to do at a concrete political level, that is, humiliating the rest of Europe by subordinating *Zivilization* to German *Kultur*.

The interview in *Der Spiegel* shows the persistence of problematic aspects in Heidegger's thinking, a pertinence that lies beyond the question of correctly interpreting his personal motivations for joining the Nazis. In the interview, Heidegger sets out to disclaim any sense of strong allegiance to Hitler, yet the reaffirmation of his nationalism points in the opposite direction. It is interesting that Heidegger thought that his Germanocentrism presented a nonproblematic, decent alternative to his previous Nazism. He thought that he was submitting an uncontroversial idea. Heidegger knew what his readers would tolerate. And he also knew that while his readers would hastily condemn Nazism, they would certainly remain undisturbed by the more familiar idea of Eurocentrism. Heidegger knew that where Hitlerism fails, Eurocentrism can easily flourish. His Germanocentrism is in some ways a hybrid of Hitlerism and Eurocentrism. It is a second level Eurocentrism; that is, it distances itself from Europe in ways similar to those in which Europe has distanced itself from non-European countries. He goes so far as to "steal" classical Greece from Europeans by tying it exclusively to Germany.

As much as Heidegger committed himself to problematic positions in the *Der Spiegel* interview, his silences were more revealing than his words. As Levinas comments, "But on the issue of Heidegger's participation in 'Hitlerian thinking,' I do not believe that any kind of historical research, archival data, or eyewitness accounts—even when they do not rest on pure misunderstandings—can equal the certainty that comes to us in the famous Testament in *Der Spiegel*, from his silence concerning the Final Solution, the Holocaust, the Shoah."³⁸

Heidegger, who at one point explicitly endorsed Nazi politics, fails to acknowledge the ultimate failure of this project, evinced in the Holocaust. Heidegger does not seem to be concerned with this radical expression of evil. Much less does he appear suspicious of the philosophical basis of Hitlerism or of the reasons for his own allegiance to it. Indeed, Heidegger pays more attention to failures in his personal life than to the consequences and implications of his commitment to Nazism. About this Levinas comments,

> Doesn't Heidegger speak of "human failing," for which, according to the same Testament, he apologized to Mrs. Husserl for not having "once more"

paid his respects at the time of his teacher Husserl's illness and death? But doesn't this silence, in time of peace, on the gas chambers and death camps lie beyond the realm of feeble excuses and reveal a soul completely cut off from any sensitivity, in which can be perceived a kind of consent to the horror?[39]

Levinas denounces a radical lack of sensitivity in Heidegger's reflections on the events that followed 1933. This point is crucial. It suggests that evil can find expression not only in open violence, but in indifference as well. The master morality of Imperial Man can afford to forget and ignore. Levinas takes this suspicion a step further and suggests that the very ideal of authenticity is suited to, if it does not actually foment, the event of forgetting. This event of forgetting is dramatically enacted in the primacy of the encounter with death:

> In the Heideggerian analysis of death, one is struck by the reduction of death to being-toward-death, to the structure of *Dasein*—that is, once again to subjectivity in its origin, as the true relationship with being on the basis of which the other man is understood. In this way, if we exaggerate somewhat, we might say that, for Heidegger (who would, no doubt, not say this), the fear of being an assassin does not manage to surpass the fear of dying. To be-to-death is to-be-to-*my*-death. . . . Consequently, the deepest desire is the desire to be, and death is always premature.[40]

Authenticity appears thus to promote either struggle or indifference. Care of the self takes primacy over the care for the Other *to the point of forgetfulness.*

As we have seen, the forgetfulness of the Other that stands behind the ideal of authenticity is not exclusive to Heidegger's earlier, more anthropological work. He may have left *Dasein* behind, but only to express in a more consistent manner an ontological turn that claimed the primacy of Being and the advent of truth (as *aletheia*) over instrumental reason and also over morals.[41] Authenticity was reintroduced at this level in a Germanocentric form. This shameful nationalism appears to be the expression of someone who stared at Being for too long and who, in a sort of hypnotic trance, remained in limbo. It is difficult to understand how, in this condition, someone could be fully attentive to the cries of others.[42]

Insofar as Heideggerian ontology is complicit with the "ideology of war" it may be argued that his ontology represents an "ontology of war." Through ontology, Heidegger reaffirms central features of a problematic vision of the search for authentic human existence. When Levinas uses the notion "ontology of war," however, he refers to something more fundamental. For Levinas the primacy of fundamental ontology itself is tied to the ideal of war.

> The primacy of ontology for Heidegger does not rest on the truism: "to know an *existent* it is necessary to have comprehended the Being of existents." To affirm the priority of *Being* over *existents* is to already decide the essence of philosophy; it is to subordinate the relation with *someone*, who is an existent, (the ethical relation) to a relation with the *Being of existents*, which, impersonal, permits the apprehension, the domination of existents (a relationship of knowing), subordinates justice to freedom. (TI 45)

The priority of ontology legitimizes a sort of "ontological imperialism" (TI 44). From this point on, everything and everyone is reduced to an element in the logic of the unconcealment of Being. In this configuration freedom and knowledge are complicit in their subordination of justice: "If freedom denotes the mode of remaining the same in the midst of the other, knowledge, where an existent is given by interposition of impersonal Being, contains the ultimate sense of freedom. It would be opposed to justice, which involves obligations with regard to an existent that refuses to give itself, the Other, who in this sense would be an existent par excellence" (TI 45).Heideggerian ontology gives expression to a preference of the Same over the Other. In reducing everything to the Same, ontology remains in line with the theoretical prejudice that Levinas found so problematic in Husserlian philosophy. By privileging the anonymous and the impersonal over the resistance of the particularity of existents this new ideal of illumination or truth gives expression to an impulse for possession and power. "Ontology as first philosophy," Levinas argues, "is a philosophy of power" (TI 46).

> A philosophy of power, ontology is, as first philosophy, which does not call into question the same, a philosophy of injustice. Even though it opposes the technological passion issued forth from the forgetting of Being hidden by existents, Heideggerian ontology, which subordinates the relationship with the Other to the relation with Being in general, remains under the obedience of the anonymous, and leads inevitably to another power, to imperialist domination, to tyranny. (TI 46–47)

Levinas points out that the Heideggerian conception of authenticity and his allegiance to nationalistic forms of politics and ways of thinking appear to relate directly to his conception of philosophy as fundamental ontology. A philosophy of power leads to a politics of power. At best, it remains silent without expressing a sense of outrage or condemnation in the presence of violence. There is thus a strong correlation between epistemic and concrete violence. The search for an alternative epistemological conception must provide an adequate answer to the problem of the propagation of violence.

The most basic problem raised by Levinas's work, as the preface of *Totality and Infinity* testifies, is the problem of the permanence and influence of the paradigm of violence and war. Levinas's work raises the question of the *overcoming* of these ideals. Moreover, since, for Levinas, violence and war make reference to the inability to evade consistently the horizons imposed by the idea of Being, this project takes the form of an overcoming of ontology as first philosophy. Beyond Heideggerian ontology, Levinas has in mind a notion of a certain "ontologism" that Western philosophy has not been able to overcome. As Levinas puts it in an essay published just a year after his reflections on Hitlerism, "In its [Western philosophy's] fight against ontologism, when it fights against it, it has fought for a better being, for a harmony between us and the world, or for the perfection of our own being. Its ideal of peace and equilibrium presupposed the sufficiency of being."[43]

The perseverance of Being, according to Levinas, leads to violence. And, for him, "every civilization that accepts Being, the tragic despair that it brings and the crimes that it justifies, merits the name of barbarian."[44] Against barbarianism, violence, and a false sense of peace that Western philosophy has not been able to overcome, Levinas proposes, as he puts it in *Totality and Infinity*, an eschatology of peace (TI 22).

The beginnings of Levinas's efforts are marked by the attempt to find a certain "need for evasion" or exit from Being in the interstices of human experience.[45] Levinas subverts the basic intuition behind Heidegger's project. Instead of laboring against the forgetting of Being, Levinas concentrates his efforts in fighting against the forgetfulness of the beyond Being.[46] This extraordinary moment is found, according to Levinas, in ordinary social experience.[47] Ordinary social life represents for him more the locus of peace than the source of alienation or violence. It is clear that in order to sustain his claim, Levinas will have to provide a conception of ordinary social life that is different from the liberal, the Nietzschean, the Husserlian, the Heideggerian, and the Hitlerian versions.[48] This is, indeed, what Levinas set out to do in the writings from the liberation up to the publication of *Totality and Infinity*.[49] The idea of ethics as first philosophy proposed in *Totality and Infinity* leads to a different conception of ordinary life. Here the ideas of human fraternity and of ordinary communication play a central role. In the next section, I will discuss Levinas's work in the light of his interest in articulating a conception of ordinary social life grounded in peace. After indicating the limits of this project, particularly in light of its inability to respond adequately to the problem of concrete violence, I will then turn to the writings after *Totality and Infinity* wherein Levinas offers a more adequate response to the paradigm of war and to the limits of Western philosophy and civilization.

LEVINAS AND THE SEARCH FOR HUMAN FRATERNITY

In order to understand the significance of Levinas's reflections on fraternity it is necessary to recapitulate the discussion presented in the first chapter. In his early essay on the philosophy of Hitlerism, Levinas notes that there are two basic connections between Hitlerism and dominant Western anthropological and epistemological conceptions, which are best represented in French liberalism. First, there is the body and bodily experience. These are aspects of the human ignored or disavowed by dominant Western anthropological and epistemological conceptions. Levinas elevates Hitlerism to the status of philosophy because it can be seen as a sort of systematic expansion of what dominant philosophy has considered irrelevant or even dangerous: the experience of the intimate link between human existence and embodiment. In some respects liberalism commits a sin by omission. The truth, however, is that the exclusion of the body as a significant element of subjectivity obeys a well-defined logic of a freedom conceived in terms of a radical separation from the natural world and from natural causes. Hitlerism becomes one of the ways in which liberalism pays for its distorted sense of priorities.

The fixation on the idea of freedom (in a way that begets decadent skepticism) partly explains the reasons for a second aspect behind the emergence of Hitlerism. The liberal conception of freedom is translated into the political conception of liberty. Liberty is, along with equality and fraternity, one of the terms that comprise the Trinitarian slogan of the French Revolution. Since freedom stands at the core of the liberal conception of the human, it is not surprising that liberalism has typically emphasized liberty and equality over fraternity. As liberty is conceived along the lines of a conception of disembodied freedom, equality refers to the identical status of abstract subjects. The subordination of the body to an abstract freedom thus seems to find a parallel in the subordination of fraternity to liberty and equality. Hitlerism exploits the double limitations of liberalism and, along with the rescue of bodily experiences, it subverts the priorities of liberalism, making fraternity the dominant element in the equation of its political principles. Fraternity becomes for Hitlerism the identity of a group united by blood ties. It refers to the unity of a race. Fraternity, thus, ultimately collapses to Aryanism. This new form of fraternity is nationalistic and anti-Semitic.

Now, unlike Aryanism—which is directly opposed to the subordination of the body in liberalism—nationalism and anti-Semitism are not completely foreign to liberal logic.[50] Both nationalism and anti-Semitism were part and parcel of liberal cultures in the West. Indeed, nationalism is the most typical form that fraternity assumes under liberalism.[51] Free and equal abstract human beings become subjects who share a language and inhabit a particular territory, that is, citizens. This concept of citizenship is tied to the notion of a community of masters to which Levinas refers in his essay on the philosophy of Hitlerism. The nationals form a community of masters. Anti-Semitism and different forms of xenophobia were not contingent dimensions of this form of life. Incidents such as the Dreyfus Affair indicated the existence of a logic of inclusion and exclusion that was constitutive of this project. Exploiting the repressed dimension of bodily experience, Hitlerism transforms liberal nationalism and anti-Semitism into racial nationalism and genocidal anti-Semitism.[52]

Reflecting in the light of the Dreyfus Affair, Nazi anti-Semitism, and captivity and genocide, Levinas ventures to elaborate a conception of human fraternity that is not racial but that is not ignorant or prejudicial of embodiment either.[53] Moreover, the renewed conception of social life must escape the pitfalls of the Heideggerian conception of *being-with*. For Levinas, sociality is not to be construed around the notion of an alienating community that militates against individuality. This way of understanding sociality arguably emanates from the inability to conceive of exteriority and multiplicity other than according to the categories through which we understand the relations between an isolated subject and things.[54] In this sense, even Heideggerian ontology would seem to give expression to the traditional metaphysical and theological picture of the world that he criticized so sharply.

The traditional picture of the world is intrinsically tied, both according to Levinas and to Heidegger, to liberal conceptions of liberty and equality.[55] For this reason liberalism offers a skewed conception of human fraternity. The limits of liberalism are clearly related to what

Levinas sees as a fundamental limitation in Western ideals of civilization—which, as we have seen before, are typically identified in this context with French political culture. As Levinas puts it, "In the reciprocity of relations characteristic of civilization, the asymmetry of the intersubjective relation is forgotten. The reciprocity of civilization—the kingdom of ends where each one is end and means at the same time, person and personal—is a leveling of the idea of fraternity. . . ."[56] Note here that, unlike Nietzsche, Levinas is primarily concerned with the leveling of human fraternity and not with the leveling of a noble or aristocratic master consciousness. From this perspective, liberalism fails not because it collapses individuality into sociality, but because sociality is understood according to a paradigm of thought that takes the isolated individual at its center.

Levinas's attempt to offer a new definition of the idea of human fraternity demands the formulation of categories of reflection susceptible to the peculiar forms of difference and multiplicity in the interhuman realm. He does not have in mind the "collectivity of comrades," but rather "the collectivity of the I-You that precedes it."[57] This collectivity, as Levinas puts it, "is not a participation in a third term—intermediary person, truth, dogma, work, profession, interest, housing, meal—that is to say, it is not a communion."[58] Levinas prefers "the formidable face-to-face of a relation without intermediary, without mediation" instead of the Heideggerian being-with.[59] Sociality is based on the relation with an Other as an alter—qua Other—and not as an alter ego—as Other who is simply equal to me.[60] The Other is essentially what is exterior—to myself, to what "we have in common," and to Being. As such, the Other introduces relations of transcendence and difference.[61] The "evasion" of Being and the overcoming of "ontologism" that Levinas proposed to articulate before find expression in the formulation of an ideal of human fraternity grounded on relations of transcendence and difference. As Levinas explains elsewhere,

> Transcendence is only possible with an Other in relation to whom we are absolutely different. . . . It seems to me that transcendence is the point of departure for our concrete relations with the Other. . . . That is why I consider that transcendence is a major notion [*une notion qui me semble première*]. . . . Men are absolutely different from each other. The concept Man is the only one that cannot be comprehended because each man is absolutely different from each other. The concept Man only has an extension: human fraternity.[62]

For Levinas, human fraternity accomplishes the evasion of Being or transcendence.

According to Levinas, ordinary social life is predicated on the extraordinariness of the relation with the absolutely Other. This idea clearly demands an account of the ways in which the abstractly conceived relation with an Other is related to concrete events of ordinary life. Moreover, Levinas also has to explain the transition from the Self-Other relation to the realm of human fraternity. Levinas attempts to do all of this through a phenomenology of eros. First, eros, understood as sexual difference, is an instance of a concrete relation to another person that cannot be conceived in intentional or ontological terms. In an erotic relationship, Levinas argues, the aim is not to comprehend, to understand, to reach the truth about, or to have power over the other person. "It is," in Levinas's own words, "neither a struggle, nor a fusion, nor a knowledge."[63] "The pathos of love," Levinas continues, "consists in an insurmountable duality of beings. It is a relationship with what always slips away."[64] The erotic relation between different genders not only represents an experience in which transcendence and difference transpire in a privileged form, but also provides the needed transition to an understanding of sociality in terms of human fraternity.[65] This transition is provided by fecundity. For Levinas, "Intersubjective asymmetry is the place of a transcendence where the subject, while conserving its structure as subject, has the possibility of not having to return fatally to itself, of being fecund, and . . . of having a son."[66] Procreation, the outcome of the erotic relation between different genders, makes possible the formation of human fraternity, that is, a community of brothers. Masculinist and heteronormative bias are clearly evinced in Levinas. In this respect, one needs to maintain a critical distance from him.

Human fraternity can only be accounted for adequately, according to Levinas, in terms of difference and transcendence. The use of other categories—from liberal forms of nationalism to open forms of racism—ends up collapsing the idea of fraternal love among mankind into different forms of life directed by the urge to form a community of masters—from plain indifference and imperial conceptions of generosity to unambiguous expressions of hate. The Levinasian account of fraternity surpasses the limitations of liberalism by assuming the embodiment of the subject. Moreover, since it is grounded on the notion of transcendence, fraternity avoids falling prey to dangerous conceptions of race and racism. The (erotic) body is the mechanism of receptivity and encounter with the Other.[67] Levinas's conception of human fraternity aims thus to offer a philosophical grounding to peace and love, not to war and blood.

Aware of the need to overcome the paradigm of violence and war, with its fixations on heroic individuality and death and with its antipathy toward ordinary social life, Levinas describes eros and human reproduction (or fecundity) in terms of the very attempt of "vanquishing death."[68] With this idea Levinas plainly rejects the Heideggerian notion of achieving authenticity through a confrontation with death. In contrast to the Heideggerian understanding of the topic, death appears to Levinas not as the climax, but as the very limit of the subject's virility. Rather than awakening the self from its loss in collective experience, death demolishes the very basis of individuality. As Levinas puts it, "Death is the impossibility of having a project.... My solitude is thus not confirmed by death but broken by it."[69] In short, death is the Other that destroys *me*. According to Levinas, eros, which is as "strong as death," offers an alternative relation to the Other that allows the existent to transcend its "originary" solitude without destroying it.[70] Breaking from its self-enclosure by entering into a relation with an Other that is not death, the existent is able to properly exist, that is, to project itself toward the future. But the subject is, for Levinas, definitely more than acts of projection. The very conditions of possibility for there to be a projection surpass the virtues and abilities of the intending subject. The opening of time in the encounter with the Other is not an accomplishment of the subject. For Levinas, temporality cannot be accounted for either in terms of the virtues of transcendental consciousness, by the movement of Being, or by the anguish of a subject who confronts death. These modes of justification occupy a privileged space in the articulation of human existence in terms of power and struggle. It is for this reason that Levinas insists that the erotic relationship is not one of power. Time, thus, appears to be not a virtue or an accomplishment but a gift.[71] The gift of time—of a time lived against the advent of death—finds a pristine expression at the level of civilized, ordinary life in the erotic relation.

The link between eros, the opening of time, and the "victory over death" is confirmed by fecundity. Eros not only introduces the subject to an alterity different from death, but through fecundity, allows him to procreate. Through procreation or paternity, the subject can survive in the son and thus "vanquish death" in a more definitive way. This does not mean that the subject can be simply identified with the son. Nor does it mean that the relation between them is one of possession or power. For Levinas, "The son, in effect, is not simply my work, like a poem or an artifact, neither is he my property. Neither the categories of power nor those of having can indicate the relationship with the child. Neither the notion of cause nor the notion of ownership permit one to grasp the fact of fecundity. I do not *have* my child; I *am* in some way my child."[72]

In *Totality and Infinity* Levinas adds: "Paternity is a relation with a stranger who while being Other ("And you shall say to yourself, 'who can have borne me these? I was bereaved and barren . . .'" *Isaiah*, 49) *is* me, a relation of the I with a self which yet is not me" (TI 277).[73] The son represents as much the continuity as the rupture of the paternal I. The paternal I can only subsist in the son, and the son "echoes the transcendence of the paternal I" (TI 278). This means for Levinas that the son is, in his relation to the father, unique and elected.[74] In all this the son embodies the dilemmas of a created freedom.

The *uniqueness* of a child who is *elected* to be *for his father* finds a counterpart in the relation of equality between the son and his brothers. "The child as elected one is," Levinas argues, "at the same time unique and non-unique. Paternity is produced as an innumerable future; the I engendered exists at the same time as unique in the world and as brother among brothers. I am I and chosen one, but where can I be chosen, if not from among other chosen ones, among equals?" (TI 279). At the point in which time is opened up definitely (in the new generation) and where the social begins to appear (the community of equal brothers) the logics of eros and fecundity give way to the logic of the ethical.[75] The ethical is reintroduced in the Levinasian discourse through the idea of fraternity. Among equals, Levinas points out, the elected I

> remains turned ethically to the face of the other: fraternity is the very relation with the face in which at the same time my election and equality, that is, the mastery exercised over me by the other, are accomplished. The election of the I, its very ipseity, is revealed to be a privilege and a subordination, because it does not place it among the other chosen ones, but rather in face of them, *to serve them*, and because no one can be substituted for the I to measure the extent of its responsibilities. (TI 279, italics mine)

The elected son is no longer only *for his father*, but also, as it were, *for his brothers*. Filiality is turned into the ethical relation of fraternity.

The transition from paternity and filiality to fraternity clearly indicates Levinas's opposition to the philosophy of Hitlerism. In contrast to Hitlerism, where a reference to biological relations justifies a politics of war and struggle, here the biological ultimately begets the ethical and the social. For Levinas the biological is hardly circumscribed to the physical. It is also tied to the ontological—and to the trans-ontological. As he puts it, "If biology furnishes us the prototypes of all these relations, this proves, to be sure, that biology does not represent a purely contingent order of being, unrelated to its essential production. But these relations free themselves from biological limitation. The human I is posited in fraternity: that all men are brothers is not added to man as a moral conquest, but constitutes his ipseity" (TI 279–80). For Levinas, the emergence of fraternity entails the idea that subjectivity is ethical, and that the social is the realm of concrete ethical experience. Therefore, it is reasonable to conclude, as Levinas set out to prove in *Totality and Infinity*, that *we are not duped by morality* and that war and *polemos* don't have to be considered as the epitome of truth, reason, or human authenticity.

Levinas argues that by virtue of fraternity the self is promised and called to goodness. But it is clear that the I would certainly be deceived if goodness were an impossible task.[76] And in a world permeated by war it would be reasonable to be suspicious. For this reason, it is important for Levinas to indicate that the fraternal self is not trapped by fate or by any particular course of events. The fraternal self can aspire to a different future in which goodness is always possible. Here again the lines between biology and ethics meet since, as we have seen, futurity is built into the very notion of fecundity. "A being capable of another fate than its own is a fecund being. In paternity, where the I, across the definitiveness of an inevitable death, prolongs itself in the other, time triumphs over old age and fate by its discontinuity" (TI 282). The idea of temporality (in terms of discontinuous time) as the achievement of a fecund being is not only intended to refute the charge of the folly of morality or to provide an alternative meaning of the biological to Hitlerism. The notion of a discontinuous time beyond fate clearly reintroduces a Judaic conception of temporality and freedom to a Christian—and more significantly in this context to a liberal—conception of Man. As I noted in the previous chapter, Levinas opposes the conception of freedom from the past obtained in pardon (for him, a Judaic conception), to the liberal conception of autonomy. Only the first makes reference to an intersubjective order and thus avoids the individualism, the aristocratic tone, and the elitism of modern conceptions of freedom such as those found in liberalism and in the formulations of Nietzsche and Husserl. In *Totality and Infinity*, Levinas ties the concept of pardon to the mode of temporality that is opened up by fecundity. As he puts it:

> The discontinuous time of fecundity makes possible an absolute youth and recommencement, while leaving the recommencement a relation with the recommenced past in a free return to that past (free with a freedom other than that of memory), and in free interpretation and free choice, in an existence as entirely pardoned. This recommencement of the instant, this triumph of fecundity over the becoming of the mortal and aging being, is a pardon, the very work of time. (TI 282)

In contrast to liberalism, which, according to Levinas, opens the doors to Hitlerism through its skewed conception of freedom and its exclusion of the biological, Levinas provides a conception of fraternity that rescues the relevance of the biological while taking an ethical rather than a racial turn. Through its links to fecundity, this notion of fraternity also provides an alternative to the Heideggerian conception of the achievement of authentic time through the encounter with death. Even the relation between Being and time must be understood, according to Levinas, not in terms of the projection of one's ownmost possibilities provoked by angst, but in terms of the time of generations opened up by the fecundity of the fraternal selves. The emergence and dynamic discontinuity of time arises not by virtue of death and struggle, but by virtue of the "victory over death" and the encounter with exteriority. The meaning of time is thus intrinsically tied to the possibility of ethics, and not to war or *polemos*. Now we shall examine more carefully Levinas's conception of fraternity to see if it successfully evades and overcomes the pitfalls of the ideology and ontology of war.

FROM EROS TO CRITIQUE

The above discussion should have made patently clear that the concept of fraternity plays a very important role in Levinas's thought. Confronting the dangers of Hitlerism and perceiving the limits of liberalism, Levinas took it upon himself to provide an alternative conception regarding the link between biology and fraternity very early on in his philosophical work. His descriptions of eros and fecundity are not only meant to show the limits of a strictly phenomenological conception of experience; more importantly, they represent major ideas in the conceptual architecture that sustain a new vision of human fraternity.[77]

Levinas's emphasis on human fraternity subverts the terms of the liberalism with which so many Jews were disenchanted in France after the Dreyfus Affair. By means of this subversion, he inserted himself in the debate regarding the appropriateness of the French Revolution's influential slogan: liberty, equality, and fraternity. This debate, as the Jewish American sociologist Immanuel Wallerstein notes, has taken the form of an inquiry into the compatibility of the ideas included in the slogan. The questions follow more or less these terms: "Is freedom possible if there is equality? Is freedom an obstacle to the achievements of equality? Do not freedom and equality lead to the opposite of fraternity? And so on."[78] More a sociologist and a political economist than a historian, Wallerstein makes reference to these debates in a way that surpasses historical interest. For him, an examination of the relation between liberty, equality, and fraternity still provides today an opportunity to reflect on utopian visions that supersede the limits of (French) liberalism.[79] These limits become evident in the increase of economic and social disparities. Exactly two hundred years after the French Revolution took place, and twenty-eight years after the publication of *Totality and Infinity*, Wallerstein concludes his essay "The French Revolution as a World-Historical Event" with an explicit endorsement of the need to pay more attention to the concept of fraternity.[80] I quote at length:

> If we are to clarify our options and our utopias in the post-1968 world-system, perhaps it would be useful to reread the Trinitarian slogan of the French Revolution: liberty, equality, fraternity. It has been too easy to pose liberty against equality, as in some sense the two great interpretations of the French Revolution have done, each interpretation championing if you will one half of the antinomy. Perhaps the reason the French Revolution did not produce either liberty or equality is that the major power holders and their heirs have successfully maintained that they were separate objectives. This was not, I believe, the view of the unwashed masses. Fraternity, meanwhile, has always been a pious addition, taken seriously by no one in the whole long post-1789 cultural arena, until in fact 1968. . . . Fraternity or, to rename it in the post-1968 manner, comradeship is a construction to be pieced together with enormous difficulty, and yet this fragile prospect is in fact the underpinning of the achievement of liberty/equality.[81]

In the aspirations of youth, women, minorities, and third world peoples in 1968, Wallerstein seems to find a way to overcome the limits of the utopian possibilities provided by the two prevailing ideologies: liberalism and Marxism. The year 1968 symbolizes what Arrighi, Hopkins, Wallerstein, and Michael Watts designate as the "great rehearsal."[82]

Other more popular accounts characterize it as "the year that rocked the world."[83] As I will use it throughout this book, 1968 refers to an international phenomenon, with significant local variants, that involved the activity of building counterinstitutions, different countercultures, and the possibility of "working against the institutions [of the modern Western state] while working within them."[84] It involved the Prague Spring, students' protests in Paris, Berkeley, and Mexico, massive protests against the Vietnam War, and the emergence of an anti-war counterculture, as well as manifestations by women and racialized minorities in the United States and elsewhere who opposed continued marginalization in modern society. I have discussed elsewhere basic differences between struggles that took place in different parts of the world.[85] I would like to use the symbolic date here primarily to point to a context in which struggles for the recognition and respect of difference (ethnic, cultural, and sexual) became prominent and gender hierarchies and traditional sexual mores were highly questioned. For Wallerstein 1968 (as a point in time but also as a symbol) represents a revolt against social and political institutions as well as ideals that came out of the French Revolution and its aftermath. In short, for him, 1968 provides important elements to assess and correct the ideals of 1789.

I argued before that the event that provoked Levinas's suspicion of French liberalism was the Dreyfus Affair. The subsequent emergence of fascism and his awareness of the important philosophical links between liberalism and fascism—along with his experience as a prisoner of war and a survivor of the Shoah—provide a horizon for the reflection on fraternity that is different from 1968. Yet, even though Levinas explicitly rejects the idea of fraternity as the "collectivity of comrades," one can perceive in his formulation of fraternity certain similarities with Wallerstein's rendering of fraternity as comradeship: "The relation with the face in fraternity, where in its turn the Other appears in solidarity with all the others, constitutes the social order, the reference of every dialogue to the third party by which the *We*—or the parti [*sic*]—encompasses the face to face opposition, opens the erotic upon a social life, all signifyingness and decency, which encompasses the structure of the family itself" (TI 280).

This conception of fraternity, which simultaneously opposes the allergy of the autonomous individual to society and the possibility of the dissolution of the self into a totality or collectivity, accentuates the similarities as well as the differences with the 1968 ideal of comradeship.

The connection is clearly established through the concept of solidarity. But solidarity is ultimately tied by Levinas to the family and to a conception of eros that finds its fulfillment in procreation. Through eros, the circle between the lovers is broken and a third person emerges—the son. For Levinas, the "we" in solidarity is the community of brothers. The social order emerges in the structure of the family. This attempt to redeem ordinary life by demonstrating the ontological pertinence of eros and by defining the family (not the autonomous subject) as the basic unit responsible for the generation of society and authentic temporality could not be more opposed to the ideas regarding eros and the family in the protests of 1968.[86] The year 1968 represented as much a political as a sexual revolution that, among other things, questioned the ultimate value of the (bourgeois) family and the (bourgeois) subordination of eros to reproduction. Judged in the light of 1968, Levinas clearly failed in examining how certain features of the Judaic experience that he wanted to recuperate were arguably complicit with these problematic concepts.[87]

The events of the year 1968 showed not only the virtues of fraternity (as comradeship) over one-sided visions of liberty and equality, but also the limits of traditional conceptions of the ideal. Fraternity is limited by its reliance on problematic conceptions of sex and gender. After all, fraternity primarily denotes a community of brothers and sons. In fraternity, as in ideological conceptions of war, women and sisters stand only in the background. War itself can be seen as an extension of the domination of women by the community of brothers. To combat the ideology of war it is thus necessary to recognize the extent to which it is the product of a *masculine* ethos of struggle.[88] That is why war typically reinforces discourses about the limits of the feminine. It also tends to reduce the role of women to the care of the wounded and to reproduction. In war, men kill other men and rape the enemy's women. Violence finds another place in the subordination of every woman to the role of reproduction. Since sexuality is tied to reproduction, and since manliness is identified with the exercise of the violent phallus, homosexuality is also typically rejected by the ideology of war.[89]

The links between fraternity and the ideology of war point to a fundamental limitation in Levinas's efforts to vindicate fraternity. He may very well have overcome Nazi racism, but he clearly failed to be critical of liberal and Nazi sexism. He failed to observe that the notion of power linked to the concept of Man as an autonomous and abstract individual cannot be separated from its specification as man. Masculinity is inscribed in the liberal conception of freedom as much as it is in the Hitlerian ideal of violence and racial unification. Heidegger's fixation with struggle and death may be also arguably traced back, as Patricia Huntington has argued, to a masculine ethos.[90] A consistent overcoming of the ideology and ontology of war thus requires a critical examination of ideals of community articulated exclusively around masculine conceptions of experience. Levinas's conception of fraternity in *Totality and Infinity* fails to address this problem in a satisfactory manner.

The challenge to traditional conceptions of sexuality and of family values in 1968 ultimately points also to the intrinsic ties between politics and ordinary life. With the sexual revolution of the late 1960s and early 1970s it became clear that the division between the public and the private is a very fragile one. The question of women's role in the home was shown to be a political problem to be discussed and assessed by the public at large and not only a private issue to be adjudicated by the family circle. This way of politicizing ordinary life does not necessarily respond to an interest in elevating politics to the status of first philosophy. The ideal of fraternity as comradeship introduces a conception of political activism directed against the ossified forms of value in ordinary life. It does not condemn sociality or advocate solipsism or heroism. But this ideal cannot simply turn to redeem ordinary life either. The events of 1968 show that the ideology of war may find a place even in the midst of ordinary social life. Its criticism is, therefore, simultaneously directed against capitalism, dominant forms of the nation-state, and the bourgeois/patriarchal family. Comradeship is therefore linked to a form of political activism that emerges as yet another attempt to counter the pervasiveness of the ideology of war.

The Levinasian conception of fraternity similarly fails to advance an adequate conception of the political. Since the ideology of war finds its most consistent expression in the exercise of a politics detached from all morals, Levinas turned to rescue the ethical. Yet, his search for the ethical was pursued at the expense of the political in some significant respects.[91] The redemption of ordinary life through the positive revaluation of dialogue (in the face-to-face encounter that takes place among the brothers) and eros may provide a response against certain basic concepts that stand behind the ideology of war, but it fails to provide an adequate response to concrete and ordinary modes of violence. If we are to follow the insights gained in 1968, particularly in the women's and minority movements that I am highlighting with this notion, we need *another* politics and praxis motivated and directed by the need for a restoration of the ethical in the political rather than by an interest in sustaining the logics of imperialism, conquest, domination, and war.

The absence of an accurate notion of the political in Levinas's articulation of fraternity is tied to a problematic split between ethics and politics. The opposition between ethics and politics is mirrored in the opposition between peace and war, and between ordinary social life and an elitist exceptionalism. That is the reason why the overcoming of the ideology of war takes in Levinas's hands the form of the redemption of ordinary life. In the end, fraternity seems to indicate more a return to or a reconciliation with ordinary life than a renewed impetus for social critique and justice. And yet, these themes find an important place in the first section of *Totality and Infinity*.[92] In an open debate against dominant conceptions of truth and the search for knowledge—we already saw how fundamental these conceptions are for the paradigm of violence and war—Levinas argues that truth does not presuppose struggle and war, but justice. The reason for this is that, according to Levinas, knowledge—like temporality—is made possible by a radical questioning of the spontaneity of the lonely subject in the encounter with the Other. For Levinas, a lonely existent may be able to taste or enjoy something, but it cannot have a concept or a knowledge of it. The possibility of conceptualization itself depends on having something in common with another. In other words, the generality of the concept makes reference to an intersubjective world and not to a lonely subjectivity. For the existent to know something it must have first encountered the Other. The Other is that which cannot be submitted to my power. I do not make the Other a theme, but I talk to him. It is in discourse that meaning for the first time emerges. The meaning or the raison d'être of knowledge originates in the rupture of the egoism of the existent by the ethical nonviolence of the Other, that is, in justice. If this is so, then knowledge is better represented by critique (as rupture) rather than by dogma.[93] And philosophy, the love of wisdom, must be understood as fundamentally a critical activity (TI 85).

The idea of philosophy as critique—of a critique that serves justice and not war—seems to locate Levinas's efforts more in line with the inspiration of 1968. The idea introduces the possibility of a critique and not only a redemption of ordinary life. Yet Levinas's reflections on truth and justice are still too ingrained in the logics of opposing the ideology of war by the redemption of ordinary social life. The relation between truth and justice ultimately demonstrates the presence of the extraordinary in the ordinary:

> The work of justice—the uprightness of the face to face—is necessary in order that the breach that leads to God be produced—and "vision" here coincides with his work of justice. Hence metaphysics is enacted where the social relation is enacted—in our relations with men. . . . The establishing of this primacy of the ethical, that is, of the relationship of man to man—signification, teaching, justice—a primacy of an irreducible structure upon which all the other structures rest (and in particular all those which seem to put us primordially in contact with an impersonal sublimity, aesthetic or ontological), is one of the objectives of the present work. (TI 78)

The extraordinary event of the emergence of signification is ethical in character and makes itself particularly evident, not in any sublime or agonistic experience, but in ordinary human discourse. With this idea of extraordinariness Levinas provides an alternative account of the links between lucidity, sociality, and ethics. He clearly shows again what he originally set out to demonstrate: that we are indeed not "duped" by morality because without ethics (as first philosophy) there is simply no sense, meaning, liberty, or human order.

As significant as an answer to the problem of the dubiousness of morality Levinas's account of extraordinariness is, it is still not sufficient to counter the pervasive influence of the ideology of war, particularly in respect to the problem of concrete violence in ordinary social life. The question raised by this predicament is not so much whether morality is possible or not, but, granting that it is possible and indeed indispensable, how it can rejoin politics and provide the basis for an ethico-political praxis that foments nonviolent relations at the concrete level of ordinary life. This question not only reflects deep concerns about extreme forms of violence, but also about the violence inscribed in the "status quo," or as Levinas himself would put it, in the "peace" of empires—which is no peace at all. This situation arguably began to emerge once again in Western Europe (and the United States) after the end of the Second World War. While Eastern Europe was submitted to a totalitarian regime, Western Europe and particularly the United States declared themselves the loci of freedom and true democracy. Liberalism assumed its role once more as the dominating ideology and political conception in the West. Indeed, the challenge of 1968 to the liberalism of 1789 was partly motivated by its opposition to the reinsertion of liberalism after 1945.

The decisive inauguration of the new liberalism occurred with the proclamation of the Universal Declaration of Human Rights in 1948.[94] Once more the principles of liberty, equality, and fraternity were declared to be the fundamental pillars of a newly established peace.[95] It was believed that a reaffirmation of these principles would prevent the repetition of any sort of barbaric Hitlerism. However positive this new reinsertion of liberalism may have been (or still is), from a Levinasian point of view it represents the confirmation of the West's commitment to the notions of freedom and autonomy that he found so problematic. To be sure, the danger that liberalism now poses cannot be simply understood in relation to the advent of Hitlerism and to the institutionalization of murder. It is now related to the comfort of a seemingly newfound peace.

To be sure, as the events of 1968 indicate, the problem with the new liberal configuration still lies in its skewed conception of human fraternity. But now the risks of the liberal notion of fraternity are not uniquely related to the emergence of nationalism and racism. Fraternity takes on demonic forms even when it dresses itself in the clothes of gentle indifference. Indifference is what allows the self to ignore or forget the condition of the other person. Indifference makes reference to a deafness that anticipates and prepares the way for the exercise of the violent vision. The advent of postwar liberalism does not lead Levinas to resign himself to new conditions and to disavow the "religious source of his love," but rather to provide a more careful diagnosis of the ways in which the paradigm of violence and war finds expression even in times of an allegedly newly found peace.

The content of the writings that appear after the publication of *Totality and Infinity* in 1961 up to Levinas's explicit reflections on human rights in the 1980s reflects a deep concern for a philosophical account that makes clear the pertinence of ethics as first philosophy to a postwar liberal West.[96] *Totality and Infinity* itself is, from this perspective, a transitional work. Two narratives emerge in *Totality and Infinity*: the narrative of eros, fecundity, and fraternity, and the narrative of philosophy as critique, justice, and proximity.[97] Levinas attempts to reconcile them, but they ultimately prove to have irreconcilable elements. While the first one points to the redemption of ordinary life—to the point of legitimating problematic views about sexuality and the family—the second one signals the need for an explicit critical engagement with forms of life that corrupt justice, even in the family. Also, while the first one seems to be motivated by the attempt to solve the predicament of death through the virtual resurrection of the father in the son, the second points to the primacy of the death of the Other and finds the challenge of the power of death in a radical transformation of the source of concern—from the self to the Other.[98] In the first, fraternity is articulated through eros and fecundity, in the second it finds expression in proximity. Gradually in his work categories of ethical experience related to the encounter with the orphan, the widow, and the stranger will take more weight than experiences and ideas directly linked with a biologically charged conception of fraternity. The problem of justice will gradually come to the forefront, and accounts of the erotic experience will become less central.[99]

OTHERWISE THAN BEING OR THE CARE FOR JUSTICE
Otherwise Than Being or, Beyond Essence, Levinas's second major work, is the product of an intense process of reflection whereby Levinas attempted to provide a more consistent response to the challenges posed by the paradigm of violence and war. From the beginning it demonstrates a more comprehensive reflection on the nature of violence. This is made apparent in his dedication: "To the memory of those who were closest among the six million assassinated by the National Socialists, and of the millions on millions of all confessions and all nations, victims of the same hatred of the other man, the same anti-Semitism." The dedication indicates that Levinas is not only concerned with the prospects of ethics in a world dominated by war, but, more generally, with a wide condition of victimization experienced by many in different parts of the world. Levinas's object of reflection now is the prevalence of a form of hatred that may or may not culminate in assassination. Although the desire to murder may motivate this hatred, it does not always have to reach such radical expressions. Hatred may find expressions in pure indifference. Sometimes, as Levinas points out in reference to Heidegger's work, the fear of one's death and the preservation of one's own being may take precedence over the anguish of committing murder.[100]

In *Otherwise Than Being* Levinas aims to articulate an account of the paradigm of violence and war and of its overcoming that is more susceptible than before to the realities of victimization in apparently "peaceful" contexts. In contrast to *Totality and Infinity* where lucidity was identified with war and politics, here Levinas defines war in terms of the "deed or the drama of the essence's interest" (OB 4). Reason and politics are conceived as the apparent opposite of war. They are related to "a rational peace" that converts the struggle of each against all into exchange and commerce (OB 4).[101] Reason and politics appear to be responsible for the transformation of war into civilization, or Hitlerism into the world of a newly found peace. They are interpreted here more in the light of Hobbes's political philosophy than in terms of the Heideggerian "ontology of war."

The main goal of *Otherwise Than Being* is not to undermine reason and politics as proper vehicles of peace. Rather, its project consists of demonstrating that the meaning or raison d'être of reason and politics is not traced back to an original condition of war (like in Hobbes), but to a pre-original moment of responsibility in which the self finds itself in proximity to the Other—to the point of substitution.[102] Thus, instead of positing a dichotomy between ethics and politics, the political appears in this context as a necessary outcome of the drama of the emergence of subjectivity. The link between the ethical and the political in *Otherwise Than Being* is justice.[103]

Levinas introduces justice in *Otherwise Than Being* through the idea of the third party. Different from *Totality and Infinity*, the third to which Levinas refers here is not the son. The way in which the subject is elevated to the realm of sociality at large is through an obsession with "all the others than the other" that I find in the face of the Other. This means that "the other is from the first the brother of all the other men" (OB 158). It is by virtue of fraternity, not by virtue of equality or liberty, that we are introduced into justice. "The neighbor that obsesses me is already a face, both comparable and incomparable, a unique face and in relationship with faces, which are visible in the concern for justice" (OB 158). With the idea of justice, Levinas refers to the transition from the asymmetry of the ethical relation where I give everything to the Other to the world of symmetry where I weigh, think, and objectify in order to be able to give to all the Others that obsess me in the face of the Other. This means, on the one hand, that before human existence indicates, as for Heidegger, "an unending concern with our daily bread," it first emerges at the point of giving oneself completely in the gift of the bread from one's mouth (OB 72, 74). On the other hand, by virtue of justice and by the establishment of symmetry, the subject is approached as an other by the others for the first time. That is, for the first time the subject has rights and not only duties. The prioritization of duties to rights indicates that rights must never take the form of an exclusive concern for finding "our daily bread," and that human existence must not be conceived primordially in terms of *care*, as Heidegger proposed. In the same way, rights must be infused with a giving that surpasses the limits of synchrony and egoism.

The priority Levinas lends to the notions of giving and response indicates that the emergence of the subject as a member of civilized society is not the achievement of any form of self-power. It is only by virtue of his responsibility that the self finds himself as a subject among others. It is, as it were, "thanks to God" that he becomes a subject and that he gains rights. "Thanks to God," as Levinas puts it, "I am another for the others. God is not involved as an alleged interlocutor: the reciprocal relationship binds me to the other man in the trace of transcendence, in illeity. The passing of God of whom I can speak only by reference to this aid or this grace, is precisely the reverting of the incomparable subject into a member of society" (OB 158).

God appears here, not as the one who calls me and allows me to reproduce, but as the one by virtue of whom I enter the world of symmetry and become a member of society. The emergence of my subjectivity gives testimony to an act of grace thanks to which I become an other for the others. Ultimately grace, not autonomy and freedom, accounts for my rights. We have seen that this theme has been present early on in Levinas's work.

Taking on his own reflections in the section "Truth and Justice" in *Totality and Infinity*, Levinas argues in *Otherwise Than Being* that not only subjectivity, but also knowledge, consciousness, work, and even the neutral notion of *being* find their "latent birth" in justice. By virtue of justice the subject emerges in the world of laws and institutions: "Out of representation is produced the order of justice moderating or measuring the substitution of me for the other, and giving the self over to calculus. Justice requires contemporaneousness of representation. It is thus that the neighbor becomes visible, and, looked at, presents himself, and there is also justice for me. The saying is fixed in a said, is written, becomes a book, law and science" (OB 159).

Written language and not discourse is linked here with justice as it is in *Totality and Infinity*. Levinas traces back the originary saying of discourse to the opening of a subjectivity that announces itself to an Other. It is the "Here I am!" The "Here I am!" is born in a position of ethical asymmetry. With justice, representation emerges and the condition of asymmetry gives way to the world of intelligible discourse. The possibility of conceptualization is linked in *Otherwise Than Being* to the appearance of the third person. Conceptualization still makes reference to the moment of giving, as in *Totality and Infinity*, but now giving only takes place when the third person appears—before there is only an announcement of a subjectivity that is prepared to give. Completing an act of giving without taking into account a third will be unjust. Thus, in giving I consider the third person, and in order to proceed justly, I think and measure. The "Here I am!" turns into the intelligible language of rules and laws (civilization) *for the sake of justice*.

Levinas believes that tracing the beginnings of subjectivity, society, and justice in ethics and the free gift of rights has important implications for our understanding of these ideas:

> The equality of all is borne by my inequality, the surplus of my duties over my rights. The forgetting of self moves justice. It is then not without importance to know if the egalitarian and just State in which man is fulfilled (and which is to set up, and specially to be maintained) proceeds from a war of all against all, or from the irreducible responsibility of the one for all, and if it can do without friendships and faces. It is not without importance to know that war does not become the instauration of a war in good conscience. (OB 159–60)

The raison d'être of the just state is found in the disinterested gift of the self to the Other and not in the eternal conflict between subjects found in a state of nature. Justice is originally demanded by goodness and not by an incurable radical egoism. Calculation and deliberation (weighing and thinking) are introduced by the demands of ethics and not by the interest in self-preservation. In short, the *spirit* of justice is found in giving more than in receiving. This means, as Levinas suggests in *Time and the Other*, that responsibility for the Other is to be maintained "even when, from the point of view of justice, no preference is any longer possible."[104] According to Levinas, the opposite of war is not the rational peace of a simultaneity in which subjects are indifferent to each other, but goodness, non-indifference, or the one-for-the-other. This is for him the true character of fraternity.

Justice is fundamentally ambiguous in character. On the one hand, it emerges in order to carry out the demands of giving to a third, while on the other hand, it encapsulates the demands of giving in laws and operates with neutral categories. It is for this reason that many consider justice to be only a matter of restraining self-interest or of conformity to the law.[105] From this perspective peace may be identified with the self-preservation of a system of laws, with the maintenance of a tradition with implicit codes of behavior, or with the survival of the self. Peace is thus confused with non-disturbance. It is identified with the lack of interruption to the order of the said and established truth.

Levinas argues that Western civilization has opted for maintaining the privilege of these conceptions of peace and of truth.[106] Since peace and truth appear to be so aligned, the love of wisdom is identified exclusively with the search for truth. With a skewed conception of peace and being absolutely committed to the demands of finding truth, Western philosophy is paradoxically led to defend war and *polemos* over peace itself. Levinas, in contrast, ties the meaning of philosophy to the search for a peace that cannot be identified with the systematic accomplishment of rationality. Levinas expands his ideas on philosophy as critique in *Totality and Infinity*. In a similar line, years later in *Otherwise Than Being*, Levinas states that the crucial task of philosophy is the *reduction* of the said to the saying (see particularly, OB 43–45). In this sense, philosophy becomes a fundamentally critical activity with a very particular telos. For Levinas, the meaning and purpose of philosophy are defined not so much by the attainment of truth as by the accomplishment of peace in a context defined by a kind of justice whose demands and expectations go well beyond liberal fairness, as Raimond Gaita has also suggested in a different context.[107] Philosophy makes sure that the imperatives of synchrony do not betray the true work of justice. It gives expression to the idea that the humanity of the human is not found either in conflict or in the stability of a well-ordered system, but in non-indifference. In this context, as Levinas himself puts it, philosophy expresses not so much the love of wisdom as the very "wisdom of love."[108]

For Levinas, philosophy, understood in this way, is aligned with the overcoming of war and with the rupture of a purely rational peace. For this reason, philosophy cannot be opposed to skepticism any more. In his later writings, Levinas complicates the conception of skepticism that he presents in his early essay on the philosophy of Hitlerism. Following Husserl, skepticism appeared to him then as a source of instability and decadence in Western civilization. Gradually Levinas becomes suspicious of such a formulation. Perhaps the problem with Europe is not so much that it was invaded by skepticism, but that it did not become skeptical enough, or skeptical in the right way. The right kind of skepticism emanates for Levinas from the "cry" of those who suffer the totalizing tendencies of those who subordinate the good to the apparently true. Levinas is thus led to a different position from Husserl: he celebrates the never-ending emergence of doubt or skepticism in the history of philosophy (see OB 20, 165–72).[109] Skepticism puts into question the adequacy and appropriateness of a given system of laws, of a systematic account of reality, or of a seemingly found truth. Skepticism ultimately testifies to the impossibility of fully betraying the *saying* in the reification of the *said*. The activity of the philosopher is to some extent skeptical: she or he questions the ossification, totalization, and reification of ideas and values based on the fundamental ethical meaning of thought and human experience.

Contrary to Husserl, Levinas does not perceive the main problem of Western civilization in terms of the emergence of naturalism, positivism, and psychologism. He believes that these postures are problematic, but not that they represent the foundation or climax of the problem. For him the problem of Western civilization is the persistence of a paradigm of war, or way of thinking that privileges conflict and violence and which finds its climax in racism and genocide. Thus, the cure that he offers is not a "rigorous science" but an ethical paradigm—which does not mean that he lacks rigor, but that for him the *reduction* of the "given" to a phenomenon constituted by consciousness is not the prime task of philosophy. Levinas keeps the concept of *reduction* to articulate the task of the philosopher, but he does not mean by it a phenomenological reduction as much as an ethical reduction. The ethical reduction refers to the clarification of the ethical meaning of human reality and to the denunciation of the betrayal of such meaning in ideas, concepts, and institutions. In this sense, the (phenomenological) *reduction* carries out a skeptical function, at least in respect to *dominant* forms of meaning. Levinas appropriates the Husserlian concept of *reduction*, but he identifies it more with the critical activity of promoting non-indifference than with clarifying the essence of things.

Philosophy, in the Levinasian sense, labors to show the faces behind impersonal systems of meaning and to call attention to an ideal of justice beyond mere fairness. As pointed out earlier, it represents not so much the love of wisdom as the "wisdom of love." Understood in this way, the emergence of philosophy cannot be explained in terms of a shift from the natural to the theoretical attitude of the observer who marvels in the face of nature or the variety of meanings in the world. This is the conception that Husserl defended, which he traced back to the emergence of philosophy in Greece. For Levinas, philosophy is born out of the exigencies of justice: to compare and assess in order to be able to "give" to all the others invoked in the face of the Other. Philosophy is also a response to cries of injustice. That is the reason why for Levinas the ear, more than the eye, is central as a metaphor for the activity of the philosopher. Philosophy, as the wisdom of love, bears witness to true communication and non-indifference. Levinas traces these different themes to Jewish wisdom, not to Greek philosophy or the European Renaissance.

Levinas's conception of infinity and exteriority are also related to Jewish monotheism. Just like God cannot be encapsulated by a name or represented by an idol, the Other is conceived by Levinas as the Infinite in relation to the subject's attempt to reduce meaning to a phenomenon. The irreducibility of the infinity of the Other to the intentionality of the "I" is the basis for Levinas's rearticulation of *reduction* in terms of what we could refer to as an ethical attitude, rather than purely a theoretical one. While Husserl provides a definition of philosophy (as the love of wisdom) in terms of the infinite tasks of knowledge, Levinas identifies Infinity itself with the other person.[110] Betrayal of the Infinity of the Other by the Western paradigm of war, rather than simply betrayal of the search for true knowledge, is the root of the crisis and violence of the West in the twentieth century. From this perspective, Nietzschean calls for a new genre of humans who can think beyond the categories of good and evil and Husserl's proposal of "lovers of wisdom" as functionaries of humankind are ill-fitted responses to the problem of modernity. There are other ideals, which, at least for Levinas, more clearly represent straightforward support of the paradigm of war—for example, Heideggerian appraisals of death and fascist conceptions of "authentic" community. Instead of individual or communal authenticity, Levinas advocates the need to maintain what I am calling here an ethical attitude, which takes place in the effective listening of others that occurs in ordinary experience, in the priority of duties to rights, and in the protest against the mechanisms that promote violence and war. The ethical attitude shows itself most clearly wherever the anguish of murdering the Other or the scandal of the Other's death is heavier than the fear of one's own death or finitude, which is different from authenticity and more profound than solidarity or comradeship.

The ethical attitude promotes philosophy as a critique of the murdering tendencies in civilization that find a ground in philosophical conceptions but that often become common sense. For Levinas, philosophy breaks decisively with the "status quo" and emerges as a form of critical discourse that promotes responsibility and the care for justice. Philosophy as critique, rather than eros and the family, becomes for Levinas the principal theme in his response to the crisis of the West in his later writings. On this point, he seems to approach the critical sensibility that found expression in the radical movements of 1968. He could not but notice it himself:

It is interesting to note how among the most imperative "sentiments" of May 1968, the dominant one was the refusal of a humanity that would be defined not by its vulnerability more passive than all passivity, by its debt toward the other, but by its self-satisfaction, its acquisitions and acquittances. Over and beyond capitalism and exploitation what was contested were their conditions: the person understood as an accumulation of being, by merits, titles, professional competence—an ontological tumefaction weighing on others and crushing them, instituting a hierarchized society maintained beyond the necessities of consumption, which no religious breath any longer succeeds in rendering egalitarian. Behind the capital of *having* weighed a capital of *being*.[111]

It is thus that Levinas answers the question as to "whether the aspirations of the youth in the world of today, despite the violence and irresponsibility in which they degenerate, do without a thought devoted to subjectivity on the basis of the responsibility and against the notion of being."[112] Youth, which was discussed in terms of the discontinuous time of fecundity in *Totality and Infinity*, now gives expression to a notion of recommencement understood in terms of the critical juncture introduced by the excess of signification. According to Levinas, youth also gives expression to sincerity—not to sincerity understood as obedience to the unconditional search for truth, but to sincerity as the very act of responsibility, as responsibility for the other.[113] Paradoxically, sincerity turns into a sort of skepticism, but unlike what Nietzsche feared, it does not translate into nihilism. In the hands of "youth," skepticism takes the form of a critique of the anti-ethical dimensions of the present order. Skepticism must be understood here in terms of the *ethical attitude*. In this sense, the emergence of nihilism in Europe testifies to a decrepit spirit that betrayed its humanity by forgetting its ethical vocation. If, as Garcia Marquez has so eloquently described, Latin America has spent one hundred years of solitude, it could be equally argued that Europe's solitude, and thus its nihilistic tendencies, have extended for a period of over five hundred years now. The protests against the capitalist and patriarchal order in 1968 raised the suspicion that postwar Europe may not be so different from the Europe of the nineteenth century, or for that matter from the Europe that began to emerge five hundred years ago after the conquest of the Americas (see chapter 6). Levinas never forgets 1492 as a significant date for the subsequent fate of the Jews and other racialized peoples in the world.[114] Yet, as we will see, he is unable to theorize the significance of the "darker" side of the Renaissance properly—in part because he was interested in showing the importance of Judaic wisdom, but not so much in unveiling the relevance of the colonial world for the understanding of modernity.[115] I will discuss this point more carefully in chapter 6.

According to Levinas the events of May 1968 gave expression, at least in some fundamental aspects, to the humanism of the other that he labored so hard to articulate. In addition to the events of 1968, Levinas was also particularly attentive to the challenges posed to the self-consciousness of the European by anti-colonial struggles.[116] In the recognition of countless particular cultures Levinas found "an interest that no longer stems from some taste for 'barbaric exoticism,' but the exaltation of a logic *other* than that of Aristotle, of a thought other than civilized. An exaltation that may be explainable as remorse fed by the memory of colonial wars and the long oppression of those once called savages, a long indifference to the sadness of a whole world."[117]

In Europe's "remorse" and in its own challenge of its centrality, Levinas saw what may be a testimony "of a Europe that is not just Hellenic!"[118] Europe searches for pardon. Here we find again the presence of a Judaic experience that Levinas attempted to give expression to at a philosophical level throughout his work. But, ultimately, what Levinas finds in this new aspect of the crisis of Europe is the testimony of the true vocation of the spirit, which is love.[119]

Levinas pointed to an ethical moment of the European crisis that finds expression in the European's bad conscience. Anti-colonial struggles, Levinas observed, were producing remorse in the European world. Here remorse and "bad conscience" must be taken as positive elements in the emergence of an ethical attitude. If so, then, with remorse Europe is finally finding the way out of its crisis and the paradigm of war. Levinas's description of this "bad conscience" summarizes many of the central points of his critique of the paradigm of violence and war, as well as many of the central elements in his own alternative position:

> That bad conscience expresses more than just a contradiction between a certain project of culture and its results. It is not made up solely of the seductions of a peace that ensures to each person the tranquility of his happiness and a freedom to own the world, and also, no doubt, even the possibility of owning, which nothing could disturb. It is not the failure of a speculative or dialectical project in the Hegelian style, a project that is indifferent to wars and assassinations and suffering, as long as they are necessary in the unfolding of rational thought, which is also a politics—as long as they are necessary

in the formation of concepts, the logic and rational completion of which are all that matter. It is not the intellectual disappointment of a system belied by the incoherence of reality that is the drama of Europe. Nor even just the danger of dying, which is frightening to each one of us. There is the anguish of committing crimes even where concepts are in agreement. There is the anguish of the responsibility incumbent upon each one of us in the death or suffering of the other. The fear of each for himself in the mortality of each does not succeed in *absorbing* the gravity of the murder committed and the scandal of indifference to the other's suffering. Behind the risk run by each for himself in a world without security looms the consciousness of the immediate immorality of a culture and a history. Have we not heard, in the vocation of Europe, before the message of truth that it bears, the "Thou shall not kill" of the Decalogue and the Bible? In *Genesis* 32, Jacob is troubled at the news that his brother Esau—enemy or friend—is marching to meet him "at the head of four hundred men." Verse 8 informs us: "Jacob was greatly afraid and anguished." What is the difference between fear and anguish? Rashi, the famous Rabbinical commentator, specifies: He was fearful for his death, but anguished at possibly having to kill.[120]

Levinas traces back the remorse of imperial Europe to the anguish provoked, not by the awareness of its death or finitude, but by the possibility of committing murder—or more precisely, by the realization that it in fact has committed murder. The anguish to which Levinas refers is the anguish of transforming fraternity into fratricide—which could serve as a provocative but quite Levinasian definition of colonialism.

The European's "bad conscience" clearly points to the need to overcome the conformism of rational peace and the ideal of autonomy that ends up promoting the exercise of power. The question is whether or not Europe consistently gave expression to that remorse in the sense of transforming its dominant natural attitude, framed by racism and imperialism as it was, to an ethical attitude such as the one that Levinas described. One must also enquire whether or not the legacy of racism and imperialism demands a more precise articulation of the ethical attitude in order to unveil the persistence of problems in Europe's basic attitudes. One thing is certain: where Levinas remained optimistic about the change in Europe's ways, other subjects observed absolute reticence and resistance to change. "When I look for man in European lifestyles and technology I see a constant denial of man, an avalanche of murders," so wrote Frantz Fanon in the aftermath of the Second World War and at the height of Algeria's war of independence with France.[121] Europe's perceived inability to turn away decisively from epistemological, social, and political ideals that are tied to a paradigm of violence and war gained it a very different judgment from this colonial subject. Addressing himself to whom he referred to as the condemned of the earth, Fanon enunciates:

> Let us waste no time in sterile litanies and nauseating mimicry. Leave this Europe where they are never done talking of Man, yet murder men everywhere they find them, at the corner of every one of their own streets, in all the corners of the globe. For centuries they have stifled almost the whole of humanity in the name of a so-called spiritual experience. Look at them today swaying between atomic and spiritual disintegration.
>
> And yet it may be said that Europe has been successful in as much as everything that she has attempted has succeeded.
>
> Europe undertook the leadership of the world with ardor, cynicism, and violence. . . . Europe has declined all humility and all modesty; but she has also set her face against all solicitude and all tenderness.
>
> She has only shown herself parsimonious and niggardly where men are concerned; it is only men that she has killed and devoured.
>
> So, my brothers, how is it that we do not understand that we have better things to do than to follow the same Europe?
>
> That same Europe where they were never done talking of Man, and where they never stopped proclaiming that they were only anxious for the welfare of Man; today we know with what sufferings humanity has paid for every one of their triumphs of the mind. (WE 311–12)

Frantz Fanon's dramatic call to abandon Europe expresses the other side of the Levinasian interpretation of the crisis of Europe. From Fanon's position it is clear that Europe has not really repented for its sins, nor has it transformed "bad conscience" into the radical conversion of its ways. The colonized others keep dying and suffering. These are the other "victims" to which Levinas dedicated *Otherwise Than Being*. Intriguingly, Fanon's sentence upon Europe dates back to 1961, the year in which *Totality and Infinity* was published.[122] And, if we consider the emergence and increasing force that postcolonial studies have taken everywhere in the academy, it is possible to say that what Fanon expressed at that time still resonates today.[123]

Like Levinas, Fanon was a French citizen who fought in the Second World War for the French.[124] But while both were fighting primarily against murderous German anti-Semitism, Fanon found the presence of anti-black racism, not only among the Germans, but also within the very ranks of the French troops.[125] As a native of Martinique, a French colony, Fanon felt that he was the "victim" of a racism linked with imperial projects. Having found the same racism and hate of the Other in French Algeria, he later participated actively in the Algerian struggle for de-colonization. This time he fought against the French. Fanon thus realized that Europe's encroachment demanded what Levinas greatly hesitated to mention in positive terms: a political intervention. When the *said* turns into possession and murder there may not be a better alternative to recruit politics as an effective way to advance the act of reduction. Politics does not only serve the need for thematization, synchrony, and control, nor is it merely "limited" by the ethical.[126] There are instances wherein politics and struggle may become the most effective means of advancing the ethical. The "youth" of 1968 pointed to something similar. But May 1968 did not show all of the perversity of Europe. It was in relation to its colonies that the liberal (not the Hitlerian) Europe showed its darkest face—to the point where talking about Europe's "bad conscience," from such a perspective, would have appeared ridiculous. Where Levinas found "bad conscience," Fanon, just like his Martiniquean teacher Césaire, read hypocrisy.[127] The confrontation with the paradigm of violence and war that found so tragic a manifestation in the West demands an examination of Europe in light of the colonial experience. The next two chapters will continue to search for an epistemological, social, and political conception capable of overcoming the paradigm of violence and war. We will see how Fanon joins Levinas, while radicalizing his effort to articulate a new humanism, a humanism of the other human being. This humanism requires for Fanon the introduction of not only an ethical but an ethico-political and de-colonial attitude as well as a de-colonial reduction, which allow the de-colonial philosopher-activist (and not only theorist or philosopher critic) to understand better, criticize, and transform a world shaped by war and colonialism.

II

OF MASTERS AND SLAVES,
OR FRANTZ FANON AND THE
ETHICO-POLITICAL STRUGGLE
FOR NON-SEXIST HUMAN FRATERNITY

3

GOD AND THE OTHER
IN THE SELF-RECOGNITION
OF IMPERIAL MAN

In this chapter we continue our ascent to a mode of criticism that reveals the inhuman pathologies of social structures and orders of knowledge. In the previous chapter I discussed Levinas's reinterpretation of the Husserlian conception of "reduction." For Levinas, as for Husserl, the "reduction" and the attitude that leads to it represent the most central components of any true philosophy. But, while Husserl, following a traditional Greco-European conception, conceives philosophy in terms of the theoretical interest of the search for truth (philosophy as the *love of wisdom*), for Levinas, it acquires a different meaning: philosophy becomes an ethical service or response, it is the very *wisdom of love*. Out of love and in accordance with the paradoxical nature of love, the philosopher criticizes. Her aim is directed against anything that betrays love. In this chapter I introduce Frantz Fanon as a paradigmatic philosopher of love; or perhaps better as a loving philosopher—not so much in the sense of someone who reflects about love, but rather in the sense of someone who is enraptured by love and who thinks and writes out of love. Put differently, I present Fanon as a philosopher of "reduction" in the Levinasian sense.

The concept of reduction does not appear explicitly in Fanon's writings. There is no evidence that he studied Husserl seriously or that he was acquainted with Levinas's work. Yet, his critical perspective and approach are very much indebted to existential phenomenology, particularly to the work of Jean-Paul Sartre. Indeed, Fanon's extraordinary effort to describe and examine the lived experience of the black and the condemned gain him the title of a philosopher of existence.[1] And it is precisely by virtue of the focus on existence and on lived experience that the reduction finds a place in Fanon's work. Consider that the reduction of reality to phenomena takes in existential phenomenology the form of an elucidation and analysis of the manifold varieties of existential postures and attitudes that define human experience. Focusing on Fanon's examination of lived experience, I aim to spell out or make explicit in this part what may be considered to be his contributions to the critical examination of the concept of reduction. Since the reduction is tied to a conception of the human being, as it was discussed previously, and since it also involves a view about the vocation of the human, I will also attempt to articulate in this part Fanon's contributions to the area of philosophical anthropology.

The closeness between Levinas's and Fanon's renditions of the reduction is made clear by the centrality of "love," ethics, and intersubjective contact in their respective works. But the Fanonian conception of "thinking," or rather, his praxis as thinker along with his loving praxis, introduces elements ignored by Levinas in his reflections. With Fanon, the "reduction" takes not only ethical but political connotations as well. This turn from the ethical to the political leads Fanon to advance a particularly pedagogical conception of social critique. He also reintroduces agonistic models of society in order to clarify the existence of pathologies in ordinary life, in political institutions, and in diverse epistemological configurations. In particular, I am going to focus here on Fanon's treatment of the Hegelian theme of the dialectics of master and slave in order to demonstrate how his critique of Hegel paves the way for a critical discourse that takes the "reduction" to unexpected horizons. In this chapter I lay out the basis for my reading of Fanon as a philosopher of reduction, while I also advance a Fanonian interpretation of the process of recognition involved in the confirmation of the identity of the master. In the next chapter, I focus on the position of the slave and spell out the basis of the Fanonian conception of subjectivity, which substantiates the claims of reading Fanon as a philosopher of reduction and as a philosopher of love. But first, I will attempt to clarify the transition from the ethical to the ethico-political, and to articulate the reasons behind the Fanonian radicalization of the "reduction."

FROM THE ETHICAL TO THE POLITICAL

Levinas confronted a world of violence where the question of ethics was at stake. He identified the world of violence with politics and attempted to find ethics in the allegedly more fundamental prepolitical dimensions of fecundity and the family. Levinas sought to make explicit the presence of the extraordinary (the religious, the ethical par excellence, the very glory of the infinite) in the most ordinary: language, eros, and procreation. In this way Levinas was opposing elitist conceptions of subjectivity that reaffirmed features of the "ideology of war" by counterpoising human authenticity and ordinary life. Fanon clearly stands with Levinas in the question of locating the source of goodness, love, and authenticity in ordinary life. But Fanon perceived the world and its pathologies in a way that was foreign to Levinas. Fanon confronted a world in which ordinary life was not opposed to the political and to violence in the ways that Levinas imagined. Fanon found that ordinary life in the colonies is constantly vitiated by violence and by the intervention of the political. That is, ordinary life in the colonies is *always already* overdetermined by the political. Language, eros, the achievement of self-identity, all of these basic features of ordinary human life are deeply marked by the political in a colonial world. As Fanon puts it, in the colonial world the normal turns abnormal.[2] The colonized cannot find refuge in ordinary social anonymity because the (perverted) extraordinary—the rupture of the ordinary through violence and misrecognition—simply tends to take the place of the ordinary.[3] In this world, psychic pathologies do not mask themselves in the symbolic; instead, they find expression in the real.[4] The colonial anti-black world in which Fanon lived was not simply formed by human beings, but by two fields: the colonizer and the colonized, the white and the black. Every form of human relation, every feature of human life exhibited the marks of this Manichean opposition. Manicheism, not simply positivism or ontology, characterizes for Fanon modern/colonial thinking and power.[5]

Fanon lived, then, in a very peculiar world: a world where the pathological came to occupy the space of the normal. But the validity or pertinence of Fanon's insights are hardly circumscribed to the colonial world. Fanon's work invites us to explore the many ways in which the violence of the political shapes our ordinary lives in the colonial, in the imperial, and in allegedly postcolonial conditions. The goodness of the ordinary is for Fanon something *given*, but at the same time it should be searched for and maintained. Effort and struggle are necessary, not so much to escape from ordinary life and to avoid the allegedly perverse effects of intersubjective existence, but precisely to be able to live with others in community. This means no less than that ethical criticism should be complemented by praxis, and that the ethical may be legitimately continued in the political. Here we find the bases to articulate *an-other politics*: an anti-hegemonic politics of struggle against the violence of the politics that militate against the ethical. An ethical politics perhaps? Fanon invites reflection on the possibility of a politics that emerges in the service of ethics.

Politics, to be sure, is hardly circumscribed by praxis alone. Politics is strongly related to discourse. Critical discourse may be considered a form of political intervention. Discourse, as praxis, however, is ambivalent and can end up hiding, rather than revealing, existing forms of oppression. This is the basis for the Fanonian critique of European humanism and of typical formulations of universal human rights. Fanon joins Levinas in his *skepticism* of the finality of a discourse grounded on the universal rights of Man.

> Well? Well, I reply quite calmly that there are too many idiots in this world. And having said it, I have the burden of proving it.
> Toward a new humanism. . . .
> Understanding among men. . . .
> Our colored brothers. . . .
> Mankind, I believe in you. . . .
> Race prejudice. . . .
> To understand and to love. . . .
> From all sides dozens and hundreds of pages assail me and try to impose their wills on me. But a single line would be enough. Supply a single answer and the color problem would be stripped of all its importance. (BSWM 7–8)

Fanon's sarcasm points to a sort of performative contradiction: talking "about" Man already betrays what is supposed to be the meaning of the discourse—that is the humanization of Man. This meaning can only find expression in the anti-hegemonic political act of talking with (not "talking about") the people and collaborating with them in the process of becoming humans. In an anti-black world the option is clear. As Fanon puts it, "In the absolute, the black is no more to be loved than the Czech, and truly what is to be done is to set man free" (BSWM 9). Although we are all "equal" there is for Fanon what may be called, using theological terminology, a "preferential option for the oppressed."[6] In this light, the problem with the discourse on the rights of Man is that it tends to lose sight of the need for this "preference." It advocates neutrality and universality, when selective participation is needed instead. The "preferential option for the oppressed" makes reference to an optics that gives priority to questions of dehumanization. It suggests the political and epistemic *priority* of such questions, and not necessarily in this case the epistemic privilege of the oppressed. The crucial point here concerns the need for a change of attitude that informs in its turn theory and critique. Accordingly, Fanon adopts a different attitude from that of liberal humanism: instead of talking about Man, he approaches black people, aiming to help them to overcome the effects of extended systematic colonial violence. As he puts it:

> Ah, yes, as you can see, by calling on humanity, on the belief in dignity, on love, on charity, it would be easy to prove, or to win the admission, that the black is the equal of the white. But my purpose is quite different: What I want to do is help the black man to free himself of the arsenal of complexes that has been developed by the colonial environment. (BSWM 30)

By approaching the black, and by addressing those who are violated, Fanon's text, *Black Skin, White Masks*, enacts the beginnings of a truly human "ordinary" world. Instead of talking about Man and love, his discourse comes into being from an intense love of the human being—which finds consistent expression in the love of dehumanized human beings. Ethics and politics, as well as discourse and praxis, are merged in Fanon's loving project of existence. The demand of the ethical "reduction" is extended by him from the level of philosophical discourse to the realm of the political and to the world of choice and human praxis. Or rather, the idea is that a consistent expression of the "reduction" demands an explicit form of political activity. This does not mean that philosophy and political praxis are for Fanon forever distanced from each other. On the contrary, philosophy and praxis are intermingled in Fanon's thought. But Fanon is not satisfied with repeating the centuries-old slogan that philosophy is "a way of life."[7] His critique of various European philosophers indicates that there are certain "ways of life" that, when examined closely, rather appear as "ways of death." As his examination of the colonial world clearly shows, there is no singular "way of life" for Fanon. For him philosophy is, or should be, first and foremost an ethical and political activity that aims to promote the very possibility of life with others in community. In a world permeated by colonial and neocolonial realities the task is clear: philosophy must fight against the persistent traces of dehumanization and empire. But how to do this? How to proceed? These questions invite us to explore what may be considered to be a particularly Fanonian rendering of the "reduction."

THE DE-COLONIAL REDUCTION

> *Conversely, if the Idea is seen as "only an idea," a representation [Vorstellung] in the realm of opinion, philosophy affords the opposite insight that nothing is actual except the Idea. For what matters is to recognize in the semblance of the temporal and transient the substance which is immanent and the eternal which is present. For since the rational, which is synonymous with the Idea, becomes actual by entering into external existence [Existenz], it emerges in an infinite wealth of forms, appearances, and shapes and surrounds its core with a brightly coloured covering in which consciousness at first resides, but which only the concept can penetrate in order to find the inner pulse, and detect its continued beat even within the external shapes. But the infinitely varied circumstances which take shape within this externality as the essence manifests itself within it, this infinite material and its organization, are not the subject-matter of philosophy. To deal with them would be to interfere in things [Dinge] with which philosophy has no concern, and it can save itself the trouble of giving good advice on the subject.* — G. W. F. HEGEL[8]

> *The architecture of this work is rooted in the temporal. Every human must be considered from the standpoint of time. Ideally, the present will always contribute to the building of the future. And this future is not the future of the cosmos but rather the future of my century, my country, my existence. In no fashion should I undertake to prepare the world that will come later. I belong irreducibly to my time. And it is for my own time that I should live.* — FRANTZ FANON[9]

Fanon did not believe in methods. He left methods "to the botanists and the mathematicians" (BSWM 12). For someone who studied human reality he found them to be of little value. Human reality is incomplete, and, as a result, it forever escapes the strictures of any one method. Methods are generally useful, but they simply cannot provide complete explanations of phenomena, at least where human beings are concerned. This is a basic phenomenological point. One of the more remarkable features of *Black Skin, White Masks* is the way in which Fanon pursues what Lewis Gordon calls "demonstration by failure."[10] An example of demonstration by failure is the way in which Fanon shows "that psychoanalysis cannot explain the black by attempting to explain the black psychoanalytically" (BSWM 76). Fanon systematically does this by taking on Freud, Lacan, Hegel, and Sartre. Fanon seems to put forward a sort of protodeconstructionism. I would rather argue that it is a particular form of the "reduction."

Fanon challenges the universality of dominant theories by testing them against the backdrop of realities marked by systematic dehumanization. A colonial and racist context represents for Fanon no less than a metaphysical transformation of the world. The methods used in one part of the world are not necessarily applicable in another. This position seems to lead to a radical relativism. But Fanon had little patience for relativist games. He was mainly concerned about relations of power that distort or pervert the life-world of human communities. And, in the colonial relation, it is clear that one group of people, a nation, or a group of nations is responsible for the condition of another people. There is more than a relativist upsurge when Fanon takes on Hegel, Sartre, or Lacan. They are European thinkers. Europe is the place where the imperial enterprise has been forged. Fanon is not satisfied with only indicating that what these thinkers say may be valid "there" in the territory of the colonizer and not "here" in the territory of the colonized. He wants to show that what happens "here" is related to what happens "there," and conversely as well. This conceptualization demands new and more sophisticated theories and critical ventures.

The colonial reality and the racist legacy of Europe appear to Fanon as the greatest crimes and pathologies of Europe. Dominant European approaches are generally mistaken not only because they do not apply in the colonies, but also, and more fundamentally, because they cannot even "see" or register how the very condition of coloniality reveals another side of themselves. Their methods simply do not appear to be radical enough. Their criticism leaves intact and sometimes even becomes complicit with configurations of power that extend the reign of the pathological and the inhuman. This means that cultural or philosophical criticism, even in the form of *skepsis* or doubt, is not in itself a progressive force that advances what Levinas calls the radical reduction of the world of the "said." Skepticism itself is ambiguous, sometimes resisting totalization and opening the path of critique, other times sustaining the status quo. Fanon alerts us to the possibility that the pre-original "saying" can be betrayed not only in the "said" of culture, legal institutions, and ideology, but in the discursive formation of critique as well. His critique of European approaches seems to apply a reduction of seemingly critical and ethical reductions, which appear to be insufficiently critical or ethical.

Fanon introduces a way of thinking that shows the ethical limitations of dominant forms of critique. For him, the colonial condition serves as an axis of reflection through which it is possible to examine the ethical limitations of law, reason, and critique. The ethical reduction takes the form in Fanon's work of what may be termed a *de-colonial reduction*. With the term de-colonial reduction I refer to the introduction of coloniality as a fundamental axis of reflection in the analysis of ideologies and of the critique of ideologies. Since the colonial condition represents for Fanon one of the insurmountable limits of the human, a condition wherein humanity itself produces its opposite, the inhuman, it serves as a referent to test the radicalism of ways of thinking and behaving that aim to give expression to what is most distinctively human. The colonial condition also appears in Fanon's writings as a world of anti-human disorder that betrays the ethical meaning of intersubjectively constituted human reality. Fanon was decisive, "There will be an authentic disalienation only to the degree to which things, in the most materialistic meaning of the word, will have been *restored to their proper places*" (BSWM 11–12, italics mine).

Colonialism is a world turned upside down. It represents, in its intentionality, a radically anti-human, anti-ethical world.[11] Fanon's main concern is not whether ethics is a non-sense. His project rather consists in analyzing the ways in which ethics is betrayed, and in articulating forms of critique and practices that aim to make possible and viable the existence of basic ethical relations. The colonial world, which includes the imperial project, is the anti-ethical par excellence. It is a world where the allegedly extraordinary event of anticipating one's own death cannot be achieved, not because the individual is lost in an anonymous "mass," but simply because death (the death of the slave, or of the indigenous population for instance) is already part and parcel of ordinary life.[12] In the colonial condition the human reaches its limits. It represents the point where humanity is made to face inhuman situations as part of ordinary life. The colonial death-world becomes the ethical limit of human reality.[13] It is a context in which violence and war are no longer extraordinary, but become instead ordinary features of human existence. This perverse expression of the conversion of the extraordinary into the ordinary represents a "limit" situation, or perhaps even a post-limit situation in the sense that the excess of abnormality goes beyond its climax and begets another reality in which it comes to define the normal. Thinking from the limits or beyond the limits becomes, in this way, a practice of de-colonial "reduction" through which the colonizing dimensions of practices, ways of thinking, and critique come to light.

One of the tasks of the *de-colonial reduction* is to show how, at different particular moments, there is a series of phenomena which cannot be explained except by bringing into light what Walter Mignolo has referred to as the *colonial difference*.[14] I have discussed elsewhere different possible meanings of this concept, as well as problems with some versions of it.[15] Here, with "colonial difference" I refer to the interpretive transformation that occurs when coloniality is introduced as an axis of reflection in the analysis and evaluation of diverse cultural forms of life, institutions, or critical discourses. The colonial difference is what is left out by approaches that ignore their own role in the dynamics of power that sustain an imperial world. The colonial difference emerges when one interprets or analyzes a problem in terms of how it contributes to or challenges a reality dominated by colonial and imperial features. It refers to the difference between traditional dominant accounts that do not take into consideration the Manichean structure of the world and those that do. It brings to light the image of the world that is left out in the effort to sustain the ideological justification of an imperial world. The de-colonial reduction leads to the recognition of the colonial difference, making explicit in the process important epistemological limitations of dominant interpretive approaches. The recognition of these limitations demands epistemological transformation. This transformation is only one side of the transgressive praxis needed to effectively oppose the forces that sustain an imperial world.

The de-colonial reduction makes explicit the challenges posed by the colonial condition to theories that assume a unified world where humans live and coexist. The colonial condition represents for Fanon a veritable reversal of the world. Due to the modern and racial imperial enterprise the world takes the form of a divide between white and black, between good and evil, and between master and slave among similar Manichean hierarchies. With colonialism the world takes the form of a divide between a master and a slave. Processes of identity formation and basic structures of the life-world take unique forms under the shadow of this perverted mode of relationality. The paradigm of the relation between master and slave thus becomes a variable that Fanon introduces to clarify different sorts of phenomena. "Though Sartre's speculations on the existence of the Other may be correct (to the extent, we must remember, to which *Being and Nothingness* describes an alienated consciousness), their application to a black consciousness proves fallacious. That is because the white man is not only the Other but also the master, whether real or imaginary" (BSWM 138).

The recognition of the constitutive character for human identity of a social realm that maintains structures of domination akin to the relation between a master and a slave is perhaps the main, or at least the most patent, contribution of *Black Skin, White Masks*. Fanon performs what in our terms may be rendered as a de-colonial reduction of phenomenology and psychoanalysis. He brings out the relevance of colonial Manichean hierarchies for the understanding of the psyche and lived experience of modern subjects such as black and white.

> The black Antillean is the slave of this cultural imposition. After having been the slave of the white man, he enslaves himself. The Negro is in every sense of the word a victim of white civilization. . . . the Antillean has recognized himself as a Negro, but, by virtue of an ethical transit, he also feels . . . that one is Negro to the degree to which one is wicked, sloppy, malicious, instinctual. Everything that is the opposite of these Negro modes of behavior is white. (BSWM 192)

The implications of the cultural imposition that Fanon describes are deep.

> The Negro is comparison. There is the first truth. He is comparison: that is, he is constantly preoccupied with self-evaluation and with the ego-ideal. Whenever he comes into contact with someone else, the question of value, of merit arises. The Antilles have no inherent values of their own, they are always contingent on the presence of the Other. (BSWM 211)

The "governing fiction" of the black, Fanon concludes, is not personal but social (BSWM 215). Fanon examines forms of life radically affected by a configuration of power that obeys the logic of the relation between master and slave. The question of the relation between the master and the slave may indeed very well be the central axis of his reflections. The de-colonial reduction consists precisely in a critical interpretation and elucidation of phenomena that brings to light the constitutive force of this binary. It is thus not fortuitous that Fanon decides to dedicate the last chapter of *Black Skin, White Masks* to a consideration of the problem of recognition and to conclude the chapter with an examination of Hegel's influential conception of the dialectics of lord and bondsman.

DIALECTICS OF LORDSHIP AND BONDAGE

Hegel's account of the struggle for recognition is familiar to many, being as it is one of the foundational milestones of modern and contemporary continental political philosophy, political theory, and of theories of human subjectivity and social conflict. For Hegel the struggle for recognition takes the form of a dialectic whose terms are those of lordship and bondsman, or master and slave. Hegel sets up an interesting drama between these two modes of self-consciousness. The ways in which master and slave relate to each other mediate the ways in which both are related to the thing, the sphere of life, or the object of desire.[16] The master is consciousness that exists *for itself* with power over the thing. He also has power over the slave, whose consciousness has the form of *thinghood*.[17] The slave, in contrast, gives expression to his active nihilating power only through the work that he carries in subjection to the master. And it is precisely through work that the slave is ultimately able to achieve a recognition denied to the master. The master's reliance on the slave and on the product of his work proves fatal as he only has the possibility to gain recognition from a dependent self-consciousness (the slave). The slave, however, who has been possessed by fear, the fear of the "absolute Lord" or fear of death, and who avoids this immediate death by entering into the service of the master, objectifies his existence in the product of his work. In this objectified existence the slave comes to recognize himself and "becomes aware that being for-self belongs to *him*, that he himself exists essentially and actually in his own right."[18] In this way, at the end, the slave has achieved recognition of his own existence as a for-itself, and the master, whose for-itself is expressed more directly through the act of subjugation and enjoyment, achieves only a defective and limited kind of recognition.

Fanon knows that "since the Negro was once a slave" and since his lived existence is marked by an institutional framework, a social imaginary, and a peculiar economy of desire that locates the black in the position of the slave, he cannot avoid taking seriously Hegel's account of the dialectic between master and slave. The condition of the black, however, is hardly a matter of serious consideration for the dominant European scholar. If one were to follow the premises of Hegel's own thinking, paying attention to the predicament of the black would entail getting lost in the particular and contingent when the idea is rather to focus on the truly universal. But Fanon had a different perception of philosophy and of critical thinking. For him "the urgent thing is to rediscover what is important beneath what is [or appears to be] contingent."[19] Fanon takes the key of his investigation from what is considered unimportant, for what seems to be also *de trop*. This approach puts him at odds with Hegel's ontology, which seeks, in contrast, to find the eternal in the temporal, and the idea in multiple and varied representations. While Hegel attempts to delineate the eternal figure of Spirit in time, Fanon takes the opposite road: situated in time he focuses on the ruptures with what presents itself as the universal or eternal. Employing the de-colonial reduction, Fanon "reduces" the imperial "said" and reveals its perverse unethical transformations. He does this by showing the insurmountable limitations of Hegelian ontology in the colonial context in light of a phenomenological investigation into the "lived experience of the black." To be sure, the epistemological act of recognizing "lived experience" in subjects who, by virtue of a racist perspective, are considered to lack one is a central element of the de-colonial reduction. In an anti-black world such acts are not only epistemological but ethical and political as well. The turn to lived experience leads Fanon away from Hegelian ontology:

> As long as the black man is among his own, he will have no occasion, except in minor internal conflicts, to experience his being through others. There is of course the moment of "being for others," of which Hegel speaks, but *every ontology is made unattainable in a colonized and civilized society*. It would seem that this fact has not been given sufficient attention by those who have discussed the question. In the *Weltanschauung* of a colonized people there is an impurity, a flaw that outlaws any ontological explanation. Someone may object that this is the case with every individual, but such an objection merely conceals a basic problem. Ontology—once it is finally admitted as leaving existence by the wayside—does not permit us to understand the being of the black man. For not only must the black man be black; he must be black in relation to the white man. (BSWM 110, italics mine)

In contexts dominated by colonial relations of power, Fanon asserts, blackness becomes a relational term that represents an area of exclusion from the reign of humanity. That is, blackness signifies something like the antithesis of being, or, using Heideggerian parlance, the veritable house of *non*-being.[20] Ontology, the "science of being," thus finds limits in this context. It is significant that Fanon defines this context not only as colonial but also as civilized, as if for him civilization were also mounted on relations of subordination that would make ontology untenable—as if civilization itself had imperial dimensions or were premised in an ontology of war. This idea would make his argument take more general forms than often thought about, becoming at the same time a general critique of ontology and a theory about the constitution of the most cherished ideals of sociality predicated by Western man.

The Fanonian critique of ontology gives expression to a most fascinating reversal: while for Hegel the dialectic of master and slave becomes a moment in the development of Spirit and cannot be properly understood without reference to it, for Fanon, it is precisely the existence of relations of subordination akin to this dialectic that makes reference to Spirit and subordination to its logic inadequate. For Fanon, the concrete existence of the master/slave relation transforms the structures of Being and meaning to such an extent that ontology does not make any sense if it does not change its tune and turn to the description of "lived existence"—rather than insisting in portraying and revealing the meaning and destiny of Spirit.[21] Non-existential ontology appears in this light not only inadequate to spell out the specificity of imperial, colonial, and civilized contexts, but also extremely conservative, if not even oppressive, as it, in its blindness, tends to mask or hide the significance of the existential tensions and the power relations that operate in empire and in contexts with imperial traces. It is for this reason that, for Fanon, beyond a "science of being" we must engage in a science of the relations between being and non-being, describing how the exclusion from being is performed and how non-beingness is lived or experienced.[22] This "science"—sociogeny—is deeply connected with a philosophy whose "bracketing" of the universal and attention to the contingent (in terms of what cannot be assimilated into the totality and also in terms of what is produced as contingent by the totality) manifests a strong relation with love. Attention to the contingent is a response to the cry of the condemned. Such attention defines a peculiar attitude, which I will refer to here as the *de-colonial attitude*. The de-colonial attitude, different from the natural racist attitude of an anti-black and colonial world and from the theoretical attitude that often serves to justify it, mobilizes de-colonial theory and critique as well as a phenomenological investigation characterized by the use of the de-colonial reduction. Fanon's *Black Skin, White Masks* can thus be read as a unique contribution to discourses on philosophy, critical theory, and "reduction."

The existential-phenomenological examination of colonialism pursued by Frantz Fanon in *Black Skin, White Masks* demonstrates how the perverse vertical distance between subjects characteristic of slavery finds new grounds and levels of expression in the colonial relation. For the colonized, Fanon writes, the colonizer "is not only The Other but also the master" (BSWM 138). Imperialism appears in Fanon's writings as the institutional and geopolitical reinscription of the master/slave relation in naturalized form. Empire becomes the world of the master, and the colonial territory the world of the slave. They are two distinct spaces, two worlds apart, yet they are deeply connected by relations of subjection and forced submission.[23] This condition gives rise to unique existential and semiotic forms that Fanon will tirelessly attempt to make explicit. This project makes a confrontation with Hegel inevitable.

As we have seen, Fanon argues that in imperialism one finds forms of bondage with existential dimensions that cannot be spelled out in relation to the Hegelian dialectic of master and slave. In a footnote to *Black Skin, White Masks* Fanon writes:

> I hope I have shown that here the master differs basically from the master described by Hegel. For Hegel there is reciprocity; here the master laughs at the consciousness of the slave. What he wants from the slave is not recognition but work.
>
> In the same way, the slave here is in no way identifiable with the slave who loses himself in the object and finds in his work the source of his liberation.
>
> The Negro wants to be like the master.
>
> Therefore he is less independent than the Hegelian slave.
>
> In Hegel the slave turns away from the master and turns toward the object.
>
> Here the slave turns toward the master and abandons the object. (BSWM 220–21)

In contexts defined by empire and colonialism, Fanon argues, the relation between lordship and bondage becomes unusually complicated. In an Imperial World, lordship is the position of a privileged self that does not even turn toward the slave to achieve recognition. The reason for this is that in this context the slave is not recognized as an other. The colonized loses all ontological weight in the eyes of the colonizer. At the same time, the colonized or colonial sub-alter,[24] Fanon adds, does not turn to the thing or transform fear into work, but only desires to be like the master.[25] We shall concentrate on these two criticisms of Hegel's conception of the dialectic of lordship and bondsman. In the rest of this chapter I will focus on the question of the self-recognition of the master or imperial man. In the next chapter I will consider the question of the struggle for recognition as it unfolds from the slave's side of the equation.

The problem to be considered in the rest of this chapter is the following: If the master/slave dialectic is not overcome by other forms of Spirit but remains a constant explicative factor of human relations defined by the experience of imperialism and colonialism, then we must ask how is it that the master, who in the colonial relation does not look for recognition from the slave, achieves recognition and sustains his position as master?[26] How is it that the master can occupy and sustain his role as privileged self without his being recognized by an other? Unfortunately, Fanon does not consider this question in *Black Skin, White Masks*.

It has been suggested that a satisfactory answer to the problem appears in Fanon's influential last book, *The Wretched of the Earth*. According to Suha Sabbagh, "It is not until *The Wretched* that the problem of white consciousness becomes the object of Fanon's analysis.... The West was able to do without the recognition of the 'non-whites' because it has created an image of this native as an inferior entity within the confines of Western discourse. Against this other, Western positional superiority and identity could then be established."[27]

Sabbagh conceives Fanon as a sort of proto-Saidian according to whom the white gains recognition by exporting the negative side of his image to the colonized: "The colonized becomes everything that the West is not, in Western discourse."[28] This radical division of the world whereby the master projects his negative image onto the slave is taken here as a satisfactory response to the question of the self-recognition of the master. According to Sabbagh, "The West has maintained a relative freedom vis-à-vis the master because it has established its identity in isolation and within the confines of Western writings."[29] This is a provocative response to the problem of the self-recognition of the master. It brings out an important element that is often forgotten and that is rescued both by Sabbagh and by the conception of the de-colonial reduction that I advanced above: that, to put it in Sabbagh's terms, "as a dehumanized entity, as a non-being, the position of the colonized Other serves less as a verdict on the nature of non-whites, and more as a means of telling us about the nature of the self defined against it."[30] Yet, while it is true that the distorted hermeneutics of the colonizer is instrumental in allowing him to maintain his identity in isolation, it is not clear that a projection of the negative elements of his own self is sufficient to account for the sustenance of identity. Here, the distinction between conquest and colonization may be relevant. The exportation of the negative image to the colonized seems to be an end result, and not a cause, of conquest. We have to account for the upsurge of violence and aggressiveness that characterizes the act of conquest. The projection of the "negative" needs to be preceded or at least accompanied by a projection of the "positive." With the "positive" I refer to a particular need for imperial self-assertion and for the certification or recognition of this identity. This alone would explain why colonizers simultaneously distinguish themselves from the colonized—instead of simply leaving them alone—while exercising their power by conquering them. It is often said that the colonizer conceives colonization as a missionary act. The question here is who or what sends or commissions conquest. I submit that this "who" or "what" is another invention or projection of the master. It comes into being out of his strong desires for recognition. But in order to uncover this, we need to focus more carefully on the process of recognition as it unfolds from the master's side of the equation. Taking on Ludwig Feuerbach's theory of projection, I will argue in what follows that, in an Imperial World, God becomes the privileged Other projected by the master in order to obtain recognition and to sustain the identity of the master and the imperial order of things. The following analysis can be read as a de-colonial reduction of the Said of the Master as he attempts to maintain imperial identity and control. The de-colonial reduction can be thus understood as a form of skepticism in regard to the master's projections and projects—it is a "reduction" of imperial projects and projections. The development of this account is particularly relevant because it substantiates my point that neither the premises nor the implications of Fanon's thought can be simply subordinated to the parameters of Hegelianism, a view that has been propagated by some influential interpretations.[31]

GOD AND THE OTHER IN THE SELF-RECOGNITION OF IMPERIAL MAN

> *Again, a son's condition is most perfect when the son, as far as his nature allows, reproduces the perfection of the father. Mankind is the son of the heavens, which is perfect in all its works. . . . Therefore mankind's condition is most perfect when it reproduces the perfection of the heavens, so far as human nature allows. And just as the heavens are governed and directed in every movement by a single mover, which is God . . . so, if our argument has been correct, mankind is at its best when all its movements*

> *and intentions are governed by one Prince as its sole mover and with one law for its direction.*
>
> *Hence it is obvious that the world's well-being demands a Monarch or single government known as the Empire.* —DANTE ALIGHIERI[32]

Influenced by Hegel's philosophy of Spirit, Ludwig Feuerbach articulated one of the most influential and powerful atheist theories of religion. His *Essence of Christianity* still stands as a classic in the field of the theory of religion. It deeply influenced Karl Marx's materialism and his conception of critique, and through him, many others as well.[33] In *The Essence of Christianity*, Feuerbach proposes the audacious idea that "religion is that conception of the nature of the world and of man which is essential to, i.e., identical with, a man's nature."[34] As a result, for Feuerbach, "consciousness of God is self-consciousness, knowledge of God is self-knowledge."[35] According to Feuerbach, God is a projection of the subjective nature of human beings. Religion is, at its very core, a form of alienation.

In a relatively recent study, Van A. Harvey claims that Feuerbach's theory of religion underwent significant changes in the writings after *The Essence of Christianity*.[36] The Feuerbachian acute and intense critique of religion finds in Harvey's analysis new and more sophisticated modes of expression, challenging the simplistic views and easy dismissals of this important figure. The Feuerbach introduced by Harvey no longer relies either on dialectical conceptions of consciousness or on the related ideas of necessary stages in consciousness's own internal development. He rather has recourse to notions of interaction between subjectivity and nature, and to desires for recognition that cannot be spelled out in relation to the internal dialectic of consciousness or in relation to Universal Spirit. As Harvey puts it,

> This Feuerbach has progressed beyond the inversion of Hegel's philosophy of Spirit to develop an original and still interesting critique of religion. Religion is no longer regarded as an involuntary projection inherent in and necessary for complete self-consciousness as it was in *The Essence of Christianity*; rather, it is an erroneous, belief-like interpretation of the all encompassing and mysterious nature upon which the self knows itself to be dependent, an interpretation that springs out of the confrontation of the I with the not-I and the desire for recognition by this other.[37]

Harvey's crucial insight is that nature is no longer seen by Feuerbach as an emanation from consciousness or Spirit. Instead, nature is properly recognized as something external that remains unfamiliar to consciousness. With this conception of nature religion can then be explained in relation to the different ways of dealing with this mystery (nature), and not in relation to necessary movements of consciousness.

The more decisive materialist dimension of Feuerbach's later theory of religion, as Harvey also points out, finds antecedents in *The Essence of Christianity*. In this book, Feuerbach challenges the idea that the otherness of nature is produced as a "moment" in the development of Spirit, arguing instead that the awareness of the otherness of nature and the world is predicated on a previous contact with "a sensuously perceived Thou."[38] As Feuerbach puts it, "I am, and I feel myself dependent on the world, because I first feel dependent on other men." And, "The first object of man is man. The sense of Nature . . . is a later product."[39] From these passages Harvey highlights the emphasis on embodiment implicit in the I-Thou encounter and the strong idea of nature. Yet these crucial ideas only appear scattered throughout the *The Essence of Christianity*, still subordinated to the theme of (infinite) consciousness. For Harvey this represents no less than a failure, leading Feuerbach to revert to the Hegelian concern with consciousness, thus falling short of the implications of his own materialist turn.[40]

It is only in his later work, or so Harvey argues, that the implications of Feuerbach's critique of Hegel unfold. In contrast to the early reductionistic view of externality and nature, Harvey argues that the renewed interpretation and critique of religion articulated by Feuerbach relies on the distinction between poles that clearly accentuate the notion of the externality of nature. Nature is taken as one of the "poles," while subjectivity becomes the other pole where feelings of dependence, egoism, and the drive to happiness find expression. The infinitude of consciousness and the notion of its necessary "moments" are set aside, and religion is explained in strictly relational terms. This move has some clear advantages over the earlier theory based on consciousness. In particular, it allows Feuerbach to account for "the religious believer's sense of being in touch with a transcendent reality outside of the self."[41] The projection only has to do with the superimposition of an image onto something that is already out there, and not with the self-development of a consciousness that embraces all and from which the notion of something exterior first derives. The projection is the result of the encounter of a mankind who desires to live, but who is surrounded by a nature that has "no heart" and that "is blind and deaf to the desires and complaints of man."[42]

In attempting to overcome the limits of the Hegelian paradigm of consciousness, Feuerbach concentrates on the traditional bipolarity of man and nature and does not develop the more interesting and innovative view, advanced in *The Essence of Christianity*, that the sense of nature is mediated by the intersubjective relation of man and man. This idea is not foreign to Hegel's work, finding expression, as we have seen above, in his view of the recognition of self-consciousness through an intersubjective struggle in a context of lordship and bondage. It thus seems that Feuerbach's more radical rejection of Hegel's paradigm of consciousness led him to an equal rejection or dismissal of the fundamental role of the I-Thou relation in the achievement of recognition. Feuerbach's conception of the exteriority of nature as a pole, therefore, seems to be achieved only at the expense of a proper consideration of the constitutive force of intersubjective struggles for recognition. This element is also ignored in his account of subjectivity as the other fundamental pole of experience. Indeed, it is possible to argue that, with the notions of man and nature as two poles, Feuerbach's materialism is still tied to the abstract and speculative form of Hegel's philosophy. That is, his overcoming of Hegel's philosophy of Spirit appears only as relative, since Feuerbach still relies on general conceptions of man and nature that tend to erase the significance of concrete intersubjective struggles for recognition. Feuerbach would have developed a more complicated view if he had considered seriously the Hegelian arguments for the idea that a direct relation with objects does not provide an adequate basis for recognition. By ignoring this question Feuerbach's theory fails to take advantage of one of the more fundamental Hegelian insights: that intersubjective forces intervene not only in human projections, but also in the constitution of human subjectivity itself.

As a result of Feuerbach's failure, he will not then consider the ways in which the projection of God may be motivated by interests of recognition that take place in intersubjective contexts defined by relations of lordship and bondage. In addition, the account of the psychological and subjective grounds of religion offered by him does not include a consideration of the ways in which the subject-subject encounter complicates the sort of motivations and feelings that give rise to and sustain religion. To be sure, Hegel does not pursue this problematic either. This, however, is to be expected since, on the one hand, Hegel does not share a projectionist conception of religion and, on the other hand, his account of the struggle for recognition is subsumed into the dialectical trajectory of Spirit. But this is precisely why Feuerbach's departure from Hegel and his conception of the primacy of the I-Thou encounter in *The*

Essence of Christianity are so significant. They brought out the possibility of approaching the question of the meaning and function of religion from the perspective of the struggle for recognition.

We find then that in *The Essence of Christianity* and in other later writings Feuerbach clearly indicates the idea that the projection of God is tied to the satisfaction of desires for recognition. But, in contrast to Hegel and Fanon, recognition for Feuerbach primarily takes place, as we have seen, in the interactions between I and non-I. Fanon's arguably more consistent and radical critique of Hegelian ontology through existential phenomenology leads him to focus on the constitutive force of desires for recognition that take place among human subjects. He is therefore more interested in the I-Thou relation than in unmediated relations between man and nature. He studies contexts defined by historical and structural forms of subjection. As a result Fanon does not talk so much of Man as of masters and slaves. The most direct and significant consequence of this turn for the theory of religion is that God can no longer be seen as a projection of human subjectivity stimulated by feelings of dependence in relation to nature, but rather as a projection of either master or slave in relation to the continuity or rupture with a context that sustains the division between lordship and bondage. This means that the projection of God does not work so much, as Feuerbach argues, in the function of the pacification of nature, but rather in terms of the tensions brought up by intersubjective relations of power. To give analytical primacy to the relations between an over-encompassing and impersonal objective pole and an equally indeterminate subjective pole would mean in this context to render obscure the strength of intersubjective relations of power in the constitution of whatever is taken as man or nature.

From Feuerbach's perspective also follows the idea of a religion that arises out of man's intrinsic subjective tensions and dealings with nature. This perspective does not offer the necessary resources to make explicit the role of religion in an imperial context. That is, it fails to reach the critical level provided by the de-colonial reduction. As a result, Feuerbach simply ignores the fact that religion is politically charged with the most varied meanings, and that conceptions of God become no less than a whole field of political tensions. In an imperial context one never finds God, but rather the God of the master or the God of the slave. Sometimes the slave has no other possibility than to turn to the religion of the master, since the master has wiped out or at least strongly devalued the religions of the slave.[43] Then we find a God with two faces. God becomes a site of contestation, the field of an incessant ontological struggle. Monotheism takes the form of Manicheism as the imperial world becomes a quasi-cosmological context divided by the ontological principles of darkness and light.

In an imperial context the dominant God is the God of the master. The very existence of empire is proof of this. *In empire, God becomes the privileged other who alone can provide authentic recognition to the imperial self.* The continued existence of this self testifies to the dominance of this God. Imperial God and imperial man become immediate proofs of the existence of each other. In other words, their existence takes a tautological form. In no other context is the assertion that man is made in the image of God more literal than in an imperial world. And the reason for this is clear: in an imperial world the conception of God is strongly overdetermined as it takes the form and effectively functions as the projection of imperial man. As Feuerbach would put it, it is not that God makes man in his likeness, but that man projects God out of his desire for recognition. This reversal has a clear consequence, that the otherness of God is extremely qualified in this context. God becomes the Other who is still part of the Same. God, as the projection of imperial man, becomes not so much an other as an alter ego. God is master like the master. And, in fact, only a master can provide authentic recognition to another master. The *difference* implicit in the monotheistic conception of God as the wholly Other, or "trans-ontological difference," is violated, making God a most fundamental structural piece in the sustenance of empire. This is only a first step in the general transmutation of meaning that the "order of things" undergoes in an imperial context.

The violation of the difference between God and man is one side of a more complicated and terrifying violation. This becomes more clear once we consider that in the act of projection there are two simultaneous processes: on the one hand, God takes the shape of man, while on the other, man takes God-like features. In short, Imperial Man takes the shape of God. But the reduction of the difference between God and Man is now reversed and augmented to such an extent that Imperial Man is taken to be qualitatively superior to other human beings. The subjugation of the slave rather than the alienation of man becomes the first evidential and experiential element of the projection. A logic of sub-alteration is contained in the process of recognition of Imperial Man. God recognizes Man, Man takes the shape of God, and then others come to be *seen* as the very incarnation of evil.[44] This logic does not respond so much to interests in the conciliation with nature as, more fundamentally, to interests in the subordination of other human beings. Modern imperial man is no pagan. He does not divinize nature, but rather becomes himself God with the sole purpose of enslaving others. Idolatry becomes egolatry, a perverse egolatry that works in the function of the rejection of otherness. At the end, narcissism becomes homicidal, and the command "Thou shall not kill" is transformed into a project of identity based on the principle "I kill, therefore I am."[45]

The proper recognition of lordship is achieved, or so I have argued, through a double violation of alterity. The interrelation of such violations is clear since the reduction of the alterity of God represents only a step in a project that culminates in obscuring and transgressing the meaning of human alterity, making it part of the homicidal logic of sub-alterity. Thus, in Empire, the phenomenological features of divinity are complicit with the degradation of peoples to a subhuman level. The projection of God is only part of a more general project that intends the collapse of the world of alterity into the world of sameness and the subjugation of otherness. In this kind of world the space between subjects is altered, leaving no space to authentic communication, ethical interaction, and dialogue, but only to imposition and domination.[46] The one under the sight and control of Imperial Man is forced to live in conditions where her and his worth augments in direct relation to her and his self-evisceration, that is, to the devaluation of her and his own body, identity, and culture. Assimilation becomes an intended reality of the structure. Since Imperial Man structurally and semiotically functions as God, the holy call to imitate God becomes an explicit act of violation. Conversion is clearly crucial to this obscure logics of identity, though it takes unique forms. The colonial logic of conversion is designed to make the colonized fail, since they will never be recognized as Lord.[47] Race plays a crucial role here, as the exteriority of the skin becomes the most basic medium through which the perverse difference of sub-alterity is raised and sustained. Through the body and skin the colonized is maintained *in his or her place*.[48] As a result, the body is lived by the colonized not so much as a prison but as an inescapable sign of murder. The codification of the skin by Imperial Man becomes much like the opposite of the biblical tale; it is a mark that signals the place where the homicidal plagues of Empire are expected to fall.

Empire appears in this light as a project that aims at the systematic eradication of difference and otherness through annihilation or assimilation. The world of empire is the world of sameness and its structure takes the form of totality. Imperial Man claims right of ownership everywhere. His cosmopolitanism works in the function of his power. That is, the whole world becomes his habitat as his rights are said to inhere in things. Being is thus coextensive with him. Wherever *there is* (*il y a*) he is, so Imperial Man cannot escape being.[49] Imperial Man is *present* everywhere, and *presence* becomes his more characteristic ontological and temporal condition. The future, as the irruption of the new, is kept from challenging the present and it becomes, as it were, only the emanation of the present. Fanon alludes to this when he points out that empire represents "a motionless movement where gradually dialectic is changing into the logic of equilibrium" (WE 314).

The link between *presence* and the *present* points to a fundamental relation between spatiality and temporality. As Levinas has called attention to, "maintenant" (now) is precisely "main-tenant" (having at hand).[50] The logic of possession defines a mode of temporality that aims to take the shape of the always present.[51] The "hand that takes" traverses the distance of space and brings the "thing" into its presence. Empire represents in many ways the highest exponential expression of this modality at the concrete historical level. Empire is the organized attempt to take the logic of possession to its most consistent level, making Imperial Man omnipresent by making the whole world, including other human beings living in it, a field of ever possible explorations and acts of possession.[52] Imperial Man invests his time in acts of classification and in the division of space and human beings.[53] The interest in preserving the temporality of the present takes sadistic dimensions: one must classify and maintain distance from those who fundamentally one would like to see *annihilated*. The temporality of the present finds its climax and most consistent expression in homicide, torture, and genocide.[54] Temporality is then radically altered by the mutation of human space into inhuman space—communication is the mode of the first, murder and dehumanization the mode of the second. Spatiality interrupts the flow of time as it enters into the logic of segregation. The segregation of people into different spaces may be seen as either the continuation or the refutation of Babel. After Imperial Man reaches the pinnacles of divinity he creates a distance between himself and others similar to that found between himself and God. Having learned how to transgress the divine space, however, Imperial Man creates a space much more insurmountable and difficult to conquer.[55] Spatiality and temporality, therefore, take precise meanings in empire. They both are inserted in an order of things that works in the function of a process of recognition that ends up sub-alterizing a group of human beings while ascribing divine features to others.

The sustenance of empire and the recognition of Imperial humanity demand a quasi-ontological transformation of the world. The notion of God is crucial for understanding empire not only because God is necessary to provide recognition to Imperial Man, but, more significantly, because empire itself may be taken as Man's most consistent attempt to be God. That is to say, Imperial Man functions structurally like God in an imperial world.[56] Imperial Man's lived experience, shaped by an imperial process of recognition, also takes theological dimensions. The Sartrean idea that Man fundamentally desires to be God clearly takes literal connotations in an Imperial World.[57] Imperial man represents perhaps the most successful attempt in this direction, being a subject whose desire to be God outweighs the desire to be recognized as human. The desire to be superior to others and to dominate them appears thus to be a motivating factor of the projection of God by Imperial Man. Indeed, God and the bondsman are the two poles by virtue of which the master constructs the edifice, both at the imaginary and at the concrete levels, that will allow him to give to his existence the shape of the necessary and all important. Imperial Man wants to become necessary Man, a man whose existence is ontologically justified. The divine, the social, and the realm of things cannot but testify to the necessity of his being. Empire is this order of things whereby Man is elevated to the status of God.

The notion of the desire to be God brings a paradoxical element in view: while the master wants to be God he still needs God as an other who can recognize him as master. This means that, at least under the basic initial conditions of recognition, the master can never truly occupy the position of God. Lewis Gordon raises a similar point in his phenomenological study of human postures and attitudes in an anti-black world: "Since whiteness is the ideal, the white man is either God or as close to God as anyone can be on earth. Therefore he needs a transcendent God simultaneously to deny his hubris and affirm his whiteness. Can he, as it were, have his cake and eat it too?"[58]

It is apparent then that while God allows the master to take the form of "God in the flesh," he signifies a purity that the master will never really be able to represent. If the master ever attempts to declare himself God, then he will not be able to obtain recognition. The process of recognition of Imperial Man leads him to confront a dilemma in which the very possibility of the future sustenance of his identity as master is at stake. For Gordon, it is precisely at this point that we find some prospects regarding the possibility of overcoming the imperial mode of reality and process of recognition: "The only alternatives are that whiteness or God itself is so ideal that no actual white man can ever achieve an identity relation with it, or that God or whiteness must be rejected, which makes humanity—Freedom—the ideal toward whom both whites and blacks aim. This freedom must, however, be approached through love, not hate, which requires respect for this freedom as Other."[59]

For Gordon, the dilemma of the master presents the opportunity for him to finally aim toward the construction of a truly human world. Feuerbach embraced a similar idea. For him, the rejection of God would lead humanity to an unprecedented self-reconciliation, thus bringing an authentic reign of love. There is, however, a fundamental difference between Feuerbach's and Gordon's approaches. While the former treats God as a general category (as the essence of man), the latter examines and critiques the God that appears and sustains a strictly anti-black world. This is the reason why "God" is said to represent pure whiteness, and why his rejection opens the possibility for an anti-racist world of love where a non-imperial divinity could find a place. But, as Gordon indicates, there is also the possibility for those who wish to further empire of making God/whiteness absolutely transcendent to continue deriving the benefits of imperial recognition. Yet such a possibility introduces a paradoxical element: radicalizing God's transcendence increases the tension between God's lordship and the ambitions of Imperial Man. With God in a position of absolute transcendence, Imperial Man appears less as a master and more as a servant to the true transcendental master. Such is the paradox of imperial recognition: its affirmation leads to its failure, unless, that is, there is a way to achieve recognition and affirm the value of whiteness without God.

RECOGNITION, THE DEAD GOD, AND THE NEW PROJECT(ION)S OF EMPIRE

In an imperial world, I argued above, the meaning and function of God are greatly determined by Imperial Man's desires for recognition. God becomes a projection that serves to recognize the master as master and to collaborate in the politics that sustain the regime of spatiality characteristic of empire. The master, however, in being recognized by God the Master, becomes a servant. To be sure this servitude is not totally negative, since it allows Imperial Man to conceive colonization and murder as altruistic acts made in the service of God. Indeed, this servitude is crucial for the initial impetus of empire. It not only allows Imperial Man to exercise his power with good conscience, it also encourages the exercise of imperial power and the extension of imperial civilization by conceiving of these actions in terms of a divine mission. Yet servitude does not fit entirely well with the consciousness of the master, and he will ultimately come to *resent* God for this. The projection of God by Imperial Man, while it allows the master to be recognized as master and thus to legitimate a morality of aggression (toward the colonized sub-other), simultaneously becomes the source of an ascetic form of valuation and existence—of life for God. The ascetic mode of valuation that for Nietzsche appeared so encompassing (see chapter 1) can thus be traced back, in this phenomenological exploration of empire, to the master and not to the slave. Or, to be more precise, it is perhaps better to say to the master as slave (of the God that he projected). This phenomenological configuration helps to explain why asceticism, in the perverse dimensions that Nietzsche observed, combines an attitude of self-submission and hate. Asceticism often works as a discipline of control in the interest of the subordination and dehumanization of others. Indeed, Imperial Man submits himself to this ascetic mode of existence only insofar as this appears indispensable to sustain a regime of power that maintains him as lord and others as slaves. As other mechanisms and ideologies of subordination develop, and as "ressentiment" against God augments, we encounter the emergence of a strong skepticism and indifference to God as well as discourses centered on the alleged "death of God." Nihilism will not be too high a price to pay for the acquired efficiency in sustaining empire—although this nihilism is soon overcome by new imperial forms of valuation.

Asceticism and nihilism gradually become the most urgent problems for Imperial Man, indeed, for him, the basic problems of humanity. The enslaved part of humanity (the colonized), however, has other kinds of fears and concerns as they are confronted not only with other aspects of imperial divinity but with Imperial Man himself. The slavery of the slave is, indeed, more terrifying than the slavery of the master. The burden of subjectivity suffered by Imperial Man under the dominance of God becomes murder and violence in the colonial context. And, while Imperial Man may be conceived as an oppressed being, the colonized remains out of the boundaries of being altogether. The most amazing feat is then attempted. The master seeks to persuade the slave that his challenge too consists in evading asceticism and overcoming nihilism. In this way, the proclamation of the freedom of "humanity" is positively charged with the lived condition of the master in his attempt to break loose of the yoke of holy servitude. The notion of Man then becomes a plausible candidate to assume the position of God, as it also becomes a *projection* of Imperial

Man. Imperial man, in any case, has achieved much simply by limiting the possibility that the slave may reflect upon the meaning of things according to the exigencies posed by his or her own condition. Imperial Man thus forecloses one major source for the possible transformation of the critique of God into a radical critique of whiteness and empire. Empire truly reaches its climax when it accomplishes this feat, making everyone think about their realities through the questions posed by the dilemmas of empire to Imperial Man.

Many are the subtle and varied forms in which the need to achieve self-recognition in a context without God has found expression. God may be dead, but it is clear that imperial Man and the imperiality of power are still rising by virtue of new and varied acts of projection.[60] Imperial Man found new ways to sustain his position as lord and to achieve what only God seemed able to offer, recognition as master. I already mentioned abstract notions of humanity or man as projections of Imperial Man in his effort to erase the significance and constitutive power of relations of lordship and bondage. Along with the concept of Man, ideas of nation, race, and the system or market have also come to fill the space left by God.[61] It is not incidental that general skepticism of God, along with ideas about the "death of God," emerged precisely when Europe came to be more consistently formed by nation-states in the nineteenth century.[62] As biologically defined ideas of race and secular conceptions of the nation provided new coordinates for self-identification, God became more and more dispensable in the process of recognition. And, in fact, once nation-states are formed imperialism finds more effective ways to legitimize itself than religion. The nation and the race become central for the identity of Imperial Man as Man, and for the idea of superiority. Then eugenics, phrenology, and the social sciences take the place of religious ideals and creeds in the legitimization of empire.[63] The divinization of the system and the theological dimensions of the market also help to sustain relations of slavery in a world without God.[64] Ideologies such as conservatism and neoliberalism, with their respective beliefs in the preservation of the system or the sustained increase of the market, offer justification to sacrificial modes of relations that assure the position of the master as the one and only lord.[65] To the "egolatrous" projection of Imperial Man to abstract man, the idolatrous relation with the system or market is added as another form of sustaining power and recognition after the "death of God." In the contemporary world, economy becomes the new theology. The logic of the market likewise becomes a new form of theodicy.⁶⁶ It is from here that the life and hunger of millions sustain an inhuman system unconditionally defended by imperial humanity.

Idolatry and the sacrificial religiosity of the modern/colonial world seem to be related not to a "slave revolt in morality," but to a "master revolt" against God and against obsolete forms of domination.⁶⁷ The imperial order of things is structured so as to hide this dimension of our contemporary reality, and it ignores that human existence is lived between the poles of lordship and bondage. This notion implicitly refers to the truism that *"the master is the master of the slave and the slave is the slave of the master."* This means that whatever the problems of the master are, they can't be understood without examining his condition as master in relation to a slave, and that whatever the slave *can't be* has to be spelled out in relation to an examination of the imperial world. Reference to man or to humanity as a single neutral entity, and reference to subjective conditions spelled out according to the internal process of particular historical conditions, must be problematized by a recognition of spatiality and the colonial difference.⁶⁸ The intellectual production of those who share a space or history with the master will remain limited if it is not complicated enough to make clear how the *sub-alterical logic* of the relation between master and slave makes of all of us *less than humans*.

Critique of the modern imperial order must involve, today, as yesterday, the critique of religion. But the critique of religion cannot be identified with a defense of atheism. Discourses on the "death of God" can become as problematic as discourses that affirm the existence of God. And sometimes the affirmation of the transcendence of God animates criticism of racism and imperialism.⁶⁹ Yet, such critiques lose their power and become dangerous when they exclude the voices of colonized and racialized subjects on the basis of such transcendence, or when they ignore the extent to which God acquires particular meanings in anti-black and colonial contexts. In such contexts one must not vacillate in declaring the need to overcome the death of the God that is complicit with the master. That is the reason why, different from the typical conception of the "death of God," Gordon advocates the death of the white God.⁷⁰ This analysis is remarkably different from Feuerbach's logic. Taking God and man as general categories untouched by intersubjective struggles for recognition erases the significance of existent relations of subordination and mistakenly identifies atheism with progressive ethical thinking. In an anti-black world love can emerge only by virtue of two occurrences: by the "death" of white God and white Man, and by the simultaneous "preferential option" for dehumanized subjects. For love to emerge, more important than an ethically ambiguous atheism is antiracism; and, more important than neutral agnosticism is a committed existence on the side of the oppressed. Love has hardly emerged as a dominant feature of our world. With all his pretended atheism or even with all his piteous religiosity, Imperial Man has found innovative ways to confirm his position as master and to sustain an imperial world. New gods, new projections, keep appearing behind the old decrepit imperial God.[71] Where, then, may the fragile possibility of love be found? It is true that the master has the option, and, indeed, the moral imperative of disavowing his position and of entering into a process of "unlearning imperial privilege."[72] But the slave, a privileged object of hate in the world, can hardly wait for this to occur. In any case, the slave has to use all her energies to accelerate the process whereby the authentic possibility of love can emerge.

So far I have attempted to spell out and expand on Fanon's contributions to understanding the project that militates against the emergence of love. Following Fanon, I described this project in terms of the master's search for recognition. We have seen that the projection of the negative image of the master to the slave or the colonized is complemented by a projection of his more positive features to an imperial God. As these projections unfold they inspire the creation of institutions and become part of common sense. The projections of Imperial Man create an aura of factuality around them. The projections are consequently directly opposed to the performance of the ethical and the de-colonial reductions, which are critical of the project of building an imperial world. To reduce means precisely in this context to show the inhuman motivations and raison d'être of the projections and to clear the space up for the emergence of love. If the slave, as was indicated above, searches for love, the reduction (as an expression of philosophy as "wisdom of love") appears to be related to her and his struggle for recognition. With this in mind we turn now to examine Fanon's account of the slave's struggle for recognition.

4

RECOGNITION FROM BELOW
THE MEANING OF THE CRY AND THE GIFT OF THE SELF
IN THE STRUGGLE FOR RECOGNITION

Let me say at the risk of seeming ridiculous that the true revolutionary is guided by great feelings of love. —CHÉ GUEVARA[1]

In the previous chapter I introduced Fanon's critical approach and then elaborated some fundamental implications of his critique of the Hegelian conception of the dialectics of lordship and bondage. In particular, I provided an existential-phenomenological analysis of the process of the master's attempt at achieving recognition. In this chapter, in contrast, I examine Fanon's conception of the process of recognition as it unfolds from the condition of slavery. If the last chapter was dedicated to the articulation and analysis of the intricate ways in which imperial modes of recognition are sustained, this chapter focuses on the search for ways to consistently overcome imperial and colonial modes of recognition from the position of sub-alterity. Here we will look for the conditions of possibility for the emergence of love in the slave's struggle for recognition.

The theme of the struggle for recognition has become fashionable nowadays either as a critique or a vindication of different efforts to obtain cultural recognition or to affirm collective identities. It is in this context that I will articulate Fanon's position on the matter. One of the most important and ignored lessons of Fanon's approach is the way in which his existential phenomenology serves to clarify the motivations and aspirations of the slave in the struggle for liberation. With this in mind, I attempt in the second section of the chapter to make explicit the Fanonian account of *desire* through a phenomenology of the "cry." Since the "cry" is, beyond questions of respect or disrespect, the first marker of an enslaved and suffering subjectivity, it provides a privileged starting point to elucidate the motivations behind the slave's struggle for recognition. As the analysis will hopefully make clear, "crying" is connected, in the struggle for recognition, with a loving subjectivity who is not able to love. Love becomes the key to articulating a Fanonian account of the colonial condition and of colonial subjects. The proper articulation of this idea constitutes the core of the argumentation in the third section of this chapter. I then conclude in the final section with an exposition of the different ways in which "love" leads Fanon to articulate a position that subverts at various levels the logics of imperial recognition. It is in the "gift," *beyond imperial recognition*, that we will find the possibility for love.

THE STRUGGLE FOR RECOGNITION

The development of modern social and political philosophy in the last two hundred years has been marked, as Jürgen Habermas has recalled on innumerable occasions, by an increasing concern for issues of legitimation and social integration.[2] The demise of overarching metaphysical conceptions that tied together cosmological, social, ethical, and political orders gave way to what is known today as "the fact of pluralism." In the effort to evade the limits of metaphysics social and political philosophy has turned procedural, not substantive; communicative, not monological; and political, not metaphysical, to use Rawls's influential formulation of the theme.[3] These are all innovative formulations in the attempt to justify a political order and to account for social cohesion in increasingly pluralistic societies. Since 1968 or perhaps even since the advent of the civil rights movement in the United States,[4] the challenges posed by the theoretical recognition of pluralism have gradually shifted, as Charles Taylor has noted in his influential essay "The Politics of Recognition," to a direct confrontation with claims for recognition from groups who feel that their cultures are endangered or not recognized as having equal value.[5] With this Taylor refers to the contemporary realities of multiculturalism, which could be understood as a considerable extension of the "fact of pluralism." What we see now emerging more and more is, as Taylor puts it, an explicit demand for recognition playing an active role in contemporary social dynamics and political struggles.

The struggle for recognition is a theme that Hegel introduced in his Jena writings and that later found a place in the influential *Phenomenology of Spirit*. Taylor is, among other things, a Hegel scholar and one would think that his taking on the theme of the politics of recognition would be an expression of his interest or indebtedness to Hegel's formulation of the theme.[6] Yet, in his essay on the politics of recognition, Taylor mentions Hegel only briefly, and only in his discussion of the concept of dignity in Rousseau.[7] When one considers Taylor's philosophical project, however, this omission does not appear as bizarre as one thinks at first. Taylor's engagement with Hegel is for the most part focused on issues related to the articulation of a moral and social philosophy anchored in the idea of *Sittlichkeit* or ethical life. Taylor is mainly interested in the understanding of ethical reason and autonomy in terms of communal conceptions of the good. That is, he appropriates Hegel insofar as Hegelian thought helps him to contest the subordination of questions about the good life to questions about justice and the right. He is more interested in the romantic Hegel who attempts to leave Kantianism behind with the articulation of a harmonic vision of subjectivity, ethics, customs, and collective life than in the more agonistic Hegel who brings up the question of struggle and recognition. The notion of the struggle for recognition, in particular as it appears in the Hegelian conception of the dialectics of lord and bondsman, brings questions and issues of its own, which cannot be subordinated to the debate about the alleged primacy of the right over the good. I am referring to issues of power relationships, of the coming to an awareness of freedom, of the process through which freedom from bondage is actualized, and to questions about the sustenance of power by dominant groups and about the struggle for hegemony. Taylor's blindness or his subordination of these issues to the discussion about the plausibility of the notion of collective rights explains why he tends to leave aside questions of power in his reflections on multiculturalism.[8]

It was up to one of Habermas's partners in Frankfurt to reveal how the idea of the struggle for recognition ultimately points to an area of philosophical inquiry located in between a de-ontological approach to ethics and politics on the one hand and communitarian concerns for the good life on the other. I refer to Axel Honneth, and to his influential work, *The Struggle for Recognition: The Moral Grammar of Social Conflicts*. In this work Honneth develops a theme with which he concluded a previous work, that an effort "to integrate the social-theoretical insights of Foucault's historical work within the framework of a theory of communicative action has to rely on a concept of morally motivated struggle."[9] It is precisely his work on Foucault that leads Honneth, in contrast to Taylor, to take into serious consideration the relevance of power dynamics in the politics of recognition. That is, in short, why Honneth refers to a *struggle for recognition*, and not simply, as Taylor prefers, to a *politics of recognition*. Taking the struggle for recognition as a theme, Honneth cannot avoid going back to Hegel. The first part of the book is dedicated to an analysis of the theme of recognition in Hegel's writings.

Honneth's critical interpretation of the Hegelian conception of recognition follows an interesting and persuasive logic. First, Honneth shows how Hegel's interpretation of recognition represents something like a paradigm shift in modern political theory. Different from Machiavelli and Hobbes, who traced social conflicts to desires for self-preservation, Hegel showed how conflict arises out of unfulfilled desires for recognition. The idea that subjects struggle to gain recognition as persons also introduces an intersubjective conception of selfhood that was absent in the vocabulary and presuppositions of early modern political theory. Honneth notes that Hegel's groundbreaking move paves the way for an examination of the moral content of social struggles. This examination requires that social and political philosophy turn to empirical social sciences in order to examine carefully the motivations behind different social movements and groups. Yet, as Honneth correctly points out, Hegel never pursues this path. Honneth argues that a series of problems in his articulation of the struggle for recognition led Hegel to develop a way of thinking and a series of concepts that inhibited the adequate empirical dimension of the research. Honneth refers to no less than Hegel's philosophy of consciousness and its trademark, the concept of *Geist* or Spirit. As Honneth puts it,

> Because Hegel gives up, along with the Aristotelianism of his early Jena writings, the notion of an intersubjectivity of human life, he can no longer conceive the process of individuation in terms of the agonistic release of individuals from already existing communicative relations. . . . If these considerations are correct, Hegel paid for the theoretical gains of his turn to the philosophy of consciousness by sacrificing his strong intersubjectivism.[10]

According to Honneth, the turn to the philosophy of consciousness has pernicious effects for Hegel's political theory. It leads Hegel to articulate sociopolitical conceptions that are at odds with his early conception of intersubjectivity and of "ethical life." At the end, Honneth argues, "Hegel is incapable of conceiving of the mode of political will-formation in terms of anything other than constitutional monarchy, because his consciousness-theoretic construction of the State requires an ultimate accumulation of all power in the hands of a single individual...."[11] Most importantly, according to Honneth, for Hegel "the construction of an ethical sphere occurs as a process in which all elements of social life are transformed into components of an overarching State. This generates a relationship of asymmetrical dependence between the State and its members similar to the one that holds fundamentally between Spirit and the products of its manifestation."[12]

Here again, as in the previous chapter, we observe the problems and contradictions that arise within the Hegelian philosophy of Spirit. At the end, Honneth, like Fanon, prefers to follow up Hegel's insights on the struggle for recognition while leaving aside the Hegelian paradigm of consciousness. Honneth offers to continue the examination of the theme of social struggles for recognition in a more empirical way, leaving behind this cornerstone of Hegel's ontological fantasies, the concept of Spirit. Honneth suggests that we need a phenomenology to develop the theme, not a phenomenology of Spirit, but a phenomenology of the social, in the sense of a description of social reality that will help clarify the nature of the struggle and specify the content of the claims made. I proceed with caution here because Honneth does not specify the sort of phenomenology that he would defend or pursue. But his critique of the Hegelian conception of Spirit and his mention of a phenomenology in the context of an examination of struggles for recognition are enough to introduce the possibility of a connection with Fanon.

Honneth's contribution to the philosophical and social-scientific analysis of the theme of the struggle for recognition is deeply marked by his simultaneous allegiance to and critique of both Foucault and Habermas. From Foucault, Honneth takes the interest in the examination of power dynamics and struggle, and from Habermas, a deep concern with normative considerations.[13] The subtitle of Honneth's study brings these two seemingly divergent perspectives into strange harmony: "the moral grammar of social conflicts." Honneth avoids the relativism of force and struggle by revealing moral dimensions in social conflicts. Once these dimensions are spelled out, he would be able, or so he hopes, to evaluate the aims and overall results of particular social movements in moral terms. Honneth is also interested in the project of articulating a view of "the struggle for recognition as a historical process of moral progress."[14] In particular, he wants to show that the bourgeois revolution of the eighteenth century has important consequences not only for historical but for normative considerations as well. Modern bourgeois legal theory is, thus, for him, both a historical event and an advancement in the formulation of moral demands.

Fanon differs from Honneth precisely at the points in which Honneth relies on Foucault and on Habermas. Fanon, like Foucault and Honneth, is interested in questions of power—and not only in questions of identity and multiculturalism. But Fanon is concerned about a particular form of power: the imperial power that creates the colonial condition. Honneth argues that recognition takes place in three spheres: love, rights, and social esteem.[15] Demands for recognition arise, for him, as feelings of disrespect in relation to the negation of rights or social esteem. Love relationships remain at the level of the private and the intimate. In the colonial condition, or so Fanon would argue, it is not possible to make these distinctions. Indeed, one of the most fundamental lessons of *Black Skin, White Masks* is that in the colonial context what happens at the level of the private and the intimate is fundamentally linked to social structures and to colonial cultural formations and forms of value. That is the ultimate reason why Fanon believed that psychoanalysis would fail to explain and to provide an adequate diagnosis of the pathology of subjects in colonial territories—unless it took the form of a sociogeny.[16] Ordinary life is infected by the colonial virus. Communication, loving relationships, and even the proper recognition of the self are distorted by a social system and by cultural forms that take blackness and other forms of sub-alterity as markers of the absence of values. Ultimately, as Lewis Gordon puts it, it is an extraordinary affair for a black person to be ordinary.[17] For Fanon, the colonial condition approximates a systematic and systemic reality of human failure. And one of the distinctive features of this reality is that dehumanization reaches stages in which feelings of disrespect gradually become either muted or transformed into desires for identification or participation with the dominant culture.[18] This is what the colonial configuration intends and what makes it so powerful: instead of taking anything in particular away from colonized subjects, it attempts to rob them of any notion of self-worth and, ultimately, of the very idea of having any rights.[19] This resembles the condition of slavery in that it involves not the stealing away of someone's property but the collapse of one's humanity into a category of property. To feel disrespect (in a way that makes reference to the lack or denial of rights or social esteem) one should have been respected first or at least know that one should be so respected.[20] But in the colonial context experiences of liberty remain buried in stories about the precolonial past, and theoretical conceptions of equality are articulated abstractly enough to easily allow or even help to promote or sustain the perversity of concrete domination. As Fanon puts it:

> The white man, in the capacity of master, said to the Negro, "From now on you are free."
>
> But the Negro knows nothing of the cost of freedom, for he has not fought for it. From time to time he has fought for Liberty and Justice, but these were always white liberty and white justice; that is, values secreted by his masters. The former slave, who can find in his memory no trace of the struggle for liberty or of that anguish of liberty of which Kierkegaard speaks, sits unmoved before the young white man singing and dancing on the tightrope of existence. (BSWM 220–21)

The point here is that in the day-to-day ordinary life of the colonized these experiences and ideas are not completely effective as producers of feelings of disrespect. That is why ultimately Fanon finds black subjects wearing white masks. To be sure, this does not mean that racialized and colonized people do not confront dilemmas of freedom.[21] What it means is that these dilemmas cannot be properly thematized in relation to spheres of culture and value that have not emerged or in which certain subjects have not been allowed to participate. Fanon has thus no other way to proceed than by raising the question of desire: what does man want, what does the black man want? This is a demand for a philosophical anthropology from the perspective of the slave. Here we may very well find a radical point of departure to pursue the project of articulating a postliberal conception of the human.

The colonial condition is thus clearly different from realities in which an independent state, a system of legal norms, and a strong "civil sphere" have already come into being. For this reason, whereas Foucault highlights how power inheres in law and how the normative character of bourgeois law is not much more than a form of self-justification, Fanon concentrates on conditions wherein law and legal subjects have not emerged or come into being in their entirety.[22] For this reason Fanon's reflections on power dynamics do not have the strong anti-normative character that they have in Foucault. But for this very reason as well Fanon is not compelled to recur to a form of neo-Kantianism to solve the problems of universality. And for him, the effort to use the allegedly normative character of feelings of disrespect to trace the historical progress behind struggles for recognition would probably seem an interesting but somewhat naïve project. It is in this respect that Fanon differs from the Habermasian strain in Honneth's project.

Perhaps the main difference between Honneth and Fanon is that for Fanon the question of the struggle for recognition is, as it was in the *Phenomenology* for Hegel, a struggle between a master and a slave. Like Honneth, Fanon strongly criticized the ontology of Spirit, but only for the sake of an existential phenomenological description of the relation between master and slave—and this primordially *from the perspective of the slave*. Since the theme of the dialectic between master and slave appears in the *Phenomenology of Spirit* under the guise of a movement of self-consciousness, Honneth does not seem to find any use for the Hegelian account. From a Fanonian point of view Honneth commits here the proverbial mistake of throwing out the baby with the bathwater. There is, indeed, a sort of internal contradiction in Honneth's approach: while he advocates an empirical turn and calls for a social phenomenology, he does not consider the extent to which concrete human reality is shaped by forces that obey the logics of a division between a master and a slave. And, if it is true, as Susan Buck-Morss has argued, that the account of the dialectic of lord and bondsman in the *Phenomenology of Spirit* was informed by the Haitian Revolution, then it is Honneth, and not so much Hegel on this point, who most frightfully fails to be in contact with history and concrete reality.[23] Indeed, Honneth seems to be in line with intellectual historians of German philosophy who discuss the emergence and development of the Hegelian theme of the relation between lord and bondsman in relation to the writings of other intellectuals in the tradition of European philosophy (most notably in the case of Honneth, Aristotle, Machiavelli, and Hobbes) and who hardly look to history—even less to historical events that take place outside of Europe—to find keys to gain some understanding of philosophical themes.[24] In a remarkable contrast to Honneth, it must be said that if Fanon was interested in anything about the struggle for recognition it was precisely in the way in which it makes explicit the basic contours of a concrete reality marked by the relation between master and slave. It could hardly be otherwise for him, a black colonized Martiniquean who aimed to analyze colonization and anti-black racism. Fanon saw the world differently from Honneth and also conceived of the struggle for recognition differently: for him there was no doubt that the struggle took the form of a confrontation between a master and a slave.[25] This is what appeared to him, what showed itself with "evidence" to him, to use the

Husserlian terminology, once he focused on the lived experience of the black on his island and abroad.[26]

For Fanon, the examination of the colonial racial context in which he lived demanded an existential phenomenological approach. His main interest was to elucidate the "pathologies of affect" that appear in conditions of subordination and to make clear the implicit demands of racialized subjects in their struggle with a racist world. He considered many problems that are extremely pertinent for social and political philosophy today—for example, social invisibility, anonymity, limitations of the "dialectic between legal and actual rights," racial dynamics, colonial semiosis, communicative action, and the constitution of the public sphere. But one of his most groundbreaking and less explored themes has to do precisely with the struggle for recognition. The driving question of *Black Skin, White Masks* is "what does the black man want?" In the colonial condition, where the black is not fully a human being, the answer is clear: the black man simply wants to become a man. The question of *desire* carries with it in Fanon's work the more fundamental question about the meaning and possibility of the human. Thinking from the limits requires an explicit engagement with the question about the emergence of humanity. Since the colonial condition is a reality of dehumanization, the answer to this question should also provide important insights as to how to overcome this condition in a consistent manner. Indeed, I believe that this is ultimately the main point of reference for Fanon's anthropological propositions. A desire to become a human being would only express a logic of delusion if it did not lead to an overcoming of the colonial condition. Therefore, the question of the human becomes in Fanon also a question about how to put an end to colonialism—understood here as a reality defined according to the logic inaugurated by the relation between master and slave.

THE CRY AND THE GIFT OF THE SELF[27]

What is it that the black wants? Our considerations must begin by recalling Fanon's criticism of the Hegelian conception of the dialectic between master and slave.

> I hope I have shown that here the master differs basically from the master described by Hegel. For Hegel there is reciprocity; here the master laughs at the consciousness of the slave. What he wants from the slave is not recognition but work.

In the same way, the slave here is in no way identifiable with the slave who loses himself in the object and finds in his work the source of his liberation.
The Negro wants to be like the master.
Therefore he is less independent than the Hegelian slave.
In Hegel the slave turns away from the master and turns toward the object.
Here the slave turns toward the master and abandons the object. (BSWM 220–21, n. 8, italics mine)

The Negro, Fanon argues here, wants to be like the master. He brings up again the condition whereby black subjects wear white masks. In another passage Fanon remarks, "However painful it may be for me to accept this conclusion, I am obliged to state it: For the black man there is only one destiny. And it is white" (BSWM 10). A world structured according to the relation between master and slave creates, as it were, a field of gravitation that makes aspirations for humanity collapse into aims for inclusion and projects of assimilation based on the ultimate value of the master's kind of life. In *Black Skin, White Masks* Fanon demonstrates how the different attempts to complete such a project end in failure. Fanon shows that the system of recognition is such that it makes it impossible for subjects to fulfill what it promises. In short, black skins will never equal whiteness.

The question of desire is complicated. There may be desires that follow or reproduce the logic of control and subordination enacted by the system of oppression. It is very significant that even in this basic deluded state of recognition "the slave turns toward the master and abandons the object." That is, the perversity of the master-slave relation does not hide what may be a positive intersubjective impulse on the part of the slave.[28] Turning toward the master and not toward the thing or object confirms the idea, examined in the previous chapter, that recognition is an intersubjective affair. Yet, this movement to the realm of intersubjectivity is vitiated by a desire for a perverse identification. The Negro wants to be like the master. The desire to simply become like the master is, of course, the main object of criticism in Fanon's *Black Skin, White Masks*. The desire for identification seems to be thus the first pathological movement of subjectivity. An interesting point here is that when Fanon says that the Negro wants to be like the master it is not entirely clear whether the Negro only wants to do this to become a master himself and to enjoy power or simply to become a "human" like the master. The confusion in part lies in that the colonial relation generates what Fanon refers to as "anomalies of affect." But what is pathological and what is not? What advances and what betrays the true aim of desire?

Clearly, Fanon's pedagogical discourse aims to shed some light on these questions, especially to subaltern subjectivities. But he is utterly aware that the colonial condition is such that colonized subjects only rarely articulate these questions or demand an answer to them. Fanon asks: "Why write this book? No one has asked me for it. Especially those to whom it is directed" (BSWM 7). Fanon finds a manifold of different attitudes in the colonized world: from the silent subjugated subject, to those who actively foment projects of assimilation, to seemingly revolutionary subjects who affirm the value of blackness in categorical terms. Silence, distorted speech, and the cry of Negro affirmation become different expressions of the black in his and her coping with the condition of slavery, colonialism, and/or anti-black racism.

In a sense, Fanon's propositions may be understood as a set of Kierkegaardian stages of sorts. Fanon, like Kierkegaard, is a pedagogical writer.[29] He assists different kinds of subjects into reaching for what for him represents the ultimate and most adequate expression of human subjectivity. But where Kierkegaard found aesthetes and ethicists, Fanon finds masters, slaves, and slaves wearing masters' masks. Both Kierkegaard and Fanon aim to provide a basic orientation in the process that leads to the proper formation of selfhood. Yet, while Kierkegaard's conception led to a defense of the hiddenness of the extraordinary (Christian) in the ordinary world, Fanon could not conceive of authentic selfhood other than in ethico-political ways that transform a political system and perverted forms of ordinary life. One thing is clear, in order to perform an adequate pedagogical role, both Kierkegaard and Fanon would have to at least envision clearly a satisfactory stage of selfhood. Thus the question of the consistent expression of the desire of the black subject may be significantly clarified if we raise the question of desire and the fulfillment of desire in respect to Fanon himself. What does Fanon, the black Martiniquean, want? Given Fanon's own testimony it appears that at least one of the things that he wanted was simply to write, even if those to whom his writing was directed had not asked him for that. In order to attempt to clarify this question consider the voice that introduces us to the body of Fanon's oeuvre:

> The explosion will not happen today. It is too soon . . . or too late.
> I do not come with timeless truths.
> My consciousness is not illuminated with ultimate radiances.

> Nevertheless, in complete composure, I think it would be good if certain things were said.
>
> These things I am going to say, not shout (*non les crier*). For it is a long time since shouting ["*le cri*"] has gone out of my life.
>
> So very long. . . . (BSWM 7, italics mine, translation modified).

Fanon's discourse opens with a clarification and with a remembrance. It comes into being only by first asserting its ineluctable, enigmatic character. Fanon adopts the "composure" of discourse. But what is a natural stance for many is for him only the result of a mysterious prehistory. A cry has preceded the emergence of words. What is the meaning of this cry, and what role does it play in the emergence of the Fanonian narrative? I will attempt to elucidate the meaning behind this enigmatic conversion of the cry into words, of crying/shouting into the serenity of discourse and pedagogical writing. What is at stake here, to put it in Levinasian terms, is the tracing of the "saying" behind what Fanon has "said," of the fundamental inspiration or passion animating Fanon's rhetoric. The question of Fanon's desire demands a clarification of why Fanon begins to write only when he is not able to cry or shout. In order to clarify this I will begin with a phenomenology of the cry.

TOWARD A PHENOMENOLOGY OF THE CRY

The remembrance of a cry long gone at the beginning of Fanon's *Black Skin, White Masks* locates the text and its author in an intriguing existential predicament. The "serenity" of organized discourse is not preceded by a period of contemplation or neutral observation of reality, but by a time of urgency in which the subject cannot take his recognition as a human being for granted and has to attract attention simply to the fact that he *is there*. The cry is, indeed, precisely that, a sound uttered as a call for attention, as a demand for immediate action or remedy, or as an expression of pain that points to an injustice committed or to something that is lacking.[30] The cry is the revelation of someone who has been forgotten or wronged. Before the word reaches the horizons of meaning, where the world is unveiled and the meaning of reality becomes clear, the cry becomes a call for the recognition of the singularity of the subject as such. The cry indicates the "return of a living subject" who impertinently announces his presence and who by doing so unsettles the established formations of meaning and challenges dominant ideological expressions.[31]

Crying is linked both with shouting and weeping. Shouting and weeping are at the same time associated with expressions of grief, sorrow, and anger on the one hand, and with joy, happiness, and love on the other.[32] A clarification of why Fanon is no longer crying by the time of writing requires the analysis of these themes in his work. The mention of the cry at the beginning of the text becomes precisely an invitation to trace the presence of these themes and to uncover dimensions of meaning that are not obvious. It is revealing that these themes appear in what may arguably be considered the backbone of *Black Skin, White Masks*—its fifth chapter, "The Lived Experience of the Black." The "Lived Experience of the Black," not "The Fact of Blackness" as the Markmann translation has it, clearly alludes to the living subjectivity of someone who alone can utter a cry.[33] If "lived experience" refers to the existence of an interiority, the cry is the call for attention to this idea, that a subject has an interiority. This affirmation only makes sense in a context wherein the subjectivity of the subject in question is denied. It is precisely in this fashion that chapter 5 begins, "'Dirty nigger!' Or simply, 'Look, a Negro!'" (BSWM 109). The signifying gaze of a subject—in this case, a white child—denies the presence of interiority in a subject who is typically defined by others according to exterior appearance alone—in this case, the most patent and obvious dimension of one's exteriority, the color of one's skin.

The *remembrance* of the objectifying gaze of the child in the opening lines of the "Lived Experience of the Black" introduces a paradoxical moment in Fanon's text. The paradox consists in, as Gordon has well put it, Fanon announcing "the absence of his interiority *from the point of view of his interiority*."[34] The description and remembrance of the event of the negation of Fanon's interiority presupposes precisely what is denied, an interiority. This interiority is what is clearly rendered invisible by "The Fact of Blackness." This invisibility is most unfortunate since the paradox is not merely a concept among others but the axis around which Fanon's ideas revolve. The paradox is at the core of Fanon's entire text/existence, which is narrated/lived in terms of the affirmation of the very possibility of affirmation and negation in a context that confines him to the status of an inanimate object. Gordon's words are also enlightening on this point: "[Fanon] experiences his historicity as a false history and his struggle with Theory, with Reason, as a cat-and-mouse game. Between Reason and History, Theory and Practice, there is experience, which in this case is the existential struggle against sedimented, dehumanized constructions."[35]

Paradox represents a challenge to reason, a self-contradictory stance that interrupts the flow of the clear and distinct logic of identity and difference. Paradox is irreducible to the abstraction and neutrality of knowledge as well as to systematic renderings of reality. The paradox is the anti-systematic resistant par excellence. That is why Kierkegaard opposed Hegel's speculative and systematic philosophy with diverse portrayals of paradox. In *Fear and Trembling*, he explores the paradoxical nature of the knight of faith, represented in its well-known father, the old Abraham. Abraham incarnates the paradoxical tension introduced by the situation in which he has been commanded by God to sacrifice the son through whom God himself promised to make Abraham the father of nations. Without allowing himself to rest on the arms of sweet resignation—that is, accepting the encroaching loss of his son Isaac—Abraham not only obeys the command, but eagerly receives the son whose life was later spared by the commander. Abraham's interiority, his faith or trust in God (that God *will make him a father of a nation through Isaac*), appears as no less than a mystery for Johannes de Silentio—Kierkegaard's pseudonym on this occasion. Abraham is paradoxical, and as such he poses a limit to a project that aims to identify the rational with the real and the real with the rational.

Fanon's subjectivity or the subjectivity of the narrator/writer of *Black Skin, White Masks* is, like Abraham's, paradoxical. His condition, however, reflects more the situation in which Abraham's son Isaac found himself: Fanon embodies the paradox of someone who is sentenced to death but who nonetheless continues living, as it were, *by virtue of the absurd*. Existence becomes in his case the negation of the negation of existence. It is "the anxiety, the distress, and the paradox" brought by this condition that is often left out in our readings of Fanon. We also forget that this paradoxical condition emerges not in a context wherein the Law and Reason call us to stop "murder," as it did in Abraham's case, but in contexts in which they ultimately justify or are complicit with murder.[36] The paradox of Fanon's existence becomes no less than a declaration against the imperial gestures and the totalitarian ambitions of a system that transforms reason into murder and interhuman contact into the evisceration of difference. Fanon's cry, the call for attention to a wrong committed, becomes here the expression of this paradoxical stance whose primary significance is posed in the form of a command, "Don't kill!" In this case, the system does not appear primarily as a prison to a subject who sees his particularity violated by the universal, but as an imperial formation that can offer the universal to some at the expense of the negation of a truly human existence to others.

The cry of Fanon is the expression of his paradoxical existential stance. The cry does not emerge out of any particular unsatisfied demand, but out of the impossibility of demanding anything whatsoever. It gives expression to a fundamental contradiction between the existence of the world at large and one's own existence. Yet, if this were the only or even the more fundamental dimension of the cry, if the cry merely reflected the desire to continue living and be recognized as a subject, then its paradoxical character would be significantly reduced—Fanon, the paradoxical subject, would be lost. Even if we could not understand why Fanon keeps on living, it would be clear to us that he cries because he wants to keep on living. The same would be true of Isaac. If Isaac had known his father's plans, it would have been simply natural for him to cry and beg for his life. Although the nature and profundity of Abraham's faith would have been untouched by this, the event would have thrown a shadow of doubt upon his successor and upon the upcoming generations born through Isaac. Isaac would be lost. But all of this would be true only if the cry were only the expression of an individualistic urge for life. In this case we would expect Isaac/Fanon to continue crying until dead or until finally liberated. Fanon, however, realizing that his liberation may not come as yet or even very soon ("the explosion will not happen today") transforms his cry into the composure of discourse. In the interval between the knife and his body, Fanon's discourse is born. The opening lines of *Black Skin, White Masks* unveil the particular temporal character of Fanon's discourse: he writes with death and suffering vigilantly on his side. There, under the knife, with a death sentence upon him, he writes. But, why write and no longer simply cry?

Fanon is clearly aware of the paradoxical nature of his act. And so he continues in the opening lines of *Black Skin, White Masks*: "Why write this book? No one has asked for it. Especially those to whom it is directed" (BSWM 7). On the altar, about to be sacrificed, Fanon writes, and he writes *for others*. He is not merely looking for an interlocutor who may carry with him the memories of a glorious but disgraced subjectivity. He is writing as if he were answering a question or responding to a demand. Yet he writes for others who have not themselves articulated a question or solicited his words. Is Fanon ultimately listening to his own cry? Is it possible that beyond a demand for individual self-recognition and for the preservation of his life, the cry represents a call for the Other? The paradox emerges again, and now in a more intensified form, as Fanon not only lives against all odds, but as he lives his life in response to Others.

THE CRY OF ETHICAL REVOLT AND
THE PARADOXICAL NATURE OF LOVE

There seems to be thus an ethical dimension of the cry that is irreducible both to the universal and to egocentric claims of the subject. The "Don't kill!" that finds expression in Fanon's cry is not properly translated merely as a demand for individual preservation, but as a general and more categorical demand to fight against a reality wherein other human beings are killed. But how is this possible? If the cry arises out of the pain of a violated subject, how is it that it ultimately becomes a call for attention to something that ultimately resides *outside* of the subject—something extrinsic, not intrinsic to him. This can only be the case if the subject is himself originally outside of himself. In this case, the cry would represent the expression of a subject who has been violated precisely in regard to the possibility of being outside of himself—that is, of loving, giving, and communicating. Fanon's main object of inquiry in *Black Skin, White Masks* is, in fact, the set of barriers that inhibit interhuman contact in a colonial world. It is not strange that the first three chapters of the book deal with language and love. It is not surprising either that Fanon opens the first chapter by proclaiming the central importance of language: "I ascribe a basic importance to the phenomenon of language. That is why I find it necessary to begin with this subject, which should provide us with one of the elements in the colored man's comprehension of the dimension of *the other*. For it is implicit that to speak is to exist absolutely for the other" (BSWM 17).

Now we can finally turn again to "The Lived Experience of the Black" in order to decipher the links between crying, shouting, and weeping, and their connection with their most basic fundamental motivations—anger and love. First, consider that in Fanon's cry (shout) there is as much anger as love—indeed, one could argue that his anger stems out of love. After the first episode of anger narrated by Fanon when he finally "makes a scene" in response to an event of degradation, he explains,

> What? While I was *forgetting, forgiving, and wanting only to love*, my message was flung back in my face like a slap. The white world, the only honorable one, barred me from all participation. A man was expected to behave like a man. I was expected to behave like a black man—or at least like a nigger. I *shouted* a greeting to the world and the world slashed away my joy. I was told

to stay within bounds, to go back where I belonged. (BSWM 114–15, italics mine)

Fanon enters the world with a clear impetus to enact a relation. He shouts, and his shout becomes like a lover's declaration of love. He greets the world as if announcing his presence, *saying*, "Here I am!" Anger—"Kiss the handsome Negro's ass, Madame!" (BSWM 114)—only emerges as a result of a most radical dismissal and violation of this loving subjectivity.

"What does the black man want?" Fanon inquires throughout the work. Here he advances his own response (as a black man): he wants "only to love." Fanon believes that ultimately what the black subject wants is to be a human—an ethico-political form of the Nietzschean call "to be oneself"—and that to be a human is to love. Given that Fanon's black body, his "Race," is the crucial element in the articulation of a system that violates the living subject and that inhibits the emergence of a world of love, Fanon decides to transform his cry of anger into a "Negro cry." The persistence of evil in face of the free offering of self and love is behind this new turn. Fanon explains, "There will always be a world—a white world—between you and us. . . . The other's total inability to liquidate the past once and for all. In the face of this affective ankylosis of the white man, it is understandable that I could have made up my mind to utter my Negro cry. Little by little, putting out pseudopodia here and there, I secreted a race" (BSWM 122).

The question of racial identity emerges out of a deep interest in the construction of a world of love. With the "Negro cry" Fanon announces a step forward in the search for recognition. Since he is not welcomed in the world, he attempts to build his own dwelling. Confronting a radical lack of hospitality, he aims to have the means that will allow him to be hospitable. After an incessant search, Fanon finally seems to find a place of his own in *Négritude*, where he can truly love.[37] Yet, his illusions are shattered as Jean-Paul Sartre illustrates how his "Negro cry," the cry of *Négritude*, represents only a movement in the Hegelian and Marxist dialectic:

> What is certain is that, at that very moment when I was trying to grasp my own being, Sartre, who remained The Other, gave me a name and thus shattered my last illusion. While I was saying to him:
> "My negritude is neither a tower nor a cathedral,
> it thrusts into the red flesh of the sun,
> it thrusts into the burning flesh of the sky,

it hollows through the dense dismay of its own pillar of patience . . ."

while I was *shouting* that, in the paroxysm of my being and my fury, he was reminding me that my blackness was only a minor term. In all truth, in all truth I tell you, my shoulders slipped out of the framework of the world, my feet could no longer feel the touch of the ground. Without a Negro past, without a Negro future, it was impossible for me to live my Negrohood (BSWM 138).[38]

In the midst of his disillusion, at the point where reason has given the final word, Fanon paradoxically rises up again and elevates his cry once more. It is his desire to love, his passionate loving subjectivity, that, stronger than logic and Reason, defies the Sartrean attempt to reduce existence and recognition to the movement of the dialectic: "But the constancy of my love had been forgotten. I defined myself as an absolute intensity of beginning. So I took my negritude, and with tears in my eyes I put its machinery together again. What had been broken to pieces was rebuilt, reconstructed by the intuitive lianas of my hands. My cry grew more violent: I am a Negro, I am a Negro, I am a Negro . . ." (BSWM 138).

Like Abraham, the knight of faith himself, Fanon resists incorporation into the System and its movements. The excess of the loving subjectivity cannot be subordinated to the order of Reason. Fanon shouts to the world, affirming his identity and wanting "only to love." Yet Fanon discovers that the cry of self-affirmation finds its limits, not in the dialectic, but in the expression of love itself: "I am a Negro, I am a Negro, I am a Negro. . . . And there was my poor brother — living out his neurosis to the extreme and finding himself paralyzed . . ." (BSWM 138).

The cry of self-affirmation suddenly comes to a stop. The moment of upsurge is interrupted as Fanon perceives that his "poor brothers" are still behind. He realizes that the cry of self-affirmation is not exempt from the powers of mystification. There are others who have not even emitted such a cry. Imagine Isaac about to be sacrificed and elevating a voice of protest. This Isaac, however, soon realizes that his brother, another prospective victim in a not much different Mount Moriah, is simply there, quiet, paralyzed. He then turns to his brother and attempts to analyze what it is that makes him remain in this condition. Suddenly, the point of reference changes and his "Negro cry" is left in the background. Fanon observes the psychological behavior of black characters in works of literature and films. They remind Fanon of the one who is behind, and who cannot even cry. "A feeling of inferiority? No, a feeling of nonexistence. Sin is Negro as virtue is white. All those white men in a group, guns in their hands, cannot be wrong. I am guilty. I do not know of what, but I know that I am no good" (BSWM 139).

Emerging out of love, Fanon's "Negro cry" survives any intellectual challenge. His love is stronger than any logical argument. Yet, it is precisely this love that, leading him to pay attention to his "poor brothers," reveals the limits of the cry and its ambiguous character. Leaving the exaltation of the cry behind, he recognizes himself in those less fortunate. About to be sacrificed, with the knife over his chest, Fanon no longer cries for his life, but decides to live—in that interval of time before the knife finally takes his life—*for the Other*. It is his brother that worries him the most, and he feels responsible for him, to the point of *substitution*.[39] At this point a new self emerges, and the cry begins to turn into a paradoxical discourse:[40] "The crippled veteran of the Pacific war says *to my brother*, 'Resign yourself to your color the way I got used to my stump; we're both victims.' Nevertheless with all my strength *I* refuse to accept that amputation" (BSWM 140, italics mine).

The "I refuse" denotes the transformation—perhaps better, transubstantiation—of a subject who now has substituted himself for the Other. A new paradox emerges here. A self confronting a vicious death and who struggles against his enemy suddenly turns toward another in a worse condition and responds to and for him. Unable to account for this (ethical) event, reason is now more baffled than before. An ethics emerges beyond the realm of the universal. The problem, to be sure, is not about the rescue of authenticity in the face of an alienating totality, but about the affirmation of life and about the very possibility of being in love with others while confronting a homicidal System. Fanon clearly opposes the forces of what is known in Heideggerian parlance as the "They."[41] But he only does so insofar as this *They* inhibits the possibility of love. By virtue of love, he ultimately is more *concerned* about the *Them*—privileged objects of hate through which the *They* gains definition—than about the preservation of his own self.[42] Yet it is precisely in this act of love that his subjectivity is truly affirmed.

Individuality and sociality emanate for Fanon out of love and responsibility. They both begin in the act of substitution whereby a loving subjectivity *gives* itself for an Other. At the end of the fifth chapter, after an intense existential struggle, Fanon finds himself again where he began, confronting the opposition between his majestic loving subjectivity and a world that resists the radical expression of love. Without a "Negro cry" to utter, beyond anger and joy, the cry turns from shouting to weeping. The cry of anger and joy is finally transformed, by virtue of substitution, into tears, but the tears are preceded by an uncompromising affirmation of love:

> I feel in myself a soul as immense as the world, truly a soul as deep as the deepest of rivers, my chest has the power to expand without limit. *I am* [gift, generosity] *and I am advised to adopt the humility of the cripple.* Yesterday, awakening to the world, I saw the sky turn upon itself utterly and wholly. I wanted to rise, but the disemboweled silence fell back upon me, its wings paralyzed. Without responsibility, straddling Nothingness and Infinity, I began to weep. (BSWM 140, modification and italics mine)[43]

From the end of the fifth chapter of *Black Skin, White Masks*, we should turn again to the initial lines of the introduction. "These things I am going to say, not shout. For it is a long time since shouting has gone out of my life. So very long . . ." (BSWM 7). Shouting has gone away, but this only indicates a deeper realization of the pain and suffering undergone by the many Isaacs of this world. As Fanon observes the situation of Others, he realizes the magnitude of the perversity and evil that finds home in this world. He weeps. He comes to terms with the situation. Only now he becomes acutely aware of the fact that "the explosion will not happen today." It is only after he weeps that his liberating pedagogical discourse can begin. It is then that he can adopt the composure of discourse. But he knows that he is still sentenced to death. Reaching a paradoxical climax, Fanon no longer shouts or weeps, but he decides to speak. The paradoxical cry turns, with patience and vigilance, into a text. Why has Fanon written *Black Skin, White Masks*? There seems to be no reason. *Black Skin, White Masks* is a *gift* as much as an act of faith—that the explosion may come one day and that a world of love may finally emerge:

> Superiority? Inferiority? Why not the simple attempt to touch the other, to feel the other, to explain the other to myself? Was my freedom not **given** to me then in order to build the world of the *You*?
>
> At the conclusion of this study, I want the world to recognize, with me, the open door to my consciousness.
>
> My final prayer:
>
> O my body, make of me always a man who questions! (BSWM 232, **bold** *italics* mine)

Black Skin, White Masks ends as it begins, with the serenity of a paradoxical subject who can only marvel us, with a prayer. Fanon prays to his (black) body (yet another paradoxical gesture), the indicator of passivity and exposure to the other and bearer of the marks that testify to the perversity of the system and the cries of those to whom his paradoxically loving subjectivity will unceasingly try to respond.[44]

FROM "DONNER" TO THE "DAMNÉS"

The drama of the Fanonian subjectivity reveals the connection between demands expressed in cries and a more fundamental (metaphysical) desire that finds expression in the act of offering and giving. The struggle for recognition finds its more consistent expression in the attempt to build a world of love. Colonialism and the master/slave relation, in contrast, represent for Fanon the most consistent effort to inhibit the creation of this world. The relation between master and slave is reinterpreted by him in light of the logic of the gift. As Fanon puts it in his last and most influential writing, *The Wretched of the Earth*, the slave is the "damné" (wretched, or better even damned or condemned).

According to Émile Benveniste, in Indo-European languages "damné" is linguistically and semantically connected with the concept of "donner" (to give). Both originally emerged from the roots *do-* and *da*.[45] While "donner" means to give, "damné" refers to "the 'loss' which is prejudicial and no longer a voluntary service."[46] The "damné," if we follow this interpretation, is the one who cannot give precisely because things are taken from him. The colonized is the "damné" in the sense that the colonial condition takes away from her, or at least radically restricts, the possibilities of giving. It is this that explains Fanon's indignation and the emergence of the cry. Consider again the following passage.

> What? While I was forgetting, forgiving, and wanting only to love, my message was flung back in my face like a slap. The white world, the only honorable one, barred me from all participation. A man was expected to behave like a man. I was expected to behave like a black man—or at least like a nigger. I shouted a greeting to the world and the world slashed away my joy. I was told to stay within bounds, to go back where I belonged. (BSWM 114–15)

Marked by the color of his skin, the colonized is made to come back where he belongs. The Manichean logic of the colonial system operates in favor of the truncation of the possibility of generous interhuman contact. To be sure, generosity is allowed, but only as an expression of the master or as an apolitical virtue. The colonial condition sets up a space of interaction where only one group is expected to give. The master makes the other a slave by taking things from him. In this way the master puts himself in a position in which he becomes the privileged giver.

In light of this examination of the meaning of lordship it is possible to assert that when Fanon complained about the negative dimensions of the seemingly revolutionary act in French history when the masters gave liberty to the slaves he was not only pointing to the need of conflict for the full realization of freedom. When the masters "decided to promote the machine-animal-men to the supreme rank of *men*" (BSWM 220) they were clearly reaffirming their privilege as givers and thus reaffirming in new ways the logic of the colonial relation. They were also making themselves sure that the former slaves felt gratitude toward them. In a way, the masters were enacting a perverse logic of substitution. They were posing themselves as the originators of the freedom of the former slaves. Since the self is a gift, the masters were trying to make the slaves feel that they had received this gift from them. And if the gift may be traced back, if we follow Levinas, to a pre-original and immemorial assignation of the self by God, it is clear that the act of giving freedom to the slaves may be very well interpreted as another chapter in the drama of the master's attempt to play the role of God.[47]

Fanon, to be sure, does not appeal to God.[48] Nonetheless, for him it is clear that freedom is given, and that it is not given by the master. He also believes, like Levinas, that the gift carries with it a burden. Subjectivity is assigned with a responsibility and an ethical task. Thus Fanon rhetorically enquires, revealing at the same time what may be considered the most original question of the inquiring subjectivity and of the subjectivity that performs the *reduction*: "Was my freedom not **given** to me then in order to build the world of the *You?*" (BSWM 232, bold italics mine). As we saw already, Fanon concludes *Black Skin, White Masks* by praying to his body that he will forever remember the implications of this question.

THE GIFT AND THE STRUGGLE FOR RECOGNITION

According to the Fanonian reinterpretation of the relation between master and slave, lordship appears to be defined according to unethical modes of taking, having, and giving. They all appear to be submitted to a logic that obeys imperatives of possession, control, and ultimately death. For Levinas, as was shown in the first two chapters, these ideals have taken hold of dominant ways of thinking in Western civilization. They form part of an ideology and an ontology of war. Consider in this light the contrast between Fanon's interpretation of freedom as a gift and the Hegelian account of freedom: "The human being, in his *immediate* existence [*Existenz*] in himself, is a natural entity, external to his concept; it is only through the *development* [*Ausbildung*] of his own body and spirit, *essentially* by means of *his self-consciousness comprehending itself as free*, that he takes possession of himself and becomes his own property as distinct from that of others."[49] For Hegel, freedom is the fundamental element in the economy of self-possession. This conception of freedom puts Hegel in an intriguing position concerning his views on slavery: "If we hold firmly to the view that the human being in and for himself is free, we thereby condemn slavery. But if someone is a slave, his own will is responsible, just as the responsibility lies with the will of a people if that people is subjugated" (88, § 57). Since Hegel interprets freedom as self-possession, and since slavery is a condition in which one's freedom is, at least formally, in the possession of another, then slavery becomes a testimony of the slave's inability to take hold of his self in freedom. In sharp contrast to this assertion, Fanon declares in the context of his critique of Mannoni's study on the alleged dependency complex of the colonized that

> Yes, European civilization and its best representatives are responsible for colonial racism. . . .
>
> The feeling of inferiority of the colonized is the correlative to the European's feeling of superiority. Let us have the courage to say it outright: *It is the racist who creates his inferior*. (BSWM 90, 93)

It is true that Hegel does not exonerate the masters of their responsibility for slavery. But Fanon's argument is different and more radical. Fanon wants the master to take all of the responsibility for the condition of slavery. I will argue now that Fanon not only is right, but that his position can be clearly articulated from unexpressed Hegelian premises.

In order to demonstrate how Fanon's conception of the responsibility of Europe in bringing about slavery may be justified using Hegelian premises, I will now refer to the final sections of the *Elements of the Philosophy of Right* wherein Hegel introduces his ideas on the nation-state. I believe that Hegel's idea about the fault of the slave is at odds with his conception of the state and his claims about the virtues of war. Consider first the Hegelian argument that "the Idea of freedom is truly present only as the state" (88, § 57). The state is for Hegel a sort of individual, and, as he clarifies, "negation is an essential component of individuality." "Thus," Hegel continues,

> even if a number of states join together as a family, this league, in its individuality, must generate opposition and create an enemy. Not only do peoples emerge from wars with added strength, but nations [*Nationen*] troubled by civil dissension gain internal peace as a result of wars with their external enemies. Admittedly, war makes property insecure, but this *real* insecurity is no more than a necessary movement. (362, § 324)

Hegel makes the point differently in a more poetical style: "The higher significance of war is that, through its agency (as I have put it on another occasion), 'the ethical health of nations [*Völker*] is preserved in their indifference towards the permanence of finite determinacies, just as the movement of the winds preserves the sea from that stagnation which a lasting calm would produce . . .'"(362, § 324). The creation of an enemy and the need for negativity can be clearly traced back to the conception of freedom as self-possession. Self-possession is not for Hegel the last movement but the first movement of the possessive free subjectivity. Indeed, the rights of the subject are primarily for Hegel rights of possession. Once rights are defined in this way, and once the state is interpreted according to the requirements of a possessive individual freedom, the outcome is clear. It is true that with his conception of self-possession Hegel relativizes the ultimate character and validity of the role of the relation of lordship and servitude in self-consciousness (87, § 57). Yet, since the state inherits the basic terms of the logic of possession, lordship and servitude are bound to emerge once again in the drama of Spirit.

> The nation [*Volk*] to which such a movement is allotted as a *natural* principle is given the task of implementing this principle in the course of the self-development of the world spirit's self-consciousness. This nation is the *dominant* one in world history for this epoch, *and only once in history can it have this epoch-making role.* In contrast with this absolute right which it possesses as bearer of the present stage of the world spirit's development, the spirits of other nations are without rights, and they, like those whose epoch has passed, no longer count in world history (374, § 347).

A few pages after this Hegel remarks, "The same determination entitles civilized nations [*Nationen*] to regard and treat as barbarians other nations which are less advanced than they are in the substantial moments of the state . . . , in the consciousness that the rights of these other nations are not equal to theirs and that their independence is merely formal" (376, § 351). Imperialism, or the geopolitical expression of the relation between lordship and bondage, it appears here, is not an accident of humanity but a fundamental feature of the logic of Spirit. The condition of slavery reappears and is now justified in relation to the progressive unfolding of the Idea. It therefore makes no sense to argue that the responsibility for slavery lies, as Hegel argues "with the will of a people if that people is subjugated." The dialectical unfolding of Spirit reinscribes the principles of lordship and bondage at a geopolitical level. It thus makes slavery a more or less permanent condition of different peoples. It also locates the virtues and rights of lordship in the territory and history of a particular kind of people: European peoples. Consider that, according to Hegel, the Spirit has unfolded giving expressions to four different principles. The last and more comprehensive, and also the more complete of these principles, finds a place in what he calls the *Germanic realm*: "The Spirit now grasps the *infinite positivity* of its own inwardness, the principle of the unity of divine and human nature and the reconciliation of the objective truth and freedom which have appeared within self-consciousness and subjectivity. The task of accomplishing this reconciliation is assigned to the Nordic principle of the *Germanic peoples*" (379, § 358). Here it is clear that, at least in one important respect, when Fanon categorically affirmed that "European civilization and its best representatives are responsible for colonial racism," he was only making explicit the truth behind Hegel's assertions.

We now see that there is much more behind Hegel's philosophy of Spirit than what Axel Honneth was able to articulate in his critical study of Hegel's account of the struggle for recognition. It becomes clear now that the problem with the paradigm of consciousness does not only have to do with the subordination of the individual to the nation. This subordination appears to be linked to a more radical form of violence that reintroduces the principles of lordship and bondage. Indeed, the sacrifice of the individual to the nation reaches its climax precisely when he gives his life in a war against others for the preservation of his nation. Fanon, in contrast, thinks from the limits. The limit is the space where human existence unfolds, but only, as it were, "against all odds"—that is, in the midst of radical conditions of subordination and dehumanization. For Fanon, this never entirely successful attempt at maintaining human beings in a subhuman state begets a Manichean colonial world, a world in which war is naturalized. It is in this context that the principles of lordship and bondage show one of their most terrifying dimensions.

As we have seen before, Fanon believes that the tragic character of the colonial condition demands counterhegemonic pedagogical acts of liberation. The call for this pedagogy is a far cry from Honneth's interests in articulating "a theoretical approach that is supposed to be able to model the struggle for recognition as a historical process of moral progress."[50] Since Honneth does not consider the full extent of the imperial dimensions of Hegel's philosophy of Spirit, he is not aware of the pernicious effects of a developmentalist view of morality and pedagogy. Also, Honneth's limited lenses allow him to search for significant moral progress only in the internal spaces of Europe. One must recall here that one of Honneth's main goals is to establish the "moral significance" of bourgeois law.[51] He adopts the developmentalist account and the interest in bourgeois law from Habermas. But Habermas's views on these matters are not themselves immune from the strong Hegelian Eurocentric bias. Consider Habermas's statements concerning the future of the European Union.

> In this context, our task is less to reassure ourselves of our common origins in the European Middle Ages than to develop a new political self-consciousness commensurate with the role of Europe in the world of the twenty-first century. Hitherto, history has granted the empires that have come and gone but *one* appearance on the world stage. This is just as true of the modern states—Portugal, Spain, England, France, and Russia—as it was for the empires of antiquity. By way of exception, Europe as a whole is now being given a *second* chance. But it will be able to make use of this opportunity not on the terms of its old-style power politics but only under the changed premises of a nonimperialistic process of reaching understanding with, and learning from, other cultures.[52]

Habermas's call for a nonimperialistic process of reaching understanding does not hide the perverse dimensions of his nostalgia for the greatness of Empire. For it is not clear in his work how a political entity other than Europe could be capable of reaching the stage of nonimperial communication. That is, it is difficult to see how in Habermas's premises peoples with non-European or non-christian cultures or religions (such as Islam or Confucianism) could really practice the sort of dialogue that Habermas considers to be rational.[53] The end result is clear: when reaching understanding renders itself impossible, given the inadequacies in the culture and religion of a certain society or nation, it will be legitimate to intervene by force and, in the process, try to form institutions that foment a truly rational form of communication. Violence, war, and intervention will be justified in the light of the Other's intrinsic fundamentalism and intolerance. Habermas's theory of communicative rationality and law is not that much different, at least in respect to an unethical Eurocentrism, from Hegel's philosophy of Spirit and Right.

It is not possible to understand fully the difference between Fanon's and Honneth's critical takes on Hegel without considering their divergent views on the human subject and on the subjective motivations behind the struggle for recognition. Honneth correctly argues that when Hegel articulated the notion of a struggle for recognition he was definitely leaving behind a tradition of social and political thought that went back to Machiavelli and Hobbes, according to which self-preservation played the primary motivating role in leading humans to form states, political bodies, and institutions. According to Hegel, conflicts among humans were not to be traced back to a motive of self-preservation, but, as Honneth describes them, to moral impulses—that is, to the recognition of one's identity and personality. What Hegel, however, continues to hold, in line with dominant trends of political theory in his time, and what Honneth does not examine in his critical reflections on Hegel, is the extent to which the "right of property" functions as the primary marker of self-identity and personality. As a result, the struggle for recognition becomes primarily a struggle to be recognized as a proprietor. Hegel inherits this idea from a liberal tradition that defined human fraternity in terms of the coexistence in a "civil society" of autonomous individuals with rights of property—Locke's felicitous definition.[54] Consider that for the Hegel of the Jena writings what initiated the struggle between persons was "theft," which made it clear that a violation of property was viewed as a violation of the person.[55] Honor could only be regained in a life-and-death struggle.[56] What changes in the *Phenomenology of Spirit* is that the life-and-death struggle, now subsumed in the dialectics of Spirit, gives rise to two modes of consciousness: one is independent and for-itself, while the other is dependent and takes the form of an object or thing; the former is lord, the latter is bondsman. Property becomes now a more complex category since even subjects can collapse into the category of objects, things, and possessions. The slave works on the property of the master and objectifies himself in it, while the master enjoys the product of the slave's work—from here comes the Marxist theory of alienation, which Marx later applied to economics and came up with the notion of surplus value.[57] We have seen all of this already. What I want to add now is that there is a presumption that the relation between the subject and property is basic. Freedom is the objectification of the subjectivity of the individual. The end result of this is that the freedom and equality of the subject tend to collapse frequently into the claim for freedom and equality in the process of coming to *possess* something. We are free to possess what we want and equal in our chances to get what we want.[58] This gives a dangerous self-referential character to the politics of recognition that threatens coalition politics and that more often than not leads only to minimal structural changes at the political and economic levels. The problem with the politics of recognition is therefore not so much that it dissolves questions of redistribution into questions of recognition as some have argued.[59] The problem, in contrast, resides in self-centered claims for redistribution. In other words, the danger is when the struggle for recognition is reduced to questions about the respect, freedom, and equality of subjects who aim to overturn the system of lordship and bondage by coming finally to possess something of their own and to be recognized as proprietors. This conception of the struggle for recognition is fated to leave untouched the basic structure of the oppressive system that creates pathological modes of recognition and to hinder the chances for the formation of what has been aptly called "a coalition politics of receptive generosity."[60]

In contrast to conceptions of the struggle for recognition articulated in terms of cultural identity or in terms of claims for possession and access to goods, Fanon discovered in his exploration of the lived experience of the black that one of the main challenges confronted by blacks in a racial society is not only that they are not recognized as people who can possess things, but that they are not recognized as people who can *give* things. Demands to be able to give are, in this respect, more radical than demands for possession. The master, under pressure, can allow the slave to have "things," but he will not recognize that he needs what the slave has. For the master, whatever the slave touches decreases in quality and value. Thus, even if he enters into commerce with the slave, the master will devalue the extent of the slave's contributions. Fanon was well aware of this dimension of the system of lordship and bondage.

> It was always the Negro teacher, the Negro doctor; brittle as I was becoming, I shivered at the slightest pretext. I knew, for instance, that if the physician made a mistake it would be the end of him and of all those who came after him. What could one expect, after all, from a Negro physician? As long as everything went well, he was praised to the skies, but look out, no nonsense, under any conditions! The black physician can never be sure how close he is to disgrace. I tell you, I was walled in: No exception was made for my refined

manners, or my knowledge of literature, or my understanding of the quantum theory. (BSWM 117)

Fanon suggests here that while coming to possess things or gaining abilities may be a necessary condition of the process of achieving liberation, it is certainly not sufficient and it should not become in itself the telos or goal of the process. The problem is that the logic of lordship and bondage may very well continue after formal concessions of rights of property. The master still resists opening himself to the Other and entering into the logic of ordinary ethical intersubjective contact. But why is it that the master resists accepting the gift or recognizing the Other as someone who can give? The answer should be clear by now: it makes evident the incompleteness of the master. Lordship requires impenetrability, while giving necessitates openness and receptivity. Giving in this sense represents the paradigmatic transgressive act. If giving is so dangerous it is not so much because it puts the other in debt, but because in the colonial context it requires an original act of openness that the master fundamentally resists.[61] The master can easily pay any debt; what he cannot do is to open himself and to be receptive to the gift of the slave. This transaction violates the very meaning and purpose of the logic of lordship and bondage.

THE GIFT BEYOND RECOGNITION: TOWARD AN ETHICAL SUSPENSION OF IDENTITY, ABSTRACT UNIVERSALISM, AND THE TELOS OF EMPIRE

> So later that year, I received another surprise.
> "Get out of the park, you fucking Puerto Rican!"
> I looked around and saw black and white boys, with sticks and pipes in their hands. Perhaps I could have told them that I wasn't a Puerto Rican. I could have told them lots of things. I could have run. But at that point I thought I had had enough. Against whom was this encounter? The "Puerto Rican Nigger"?
> I didn't realize it then, but I had decided at that moment to be, for that moment, a Puerto Rican because "they"—those anonymous, hating "they"—yes, those they whose anonymous, hating consciousness is saturated with American false identities promising them, at the end of all the misery and suffering, a promised land of the "we," for them I shall be whoever they hated. —LEWIS GORDON[62]

For Fanon, as we have seen, the initial movement of subjectivity is an upsurge of givenness. The logic of the relation between lordship and servitude represents a radical attempt at subverting and perverting the logic inaugurated by the gift of the self. We saw that for Levinas the subject first emerges when he takes the bread out of his mouth and extends his hands, giving his bread to the Other. Colonialism is the drama that best reflects the attempt to stage the opposition of this original ethical movement. The colonized "damné" is the one who wants to give but who cannot give because what he has has been taken from him. Colonialism creates a reality in which some subjects become privileged givers while others do not even have bread to eat or to give. And if one of the main goals of the master is to possess, as it were, the monopoly of the human, it is clear that this situation confirms, albeit in an indirect manner, the Levinasian and Fanonian suspicion that giving and loving are fundamental traits of the very humanity of the human.[63] In this light it is perfectly consistent for the master to advocate a religion of love and generosity—something that facilitates his maintenance of the monopoly of love.[64] The slave, in contrast, struggles to create a condition in which he too can express the full extent of his or her loving subjectivity. The religion of the slave (many a time the very religion of the master turned against him) often reflects this interest in coming to be recognized as someone who can give and love—but giving and loving in different ways from the master.[65] The task is, as Fanon puts it, *to restore things to their proper places* (see BSWM 88). The struggle for recognition becomes in this way a struggle for liberation motivated by interests in forming an (ordinary) ethical community. Liberation becomes then not so much a struggle for freedom and equality as a struggle for human fraternity.

The idea that the struggle for liberation is primarily a struggle for fraternity does not mean that liberation does not involve claims of freedom and equality. What it means is that the ultimate aim of the struggle hardly consists in achieving these ends alone. In short, the idea is that the telos and most fundamental aim of the struggle for liberation is the formation of a human community where subjects are not only recognized as possessors but as givers as well. The demand for liberation is indeed the demand to be free and equal, but free and equal not only to have things, but to give and receive as well. Possession, thus, enters the logic of the gift. "Having" represents a necessary moment in the process of giving. But "having," here, does not denote so much an "entitlement" as simply the access to goods that allow for the preservation and reproduction of one's life.[66] The telos of whatever "I have" is not accumulation but the enactment of intersubjective contact through giving and receiving.

The demand for liberation is also a demand for the recognition of identity. If the most radical gift is not any kind of possession but one's own self, then it is clear that struggles for liberation entail claims about the identity of the self. In this light it becomes obvious that demands for the recognition of identity are hardly limited by egocentric interests for recognition or for the preservation of identity. The ultimate telos of the struggle for liberation is the creation of a community wherein people can give themselves completely as who they are and others are receptive to this gift. Claims for the recognition of identity play a positive role in the process of *restoration*, but they also have their limits. Fanon confronted this limitation when he was raising his "Negro cry": "And there was my poor brother—living out his neurosis to the extreme and finding himself paralyzed . . ." (BSWM 138).

An act of fraternity, perhaps even more of *altericity*, dislocates the act of identity affirmation and throws him out of himself to someone in a worse condition than him.[67] Fanon raises a similar alert to black intellectuals who attempt to redeem blackness by identifying the Negro with the universal. Applying the insight that he gained in his confrontation with Sartre's critique of Négritude, Fanon responds to these intellectuals: "What? I have barely opened eyes that had been blindfolded, and someone already wants to drown me in the universal? What about the others? Those who 'have no voice,' those who 'have no spokesman.' . . . I need to lose myself in my negritude, to see the fires, the segregations, the repressions, the rapes, the discriminations, the boycotts. We need to put our fingers on every sore that mottles the black uniform" (BSWM 186–87).

Fanon opposes the move to an abstract universalism with an emphasis in concrete particularity. But this emphasis in particularity is not motivated either by liberal concerns for the loss of individuality or by supposedly anti-liberal or even radical ideas about the links between subjectivity, community, and culture. Fanon's main concern signals the ethico-political movement from slave to slave. Ultimately, the need to suspend the universal and to lose himself in his Negritude obeys the imperative of restoration: of working for the "damné." Fanon claims an exception from the universal only insofar as blackness becomes the locus of dehumanization and inhumanity and as he tries to respond in an ethico-political manner to that situation: "One can already imagine Alioune Diop wondering what place the black genius will have in the universal chorus. It is my belief that a true culture cannot come to life under present conditions. It will be time enough to talk about the black genius when the man has regained his rightful place" (BSWM 187).

Fanon is interested in the restoration of an ordinary human world. And a human world includes the possibility for self-expression, for the formation of diverse communities, and for the flourishing of a culture. Fanon is thus more interested in creating the material conditions of possibility for the emergence of a culture than in claiming the intrinsic value of particular contents or ideas of any particular culture.[68] The content of a culture is important, but before we fall into the warm embrace of any particular tradition we first need to be sure that subjects can produce and reproduce their culture in an ethically ordinary way, that is, without confronting the pathologies created by systematic conditions of oppression and subordination. Otherwise we fall victim to the fundamentally misanthropic gesture of loving the culture of a people while simultaneously hating or being indifferent to them. Beyond this, it is clearly possible, and, indeed, necessary, to be aware of the processes by which different cultures can contribute to the envisioning of innovative methods for advancing more humane ways of thinking and acting. By the same token, different cultures can be harshly criticized when they promote violence rather than peace.[69] It is important, however, to recognize that the struggle for humanization does not leave cultures untouched. The fight for humanization and for establishing the basis of non-sexist human conviviality provides the condition for a positive (more humane and humanistic) transformation of the values and ideas of subjects and cultures.[70]

Recognition involves then an ethical act of giving *beyond recognition*.[71] This is the initial upsurge of an emergent subjectivity. The loving subjectivity emerges in the world and is confronted by two camps. There are the masters and there are the slaves. The masters are primarily the ones who will let this subject know where he belongs. If the subject is rejected by the masters, then he may try to become like them or to be recognized by them. But the subject may also, in a fantastic ethical subversion of the logics of recognition, turn to the slave and recognize the slave as a br*other*: "It was my philosophy professor, a native of the Antilles, who recalled the fact to me one day: 'Whenever you hear anyone abuse the Jews, pay attention, because he is talking about you.' And I found that he was universally right — by which I meant that I was answerable in my body and in my heart for what was done to my brother" (BSWM 122).

Fanon turns the tables here; the logics of recognition give space to the paradox of substitution. The loving subjectivity emerges in the world and finds itself "answerable" for its brother, the slave.[72] In a paradoxical act Fanon assumes responsibility for the Jew and transforms his life into the pursuit of the consistent overcoming of the logics of lordship and bondsman. The subject lives and works *for the Other*. As Fanon puts it: "This means that there is work to be done over there, human work, that is, work which is the meaning of a home. Not that of a room or a barrack building. It means that over the whole territory of the French nation . . . there are tears to be wiped away, inhuman attitudes to be fought, condescending ways of speech to be ruled out, men to be humanized."[73]

Anticipating the concerns of someone (and there is always someone with such concerns) who thinks that what Fanon is saying is a matter of following directions or of simply applying abstract methodologies to concrete realities, Fanon writes,

> Your solution sir?
>
> Don't push me too far. Don't force me to tell you what you ought to know, sir. If YOU do not reclaim the man who is before you, how can I assume that you reclaim the man that is in you?
>
> If YOU do not want the man who is before you, how can I believe the man that is perhaps in you?
>
> If YOU do not demand the man, if YOU do not sacrifice the man that is in you so that the man who is on this earth shall be more than a body, more than a Mohammed, by what conjurer's trick will I have to acquire the certainty that you, too, are worthy of my love?[74]

The master, at least for a moment, sees a human face in the Other and asks something. He steps, momentarily at least, out of the perverted logics of imperial recognition. Yet, while questioning clearly points to the incompleteness of the master, he still takes the recognition of his humanity for granted. Moreover, he asks something that, as Fanon indicates, he should already know. "Asking" here works as a form of evasion or at least it indicates strong resistance to accepting and doing what one knows one should do. Fanon's point is that putting a question to the slave already enacts a logic of humanization that the search for an answer to the question betrays. The master enters into a performative contradiction. Fanon, as the revolutionary pedagogue that he is, answers the question only by raising other questions. With these questions he only makes explicit what the master is trying to "forget" or ignore: that the humanization of the slave demands no less than the end of the imperial world. By virtue of substitution, Fanon recognizes the slave as a brother and then refuses to recognize or to take for granted the humanity of the master. In an unexpected turn, Fanon puts the master in a position where he is the one who has to struggle for recognition (as a human being). No less is expected from the master than giving expression to his loving subjectivity by entering into the paradox of love taking responsibility for the slave *to the point of substitution*, and not only to the point of questioning or critiquing.

The previous chapter concluded with the question of the possibility of love. A consistent account of this question entails an innovative view of subjectivity. For Fanon, as for Levinas, the self is primarily *a gift that gives*, and who, as embodied, is also able to receive and to be hospitable. The consistent expression of this subjectivity entails the restoration of an ordinary world where the self can unfold—that is, where giving and receiving can find non-pathological forms. Subjectivity also means for Fanon agency and freedom. But this agency and freedom are not those of a monad or an egocentric subjectivity. Freedom and agency show themselves in *work*, and primarily in the loving humanizing work that Fanon took so seriously (see BSWM 222). It is in this way also that Fanon provides a response to the question of desire: "As soon as I *desire* I am asking to be considered. I am not merely here-and-now, sealed into thingness. I am for somewhere else and for something else. I demand that notice be taken of my negating activity insofar as I pursue something other than life; insofar as I do battle for the creation of a human-world—that is, of a world of reciprocal recognitions" (BSWM 218).

From love to action and work we are led then to political revolutionary activity.

> I do not carry innocence to the point of believing that appeals to reason or to respect for human dignity can alter reality. For the Negro who works on a sugar plantation in Le Robert, there is only one solution: to fight. He will embark on this struggle, and he will pursue it, not as the result of a Marxist or idealistic analysis but quite simply because he cannot conceive of life otherwise than in the form of a battle against exploitation, misery, and hunger. (BSWM 224)

Confronting a reality where imperial politics violate the ordinariness of the extraordinary, Fanon defended an ethico-political praxis of liberation. This praxis entails a sort of teleological suspension of identity and of universality in the interest of the humanization of the world. In this case, the suspension is not, as in Kierkegaard's formulation, a suspension of the ethical.[75] Both the suspension and the telos are ethical for Fanon. The teleological suspension of identity and universality is at the same time an ethico-political defiance of the telos of empire. The formation of a truly human world can only follow from committed, radical, and paradoxical acts of love. Fanon unveils the need for a pathos of love that stands against the ethos of empire. There are no recipes for political action. But Fanon gives a clear sense of the priorities. He proposes that the struggle for recognition be taken primarily in the sense of a struggle for genuine human intersubjectivity. Fanon anchors ideas of fraternity and intersubjectivity not in equality, in common natural kind or in fecundity, but in the upsurge of a loving subjectivity toward one who is "below." In Levinasian terms, metaphysical desire toward the Other who is "above" (in a position of highness) manifests itself concretely in the commitment for the improvement of those who are "below" (faceless creatures of the world of empire)—to the point of giving one's life *for the Other.*

Life and death acquire new meaning under the paradox of substitution. Risking one's life surpasses the economy of recognition. At the end, Fanon is more concerned about the death of the slave than about his own death. He is more concerned about being an accomplice to murder than of confronting his own demise. Nothing less is what he means when he says that he is "answerable in [his] body and in [his] heart" for what happens to the Jew. His participation in the Second World War should leave no doubt about this. Fanon lives his life, not anticipating his own death, but rather, as it were, going against it so that he can have the time to respond to the Other. The teleological suspension of identity ultimately involves then a teleological suspension of the destructive powers of death. Life in this sense is not defined, as Levinas insistently argued, by anguish over one's own death, but by "an affection more passive than a trauma."[76] The death of the Other becomes the veritable *scandal.* For Levinas, "Death—as the death of the other [*autrui*]—cannot be separated from this dramatic character; it is emotion *par excellence,* affection or being affected *par excellence.*"[77] Fanon's existence gave clear expression to the trace of this affection. This is made evident in a letter he wrote to a friend four weeks prior to his death:

> Roger, what I wanted to tell you is that death is always with us and that what matters is not to know whether we can escape it but whether we have achieved the maximum for the ideas we have made our own. What shocked me here in my bed when I felt my strength ebbing away along with my blood was not the fact of dying as such, but to die of leukemia, in Washington, when three months ago I could have died facing the enemy since I was already aware that I had this disease. We are nothing on earth if we are not in the first place the slaves of a cause, the cause of the peoples, the cause of justice and liberty. I

want you to know that even when the doctors had given me up, in the gathering dusk I was still thinking of the Algerian people, of the peoples in the Third World, and when I have persevered, it was for their sake.[78]

In the deathbed, without having to anticipate death because it appears to be simply on his side waiting for him, Fanon is primarily concerned for the Other.[79] Once again the logics of recognition are dislocated when, in a paradoxical act of love, Fanon declares that life is nothing if we do not make ourselves *the slaves* of a cause. The desire to be master finds here its most direct and radical opposite. It is as if Fanon has been taken *hostage* by the Other, living for him *to the point of substitution*. It is as if he had become, out of love, the slave of the slave.[80] It is this paradoxical position that I have been referring to as *altericity*. Altericity defines, beyond Heideggerian *care* and the Hegelian life and death struggle, a unique mode of ethical and ethico-political subjectivity.[81] In Levinas's formulation, "being affected by the death of the Other is a remarkable and essential event of my psychism insofar as it is a human psychism."[82] Accordingly, Levinas argues,

> We are taking up this term desire; to a subject turned to itself, which, according to the Stoic formula is characterized by . . . the tendency to persist in its being, or for which, according to Heidegger's formula, "there is in its existence question as to this very existence," a subject thus defined by care for itself, which in happiness realizes its *for itself*, we are opposing the desire for the other which proceeds from a being already gratified and in this sense independent, which does not desire for itself. It is the need of him who no longer has needs. It is recognizable in the need for an other who is another [*Autrui*], who is neither my enemy (as he is in Hobbes and Hegel) nor my "complement," as he still is in Plato's *Republic*, which is set up because something is lacking in the subsistence of each individual. . . . In desire the I is borne toward the other in such a way as to compromise the sovereign self-identification of the I, for which need is but nostalgia and which the consciousness of need anticipates.[83]

Desire is primarily, for Levinas as for Fanon, desire for the Other.[84] When this desire takes the form of a political struggle against the structures of dehumanization then we can refer to it, following Chela Sandoval, as "de-colonial love."[85] De-colonial love is positive, and not, like traditional conceptions of critique, only negative. Fanon makes clear his disagreement with conceptions of subjectivity that privilege negativity: "Man is not merely a possibility of recapture or of negation. If it is true that consciousness is a process of transcendence, we have to see too that this transcendence is haunted by the problems of love and understanding. Man is a *yes* that vibrates to cosmic harmonies" (BSWM 8).

Desire is the upsurge of the loving subjectivity. It is a *Yes*, or a radical affirmation of sociality and interhuman contact. Altericity is the *Yes* of love expressed as *non-indifference* toward the Other, primarily toward the Other who is "below" (also sub-Other or sub-alter). The *Yes* of love thus leads to a conception of ethical struggle against the dehumanization of the sub-alter. In this sense, altericity is another way of conceiving the de-colonial attitude, out of which the de-colonial reduction emerges and is sustained. As simultaneously affirmative of generosity and critical of damnation, altericity and the de-colonial attitude are both affirmative and negative:

> I said in my introduction that man is a *yes*. I will never stop reiterating that.
> *Yes* to life. *Yes* to love. *Yes* to generosity.
> But man is also a *no*. *No* to exploitation of man. *No* to the butchery of what is most human in man: freedom. (BSWM 222)

Altericity is the subjective modality that best gives expression to Fanon's new humanism. This humanism is grounded not so much in abstract universality as in the ethical and de-colonial suspension of the universal. For this reason it is not a classical humanism, but, I would argue, a *humanism of the Other*. I believe that Fanon would fully endorse this Levinasian characterization of the fate of humanism and of its critique by anti-humanists in the contemporary world:

> Modern anti-humanism, which denies the primacy that the human person, free and for itself, would have for the signification of being, is true over and beyond the reasons it gives itself. It clears the space for subjectivity positing itself in abnegation, in sacrifice, in a substitution which precedes the will. Its inspired intuition is to have abandoned the idea of person, goal and origin of itself, in which the ego is still a thing because it is still a being. Strictly speaking, the other is the end; I am a hostage, a responsibility and a substitution supporting the world in the passivity of assignation, even in an accusing persecution, which is indeclinable. Humanism has to be denounced only because it is not sufficiently human. (OB 127–28)

Fanon's humanism is not the abstract humanism that interferes with the activity of humanization, but the humanism of the ethical suspension (with a de-colonial intent) whereby the universal is suspended in favor of a higher telos. This humanism is grounded on love, which finds consistent expression in the preferential option for the "damnés." Fanon was concerned for the "damnés" in Martinique, in Algeria, and all over the Third World. It was just a matter of time until the peoples in the Third World would come to adopt Fanon as one of their own. Given the conceptual connections between the work of Levinas and Fanon, it is not strange that particular expressions of Third World philosophies, such as the Latin American "philosophy of liberation," found in them philosophical allies. In the next part I examine the work of the philosopher and religious thinker Enrique Dussel and evaluate his philosophical project in the light of his appropriations of both Levinas and Fanon.

FROM THE ETHICAL
TO THE GEOPOLITICAL

A LATIN AMERICAN RESPONSE
TO COLONIALITY, NEOLIBERAL
GLOBALIZATION, AND WAR

ENRIQUE DUSSEL'S ETHICS AND PHILOSOPHY OF LIBERATION

> *One of those refreshing nights in our poor barrack at a building co-op for Arab workers who built their own houses in Nazareth, I was narrating Latin American history and became enthusiastic about the figure of Pizarro, who conquered the Inca Empire with just a few men. Looking me in the eyes, Gauthier asked me: "Who were the poor at that moment, Pizarro or the Indians?" That night at candlelight I wrote to my historian friend from Mendoza, Esteban Fontana: "We shall write one day the History of Latin America from the other side, from the underside, from the position of the oppressed and the poor."* —ENRIQUE DUSSEL[1]

It was 1959 when Enrique Dussel had what he refers to as the "originary experience" that made him acutely aware of the links between poverty and geographical location, and that compelled him to prepare himself to one day rewrite the history of Latin America from the perspective of the poor and the dispossessed in the continent. At that point Frantz Fanon was fighting with the Algerian National Liberation Front against France, and Levinas was developing what would later be published as *Totality and Infinity*. It was about ten years later when the works of these two greats found their way into Dussel's thought, having a tremendous impact on the elaboration of what he would come to call a philosophy of liberation.

The ten years that go from Dussel's sojourn in Israel in 1959 to his return to Argentina in 1967 and then to the initial articulations of his philosophy of liberation in 1969 were accompanied by important events in Latin America. First among these events was the Cuban Revolution of 1959. The Cuban Revolution represented for many a possible way out from the predicament of Latin America since at least 1898. This situation prompted a massive expansion of the U.S. economy to Latin America. Against the advocates of such "development," some theorists argued that there were necessary links between development in the North and underdevelopment in the South. This is one of the main tenets of what was later called dependency theory. In this sense it is possible to say, as Walter Mignolo puts it, that "dependency theory brought to the foreground and into the discussion a concern with the marginal, the poor, and the miserable as the victims of capitalism."[2] As was clear at least since his work in Israel with the French priest Paul Gauthier, Dussel was particularly interested in the problem of marginalization and systematic poverty. It was not, however, precisely until 1969 that Dussel heard about dependency theory for the first time. At that point, the dictatorship in Argentina was confronting strong opposition from popular groups. In an event reminiscent of the events of 1968 in France, Mexico, and elsewhere, workers and students took the Argentinean city of Córdoba in 1969. It is in this context that Dussel discovered the work of Emmanuel Levinas.

When Dussel discovered Levinas he was teaching a course in ontological ethics. Dussel had completed by then a doctoral degree in philosophy from the Universidad Complutense in Madrid, and another one in history from La Sorbonne in Paris. Yet it was in Paris, Dussel comments, where his philosophical experience truly began.[3] Dussel arrived in Paris in 1961, the year in which both Levinas's *Totality and Infinity* and Fanon's *The Wretched of the Earth* were published. Among his fellow students there were young veterans from the Algerian war. It was in this context that Dussel was introduced to phenomenology. He read Merleau-Ponty, Husserl, and Ricoeur, whose seminars he was able to attend. In this same period, Dussel reflected carefully about the problem of the position of Latin America in history through a careful reading of Leopoldo Zea's *America en la historia* (originally published in 1957). Dussel's reading of Levinas's *Totality and Infinity* in 1969 had a strong effect on his project: the ontological ethics in Heideggerian style that he found himself articulating at that point turned into a Latin American ethics of liberation.

Levinas's work had a tremendous impact on Dussel's project of articulating the specificity of Latin America in history and in the philosophy of history. It also played a fundamental role in Dussel's shift, to use his own terms, from phenomenology to liberation, and from a cultural hermeneutics to a critical ethics of liberation. In this chapter I analyze Dussel's critical appropriation of Levinas. Since Dussel's ethics and philosophy of liberation are grounded on notions of exteriority and otherness that

Dussel takes from Levinas, I will explain Levinas's treatment of these themes. Like many topics and analyses in the Levinasian literature, the way in which Levinas articulates the idea of the Other cannot be properly understood without a critical reflection on phenomenology. I therefore include in this chapter a brief discussion of the phenomenological treatment of objectivity and otherness. Only in this way will we be able to assess to what extent Dussel's conception of exteriority surpasses, as he alleges, the limitations of phenomenology and of Levinas's own conceptions. The discussion of phenomenology and of Levinas's treatment of the Other are also important in that they provide the necessary background to assess the idea, submitted by a Dussel scholar, that many of the alleged problems in Dussel's mode of argumentation dissolve with an appropriate understanding of Levinas's philosophy and of Dussel's indebtedness to Levinas.[4]

The critical assessment of Dussel's appropriation of Levinas begins in the second section of this chapter. In this section I also evaluate Dussel's alleged overcoming of phenomenology in light of Fanon's existential phenomenology. Dussel was acquainted with Fanon indirectly through his encounter with dependency theory and directly through a reading of *The Wretched of the Earth*. In his *Philosophy of Liberation* Dussel credits Fanon with having anticipated a philosophy of liberation.[5] Following Lewis Gordon, in the previous two chapters I have suggested that the moment has come to recognize Fanon seriously as a philosopher of liberation with a fresh existential phenomenological perspective.[6] This position, however, puts me at odds with Dussel, who declares a divorce between phenomenology and liberation. I will argue not only that phenomenology is not antithetical to liberation, but also that Dussel's philosophy of liberation itself would have strongly benefited from an existential phenomenological approach. In short, I will argue here that there are points in Dussel's ethics in which he tried to be Levinasian, but where, in contrast, he should have been Fanonian. The critique of Dussel in this chapter from a phenomenological perspective (both genetic and existential) paves the way for an appropriation of relevant historical and geopolitical considerations that complement the critical work of de-colonial reduction (simultaneously ethical, political, and geopolitical) that I have attempted to formulate through the works of Levinas and Fanon. I move from an examination of Dussel's contributions in history and geopolitics to the de-colonial reduction of modernity in the next chapter.

THE PROBLEM OF THE OTHER OR THE OTHER AS PROBLEM: TOWARD A GENETIC PHENOMENOLOGICAL ACCOUNT OF OTHERNESS

> *Precisely thereby every sort of existent itself, real or ideal, becomes understandable as a "product" of transcendental subjectivity, a product constituted in just that performance. This kind of understandableness is the highest imaginable form of rationality.* —EDMUND HUSSERL[7]
>
> *Phenomenology is a method for philosophy, but phenomenology—the comprehension effected through a bringing to light—does not constitute the ultimate event of being itself. The relation between the same and the other is not always reducible to knowledge of the other by the same, nor even to the revelation of the other to the same, which is already fundamentally different from disclosure.* —EMMANUEL LEVINAS[8]

"To the things themselves." Thus, Husserl announced the beginning of a new philosophical movement that was to take hold of the twentieth-century Western philosophical imagination. Through a particular method, the phenomenological reduction, a new field opened itself to philosophical investigation, and the possibility of making of philosophy a "strict science" finally seemed to be fulfilled. Transcendental consciousness, its eidetic structures, and the meanings constituted form this new field, a horizon of meaning the extent of which covers the whole "world." In the first chapter, I discussed the contributions of the Husserlian project to the articulation of an epistemology and a philosophical anthropology that aimed to take European humanity out of its deep crisis. While I focused there on subjectivity and freedom, I will focus here on objectivity and exteriority. In the treatments of these themes I find the key for the emergence of new approaches in the phenomenological tradition: from static analyses of intentionality I trace the emergence of ontology, genetic phenomenology, and of Levinas's own conception of metaphysics. This section, thus, supplements in important ways the discussion of phenomenology in the first part of this work. I include it here because it is directly connected with my critique of Dussel's appropriation of Levinas. I will argue that it is not possible to understand the problems behind Dussel's appropriation of Levinas without being aware of how Levinas's ethical metaphysics is located at the level of a genetic phenomenological investigation.

The ideas that the meaning of reality is fully dependent on the intentionality of consciousness and that philosophy operates only in the realm of phenomena provide original and fascinating answers to the problem of skepticism and European nihilism, but they also open a whole field of questions and concerns, particularly at the ontological level. They raise questions about the ontological status of reality and of its import, not only for the formation of meaning, but also for the very emergence of consciousness. Phenomenology also has to explain how the ego-monad is not solipsistic, and how precisely is it able to recognize the "other," not as any phenomena or object in the world, but precisely as an other. The problem of the adequate recognition of exteriority may very well be, in short, the Achilles' heel of Husserlian phenomenology.

One of the earliest and strongest critiques of what appeared to many as a problematic immanentism and idealism in Husserlian phenomenology was presented in Jean-Paul Sartre's treatise on phenomenological ontology, *Being and Nothingness*.

> But, we are told, Husserl defines consciousness precisely as a transcendence. In truth he does. This is what he posits. This is his essential discovery. But from the moment that he makes of the *noema* an *unreal*, a correlate *of* the noesis, a noema whose *esse* is *percipi*, he is totally unfaithful to his principle. Consciousness is consciousness *of* something. This means that transcendence is the constitutive structure of consciousness; that is, consciousness is born *supported by* a being that is not itself.[9]

According to Sartre, Husserl's account of the noema or "the perceived as perceived" distorts the meaning of transcendence, which entails the recognition of something that is *for consciousness*, but that at the same time is something *in itself*. In other words, Sartre argues that Husserl denies the transcendence of consciousness by reducing the character of the given to a component of consciousness. Rather than with transcendence we are left, or so Sartre argues, only with immanence.

Sartre's criticism is a defense of the transcendence of consciousness based on the difference between consciousness and that toward which it is directed. This distinction is fundamental for the articulation of Sartre's ontology, yet it reflects a mistaken conception of the Husserlian noema. Sartre presupposes here that the noema has to be conceived as real and as other than consciousness in order for the transcendence of consciousness to be maintained. Sartre ignores with this two fundamental points: (1) the noema cannot be something extra-phenomenal because it is precisely that of our perception of the world that survives the transcendental reduction, and (2) this interpretation does not deny in any manner that that toward which consciousness is directed is extra-phenomenal. The noema is the *intended as intended*, the *perceived as per-*

ceived, and not the perceived as such or the object of the intentional act. As Husserl's formulation has it,

> The *tree simpliciter*, the physical thing belonging to Nature, is nothing less than this *perceived tree as perceived* which, as perceptual sense, inseparably belongs to the perception. The tree simpliciter can burn up, be resolved into its chemical elements, etc. But the sense—the sense *of this* perception, something belonging necessarily to its essence—cannot burn up; it has no chemical elements, no forces, nor real properties.[10]

As mistaken as Sartre's criticism may be, I believe that the import of his critique surpasses the limits of the all too familiar depiction of Husserlian phenomenology as a kind of Berkeleyan idealism. Sartre's criticism points to a different problem, that is, to the articulation of the relation between consciousness and reality exclusively in terms of *senses* that pertain to consciousness.

The difficulties of a philosophical posture according to which every relation of consciousness is exclusively thematized in terms of constitution of meaning and expansion of horizons become most obvious in the treatment of the constitution of the other person. This exclusivity is arguably related to the primacy of the epistemological in Husserl's thought. Already found in Levinas's early work, this idea is also recognized by Sartre. "Because," Sartre argues, "Husserl has reduced being to a series of meanings, the only connection which he has been able to establish between my being and that of the Other is a connection of *knowledge*. Therefore Husserl cannot escape solipsism any more than Kant could."[11] The conception of the relation between consciousness and everything else exclusively in terms of the active constitution of meaning by consciousness eliminates the possibility of recognizing at least three things: first, that an encounter with the Other is irreducible to knowledge; second, that the encounter is precisely that, an encounter; and, third, that out of the encounter, dynamics of recognition and self-identity are going to take place. These ideas are clearly behind Sartre's analysis of the ontological significance of the gaze of the Other, and of the resulting interplay of masochism and sadism in intersubjective relations of bad faith.[12]

The problem of accounting for the relations between consciousness and that of which consciousness is conscious introduces the problem of passivity. The point is not simply, as it was not before, that transcendental phenomenology fails in recognizing the ontological significance of the existence of the external world (the *in itself*); the problem now is rather determining the extent to which phenomenology accounts adequately for the ways in which the *in itself* impinges on consciousness. The problem is also about the role of the given in the very constitution of meaning. In short, what seems to be missing in the phenomenological account is what Jaako Hintikka has referred to as "a level of self-givenness in experience," and a view that relates from the outset what is given to the very "constitution of the noema."[13] Perhaps what Sartre ultimately points to is that peculiar obscurity between Husserl's description of the noema as, on the one hand, that which is *bestowed by consciousness*, and, on the other, *the perceived as such*, one element seemingly indicating the activity of consciousness and the other its receptive capacity. We are pointing here to the problem of the emergence of meaning, a problem that Husserl addressed with the concept of constitution, more in particular, with the development of genetic phenomenology.

That the problem of the origin of sense—a problem that can be traced back to the issue of the contact between consciousness and something that is external to it, and that makes the notion of *constitution* appear more as a problem than as a solution—is internal to phenomenology has been made clear by Robert Sokolowski:

> In the *Investigations*, we saw that the meanings contained in intentional acts are posited, but their origins are not given. They are always assumed as already there. The same is true in the noematic analyses of the *Ideas*, where the senses of things are all posited as ready-made in perception. In our perception, we find such and such predicates belonging to one region, others belonging to another. But how are these senses constituted in themselves? Where do they arise from? Husserl does not explain the content of the senses of objects constituted by intentionality. The content is accepted as simple facticity, as something that consciousness is faced with.[14]

According to Sokolowski, Husserl does not provide in his early work an explanation of the relation between the "advent" of sense and the presentation of the given. It is necessary to clarify here that Husserl's account of *hyletic* data, of the "stuff" formed by the noesis in the intentional act (something like *sense data* but without its positivistic overtones), would not do to solve this problem. *Hyletic* data, at most, would *limit* but not actively participate in the generation of *sense*.[15] With such a limited role it is not clear how sensations would come to be connected with sense. Sokolowski explains,

> In the *Logical Investigations* as in *Ideas I*, the role of sense data is incorporated into a theory of intentionality, under the matter-form schema. Sensations are the raw material which serves as the basis for the constitution of objects and meanings. We are not completely free in forming objects and senses. We are limited by what is given in sensation, for the passive, material element imposes restrictions on the activity of intentionality. The manner in which this happens, however, is not explained. It calls for an explanation, because it is not self-evident how sensations, which are radically different from noeses, can enter into the realm of intentions and exercise an effect on them. No explanation is forthcoming as long as we hold to the schema, because the correlation of sensations and noeses has to be simply accepted as a fact expressed in this schematism.[16]

According to Sokolowski, the matter-form schema adopted by Husserl in *Ideas* cannot offer a solution to the problem raised here because it excludes an explanation of constitution as a (temporal) process.[17] It would only be when Husserl came to integrate his doctrine of inner time with that of the higher level constitution achieved in acts (such as those explained by the matter-form schema) that the problem of the role of sensations in the formation of meaning, and that of the link between the given, the noema, and what is intended, would come to be addressed more adequately.[18]

Part of Sokolowski's argument is that a study of Husserl's writings shows that the integration of genetic constitution, a doctrine that introduces the historical or temporal element into the higher spheres of the constitution of meanings, can be understood as a response to the problems that arose through his early approach and, I would add here, at least partially to criticisms such as those later articulated by Sartre. Sokolowski thus attempts to portray the trajectory of Husserl's writings in the light of a response to the problem of the givenness or "facticity" that is an essential component of perceptual acts—a givenness that influences the formation of meaning from the very outset of the perceptual encounter. According to him,

> Once the historical dimension is brought in, Husserl will be forced to treat the first establishment (*Urstiftung*) of a given meaning or type of object. Genetic constitution points back to first occurrences as a particularly important problem, which does not make itself felt as long as we remain in static analyses. The theory of genetic constitution thus provides the first possibility of solution for a problem and a defect in Husserl's phenomenology which

appears as far back as the *Logical Investigations*. Husserl's probe back into the very beginnings of a meaning or object as established will bring into relief the role of sensory data as the stuff from which it arises, and in which it must somehow be pre-formed before it actually appears. In this way, he will be able to give a certain explanation of the origins of the content of the senses and objects constituted by intentionality.[19]

Sokolowski makes clear here that the importance of adopting an approach that focuses on the temporal development of the constitution of "senses" lies in that it permits one to establish a connection between what is given to consciousness and the formation and bestowal of a "sense" that is said to pertain to a particular intended object. If it were possible to establish the exact role of the object in the constitution of its meaning, then the problem of the connection between noema and object would be clarified and the idealistic connotations of transcendental subjectivity would be avoided or reduced to a minimum.

Husserl integrates his views on inner time in his *Formal and Transcendental Logic* and in the *Cartesian Meditations*. In these works, Husserl traces the origin of sense to the processes of one's conscious life. That is to say, for him, the emergence of "every sense" becomes clarified by an account of "my life's constitutive syntheses."[20] These syntheses are referred to in terms of "active" and "passive geneses." While "active genesis" refers to the *constitution of new objects originally*, objects that present themselves *as products* (for example, inferences, cultural objects, and so forth), "passive genesis" is described as "a passivity that gives something beforehand."[21] Sokolowski sums up Husserl's views on the various sublevels involved in "passive constitution" as follows: "There is first a stage of pure sensation, then a stage in which sensations are externally spatialized, when they are constituted into what Husserl calls 'phantoms,' and finally a stage in which things are constituted: fixed identity points that solidify within the world of phantoms."[22] The significance of the concept of passive genesis lies in that it serves Husserl's explanation of the role of sensations in the formation of meaning. As Sokolowski points out, this approach sheds light on "the constant interplay of conceptualized senses with pre-predicative encounter, and [on] the stimulus this has on the growth of constitution."[23] However, Sokolowski himself doubts that genetic phenomenology will solve all of the problems confronted by phenomenology in relation to the recognition of the given and its role in the formation of sense. He believes that it is necessary not only to investigate the structures of subjectivity working in the formation of meaning, but that, in addition, "Husserl's philosophy needs an examination of what the condition *sine qua non* is for reality to reveal itself, in constitution, as that which it actually is. In other words, the fundament in reality which allows reality to emerge in constitution has to be investigated."[24] Sokolowski believes that the Heideggerian concept of *das Sein der Seinden* (the Being of beings) may be understood precisely in light of the concern with accounting for "the fundament in reality which allows reality to emerge in constitution."

Sokolowski's reflections on the limits of Husserlian phenomenology indicate yet another aspect in which Heidegger's thought seems to supersede that of his teacher. While the early Levinas pointed out how Heidegger's conception of *Dasein* is a less intellectualistic version of the subject than the Husserlian one, Sokolowski suggests that it is rather Heidegger's shift from subject and intentionality to Being that marks a significant progress in respect to Husserl. It is Heidegger's conception of Being as *es gibt* ("there is," or literally "it gives") that most radically responds to the limits in Husserlian phenomenology. From a Levinasian point of view, however, there is nothing more problematic in Heidegger's thought than the idea that meaning can be accounted for in impersonal terms—that is, that *it* gives, that Being gives itself. Moreover, according to Levinas, it is precisely Heidegger's ontological turn that anchors his thought more radically in the tradition that privileges theory and knowledge in the articulation of basic philosophical problems. Levinas argues that for Heideggerian ontology everything becomes ultimately a matter of the opening and unconcealedness of Being. The *understanding* of Being remains in this way precisely that—understanding. According to Levinas, Heideggerian ontology is therefore still tied to epistemology.

The questions raised by the problem of objectivity in relation to the passivity of the subject are radicalized in respect to the question of accounting for the exteriority of the other person. The reason why Husserl's reflections on the constitution of the "Other" come at the end of his *Cartesian Meditations* is not mere coincidence. The constitution of the "Other" becomes perhaps the more difficult problem for phenomenology insofar as this otherness seems to challenge the very basis of the Husserlian attempt to spell out the encounter between consciousness and what is external to it in terms of the constitution of meaning.[25] Both Sartre and, as we have seen, Emmanuel Levinas challenge Husserlian phenomenology on this point. In contrast, Heidegger, if we follow Levinas's interpretation, ended up subordinating the question of the other to an ontology that accounted for the possibility of truth primarily in impersonal terms. At the end, both the self and the other person are subsumed in a play of ontological significations. Here perhaps lies one of the essential differences behind Heidegger's criticism of Sartre in the "Letter on Humanism." Unlike Heidegger, Sartre maintains human beings at the center of his philosophical account of the emergence and unfolding of meaning. Sartre defended the primacy of a freedom committed to praxis against dehumanization. For this reason his philosophical anthropology and his humanistic ideal also surpass, along with Heideggerianism, the limits of liberalism. At least this is the way in which Levinas conceived of Sartre's contribution:

> The idea that human freedom could be retrieved in the midst of everything that is imposed on man came from Sartre like a message of hope for a whole generation that grew up under fatalities through all the expectation of our century and for which the humanism of eloquence, however much it glorified human rights, was totally unconvincing. A new philosophy is, first and foremost, the word given back to those who had lost it in the rhetoric where great projects founder. That this freedom never turn[ed] to evocation of outworn pagan myths related to the ideal of personal salvation, that Sartre immediately heard it as concern "for others," as a source of responsibilities to assume with regard to one who, by all evidence, *"does not concern us"* [ne nous regarde pas], certainly touched a most sensitive chord in Jewish conscience. Angst for a freedom straightaway devoted to others and not, as for the pre-genocide philosopher Heidegger, angst for *my* death, angst for that which is *"most mine"* in concern for the human that I am for my own being. For us, survivors of the extermination camps, survivors of universal history, for many of us this new language suddenly rang out as familiar or very close.[26]

In short, for Levinas, Sartre's ontology and existential philosophy are, unlike Heidegger's, post-genocidal.

Perhaps the main difference between Sartre and Levinas is that while Sartre raises the problem of the Other in terms of the dialectics of recognition between two subjects whose most basic character is to be free and embodied, Levinas appropriates and radicalizes Husserl's own genetic phenomenology and argues that the contact between the self and the other precedes the very formation of the self as a free subject. For Levinas the free subject has a vocation: it has been *elected* to serve other human beings. Freedom is thus for Levinas a positivity and not only a negativity. Freedom is an upsurge of love. It is here that Levinas's genetic phenomenology and Fanon's existential phenomenology join forces.[27] The Other is not only that by virtue of whom I become aware of my objectivity, as Sartre insightfully points out; the Other is also that to whom I am *called* to serve.[28] Bad faith in this sense becomes an attempt by the self to hide from itself its transcendence as nihilating freedom, its objectivity as embodied consciousness, and/or its transcendence as a positive movement toward exteriority. The exercise of violence, which represents nothing less than the radical negation of love and which expresses an allergy to otherness, may be therefore understood as a betrayal of the very humanity of the human.

Accounting for the conditions of possibility for the emergence of the loving subjectivity became for Levinas a lifelong project through which he aimed to provide the bases for a post-genocidal and postliberal conception of the human. The adoption of a genetic phenomenological approach responds to this interest. The themes of exteriority, metaphysics, and otherness will find a place in the very genesis of the self. Levinas's ethical metaphysics refer then, not to the origin of the cosmos, but to the "hither side" of human experience. We will explore now more carefully the presence of a genetic phenomenological approach in Levinas's work. This exploration will provide important considerations for an adequate interpretation of Levinas's conception of otherness. In this discussion, the difficulties of adopting Levinas's categories directly for the articulation of a philosophy of liberation will become clear, and we will be in a better position to assess the limits and the relevance of Dussel's project.

The presence of a genetic phenomenological approach is patent in Levinas's work early on. Richard A. Cohen begins his "Translator's Introduction" to *Time and the Other* with a very significant remark, which is something to have in mind not only when reading this text, but in reading any of Levinas's other philosophical works as well.

> *Time and the Other* has a genetic phenomenological structure. It begins with existence without existents, describes the origination of the distinct existent, the subject, then moves to the progressively more complex constitutive layers of subjectivity, its materiality and solitude, its insertion in the world, its labor and representation, its suffering and mortality, to conclude with the subject's encounter with the other person, dealt with specifically in terms of eros, voluptuosity and fecundity. . . . Thus the analyses begin with what so lacks alterity that it is anonymous like the night itself, existence without existents, what Levinas calls the "there is," and end with what is so radically and irreducibly other that it is the very paradigm of alterity, what Levinas calls in *Time and the Other* the "mystery" of the other person.[29]

The significance of Cohen's introductory remark is twofold: (1) it specifies the mode of Levinas's argumentation—genetic, that is, it describes a reality or an activity by narrating its development, and (2) the development being narrated is not one striving toward conciliation of contraries into a total unity, but one that points to the irreducible character and fundamental status of alterity.

Genetic phenomenology refers to an account concerned not only with the emergence of meaning, but also with the emergence of the subject itself. Instead of departing from the conditions given by a transcendental subject or by Being in general, Levinas begins with an "existent." He will then attempt to provide an account of the process whereby this "existent" becomes a (human) subject. The crux of Levinas's exploration is this: an encounter with otherness is necessary for the formation of the human subject. The Other cannot be simply constituted by the self because the encounter with the Other is a condition of possibility for the emergence of the self. That is why for Levinas the self is always more than acts of sense bestowal or projection of possibilities. The unilateral conception of the subject as the ultimate source of all meaning carries for him possible dangerous consequences.

> Presence, the production of Being or its manifestation, is *given*, is a mode of being-given (*Gegebenheit*). Husserl describes this as filling a void, as satisfaction. He who himself lays stress on the role of human incarnation in the perception of what is given, and on the "lived body" (*Leib*) as the organ of consciousness... will certainly authorize us to insist on the primary role played by the hand: Being is *bestowed* and this bestowal is to be understood in the literal sense of the world. The Bestowal is completed by the *hand that takes* (*la main qui prend*). It is therefore in this taking of possession (*mainmisse*) that presence is "presence proper," presence in "flesh and blood" and not only "in images": presence is produced as a *hand-holding-now* (*main-tenant*).[30] It is in the taking-in-hand that the "thing itself" matches what the intention of thought willed and aimed at.[31]

In order to avoid the idea of the capture of the Other by "the hand that takes" Levinas has to formulate otherness as that which is fundamentally non-presentable or invisible. But, for the intending subject everything becomes an object to be illuminated by its light. Thus Levinas had no other recourse but to adopt a genetic phenomenological standpoint and venture to show the ways in which the encounter with the Other precedes the very emergence of the self.

The adoption of a genetic approach can be thus traced back to Levinas's interest in successfully evading the dominance of epistemology in philosophy, which, as we have seen, is strongly associated with the paradigm of violence and war that I have been describing and criticizing throughout this work. Against the primacy of epistemology, and against the dominance of an ontology that remains enslaved to epistemological needs, Levinas attempted to formulate an account of "ethics as first philosophy." The idea of "ethics as first philosophy" cannot be properly understood without considering the presence of a genetic approach in his work. What Levinas means by this is that the emergence of subjectivity, along with the very conditions of possibility for the formation of meaning, are dependent on the encounter between a self (qua existent) and an Other. And the relation between these two is far from collapsing into the relations between a self and an object or objects. Beyond the impersonal vocabulary of science or epistemology, it is in ethics that Levinas finds the possibility for the appropriate articulation of these themes.

Now, ethics is clearly and correctly associated with practical philosophy. It is typically linked with the realm of human action, either in terms of moral imperatives, or in terms of customs that orient praxis. Levinas's conception of "ethics as first philosophy," however, is not encapsulated by any of these ways of understanding ethics. The main reason for this is that while practical philosophy presupposes the existence of the acting subject, Levinas uses ethics in order to account for the formation of the self. That is, for Levinas ethics becomes instrumental for the articulation of a philosophical anthropology that also clarifies the conditions of possibility for the emergence of meaning and freedom. In short, Levinas's conception of "ethics as first philosophy" locates ethics at the transcendental level. More than ethics proper, what we have then is an ethical metaphysics. The relation between the self (qua existent) and the Other surpasses for Levinas the epistemological and ontological molds. Beyond objectivist relations of knowledge and beyond struggles for recognition between two alter egos, what we have, at least initially for Levinas, is the (ethical) encounter between the Same and what forever remains exterior to it. Levinas will adopt categories and concepts used in practical ethics in order to enunciate the sorts of relations that take place at this metaphysical and genetic level of the formation of subjectivity.

The use of concepts and ideas associated with ethics (at the concrete level of human existence) to spell out the transcendental dimensions of the subject does not mean that these levels are coextensive. There is a difference at the level of categories here. Even though the concepts may be the same, what holds at the transcendental level does not necessarily apply to the concrete level. One would need to articulate mediations between the two levels. Moreover, the concrete here is not limited to practical ethics but encapsulates the totality of human experience. We can find the traces of the transcendental—as adequate expressions or as futile attempts at escaping or hiding from it—everywhere.

One of the risks of the elevation of ethics to the transcendental level is that since we can find the traces of ethics everywhere, then it would seem that practical ethics loses specificity and, thus, its normative power to regulate conduct. In this sense the genetic-transcendental turn introduces a problem more radical than the usual concern about the reduction of politics to ethics. What we find is a gap between ethics (at the transcendental level) and ethics (at the concrete level). Insofar as Levinas, in his attempt to evade phenomenology, recedes back into the prephenomenalistic formation process of the subject, ethics seems to lose any connection with the phenomenal-practical world. In a sense, the overcoming of phenomenology through ethics becomes the confinement of ethics to the pre-phenomenal. In this context it is pertinent to ask to what extent the idea of "ethics as first philosophy" implies not so much an overcoming of phenomenology as the very displacement of ethics into an obscure zone of practical inapplicability.

This problem is evinced in *Time and the Other*, wherein Levinas goes from the encounter between self and Other at the transcendental level to a description of eros (not ethics) at the concrete level. It was only through eros that Levinas found his way to the concrete realm of sociality and of human fraternity where practical ethics finds a space. We have already seen how Levinas's account of eros ends up introducing unethical considerations—for example, in his conception of the feminine. But *Time and the Other* also offers a different and seemingly less problematic view of the relation between self and Other. This view is important because it has been central for the articulation of Dussel's philosophy of liberation.

For Levinas, "The Other as Other is not only an alter ego: the Other is what I myself am not. The Other is this, not because of the Other's character, or physiognomy, or psychology, but because of the Other's very alterity. The Other is, for example, the weak, the poor, 'the widow and the orphan,' whereas I am the rich or the powerful."[32] This passage exhibits clearly the tension between the transcendental and the concrete in Levinas's account of ethics as first philosophy. It would seem that the Other qua metaphysical exteriority is simply found directly face to face in concrete experience. The problem with this is that this situation can easily be accounted for in phenomenological terms in relation to the problem of the constitution of the meaning of "weak and poor" by an "I" that functions as a transcendental subject. The Other qua metaphysical exteriority thus cannot simply be the poor or the weak in front of me. If this were not the case then we would not find the Other qua Other, but the Other qua poor. This will introduce a series of problematic questions about the precise concrete location of the Other—as if the status of otherness could be associated with a particular position in the realm of concrete ordinary life. I submit then that the relation between the rich and the poor serves here as a sort of metaphor to indicate one of the modes of the relation between the Other qua metaphysical exteriority and the self as egoist existent. Levinas adopts concepts and ideas linked with experiences that occur in ordinary life to describe the movements by virtue of which subjectivity is born. This does not mean, however, that the two levels, or the meaning of the concepts used at each level, can be simply identified to one another. It is necessary to articulate the mediations between the genetic level and the realm of experience. The dismissal of this point is one of the strongest temptations and one of the gravest mistakes in the interpretation of Levinas's work.

The problem with collapsing Levinas's description of the events at the transcendental level to concrete ordinary existence is that at the concrete level we are, first and foremost (though not uniquely for Levinas), in the realm of the phenomenon and of presence, whereas, as we have seen, one of Levinas's main aims is to overcome what he sees as the limits of discourses fixed on the alleged irrefutable primacy of this level. This is the tension that any attempt to adopt Levinas's philosophy for ethico-political purposes confronts: on the one hand, Levinas's consistent evasion of phenomenology seems to confine his ethics to a level in which its significance for practical matters becomes obscure, if not dubious; on the other hand, if this were not the case and his ethics were directly applicable to practical issues, then one would have to deal with the presence of a series of difficult moral notions, and with the recommendation of what could be deemed as anti-ethical intersubjective relationships. Put differently, "ethics" becomes first philosophy at the price of becoming insignificant, and it becomes significant to the extent that it reaches ahead to the shores of the phenomenon, therefore subsuming itself again into the deep waters of phenomenology. The irony is that at this moment not only the supposed primordiality of "ethics" but also its very ethical character are at stake.

Unfortunately, the appropriation of Levinas for the articulation of a concrete ethics and politics has tended to ignore the complexities of his discourse. This is due in great part to the dominant role of *Totality and Infinity* in the formulation of practical and political philosophies grounded on Levinas's philosophy. This should cause little surprise since *Totality and Infinity* was the only major book published by Levinas during the time in which Dussel began to articulate his philosophy of liberation. The problem with *Totality and Infinity* is that the relation between self and Other is put in terms of a traditional metaphysical opposition that can only relate two elements by first granting them total independence. Even though the self can never possess the Other, the Other seems to appear and confront the self. The account of the relation between self and Other as a face-to-face encounter still seems to carry with it the traces of the description of the encounter that can be reduced to the question about the expansion of the subject's horizons of meaning. From here, Levinas's restatement of the relation between self and Other in terms of the relation between the rich and the poor in *Totality and Infinity* clearly invites a literal, and not a metaphorical, reading.

These are some of the pitfalls that an attempt to link Levinas's work with ethico-political dynamics needs to overcome. Dussel's philosophy of liberation, however, has tended to reduplicate and intensify the problems in Levinas's account instead of overcoming them. In the next section I will critically revise Dussel's appropriation of Levinas. I will attempt to show that while Dussel's appropriation is deeply problematic in many respects, he nonetheless uncovers another area of enquiry into which the work of Levinasian *reduction* must be extended. In this sense, Dussel's work becomes indispensable for the proper articulation of a critical discourse that aims to reduce the Said and to open possibilities for more humane ways of being in the world with other human beings.

ENRIQUE DUSSEL: FROM PHENOMENOLOGY TO LIBERATION

> *What are phenomenology and existentialism if not the description of an "I" or a Dasein from which opens a world, always one's own? What are all the critical schools, or even those that launch themselves in search of utopia, but the affirmation of the center as the future possibility of "the same"?* —ENRIQUE DUSSEL[33]

The path from phenomenology to liberation is worked out in Dussel's *Filosofía de la liberación* (Philosophy of liberation). Like Levinas's *Totality and Infinity* this text begins with a reflection on the role of the idea of war in dominant Western thought.

> From Heraclitus to Karl von Clausewitz and Henry Kissinger, "war is the origin of everything," if by "everything" one understands the order or system that world dominators control by their power and armies. We are at war—a cold war for those who wage it, a hot war for those who suffer it. . . . Space as a battlefield, as a geography studied to destroy an enemy, as a territory with fixed frontiers, is very different from the abstract idealization of empty space of Newton's physics or the existential space of phenomenology. (PL 1)

The ideal of war finds direct expression, according to Dussel, in the emergence of an imperial cartography that delineates the contours of the world according to its violent intentionality. Like Levinas in *Totality and Infinity*, Dussel reflects on the ties between the ideal of war and the search for knowledge. In the metropolis of the empire, philosophy becomes the expression of the dominating and violent subject. The philosophy of the *ego cogito* expresses for Dussel the experiential dimension of an imperial subject that takes other subjects and cultures as manipulable objects. True creative and critical philosophy, in contrast, is born, for Dussel, in the periphery. For Dussel, the periphery becomes the space in which it is clear that the oppressed cannot be conceived as a thing but as a suffering human being. Initially born in the periphery, philosophy is critical at first, but then it becomes dogmatic when it turns to the center and takes the form of a rationalization of the experience of Imperial Man.

The philosophy of the center tends, for Dussel, to interpret Being as the totality of the limited experience of subjects in a position of power. Its myopic point of view leads it to propose and defend a peculiar formulation of ontological relations in political terms. Ontology therefore becomes a rationalization of the world of war in which the politics of empire reigns. For Dussel, as for Levinas, though for different reasons, ontology becomes a philosophy of power and war. In contrast, the philosophical thought that emerges from the periphery expresses the reality of being an outsider. With the ensuing heightened critical perception philosophers from the periphery are able to articulate a more comprehensive and adequate account of reality. According to Dussel, "The philosophy that knows how to ponder this reality, the de facto world reality, not from the perspective of the center of political, economic, or military power but from beyond the frontiers of that world, from the periphery—this philosophy will not be ideological. Its reality is the whole earth;

for it the "wretched of the earth" (who are not non-being) are also real" (PL 10–11). The reference to the "wretched of the earth" in this passage announces the presence of Frantz Fanon, who is invoked later in the text as a precursor of the philosophy of liberation (see PL 13). It is clear, then, that Dussel's own *Philosophy of Liberation* is taken by him as the most systematic and self-reflective work in liberation thought. Dussel decidedly attempts to leave ontology and phenomenology behind, and, by departing from the periphery, to articulate a genuine critical metaphysics. Dussel's pretensions are clear: "Against the classic ontology of the center, from Hegel to Marcuse ... a philosophy of liberation is rising from the periphery, from the oppressed, from the shadow that the light of Being has not been able to illuminate. Our thought sets out from non-Being, nothingness, otherness, exteriority, the mystery of no-sense. It is, then, a 'barbarian' philosophy" (PL 14).

Dussel's conception of metaphysics is grounded, like Levinas's, in a peculiar conception of exteriority. Exteriority is for Levinas that which characterizes the "otherwise than being, or beyond essence." It is alterity, or the Other qua Other. Insofar as alterity surpasses totality and Being, it is, as Dussel puts it so well, trans-ontological. While Heideggerian ontology highlights the relevance of the difference between beings and Being, or ontological difference, Levinas points to the difference between Being and what remains beyond Being, or, following Dussel's own terminology, what may be referred to as the trans-ontological difference. For Levinas we can find the traces of the trans-ontological difference in the lived existence of the human. Ultimately resistant to a domestication by any given form of meaning, exteriority itself, or the Other qua Other, is, however, never present. In order to maintain exteriority it must remain, as it was previously pointed out, invisible. These peculiar features of exteriority account for Levinas's adoption of a genetic approach: the Other does not appear to a subject but rather intervenes in the process of the emergence of the self. The Other is, thus, not present, but it is always already disturbing and dislocating the contentment of the self. The Other thus becomes a continuous source of destabilization. That is why the Other in Levinas never becomes a ground and can only inspire a critical philosophy of reduction.

Dussel's conception of exteriority is remarkably different from that of Levinas. While for Levinas the Other is ultimately never present to the self, for Dussel the Other is a concrete human subject in a position of subordination. The Other for him is precisely the subject who lives on the periphery. It is the poor and the oppressed (PL 59). In this way Dussel identifies metaphysical exteriority with exclusion. The Other is not so much the Other qua Other but the Other qua poor. Dussel (con)fuses here the "beyond Being" with the non-being. In our own terms, Dussel fuses the trans-ontological and the sub-ontological difference. The sub-ontological difference refers to the distinction between Being and that to which its very being is denied. More precisely, it highlights the appearance of the non-being/non-Other, or, what I would refer to as the sub-alter. The sub-alter is not the Other qua Other, not even the alter ego—the Other like myself—but that "other" that is no-Other; it is not the irreplaceable and loved, or the replaceable and respected other, but the eliminable Other. It is the object of indifference and hate. The sub-alter is that "thing" without which, from the perspective of the master, meaning would flow uninterrupted. The sub-alter is the concrete human being who is rendered as less than a "thing" or as an animal. At best, it is *seen* as the combination of a man and a beast. The sub-alter is created by a system of subordination. It therefore appears in reality not so much as another human being but as someone who is somehow less than a human being. Levinas's work raises the problem of how to connect the relation between the self and the trace of the Other with a reality shaped by dehumanization, that is, a reality in which we do not find only alter egos, but sub-others. I have suggested that while an account of the constitutive role of the Other qua Other in the formation of subjectivity requires a genetic approach, an examination of the world of subordination requires, among others, an existential phenomenological approach. The proper thematization of oppression and suffering requires an enquiry into the lived experience of those involved. The point of contact between the genetic and the existential approach is found, then, in the formulation of the many ways in which the ethical contact between human beings is both constitutive of their humanity and betrayed by them in different contexts, situations, as well as in sociopolitical and economical systems. I am referring to a productive elaboration of the contacts between the trans-ontological and the sub-ontological difference. I have suggested that this elaboration is pursued in the task of reduction, and more specifically in the de-colonial reduction, a reduction that seeks not only to understand but also to change the conditions of lordship and bondsman.

In his *Philosophy of Liberation* Dussel takes a more direct path, but also, in my view, a more problematic one, to spell out the connections between the trans- and sub-ontological levels. He discards phenomenology as a suitable area of enquiry and then proceeds by applying

Levinasian categories to concrete experience. It is only by doing this that he can propose a direct opposition between phenomenology and liberation. The collapse of categories articulated at the genetic level to the concrete existential and geopolitical level is bound to create a series of problematic articulations. First, it is precisely by applying Levinas's terminology directly to geopolitics that Dussel becomes most radically anti-Levinasian. For Dussel, the Other becomes first a concrete subject, then a certain people with a history, and finally *myself*, that is, the poor of Latin America and the philosophy of the periphery. For Levinas, in contrast, the Other qua Other is always Other than myself. That is why the Other remains for Levinas a constant disrupting factor and never becomes a ground for knowledge. In Dussel's *Philosophy of Liberation* the geopolitical regions where dehumanization reigns immediately gain epistemological privilege. His own philosophy of liberation is, indeed, authenticated by this defensive strategy. It is because of this characteristic that Dussel's thought has appeared as dogmatic and arrogant for some.[34] Michael Barber has defended Dussel from such attacks by spelling out the Levinasian roots of Dussel's philosophy of liberation.[35] He argues that the "foundationalism" in Dussel's thought can be related to the "indemonstrability" of Levinas's own discourse. Barber, however, does not consider the differences between Levinas's genetic phenomenology and Dussel's geopolitics of knowledge. He also fails in distinguishing between trans-ontological and sub-ontological alterity. Contrary to what Barber thinks, Dussel's "foundationalism" is different from Levinas's "post-foundational foundationalism" because, ultimately, for Levinas, unlike for Dussel, the Other never becomes the ground for the articulation of a new philosophy. In contrast, Dussel validates his own work and gives himself authority by portraying the role of the Other himself. And, since, for Levinas, the Other elicits a responsible response, then Dussel's own words acquire the force of moral commands. His discourse gains normative force a priori. Here Dussel, without intending to, repeats the gesture of the master, which consists precisely in legitimizing his own discourse a priori. In all of this, Dussel ignores the realization that the normative aspects that Levinas articulates in his conception of ethics as first philosophy are, as we have seen, hardly justified outside of the realm of genetic considerations and deeply problematic when they are applied directly to concrete reality.

Dussel's direct application of Levinas's ethical metaphysics to concrete historical reality is clearly behind some of the epistemological and ethical problems in his work. Santiago Castro-Gómez has pointed out some difficulties in the portrayal of Latin America as the Other of Europe. He argues that the category of the Other is overly generalizing and that it ends up fomenting a forgetfulness of the particular "others" in Latin America.[36] Depicting Latin America as the Other of Europe has thus a double role: on the one hand, it opens the space for an allegedly new way of thinking, and, on the other, it unifies the diversity of a continent into a single subject. In both ways, Castro-Gómez argues, Dussel's work stays within the boundaries of the binary and totalizing European modern thought. Nowhere is this problem more clear than in Dussel's foreword to the first volume of his *Filosofía ética de la liberación*: "From 'Alterity' emerges a new thinking which is not dialectic but analectic. Gradually, we introduce ourselves in what is unknown to modern philosophy . . . , creating a Latin American anthropology with the pretension of representing the fourth age of philosophy and the authentic post-imperial contemporary philosophy."[37]

The categories of Levinas's thought help Dussel to legitimize his own thinking in unconvincing and problematic ways. The same categories lead him to articulate disturbing ethical statements. This is most clear in his association of ontology, the philosophy of the Same, and homosexuality. He argues that the homosexuality of the ancient Greeks was clearly related to their fascination with the philosophy of the Same and with ontology.[38] The metaphysics of liberation ends up becoming not only the Other of Europe, but also the Other of traditionally excluded groups of human beings. It claims a privileged status as an other, and then it proceeds to create its own others.

Dussel's analyses are marked by a problematic interpretation and appropriation of Levinas's work. He rejects a phenomenological approach and proceeds to apply Levinasian categories to the concrete level. Even though Dussel cites Fanon as a precursor of a philosophy of liberation, he fails to learn from him that existential phenomenology is crucial for the proper articulation of the problem of oppression. Accounting for the intricate ways in which domination takes place requires an examination of the lived experience of dominated subjects. Following this approach, Fanon, in contrast to Dussel, makes a distinction between normal and abnormal homosexuality. Abnormal sexuality, either homosexual or heterosexual, is for Fanon that which obeys a racist dynamic of desire. This dynamic appears in unsuspected places. As Fanon points out, "The Negrophobic woman is in fact nothing but a putative sexual partner—just as the Negrophobic man is a repressed homosexual" (BSWM 156). Since for the anti-black racist the black symbolizes the biological (BSWM

167) and, in particular, the genital (BSWM 170, 180), the fear of the black man represents at the same time a fascination with him. Fanon believes that this perverted dynamic of desire explains why ultimately prostitution becomes, for homosexual Martiniqueans, a means of livelihood in Europe (BSWM 180). The complexities of the logics of oppression clearly indicate that the indiscriminate application of metaphysical categories to social practices obscures, rather than illuminates, the true sources of oppression and domination.

What we have then is that, instead of superseding Levinas and Fanon, Dussel not only seems to betray a fundamental part of their contributions, but also puts at risk the very liberating aspirations of his own work. When examined from the perspective of Levinas's critical interventions, Dussel's early liberation philosophy appears to (con)fuse the metaphysical aspect of Otherness with the hierarchical relation between selves and concrete others. This (con)fusion takes new aspects as the Levinasian conception of the self-Other relationship is then used as a trope to interpret, diagnose, and critique existing social and geopolitical relations. But the problem is not only that Levinasian ethics cannot be directly applied to concrete ethical relations. Another issue to consider is that, as Fanon suggested, ethics finds problematic expressions in the colonial world. Rather than self and enslaved Others, racialized and colonial subjects take the form of non-self/non-others.[39] Thus, ethics is suspended and ethical categories lose their efficiency. From this point of view, Dussel seems to commit a double error: first he mistranslates Levinasian ethics to concrete reality and then he uses the translated terms for the analysis of a context in which ethical categories do not seem to apply in the first place.

In response to the Fanonian critique, one must indicate that Dussel is fully aware that what is needed in the colonial world is not ethics as such but political action. Fanon and Dussel coincide in the idea that politics must be oriented by ethics—although Dussel has added more recently that politics has its own autonomous principles.[40] Where they depart from each other is in how to go about doing this, particularly in regard to the use of phenomenology. Inspired by Levinas, Dussel reaches the conclusion in his *Philosophy of Liberation* that phenomenology was irreparably tied to the ontology of the Same and that it did not serve to advance a project of liberation. In order to escape such complicity with ontology and power, Dussel appropriates Levinas's ethical categories and applies them to the understanding of cultural dynamics, social relationships, and geopolitical structures. For Levinas, however, it was clear that phenomenology still occupied an important role in elucidating lived experience. And it was precisely in this way that phenomenology was central to Fanon. For Fanon, the critical analysis of a world deprived of ethics needs to begin with an elucidation of the lived experience of the non-self/non-others. This was his radical humanistic insight. And in this, his position was different from that of Levinas, who focused quite exclusively on showing the relevance of Jewish contributions to Europe without adopting a more consistent *de-colonial attitude*. Yet while Fanon articulates with detail the existential dimensions of the colonial drama, he does not articulate with depth its historical roots and its complex geo-political dimensions. It is here that one of Dussel's main strengths lies. We will see this in the next chapter.

6

ENRIQUE DUSSEL'S CONTRIBUTION TO THE DE-COLONIAL TURN
FROM THE CRITIQUE OF MODERNITY TO TRANSMODERNITY

The elucidation of Dussel's contribution to the ethico-political de-colonial turn—which finds partial expression in the work of Levinas and a more explicit articulation in the work of Fanon—can only begin on the basis of Levinasian and Fanonian critiques of Dussel's early efforts. At the same time, a precise formulation of the de-colonial turn and the critique of modernity as a paradigm of war would be fundamentally incomplete without engaging Dussel's work and locating the relevance of his philosophy and ethics of liberation. In the last chapter, I critically analyzed core ideas in Dussel's philosophy of liberation, arguing that Dussel's appropriation of Levinas collapses metaphysics all too readily into geopolitical relations, and that the unmediated application of Levinasian categories to social reality leads Dussel to problematic arguments that could have been avoided through a consideration of existential phenomenology, and more specifically Fanonian sociogenesis. Dussel overextends Levinas's utility and radically minimizes Fanon's contributions to the project of formulating a philosophy of liberation. In this chapter, we will see that there exists a prehistory to Dussel's philosophy of liberation, which explains Dussel's reliance on Levinas's Jewish intervention into phenomenological and ontological discourse. This prehistory also explains Dussel's interest in history and geopolitical relations, which leads him to contribute uniquely to the critique of Hegel and to the formulation of the geo-political dimensions of the de-colonial turn.

Both Levinas's ethical metaphysics and Fanon's sociogenesis of master and slave forms of consciousness in modernity can also be understood as critical responses to Hegel in that they focus on philosophical accounts of subjectivity and sociality. Where Hegel saw dialectical movement, Levinas and Fanon point to the paradoxical character of ethics, and in the case of Fanon, to the need for a political inauguration of the ethical in conditions of sub-alterity. Levinas and Fanon also reflect critically on Hegel's philosophy of history, but they do so in a very limited manner. Levinas aims to legitimate what he regards as the holy history of the Jewish people beyond Hegel's account of history as expressed in terms of the unfolding of Spirit.[1] Fanon protests vigorously against the idea of European superiority (in any form, with exclusive reference to Greek roots or in a more open-minded way) and calls for a new humanism beyond modern conceptions of the nation-state, as Hegel articulated them. Like Levinas and Fanon, Dussel is critical of Hegel's ontology and philosophy of history, but he expresses more clearly and to a greater extent than the others the limits of Hegel's conception of history and geopolitical imaginary.

This chapter begins with an exploration of Dussel's interest in history—an interest that is not only academic but also very personal—before then turning to an explanation of his philosophy of liberation. There are questions of identity at stake in Dussel's historical reflections, questions that point Dussel in the right direction, but that ultimately limit his explorations. It is only through a "teleological suspension of identity" that he is able to overcome the limits of his identitarian questions. It is precisely at the point where identity is suspended that phenomenology once again becomes an important tool for Dussel. After exploring the virtues and limitations of Dussel's concerns with identity, and the (albeit relative) overcoming of those limits, I compare his reflections on the genesis of history or genealogy with other such views. Although I make reference to Hegel and Husserl, understanding Dussel's critique of them leads me to focus on Reinhart Koselleck's account of the pathogenesis of the Enlightenment. Koselleck's account emphasizes the relevance of the philosophy of history in the aftermath of the Enlightenment and its role in generating serious pathologies in European society. Dussel broadens the scope of Koselleck's investigations and provides crucial links between the pathogenesis of Europe and the colonial reality. My account of Dussel's own genealogy of modernity is based on *The Invention of the Americas: Eclipse of "the Other" and the Myth of Modernity*. I interpret *The Invention of the Americas* as a "de-colonial reduction" of European philosophy of history that opens up a temporal and spatial imaginary that is essential to understanding the meaning and significance of the de-colonial turn. As a result, after the Levinasian and Fanonian critiques of Dussel, it is Dussel's reflection on history that allows one to understand better the revolutionary nature of Levinas's and Fanon's interventions, along with those offered by other figures of the de-colonial turn. *The Invention of the Americas* also offers a phenomenology of the "I conquer," which complements Fanon's phenomenology of the racial self in *Black Skin, White Masks*, and these combined phenomenologies—alongside Dussel's genealogy of modernity and Levinas's genetic phenomenology—provide a view of hegemonic modernity as a paradigm of war.

DUSSEL AND THE QUESTION OF LATIN AMERICAN IDENTITY

Dussel's central contribution to the epistemological and political project that emerges from the intersection of Levinas and Fanon resides in his view of history, the relevance of geopolitics, and the critique of Eurocentrism. But, like many of his other views, his ideas about these topics are partially shaped by his appropriation of Levinas, as well as—one must add here—a peculiar concern with identity. A concern with identity and legitimate belonging is central to many of the figures whose work has been analyzed in this text. This should not be surprising. Most of these figures are responding to a situation of crisis that is intimately bound up with ideas and values that have served as sources for modern subjectivity and identity, defining the identity of Europeans, Jews, "black folk," Latin Americans, and others.

For colonized and racialized peoples identity is always contested, since it is tied to a power structure and an imaginary that militates against their very existence. For this reason, questions of liberation and identity are central to philosophical discourses articulated from the position of sub-alter peoples. As Lewis Gordon has pointed out, some authors who work on this subject highlight one of these elements over the other, while others attempt to strike a balance between the two.[2] While Dussel's philosophy of liberation focuses on the question of liberation, his historical investigations have for the most part been shaped by the question of identity, responding as they do to the question: "Who am I as a Latin American?" It is this question that leads him firstly to reflect on the roots of Latin American culture and to identify the place of Latin America in world history, and later on to the articulation of a philosophy of liberation that is deemed to be explicitly Latin American. Thus, even though Dussel's philosophy accentuates the problem of liberation, it also aims to provide a response to questions of identity, particularly in his historical accounts. His work seeks to show that Latin America not only has a place in history but also its own distinct philosophy, and in this respect his project is not so different from Levinas's attempt to uncover the Jewish roots of Europe. Both figures attempt to gain recognition and to grant ontological weight to their cultures through philosophy. However, as we will see, there are still significant differences between them, which allow Dussel to overcome some of Levinas's limits and problematic formulations.

The centrality of questions regarding cultural roots and identity in Dussel's work can be traced back to different elements in his intellectual formation. In many ways, Dussel's concern for these questions reflects the position of a Latin American *mestizo* who no longer believes that he is simply or primarily European. At various points, Dussel explains the effect that his first trip to Europe had on him. Before reaching Europe, he had stopped in different parts of the Americas and the west coast of Africa, and by the time that he got to Lisbon and then on to Spain he had concluded that he was not European.

> With my trip to Europe—in my case, crossing the Atlantic by boat in 1957—we discovered ourselves to be "Latin Americans," or at least no longer "Europeans," from the moment that we disembarked in Lisbon or Barcelona. The differences were obvious and could not be concealed. Consequently, the problem of culture—humanistically, philosophically, and existentially—was an obsession for me: "Who are we culturally? What is our historical identity?" This was not a question of the possibility of describing this "identity" objectively; it was something prior. It was the existential anguish of knowing oneself.[3]

Dussel's surprise at not being European presupposes the strong identification with Europe that he had derived partly from his family and partly from his studies, and it would be difficult to overestimate the impact of the latter:

> The philosophy that we studied set out from the Greeks, in whom we saw our most remote lineage. The Amerindian World had no presence in our studies, and none of our professors would have been able to articulate the origin of philosophy with reference to indigenous peoples. Moreover, the ideal philosopher was one who was familiar with the precise details of classical western philosophers and their contemporary developments. There existed no possibility whatsoever for a specifically Latin American philosophy. It is difficult to evoke in the present the firm hold that the European model of philosophy had on us (since at that moment in Argentina, there was still no reference to the United States). Germany and France had complete hege-

mony, especially in South America (although this was not the case in Mexico, Central America, or the Hispanic, French, or British Caribbean).[4]

The irony of the situation is that it was not until his first trip to Europe that Dussel came to realize that he could not consider himself European, and that he was not going to devote any more energy toward trying to become one. Instead, he took on the task of elucidating Latin American identity.

This rejection of assimilation into European standards and interest in finding the meaning of Latin American identity represented a step forward in the establishment of a de-colonial consciousness, but they were by no means sufficient. For the very question of a *Latin* American identity already privileges European roots. Dussel's disenchantment with European philosophy reflected the anxiety of a descendant of European immigrants whose rejection of Europeanness was premised on an implicit identification with it. The fact that he focused during the 1960s on writing three volumes on Hellenic, Semitic, and Christian humanism certainly strengthens this impression. The roots that Dussel was concerned with—Semitic roots that are to some extent disavowed by many Europeans—remained European roots nonetheless.

Of the three conceptions of humanism that Dussel studied, he was most critical of the Hellenic and the Christian and quite positive toward the Semitic. To some extent, that put him close to Levinas's position, but Dussel had not read or known Levinas at that point. However, Dussel was, like Levinas, responding critically to Heidegger, who arguably overvalorized Greek philosophy. While Dussel was still under the influence of Paul Ricoeur's cultural hermeneutics and to some extent Heidegger's ontology, the value that he found in Semitic humanism would lead him in a different direction. The importance of embodiment, the appreciation of materiality, and prophetic critique would gradually become central for Dussel's work, from his *Philosophy of Liberation* and his studies on Marx to his most recent *Ética de la liberación en la edad de la globalización y de la exclusión*.[5] And, at least initially, this orientation hinged on his question about Latin American identity. As he puts it in the prologue to *Semitic Humanism*:

> We are going to analyze here a totally different tradition [from the Hellenic]. ... This study concerns a series of problems, which at first sight might look completely disconnected from the concerns of contemporary Latin Americans; but, if we reflect deeper on the very contents of our own actual consciousness, if we want to found the values of our own culture, then we will

understand that this is not a gratuitous and futile investigation, but one that is of great necessity to explore scientifically the bases of our own Latin American "world."[6]

This investment in *Latin* Americanness and the efforts to examine European roots—even though this was done critically and in certain respects counter to the current of the times—testify to a certain complicity with the European vision of history and being. Dussel's trip to Europe decentered his identification with Europe, but only partially. This becomes clear in an interesting episode in Dussel's life already alluded to in chapter 5 when, while working as a carpenter in Israel, he recounts Latin American history to Paul Gauthier. Dussel states that he became very enthusiastic about the virtues of Fernando Pizarro, who conquered the Inca empire with only a few men. Even though Dussel had come to question the character of his assumed affiliation with Europe, it was clear where his sympathies lay. It was, however, in that moment—his conversation with Gauthier—when his sense of identification would suffer another blow (the first having occurred on his trip to Europe). Dussel realized that he had yet to understand Latin America from the point of view of its underside. Dussel refers to this point as the "'originary experience' that became the base for every other future epistemological and hermeneutic transformation."[7] From this point on, the question of identity would be fundamentally tied to the question of an ethics and politics of liberation. His appreciation of the Semitic ethos—a cultural source that gave value to the materiality of life and that offered resources to criticize poverty—would from that point on relate not only to the question of identity but also to the question of liberation.

While it is clear that Dussel's interest in Semitic humanism cannot be reduced to matters of faith or identity, one might point out that his clarifications and celebrations of the Semitic ethos were achieved at the expense of the invisibility of other cultural elements in the Americas, such as the indigenous and the black. And indeed, Dussel sometimes writes as if it is *only* Semitic cultures that have an appreciation for corporeality and a concern for the poor. In Dussel's work, there is a tendency to privilege Semitic ethics to the point that it sometimes gives us the impression that he opposes Hellenocentrism by offering Semitic-centrism as an alternative. Yet, while some of this may be true, the situation is more complex, as Dussel makes clear in his preface to *Hellenistic Humanism*:

> Our work is only a prolegomenon because it allows us to "know how to situate" ourselves, that is to say, it is a history of philosophy, or even history

of pre-philosophy. The work that we present here represents the beginning of such prolegomenon. It will be necessary, after having exposed the pre-philosophical structures of the Greek and Semitic world, to face the evolution of such structures in the world of Roman-European Christendom and then arrive in the Iberian Peninsula. *With that, we will only offer an account of the historical position of the conqueror. We will still need to study the Amerindian world, the "clash" with the Hispanic world, the constitution of Latin America, as well as the evolution of colonial Christendom and neocolonial nations in order to adequately work on the current pre-philosophical world in our America, which is the ultimate object of our investigations.*[8]

Dussel penned these lines in 1963. *Hellenic Humanism* was already completed by 1961, and *Semitic Humanism*, the second volume of the trilogy, was completed in 1964. The third part of the trilogy, *Dualism in the Anthropology of Christendom*, was finished in 1968, but before that—in 1966—Dussel wrote an unpublished volume of almost three hundred single-spaced pages with the title *Hypotheses for the Study of Latin America in Universal History*. In this volume, Dussel touches upon what he had suggested in 1963: the cultural roots of the indigenous world that later came to be known as the Americas.

Hypotheses is divided into two parts. At the end, Dussel promises a third part, but this never materialized during the subsequent two decades. The first part focuses on the historical trajectory and cultural roots of the inhabitants of the Americas prior to the arrival of the Europeans. The second focuses on the historical trajectory and cultural roots of so-called indo-Europeans and Semitic peoples, who were present on the Iberian Peninsula at the time of the conquest—he refers to Christians, Muslims, and Jews. This volume is, in general terms, very ambitious and erudite, but it is also deeply problematic at some points. This is due to the fact that indigenous cultures appear as irremediably prehistorical forms that, while essential for Latin American being, are immeasurably distant from Latin American historical consciousness and a universal civilization of technology and science. For Dussel, history, properly speaking, only emerges with the Semitic world, and hence Latin America owes its historical consciousness solely to the latter. Thus while the first part of the *Hypotheses* concludes with a section entitled "Amerindia in Universal Pre-History," the second finishes with a section entitled "Significance of Judeo-Christianity for Latin American Culture." The problem with Dussel's approach in this project lies not only in his Semitic-centrism, but also in the fact that Latin America had become for him by this point what Europe had represented for the defenders of the Eurocentrism he criticized: the center, telos, and goal of a historical process that culminated in the consciousness of whoever was considered the most adequate representative of that spiritual and geographical figure called Latin America.

In *Hypotheses*, Dussel criticizes the Eurocentrism of Hegel's philosophy of history, but he ends up reproducing his own "continentalist" vision. By a "continentalist" vision, I mean the conception of a heterogeneous group of human beings in terms of the unity of a spiritual shape or form, which tends to be associated with the geographical notion of a continent.[9] The continent encompasses the nation-state, so it is not defined by unity of language or religion, and in Dussel's case it is defined by an allegedly common historical consciousness, that of being Latin Americans. It is on this basis that Dussel regards indigenous cultures as prehistorical, which leads one to suspect that surviving indigenous peoples do not entirely belong in the spiritual shape that we call Latin America. This view thereby results in an image of a "past" that survives in the "present."

In his early historical narrative, Dussel reproduces some of the problems identified with the philosophers that he criticizes. The impetus toward continentality is found in philosophers such as Hegel, but it also appears in thinkers such as Husserl. In Hegel, Spirit moves through time from region to region (excluding Africa) until reaching its climax in Western Europe. Western European humanity is characterized by mature notions of freedom that culminate in the formation of the nation-state. Husserl does not give any credence to Hegelian Spirit, but for him Europe represented a "spiritual shape" oriented by the ideas of reason and critique. The implications of this view were profound for Husserl: "No matter how hostile they may be toward one another, the European nations nevertheless have a particular inner kinship of spirit which runs through them all, transcending national differences. There is something like a sibling relationship which gives us all in this sphere the consciousness of homeland."[10] Husserl goes on to argue that the "something" in question is an idea and a set of goals that make Europeans different from other nations and that make other nations want to Europeanize themselves, while Europeans, "if they understand themselves properly, would never desire to Indianize themselves," for example.[11] There are profound problems with Husserl's formulations of his continentalist vision. He states, for instance, that by virtue of the universality of reason, "even the Papuan" must be considered a man as opposed to a beast, but that "the humanity of higher human nature or reason requires . . . a genuine philosophy," and this is precisely what Europeans have come to possess.[12] Appeals to the uniqueness of continental spiritual shapes thereby serve to transpose racism from biology and culture to philosophy itself.

Continentalist visions are centered on a definition of space, but they are grounded on notions of time. Hegel cemented his own view of the superiority of European civilization and culture in "the philosophy of world history." Dussel's own project is partly inspired by Hegel's efforts, although in a negative way. He seeks to contest the Hegelian view that regards Europe as the climax of world history and that regards other regions as secondary or totally insignificant. Dussel's reproduction of a "continentalist" vision is clearly tied to Hegel's philosophy of world history, which brought together different elements that had already existed in the discourse of the philosophy of history and the Enlightenment. We should take a careful look at these discourses in order to determine more precisely the limitations and the advantages of Dussel's critical response to them.

THE PHILOSOPHY OF HISTORY IN THE AGE OF ENLIGHTENMENT

Hegel's "philosophy of world history" was clearly tied to the philosophy of history, which according to Reinhart Koselleck, was an expression of the Enlightenment in its "hypocritical stage."[13] For Koselleck, the philosophy of history was born as a tool of the rising bourgeoisie in their opposition to absolutism. It allowed the bourgeois critics of absolutism to claim the end of the latter as a result of the inexorable forces of a process defined in terms of moral progress. What began as "critique" ended up as the idea of the future as a moral utopia in which the bourgeoisie found a refuge, but also under whose auspices it obtained self-certainty, security, and power.[14] However, with the philosophy of history, what provided power and certainty also led to self-deception, since it was believed that political changes were going to come about as part of an inexorable moral progress within European civilization. According to Koselleck, the philosophy of history represented a "qualitative step . . . which prevented all participants from gaining insight into their own delusion."[15] This lack of insight and ambiguous relation to politics was costly: thanks in part to the work done by the philosophy of history at the time, "the Enlightenment succumbed to a Utopian image which, deceptively propelling it, helped to produce contradictions that could not be resolved in practice and prepared the way for the Terror and for dictatorships."[16]

What Koselleck has in mind is nothing less than German National Socialism, "whose loss of reality and Utopian self-exaltation had resulted in hitherto unprecedented crimes."[17]

With his description of the dialectic of enlightened criticism, Koselleck seeks explicitly to offer a "genetic theory of the modern world" that links the ambiguities of the Enlightenment with Nazism. The text is a product of the early period following the Second World War, when many Europeans were trying to explain the root causes of what they had lived during the war. Koselleck explains that he was also thinking about the cold war and the increasing utopianism of the two emerging superpowers. What is surprising about the text is that while the author partially chronicles a path that goes from critique to utopia to racist terror and genocide, race is not mentioned; nor does it form a part of his analysis of the "pathogenesis of modern society." Koselleck states that "bourgeois society was the first to cover the globe,"[18] but there is little reference to the ways in which the emerging bourgeois society conceived of itself in relation to other peoples, including marginalized and racialized groups in its midst. Yet, as Koselleck himself explains, the bourgeois philosophy of history was from the outset a global philosophy of history, which made direct reference to places outside of Europe. For example, Koselleck writes about the influence of the work of Guillaume-Thomas-François Raynal (Abbé Raynal), who proposed in his influential *Histoire philosophique et politique des établissements et du commerce des Européens dans les deux Indes* (1770) that the relationship between the so-called New and Old Worlds forms the basis of an articulation of a philosophy of history that posits an irreparable breach between the *ancien* and the *nouveau* regimes.[19] Abbé Raynal understood the New World as one of "natural innocence" and the Old World as characterized by tyranny. The struggle of the American colonists against the European metropoles represented the divide between the emerging bourgeoisie in Europe and absolutism. And just as the innocent colonists were destined to win, so too were the European bourgeoisie. The lesson that Abbé Raynal derived from the War of Independence fought between the United Kingdom and what is now the United States was, in Koselleck's words, that "the end of military conflict lay in the moral starting point, and thus its morally certain outcome justified the civil war."[20]

While Koselleck notes the crucial role played by the New World in the philosophy of history articulated by the European bourgeoisie, he does not examine its full implications. One must not forget that settlers in what is now the United States as well as in other places in the Americas were simultaneously looking, as it were, "up" to Europe and "down" to the indigenous populations and black slaves in their midst. Abbé Raynal's contribution was to argue that while settlers in what later became the United States may have been looking "up" to the absolutist European order, morally speaking it was they who were "up." And those who were "down" morally speaking—that is, the European kings—had their days numbered. The supposedly superior moral position of the settlers and their subsequent revolution and victory were seen as an anticipation of the achievements of the European bourgeoisie itself. The settlers' victory, however—and this is what Koselleck fails to analyze—implied not only "independence" from the European absolutist order, but also a direct dominion over their indigenous and enslaved populations. Indigenous peoples and black slaves continued to be subjugated, but this now took place under the auspices of the independent and secular nation-state, and not by the decrees of European kingdoms. The depiction of settlers as "innocent" thus legitimized not only their victory over the colonialism of the absolutist order, but also the subjugation of racialized populations in their territories. And one thus wonders if the perception of the bourgeoisie in Europe as "innocent" and their comparison to the American settlers was not actually serving a double purpose: a simultaneous legitimization of their struggle against absolutism and of their own forms of colonization and racialization elsewhere in the globe.

To be fair to Raynal, it must be noted that his legacy is in this sense ambiguous. His *Histoire philosophique* included a harsh critique of slavery and a justification of anti-slave revolt that was widely known at the time. In his *Black Jacobins*, C. L. R. James hypothesizes that Raynal's work could have influenced the leader of the Haitian revolution, Toussaint L'Ouverture.[21] Others, such as Michel-Rolph Trouillot, however, doubt the possibility.[22] In any case, what is clear is that which parts of Raynal's *Histoire philosophique* were of influence and how those parts would be interpreted could evoke different philosophies of history according to the reader, particularly if he or she belonged to such contrasting positions as the European bourgeoisie on the one hand and slaves of the African Diaspora in the Americas on the other. Koselleck exclusively focuses on the impact of Raynal's work in the emerging philosophy of history of the European bourgeoisie. If he had been more attentive to other dimensions of the *Histoire philosophique*, he would probably have noted the serious problems to which the bourgeois philosophy of history was giving rise, beyond the effects that it had in Europe.

What Koselleck misses is what would become one of the central points in Mary Louise Pratt's influential study of travel writing and European expansion since the eighteenth century.[23] She shows that at least since 1735 there emerged in Europe a new planetary consciousness that looked at the world through the lenses of science. Following the work of Linnaeus, Europeans conceived of nature as a system that could be classified under precise typologies. This method was scientific, and thus the production of the typologies was understood as value neutral and objective. Scientific expeditions appeared as disinterested activities, even though they served specific commercial and political interests. Pratt shows that this new planetary consciousness, grounded on a scientific perspective, became a means to establish a distinction between the bourgeois perception of the world and its manner of dealing with it, and the violent acts of conquest and enslavement perpetrated by the absolutist order. An anti-conquest discourse became part of scientific discourse, and we see this in the travel writing of the time, which portrayed the emergent bourgeoisie as "innocent" and well intentioned. At this point, two things became clear: first, given its new planetary consciousness, bourgeois authority had a wider scope than that of the absolutists; and second, the new form of colonial rule would increasingly rely on a scientific point of view vis-à-vis a religious one, as the latter had sustained absolutist authority. Thus, appeals to "innocence" were perhaps first made in reference to the differences between absolutist colonial rule and the supposedly disinterested point of view of the bourgeoisie and its new planetary consciousness, which provided new justifications for colonization. Therefore, there is no doubt that the bourgeoisie was interested as much in vanquishing the absolutist order as in redefining and expanding colonial rule. For them, these two things went hand in hand.

To be sure, the association of the European bourgeoisie with the American settlers may have played yet another unmentioned role: making clear that, unlike absolutism, the bourgeoisie were prepared to expand the circle of "lordship" to settlers such as those found in the area that became the United States, who would now begin their own imperial ventures. That is to say, the bourgeoisie were willing to expand the fold of racial and imperial privilege, at least to some extent. Yet, as ironic as it may sound, they were simultaneously cementing their view of inferior races through racial classifications of various kinds. The irony increases if one considers that those who declared themselves innocent because of their allegedly disinterested perspective were precisely those responsible for elevating racism to a previously unseen level, formalizing racist perspectives into a science. Science was, of course, a fundamental part of the secular disciplines that had gained some space in Renaissance-style universities under the absolutist order, and science gradually became the most legitimate form of producing knowledge. Anthropology and Orientalism—as well as the rest of the social sciences—emerged as part of this liberation of science, alongside the solidification of the nation-state form in Europe.[24] In the nineteenth century, as the American settlers in the United States and other places were building nation-states and re-colonizing their racialized subjects, Europe was redefining the way in which it conceived of and related to the rest of the world. In some ways it makes sense to state that there existed a parallel between what American settlers began to do at the national level and what the European bourgeoisie continued to do, in a renewed way, at the international level. Both redefined racial hegemony in light of nationalization and secularization processes at different levels in their societies and, in the case of European countries, at the global level as well. Travel writing and the philosophy of history provided the foundation for understanding these processes not in terms of the achievement of naked power, but in terms of innocence and moral superiority. Perhaps both discourses find a climax in Hegel's philosophy of world history, in which European superiority and the fate of colonial peoples are spelled out not as the result of ideological, economical, and political dynamics, but as the expression of the "travel" of Spirit through different cultures and nations. For Hegel, European dominion is not only a matter of innocence, but also of historical responsibility.

It should be clear by now that understanding the settlers of the thirteen colonies as innocent served to exculpate European bourgeois sins and legitimate a sense of superiority not only in regard to the *anciens*, but also to non-Europeans and people of color. But just as the category of innocence was deployed at the time to legitimize bourgeois opposition to absolutism, the same occurred with the concept of guilt. Immanuel Kant made this point most clearly in his response to the question of the Enlightenment:

> *Enlightenment is mankind's exit from its self-incurred* [or culpable; *verschuldeten Unmündigkeit*] *immaturity. Immaturity is the inability to make use of one's own understanding without the guidance of another. Self-incurred is this inability if its cause lies not in the lack of understanding but rather in the lack of the resolution and the courage to use it without the guidance of another. . . . Laziness and cowardice are the reasons why such a great part of mankind, long after nature has set them free from the guidance of others (nat-uraliter*

majorennes), still gladly remain immature for life and why it is so easy for others to set themselves up as guardians. It is so easy to be immature."[25]

Kant's definition of the Enlightenment shaped the terms of debate beyond what could have been his original intentions: insofar as the absolutist regime resisted the force of enlightened critique it was "guilty" and immature, while the enlightened bourgeoisie was "innocent" and mature. The terms of the Enlightenment view of history were clear by that point: the self-conception and justification of the newly emerging Europe were provided by notions of maturity, and thus historical development, as well as innocence and moral superiority.

It is through this analysis that the relevance of Dussel's intervention becomes clear, for the idea of the "innocence" of enlightened Europeans—and the intrinsic culpability of non-enlightened peoples—is the crux of Dussel's analysis of what he refers to as the "myth of modernity." This "myth" is the core of what Dussel calls Eurocentrism, which is evident in Kant's definition of the Enlightenment: "For Kant, immature culture is culpable and its ethos lazy and cowardly. Today one needs to ask Kant: Ought one to consider an African in Africa or a slave in the United States in the eighteenth century to be culpably immature? What about an indigenous person in Mexico or a Latin American mestizo at a later period?"[26]

Dussel's analysis of the "myth of modernity" suggests that the other side of the "innocence" of the bourgeoisie was precisely the presumption of the culpability of the colonized and the enslaved. By "colonized" I mean, of course, not settlers who were unfairly treated by the European kingdoms and who demanded independence, but rather groups of people who were seen as intrinsically inferior and whose "nature" would be formalized by racial discourse: that is, people of color in general and not, for instance, the American settlers to whom Abbé Raynal primarily referred, who were for the most part Christian and white. These features took on an aura of absolute legitimacy not only in scientific discourse on race but also in the philosophy of history. It is this aura that Dussel has in mind in his critique of Eurocentrism:

> This Eurocentric position—first formulated at the end of the eighteenth century by the French and English "Enlightenment" and the German "Romantics"—reinterpreted all of world history, projecting Europe into the past and attempting to show that everything that happened before had led to Europe's becoming, in Hegel's words, "the end and center of world history." The dis-

tortion of history begins with the Encyclopedists (Montesquieu's *The Spirit of Laws* [1989 (1748)] is a good example) but continues with the English "Enlightenment" thinkers, Kant in Germany, and finally Hegel, for whom the "Orient" was humanity's "infancy" (*Kindheit*), the place of despotism and unfreedom from which the Spirit (*Volksgeist*) would later soar toward the West, as if on a path toward the full realization of liberty and civilization. Since the beginning, Europe had been chosen by Destiny as the final meaning of universal history.[27]

Dussel, like Pratt, draws connections between Enlightenment discourse and the aims of the bourgeoisie on the one hand, and shifts in the perception and justification of enslavement and colonization on the other. While Pratt focuses on travel writing and the discourse of science, Dussel focuses on philosophical writings and the philosophy of history, which situate him closer to Koselleck's interests. Indeed, Dussel's ultimate aim is to offer, like Koselleck, a "genetic theory of modernity," but one that does not ignore the links between the idea of Europe and its intimate connections to the colonial world.

In sum, while Dussel's early reflections on world history were shaped by questions of identity and by a hermeneutic methodology that sometimes led him to fall into essentialist and culturalist arguments, his suspicion of the traditional account of history and Europeanness led him to uncover other problematic aspects of the philosophy of history that do not appear, for instance, in an analysis such as Koselleck's. Koselleck makes clear that there is a need to review critically the meaning and function of the philosophy of history in the late eighteenth century and the nineteenth, since he saw these as connected in his "genetic theory of the modern world" to the criminal utopias that defined political projects in the first half of the twentieth century. Dussel's sojourn to Europe began in the 1950s, and he belonged to the first generation of Latin American intellectuals who went to Europe after the Second World War. Both Koselleck's and Dussel's intellectual projects came to be defined by a new sense of the meaning and possibilities of Europe, after that continent had received a strong blow to its images and promises. Aimé Césaire put it best when he wrote in his *Discourse on Colonialism* (also around the same time) that "Europe is indefensible."[28]

> The fact is that the so-called European civilization . . . as it has been shaped by two centuries of bourgeois rule, is incapable of solving the two major problems to which its existence has given rise: the problem of the proletariat

and the colonial problem; that *Europe is unable to justify itself before the bar of "reason" or before the bar of "conscience"*; and that, *increasingly, it takes refuge in a hypocrisy which is all the more odious because it is less and less likely to deceive.*[29]

Four years before Koselleck had published his critique of the "hypocrisy" of the enlightenment, Césaire was pointing out that "hypocrisy" had characterized bourgeois rule for the last two hundred years (roughly from the beginning of the Enlightenment up to the conclusion of the Second World War), and he added that such "hypocrisy" was "all the more odious" now because "it is less and less likely to deceive." If the philosophy of history represented, as Koselleck argues, the climax of enlightened and bourgeois "hypocrisy," it was just this sort of historical vision that would naturally be undermined and become less and less convincing after the war. Koselleck's own critical analysis of it is an expression of such a lack of conviction. He unveiled the philosophy of history and showed it to be a mechanism of mystification that provided the basis for lethal utopias. Dussel's profound concern with revising the Eurocentric account of history is an expression of the general disenchantment with Europe that emerged after the war. His efforts to critically revise presupposed ideas about the emergence of modernity do not respond purely to questions about identity but reflect larger concerns as well. I propose here that Dussel's work is most successful not when it is driven or strictly defined by a Latin American or a Christian aim to respond to the question of identity in Latin America, but rather when he reflects critically on the larger issue of bourgeois hypocrisy, which was so central in the work of Césaire and Koselleck, among others. To be sure, Césaire's and Dussel's interests are different from those of Koselleck in that the "colonial problem" is of utmost importance for them. And so, Dussel's own "genetic theory of modernity" is one that aims to show the hypocrisy of European bourgeois rule and the production of its lethal ideologies through careful consideration of their effects on the colonial world. Indeed, for Dussel, the genesis of modernity cannot be fully understood without a consideration of the colonial relations that preceded the emergence of the bourgeoisie.

Dussel traces the emergence of modernity as a world system back to the sixteenth century, and according to him, the conquest of the Americas played a crucial role in this process. But so far we have seen that his focus in the 1960s was not so much on modernity as such or the conquest, but rather on premodern sources in the Hellenic, Christian, and Semitic worlds. His *Hypotheses* concluded precisely at the point where he would have elaborated on the meaning and significance of the conquest for Latin American identity. It took him more than two decades to provide this promised step in his project, but by this time it was no longer framed so much by the question of Latin American identity as by a concern for the meaning of the "discovery" and conquest for the native populations. This shift in perspective—perhaps the closest to his pledge after the conversation with Gauthier—was not so much a matter of a personal or individual achievement. Questions about the meaning and significance of the "discovery" and conquest became central in many parts of the Americas and Europe as the five-hundredth anniversary of such events approached. In the years before and after 1992 there appeared a vast quantity of writings on the "discovery" and conquest of the Americas, including Pratt's own *Imperial Eyes* and Walter Mignolo's *The Darker Side of the Renaissance*, among many others. By this time, these represented not only European and *mestizo* voices, but also powerful interventions by indigenous peoples. Here, Dussel sides with indigenous perspectives without identifying himself as or pretending to be indigenous, and as a result the strong concern with *Latin* American identity recedes into the background, and different concerns and questions come to the fore. His reflections on the "covering over" of the faces and voices of the indigenous peoples during the "discovery" and conquest represent his most sophisticated critical analyses of modernity to date. These analyses also represent to some extent a complement and to another extent an alternative to Koselleck's account of the genesis of modernity and to other such accounts articulated, for instance, by the group of thinkers associated with the Frankfurt school, originally established by Felix Weil in 1923. It is to some extent significant, then, that Dussel presented his newly revised "genetic theory of modernity" precisely while he was a visiting professor at Frankfurt.

DUSSEL'S FRANKFURT LECTURES

Dussel's contribution to the critique of Eurocentric accounts of world history is clearest in his Frankfurt lectures, later translated and published under the title of *The Invention of the Americas: Eclipse of "the Other" and the Myth of Modernity*. These lectures were given and originally published in 1992, which marked the fifth centenary of the "discovery" of America. The advent of this important date provoked Dussel to return to the question of locating the position of Latin America in world history, not from the perspective of Pizarro or Cortés, but from the perspective of the Indians. The text is divided into three parts. In the first part Dussel shows the ways in which the "discovery" of the Americas became instrumental in the self-definition of the modern European subject and its history. The year 1492 represented the beginning of the conception of Europe as the center of the world, and European modernity cannot be understood adequately without considering the extent to which this concept has impinged upon the ideas and experiences of the European. Among these we find the ideas that history progresses geographically from east to west and that Europe represents the climax of human civilization. For Dussel, these ideas underlie the ideological and mythical character of European modernity. This myth accomplishes the "covering over" of the otherness of the subjects in the periphery and leads to their depiction as subhumans to whom Europe renders a service by civilizing them and bringing them to God and civilization.

In the second part of the book, Dussel introduces a more direct critique of the myth of modernity. He first describes what he considers to be the "maximal critical consciousness" of Europe with regard to the act of conquest and colonization, locating this critical consciousness in the work of Fray Bartolomé de Las Casas. In the latter's critique of the ways in which Europe "covered over," enslaved, and killed non-Europeans, Dussel finds the articulation of a critical vision that surpasses the views of Enlightenment and post-Enlightenment philosophers such as Kant and Hegel (and Dussel also includes Habermas on this list). Without finding much support from modern European voices, Dussel turns in the second chapter of this part to articulating an account of the "discovery" of America from the perspective of the native populations.

> It is now time to change skins and to see through new eyes. It is now time to put off the skin and the eyes of the *I conquer* which culminates in the *ego cogito* or the will-to-power. One's new hands are not those that clutch iron arms, and one's new eyes are not those looking out from the caravels of the *European intruders*, who cry Land! with Columbus. The new skin is the soft, bronzed skin of Caribbeans, of the Andean people, of the Amazonians. The new eyes are those of the Indians who, with their bare feet planted on soft, warm, island sands, saw in wonderment new gods floating on the sea as they approached.[30]

Dussel now begins a reconstruction of history from the perspective of the Indians. For him, "a historically and archeologically acceptable reconstruction is needed to correct the Eurocentric deviation that excludes Latin America from world history. Such a reconstructed and full account of the histories of the civilizations that produced occidental Europe will unmask Hegel's vision not merely as a Eurocentric ideological invention but also as an inversion of the facts."[31] With this in mind Dussel begins to articulate an innovative vision of history that traces the propagation of civilization from west to east. The Pacific Ocean and not the Atlantic, Dussel persuasively demonstrates, was the place where the great civilizations initially moved. It was precisely through the Pacific Ocean that the Americas were substantially populated for the first time. The great civilizations of the pre-Columbian Americas were not located in the west but, as it were, in the east of the east.

In the third part of the lectures Dussel explores the significance of 1492 for the indigenous populations, especially the Aztecs. According to Dussel, 1492 took on mythical proportions for them since it represented the arrivals of new gods. As soon as those gods were discovered to be human beings, they were taken as bestial invaders. At that point the Aztecs realized that they were confronting nothing less than the *end of the world*. The cosmovision of the Aztecs ended when they realized that their sacrificial system had been replaced by one in which entire civilizations were subdued and annihilated, not for the sake of a new dawn, but for gold and silver, and, ultimately, for accumulation. As Dussel puts it,

> A new god ascended on the horizon of this new epoch. He began his triumphal march in the heavens, not under the sacrificial sign of Huitzilopochli, but under the auspices of modernity's sacrificial myth. This new god was *capital* in its mercantilist phase, which prevailed in Spain in the sixteenth and seventeenth centuries and after in Holland. This new fetish metamorphosed, acquiring its industrial face in eighteenth-century England and its transnational embodiment in the twentieth-century United States, Germany, and Japan.[32]

Dussel extends this critical vision of the Aztecs to a judgment about contemporary ideological and institutional realities that endanger the lives of their descendents and many others throughout the world.

In this text Dussel, like Fanon, makes explicit how the reality of colonization reveals another side of the European subject. The ideas of taking off the "skin and the eyes of the *I conquer*" and of "changing the skin and seeing through new eyes" are significant because they allude to a phenomenological process of *reduction* in which certain presuppositions are suspended and others are imaginatively and creatively taken on. In this text Dussel suspends to a greater degree than before the views and interests that emerge more directly from his *mestizo* identity. The view of the inhabitants of Tenochtitlan at the moment of Cortés's arrival and conquest take *priority* for him. In this, Dussel takes a fundamental step toward the formation of the *de-colonial attitude*: he suspends the ontological priority of his identity and adopts a "preferential option" for the point of view of the condemned. In contrast to Husserl, Dussel looks at the phenomenon "Europe" not from the perspective of Europe itself but rather from a perspective that is for the most part considered alien to and irrelevant for it. Dussel's *The Invention of the Americas* should be read side by side with Husserl's reflection on the Renaissance in *The Crisis of European Sciences and Transcendental Phenomenology*, since they are both talking about the same phenomenon—Renaissance Europe—but doing so from different perspectives. To some extent, these expositions may be complementary, but to another extent they exist in tension to one another. For as much as Husserl aims to shed light on the essential meaning of Europe, he does not bracket his commitment with Europeanness or the historical conceptions crafted by the nineteenth-century philosophy of history.[33] Husserl complains about the excesses of positivism, naturalism, and psychologism, but he never seriously confronts or suspends the claims of Eurocentrism. He was therefore unable to spell out the links between science and colonization as well as between Renaissance ideals and the idea of the non-homogeneity of the human species.

None of what I have stated above about Husserl implies that his diagnoses and responses to the crisis of the European sciences are devoid of any value. One must not forget that he was reacting against naturalistic and positivist conceptions of selfhood and human existence, which turned subjectivity into a fact of nature or datum. Excessive naturalism, positivism, and psychologism turned the European subject into an inert form and made him appear as a sort of slave. One could therefore argue that phenomenology is a response to a certain form of slavery and colonialism that could easily lead to or legitimize oppressive and violent epistemic, social, and political forms, even to the point of genocide. Phenomenology seeks to provide an alternative to this, but, as we have already seen, Husserl's reflections remained shortsighted. He ignored or downplayed the extent to which European reason does more than produce slavery, colonialism, and genocide *in the present or future*, but rather functions in complicity with and helps to generate and justify all of them—particularly in relation to non-European populations since the Renaissance. Husserl, in short, remained blind to the Eurocentrism that Dussel analyzes as well as to Du Bois's "color line."[34] His phenomenological reduction was not radical enough to see "the veil" of ignorance and racial prejudice that Du Bois analyzes. By conceiving the crisis of the European sciences primarily as a European crisis, and not as a human crisis in which non-Europeans were heavily involved, Husserl misses the opportunity to articulate a more radical and humanistic phenomenology. Fanon, Dussel, and to a certain extent Levinas seek to decolonize phenomenology (or at least to provide fundamental insights in how one might do so), and, along with that effort, to similarly decolonize other European responses to the crisis of reason: psychoanalysis in the case of Fanon and communication ethics in the case of Dussel, among others. In the case of phenomenology, Husserl's diagnosis of Europe and his conception of subjectivity would arguably have accomplished a more radical expression if his phenomenology of the historical phenomenon—Europe—had involved a phenomenology of colonization as well as an examination of the lived experience of the colonized. This is what Dussel's *The Invention of the Americas* and Fanon's *Black Skin, White Masks* would later seek to provide. Husserl's critique of objectification and skepticism required an ample investigation of these problems, but the objectification that Husserl considered was that of European man, taken as a model for humanity as a whole. As a result, responses to the challenges confronted by this figure were conceived as solutions to the problems of humanity, a rhetorical gesture that reproduced imperialism and was complicit with other forms of objectification and dehumanization.

Several years after Husserl wrote *The Crisis of European Sciences and Transcendental Phenomenology*—when the Second World War was already over, the decay of Europe was all the more obvious, and the cold war had begun—Koselleck wrote his reflections on critique and crisis. As we have seen, Koselleck traced the origin of the crisis back to Enlightenment forms of critique and utopias. Although Husserl admired the Enlightenment's commitment to reason, he still believed that there was a "hidden absurdity" in Enlightenment views of rationality.[35] He also criticized Kant, whom he considered "a child of his time," for sustaining a naturalistic psychology that led him to "mythical conceptions."[36] However critical he was of Kant, Husserl did not see the mythical side of Kant, which derived not from sharing naturalistic presumptions with other eighteenth-century thinkers, but rather from holding views about modern enlightened Europe that led to its destructive utopias. Koselleck highlights what he calls the "hypocrisy" of Enlightenment forms of critique, which at the Enlightenment's height took the form of the philosophy of history. The "myth" that Husserl did not observe relates to Kant's complicity with the emerging philosophy of history, which, if we follow Koselleck and Dussel, began to be constructed around the time of the Enlightenment. Dussel makes explicit that the crisis of Europe must be related to a "myth" that achieved philosophical status with the philosophy of history that emerged in the Enlightenment, to which Kant contributed in important ways. This "myth" would pass unnoticed through generations of European thinkers and other defenders and critics of European modernity. A fundamental premise of this emergent myth is that Europe is the result of a rather linear progression, which goes through selected cultures according to their connection with classical Greece and Rome. This view began to emerge in the Renaissance, but it achieved philosophical status through the philosophy of history that was formulated beginning in the Enlightenment. As Dussel puts it,

> The "Enlightenment" vision would block off like a cement wall the old "disconnected Europe," the "Dark Age" Europe that until the fifteenth century, in the most optimistic scenario, was a periphery of the Islamic, Chinese, and Hindustani world—that "Oriental" world, much more "refined" and developed, from all points of view, that was the "center" of the old world, and the densest part of the world-system until the end of the eighteenth century.[37]

The influence of this view cannot be underestimated:

> From Hegel, Marx, and Comte to Weber—including Freud, Husserl, Heidegger, Popper, Levinas, Foucault, Lyotard, and Habermas—Eurocentrism shines unopposed. And it would dominate the colonial world with the brilliance [brillo] of "Western culture," as humanity's most developed center "since the beginning" (even though it may be a qualitatively irreplaceable critical conscience, as in the case of Habermas until the present).[38]

Like Koselleck, Dussel begins to articulate a critical view of the philosophy of history after the Second World War, in a context in which Europeans and non-Europeans became generally more skeptical toward the promises of the European Enlightenment and European civilization than ever before. Unlike Koselleck, however, Dussel—as well as other critics of modernity such as Césaire and Fanon—began to make connections between the recent barbarities internal to Europe and the barbarities perpetrated by European civilization in its colonial territories. Giving expression to his main concerns as a black subject in the French colonies, Césaire pursued an analysis of power and history that focused on the French Revolution and the colonial problem.[39] As a Latin American *criollo*, Dussel's more immediate concerns were different: he wanted to understand the history of Latin America beyond Eurocentric prejudices. It is true that the suspension of some Eurocentric prejudices left his *mestizo* prejudices untouched, and that a "continentalist" vision blinded Dussel as much as it had blinded Husserl. Their differences cannot hide that complicity, but there was nonetheless in Dussel's intervention the beginning of a rupture that, when aligned with other views such as those of Césaire and Fanon, has the potential for further radicalization. Dussel himself took these efforts to another level when, in the context of the five hundredth anniversary of the "discovery" of the Americas, he suspended more than ever before his *mestizo* point of view and took more seriously the standpoint of the inhabitants of the Americas at the time of contact. I have commented on the general outline of the book already, but now I would like to articulate two of its main contributions toward the understanding of European modernity.

Dussel argues that it was not until the Enlightenment that European intellectuals finally formalized a Eurocentric view of the world in their philosophy of history. Like Koselleck, he finds a constitutive "hypocrisy" in the philosophy of history, but Dussel's understanding of this "hypocrisy" was articulated in different terms. It was more related to the kind of "hypocrisy" that Césaire referred to in his *Discourse on Colonialism*: the hypocrisy of European depictions of Europe as a self-giving and sacrificing continent that generously imparted the gift of critique, rationality, freedom, autonomy and the like, while in reality sacrificing the colonized on the altar of capital and European superiority. Mary Louise Pratt's work allows one to trace this constitutive hypocrisy of the Enlightenment back to at least 1735, at which point there emerged in Europe a new planetary consciousness that looked at the world through the lens of science, a lens that allowed Europeans to declare neutrality and innocence in their new colonial adventures. However, one must interrogate the extent to which science was connected with a planetary perspective that allowed the bourgeoisie to differentiate itself from absolutism even before the Enlightenment. This much is suggested by Anthony Pagden in his reflections on the idea of Europe:

> After Columbus's discovery of America and the rounding of the Cape of Good Hope (famously declared by Adam Smith to be "the two greatest and most important events recorded in the history of mankind"), the European belief in the capacity of European science to dominate the world became even more assertive. Both of these oceanic journeys had been made possible by the

use of the compass and the skill of European navigators and cartographers. Only those whom Punchas described as "we in the West" had been able to achieve such triumphs. Asians and Africans had been capable of limited navigational feats. But only Europeans had managed to cross oceans, to settle and to colonize. Only the Europeans had "civilized" peoples from distant and inferior worlds.[40]

It is true that European "planetary consciousness" and the investment in science would take different forms in the eighteenth century, but it is nevertheless possible to identify important precedents in the world view that emerged with the "discoveries" and conquests a few centuries before. Science, colonialism, Eurocentrism, and the emergence of a new world view were intrinsically connected in such moments of "discovery" and conquest. The "discoveries" and conquests helped to cement the idea of successful scientific knowledge just as the later scientific point of view would produce a new discourse that would redefine colonialism: racial discourse. The success of scientific knowledge and colonial power were related both in the Renaissance and later on during the Enlightenment.

For Dussel, it is clear that while it was not until the Enlightenment that Eurocentrism's "imperial eyes" gained an elevated status in the philosophy of history, the "sacrificial myth of modernity" that is constitutive of its hypocrisy can be traced back to the late fifteenth century and the sixteenth. Dussel's view is that modernity is "originally European—and it is evident that its sources date back to the Egyptian, Babylonian, Semitic, Greek worlds, but that only in the 15th century it reached world implementation; and that it constitutes and reconstitutes itself simultaneously by a dialectical articulation of Europe (as center) with the peripheral world (as a dominated sub-system) within the first and only 'world system.'"[41] This counterpunctual understanding of modernity with reference to the "discovery" of the Americas is remarkably different from traditional accounts that conceive of European modernity as the result of a linear progressive development that goes from the ancient Greeks through the Roman Empire and the Christian world to the European Renaissance. These sorts of accounts inform Husserl's phenomenology of the historical shape of Europe, and I mention Husserl because, as I have already suggested and make clearer in what follows, Dussel aims to provide an alternative phenomenology of the history of Europe and modern subjectivity. Husserl posits a direct and uninterrupted link between the philosophy of the Greeks and the philosophy and scientific perspectives that began to emerge in the Renaissance. In his analysis, the work of Galileo and Descartes continued a way of thinking and a perspective that Europe inherited from the Greeks, and for Husserl their work must equally be taken as a model to address the crisis of European humanity and the European sciences. While Husserl's phenomenology was widely contested, this was not so much the case with his general views about the essence of Europe (which was related to Heidegger's, though in a critical way), which already form part of a certain philosophical common sense. Thus we find in 1989 a book by Charles Taylor on the "making of the modern identity," which traces the "sources of the self" to a line of thinkers that go from Plato, to Augustine, Descartes, Locke and others who followed them. For both Husserl and Taylor the virtues as well as the dilemmas that modern subjectivity confronts can be spelled out and elucidated, if not also solved, with exclusive reference to these sources.

Dussel contributes to accounts about the "making of modern identity" both by introducing a different conception of modernity and by commenting on unsuspected sources. He makes his difference with Taylor explicit:

> Just as in the case of Hegel—who was philosophically the initiator of this question in the history of philosophy—for Taylor the originary diachronic process of modernity also follows the linear movement Augustine-Descartes-Locke, et al. In short, I argue that this manner of interpreting modern identity is eurocentric, that is to say, provincial, regional, and does not take into account modernity's global significance and, thus, the inclusion of Europe's periphery as a "source," also constitutive of the modern "self" as such. This will allow us to discover certain aspects (and to occlude others) of "modern identity" and the "sources of the self."[42]

Against the (imperial) "planetary" perspective of European imperial eyes that became instrumental for bourgeois colonial adventures, Dussel deploys another "planetary" perspective to demonstrate the complex constitution of modern subjectivity and the precise unfolding of modernity. Instead of serving imperialism, this "planetary" perspective aims to overcome Eurocentrism and seeks to advance de-colonization by helping to elucidate the role of colonization as well as the contributions of non-European cultures to the formation of modernity. In this sense, *The Invention of the Americas* is not simply an interdisciplinary study with a regional orientation—that is, a book in the tradition of "area studies"—but rather a direct intervention into discourses of modernity, its crisis, and the sources of the self.

The first chapter of *The Invention of the Americas* begins with an examination of Eurocentrism in the Enlightenment, but Dussel immediately turns his attention to the Renaissance. For Dussel, "modernity *originates* in the Europe of the free cities (within the context of the feudal world) from the 10th century on, approximately, but is born when Europe constitutes itself as center of world system, of world history, that is inaugurated (at least as a limit date) with 1492."[43] Dussel later regarded his own thesis that Europe becomes the center of the world system in 1492 as Eurocentric, since Europe was still marginal then in comparison with geopolitical regions such as China; yet the experience of the Renaissance, particularly its darker side of conquest and colonization of the Americas, provided the central coordinates for Europe's self-definition and continued expansion in and after the Enlightenment.[44] The experiences, ideas, and conceptions that derive from the acts of "discovery" and conquest are a constitutive part of modernity and define the moment when it expands beyond European shores, giving Europe a sense of centrality. It was precisely at the moment of the "invention of the Americas" that the "myth of modernity" first came clearly into view. Dussel argues that "because of [Columbus's] departure from Latin anti-Muslim Europe, the idea that the Occident was the center of history was inaugurated and came to pervade the European life world."[45] From the different "discoveries" that took place during the Renaissance by the Portuguese and Spaniards, to conquest, and later on to colonization, Dussel observes the formation of a characteristically new form of being in the world that would become constitutive of modernity and give shape to its "myth."

Dussel's analysis of the limits and possibilities of modernity focuses on three figures, none of which plays any role in traditional accounts of modernity: Hernán Cortés, Bartolomé de Las Casas, and Moctezuma. Cortés is the prototype of modern subjectivity, embodying its darker side or mythical dimensions. Las Casas responds critically to the new sense of subjectivity that is being forged by the conquest, and to the violent civilizational project that unfolds before his eyes. He is a critic of the perverse logic of modernity. Moctezuma represents for Dussel a different point of view altogether, one that is critical of modernity's darker side but that also introduces a non-Western diagnosis of Europe's excesses that is fundamental to overcoming modernity's limitations. Cortés, Las Casas, and Moctezuma represent types, which incarnate forms of subjectivity, knowledge, and critique, each in different degrees. The idea that derives from this proposal is clear: in order to understand the complexity and ambiguous character of modernity it is necessary to consider the actions of the conquerors and the work of the defenders and critics of colonialism, and not only the work of Augustine, Galileo, or Descartes. The experience of the conqueror—and not only that of the religious self, the scientist, or the philosopher—left an imprint on modern subjectivity. The "mythical" dimensions of modernity that Dussel identifies can be traced back to the warring subjectivity when it assumes the role of God. Without being explicitly aware of this dimension, or taking it seriously as a problem, other accounts of subjectivity were shaped by this view of the self and perpetuated its problematic tendencies in different ways.

The description of modernity as a paradigm of war can only be fully understood when we relate it to the experience of warriors and conquerors at the birth of modernity. Following the geographical recognition of a territory, conquerors proceeded to take control of the bodies of the inhabitants, since they needed to be *pacified*, as it was customary to say in that epoch. In the Spanish world, and later on in the European world more generally, it fell to the warrior to establish dominion over others, and the conquistador was the first modern, active, practical human being to impose his violent individuality on the Other.[46] As Dussel makes clear when he traces the origin of modernity back to the tenth century, it was not that ideas about modern subjectivity were totally absent before Cortés became a conqueror, or that the emerging model would become hegemonic without any precedents or background that facilitated its expansion. What emerges from his analysis is the idea that modern subjectivity combined some of the features of the existing humanism of the time with ideas that emerged from the "discovery" of a "new" world and the experience of warriors and conquerors (not kings or clergy) vis-à-vis peoples regarded as inherently inferior. From then on, a particularly modern sense of human freedom was linked to certain relations of power that affected not only the way in which subjects perceived themselves, but also the way in which they related to others whose bodies presumably carried the marks of inferiority. The "myth of modernity" is therefore simultaneous with the emergence of modern subjectivity itself: freedom and the ensuing sense of rationality that emanates from it were tied to a peculiar conception of power that is premised on the alleged superiority of some subjects over others.

Dussel focuses on elucidating a peculiar conception of self and others (that of the warrior and conqueror) as well as a praxis that bears the mark of modern subjectivity. By emphasizing phenomenology and *subjectivity* in his analysis, Dussel makes it clear that his argument concerns a way of conceiving of the self and the world and not the systematization of that sense into a paradigm. As he puts it elsewhere, "Modernity originates a century before it becomes a paradigm . . . that corresponds with the new experience."[47] This experience begins to emerge in the transition of a poor noble who turns into a rich general captain, leading more than five hundred soldiers with the task of conquering a large territory in the so-called New World, the humanity of whose inhabitants is uncertain for them. Hernán Cortés went from being a poor noble from Spanish Extremadura to a plantation owner (*encomendero*) in Santo Domingo, to becoming rich after accompanying his brother on the conquest of Cuba, to finally leading the conquest of Yucatán. Once Cortés enters into contact with the Aztecs and is received by Moctezuma's ambassador, he realizes "for the first time that these people considered him a god."[48] According to the account of Fray Juan de Torquemada: "Hernán Cortés heard this, and with all his people he thought carefully about the situation."[49] The Spaniards response to the situation in which they found themselves initiated a process that would change the world forever, both for the Aztecs and for the Spaniards themselves. The European ego would emerge as a "quasi-divine superiority over the primitive, rustic, inferior Other."[50] Clearly, such a sense of being divinely endowed had existed before: to be sure, both the Aztec emperor and the king of Spain enjoyed similar privileges. In contrast to both, however, this new "god on Earth" had not gained its status through a traditional process of endowment that tied him to customs that sustained an already established social and political order. This new situation became clear in Cortés's exchange with Moctezuma:

> One can only imagine Moctezuma's feeling when he stood face to face with the conquistador who had freely and personally decided to confront the emperor who was considered a quasi god by his empire. Moctezuma, in contrast, was absolutely determined by the auguries, sorceries, astrological definitions, myths, theories, and other sources that revealed the designs of the gods. The free, violent, warlike, politically adept, juvenile modern ego faced an imperial functionary, tragically bound by communal structures like a chained Prometheus. Everyone else stared at the earth in front of the emperor. The "I-conqueror" was the first ever with the freedom to look him in the face.[51]

Tzvetan Todorov makes a similar point.

> Far from the central government, far from royal law, all prohibitions give way, the social link, already loosened, snaps, revealing not a primitive nature,

the beast sleeping in each of us, but a modern being, one with a great future in fact, restrained by no morality and inflicting death because and when he pleases. The "barbarity" of the Spaniards has nothing atavistic or bestial about it; it is quite human and heralds the advent of modern times. . . . What the Spaniards discover is the contrast between the metropolitan country and the colony, for radically different moral laws regulate conduct in each: massacre requires an appropriate context.[52]

For Todorov, the birth of the modern self is dependent upon the awareness of a fundamental difference between the metropolitan country and the colony. The colony is the place where laws are suspended and the warring subjectivity can fully unfold, and where the conqueror even has more freedom than the king himself. Indeed, in a sense, the conqueror's position was more similar to that of a god than that of either of the two emperors, Charles V or Moctezuma. The conqueror faced an entirely new world, and thus had more freedom in how he would proceed. He did not owe his new position to tradition, nor was he bounded by it as strongly as were the emperors. There was a new margin of freedom and detachment from tradition, accompanied by a power that was not given directly by God but which originated in an encounter with someone regarded as inferior.[53] This new situation prefigures the idea of a self who is in control of his own destiny and whose authority resides in his own power rather than in the will of an omniscient and all-powerful god. The "I conquer" exhibits key elements of modern subjectivity: a certain distance from established customs, a new sense of freedom, and a peculiar ambiguity toward God that comes from recognizing him as Lord but at the same time knowing that new earthly lordship does not ultimately rely on His authority.[54]

Once in the colony, away from home, the conquerors had the liberty of radicalizing and naturalizing the behavioral codes that had governed the relations between Christians and their enemies in the Middle Ages. This gesture became clear at the very beginning of the "discovery" expeditions, even before Cortés had arrived in Mexico. Consider that Columbus's first reaction upon seeing the "natives" is to assert that "y yo creí e creo que aquí vienen de tierra firme a tomarlos por captivos. Ellos deven ser buenos servidores y de buen ingenio, que veo que muy presto dizen todo lo que les dezía" [I thought that others come here from firm land to take them as captives. They should be good servants and intelligent, since they do very promptly everything that one tells them].[55] In order to understand the significance of this statement, in which Columbus attaches to the idea of the natives the notion of servitude and the possibility of enslavement, it is necessary to bear in mind that while early Christians criticized slavery in the Roman Empire, later Christians considered enemies vanquished in war to be legitimately enslaveable.[56] Indeed, in the ancient world and the Middle Ages it was for the most part legitimate to enslave people, particularly prisoners of war and the vanquished. Many of the conflicts that led to war and the enslavement of combatants and prisoners were motivated or justified with reference to religious differences. After the fourth century, European Christians inhabited a world also populated by infidels, heretics, "pagans," Jews, and later on, Muslims. The difference between Christians and others was primarily religious: Christians believed in the one true God and practiced the true religion, while others worshiped false gods. This form of conceiving difference and justifying war would change dramatically after the encounter with and invention of the "indigenous" person and later on the "black" in the Americas.[57] For the difference between Christians and the latter groups was not based primarily upon religion, but rather on differing degrees of humanity. As Sepúlveda put it, drawing from and reinterpreting Aristotle, indigenous peoples were servants by nature.[58] The justification of their enslavement did not rely so much on religious differences as it did on natural ones. This naturalization of religious hierarchies and their expression in situations of conflict between Christians and non-Christians is arguably part of the emergent scientific, secularizing, and particularly modern world view that accompanied the conquest and predated the scientific expeditions of the eighteenth century or the Enlightenment. Here the "discoverer" was also a warrior and a conqueror, more often assisted than opposed by the philosopher and the theologian.

For Dussel, the phenomenology of the "I conquer" helps to clarify the constitutive ambivalence of modernity and its bifurcation between its more consistently emancipatory ideals and its "mythical dimension." The freedom of the "I conquer" is simultaneously freedom *from* the Christian medieval order of symbolic representations and freedom *for* the exploitation of nature and the domination of subhuman others. As Sylvia Wynter has put it, the conquest inaugurated a poetics of the *propter nos*, which established a new relation toward the world.[59] The secular search for financial advancement as well as ideas about how to obtain it (exploitation of resources) and who would obtain it (those considered to be fully human) became entangled and constitutive parts of modernity's principle of expansion and reproduction. Aníbal Quijano refers to this as the coloniality of power, by which he means the relation between modern forms of exploitation (structured around the dominance of capital) and domination (articulated around the idea of race). For Quijano, the centrality of these forms of exploitation and domination, as well as their interconnection, were the result of forms of power that were first put in place in the Americas. He is very explicit about the role of the conqueror's ideology in this process. First there was

> the codification of the differences between conquerors and conquered in the idea of "race," a supposedly different biological structure that placed some in a natural situation of inferiority to the others. The conquistadors assumed this idea as the constitutive, founding element of the relations of domination that the conquest imposed. . . . The other process was the constitution of a new structure of control of labor and its resources and slavery, serfdom, small independent commodity production and reciprocity, together around and upon the basis of capital and the world market.[60]

Dussel, Quijano, and Wynter lead us to the understanding that what happened in the Americas was a transformation and naturalization of the *non-ethics of war*—which represented a sort of exception to the ethics that regulate normal conduct in Christian countries—into a more stable and long-standing reality of *damnation*, and that this epistemic and material shift occurred in the colony. Damnation, life in hell, is colonialism: a reality characterized by the naturalization of war by means of the naturalization of slavery, now justified in relation to the very constitution of people and no longer solely or principally to their faith or belief. That human beings become slaves when they are vanquished in a war translates in the Americas into the suspicion that the conquered people, and then non-European peoples in general, are constitutively inferior and that therefore they should assume a position of slavery and serfdom. Later on, this idea would be solidified with respect to the slavery of African peoples, achieving stability up to the present with the tragic reality of different forms of racism. Through this process, what looked like a "state of exception" in the colonies became the rule in the modern world. However, deviating from Giorgio Agamben's diagnosis, one must say that the colony—long before the concentration camp and the Nazi politics of extermination—served as the testing ground for the limits and possibilities of modernity, thereby revealing its darkest secrets.[61] It is race, the coloniality of power, and its concomitant Eurocentrism (and not only national socialisms or expressed forms of fascism) that allow the "state of exception" to continue to define ordinary relations in this, our so-called postmodern world.

Race emerges within a permanent state of exception where forms of behavior that are legitimate in war become a natural part of the ordinary way of life. In that world, an otherwise extraordinary affair becomes the norm and living in it requires extraordinary effort.[62] In the racial/colonial world, the "hell" of war becomes a condition that defines the reality of racialized selves, which Fanon referred to as the *damnés de la terre* (condemned of the earth). The *damné* (condemned) is a subject who exists in a permanent "hell," and as such, this figure serves as the main referent or liminal other that guarantees the continued affirmation of modernity as a paradigm of war. The hell of the condemned is not defined by the alienation of colonized productive forces, but rather signals the dispensability of racialized subjects, that is, the idea that the world would be fundamentally better without them. The racialized subject is ultimately a dispensable source of value, and exploitation is conceived in this context as due torture, and not solely as the extraction of surplus value. Moreover, it is this very same conception that gives rise to the particular erotic dynamics that characterize the relation between the master and its slaves or racialized workers. The condemned, in short, inhabit a context in which the confrontation with death and murder is ordinary. Their "hell" is not simply "other people," as Sartre would have put it—at least at one point—but rather racist perceptions that are responsible for the suspension of ethical behavior toward peoples at the bottom of the color line. Through racial conceptions that became central to the modern self, modernity and coloniality produced a permanent state of war that racialized and colonized subjects cannot evade or escape.

The modern function of race and the coloniality of power, I am suggesting here, can be understood as a radicalization and naturalization of the non-ethics of war in colonialism.[63] This non-ethics included the practices of eliminating and enslaving certain subjects—for example, indigenous and black—as part of the enterprise of colonization. From here one could as well refer to them as the death ethics of war. War, however, is not only about killing or enslaving; it also includes a particular treatment of sexuality and femininity: rape. Coloniality is an order of things that places people of color within the murderous and rapist view of a vigilant ego, and the primary targets of this rape are women. But men of color are also seen through these lenses and feminized, to become fundamentally penetrable subjects for the *ego conquiro*. Racialization functions through gender and sex, and the *ego conquiro* is thereby constitutively a *phallic ego* as well.⁶⁴ Dussel, who presents this thesis of the phallic character of the *ego cogito*, also makes links, albeit indirectly, with the reality of war.

> And thus, in the beginning of modernity, before Descartes discovered . . . a terrifying anthropological dualism in Europe, the Spanish conquistadors arrived in America. The phallic conception of the European-medieval world is now added to the forms of submission of the vanquished Indians. "Males," Bartolomé de las Casas writes, are reduced through "the hardest, most horrible, and harshest serfdom"; but this only occurs with those who have remained alive, because many of them have died; however, "in war typically they only leave alive young men (mozos) and *women*."⁶⁵

The indigenous people who survive the massacre or are left alive have to contend with a world that considers them to be dispensable. And since their bodies have been conceived of as inherently inferior or violent, they must be constantly subdued or civilized, which requires renewed acts of conquest and colonization. The survivors continue to live in a world defined by war, and this situation is peculiar in the case of women. As T. Denean Sharpley-Whiting and Renée T. White put it in the preface to their anthology *Spoils of War: Women of Color, Cultures, and Revolutions*:

> A sexist and/or racist patriarchal culture and order posts and attempts to maintain, through violent acts of force if necessary, the subjugation and inferiority of women of color. As Joy James notes, "its explicit, general premise constructs a conceptual framework of male [and/or white] as normative in order to enforce a political [racial, economic, cultural, sexual] and intellectual mandate of male [and/or white] as superior." The warfront has always been a "feminized" and "colored" space for women of color. Their experiences and perceptions of war, conflict, resistance, and struggle emerge from their specific racial-ethnic and gendered locations. "*Inter arma silent leges*: in time of war the law is silent," Walzer notes. Thus, this volume operates from the premise that war has been and is presently in our midst.⁶⁶

The links between war, conquest, and the exploitation of women's bodies are hardly accidental. In his study of war and gender, Joshua Goldstein argues that conquest usually proceeds through an extension of the rape and exploitation of women in wartime.⁶⁷ He argues that to understand conquest, one needs to examine: 1) male sexuality as a cause of aggression; 2) the feminization of enemies as symbolic domination; and 3) dependence on the exploitation of women's labor—including reproduction.[68] My argument is, first, that these three elements came together in a powerful way in the idea of race that began to emerge in the conquest and colonization of the Americas. My second point is that through the idea of race, these elements exceed the activity of conquest and come to define what from that point on passes as the idea of a "normal" world. As a result, the phenomenology of a racial context resembles, if it is not fundamentally identical to, the phenomenology of war and conquest. Racism posits its targets as racialized and sexualized subjects that, once vanquished, are said to be inherently servile and whose bodies come to form part of an economy of sexual abuse, exploitation, and control. The coloniality of power cannot be fully understood without reference to the transformation and naturalization of war and conquest in modern times.

Hellish existence in the colonial world carries with it both the racial and the gendered aspects of the naturalization of the non-ethics of war. "Killability" and "rapeability" are inscribed into the images of colonial bodies and deeply mark their ordinary existence. Lacking real authority, colonized men are permanently feminized and simultaneously represent a constant threat for whom any amount of authority, any visible trace of the phallus is multiplied in a symbolic hysteria that knows no limits.[69] Mythical depiction of the black man's penis is a case in point: the black man is depicted as an aggressive sexual beast who desires to rape women, particularly white women. The black woman, in turn, is seen as always already sexually available to the rapist gaze of the white, and as fundamentally promiscuous. In short, the black woman is seen as a highly erotic being whose primary function is fulfilling sexual desire and reproduction. To be sure, any amount of "penis" in either one represents a threat, but in his most familiar and typical forms the black man represents the act of rape—"raping"—while the black woman is seen as the most legitimate victim of rape—"being raped." In an anti-black world black women appear as subjects who deserve to be raped and to suffer the consequences—in terms of a lack of protection from the legal system, sexual abuse, and lack of financial assistance to sustain themselves and their families—just as black men deserve to be penalized for raping, even without having committed the act. Both "raping" and "being raped" are attached to blackness as if they form part of the essence of black folk, who are seen as a dispensable population. Black bodies are seen as excessively violent and erotic, as well as being the legitimate recipients of excessive violence, erotic and otherwise.[70] "Killability" and "rapeability" are part of their essence, understood in a phenomenological way. The "essence" of blackness in a colonial anti-black world is part of a larger context of meaning in which the death ethics of war gradually becomes a constitutive part of an allegedly normal world. In its modern racial and colonial connotations and uses, blackness is the invention and the projection of a social body oriented by the death ethics of war.[71] This murderous and raping social body projects the features that define it onto sub-Others in order to be able to legitimate the same behavior that is allegedly descriptive of them. The same ideas that inspire perverted acts in war—particularly slavery, murder, and rape—are legitimized in modernity through the idea of race and gradually come to be seen as more or less normal thanks to the alleged obviousness and non-problematic character of black slavery and anti-black racism. To be sure, those who suffer the consequences of such a system are primarily blacks and indigenous peoples, but it also deeply affects all of those who appear as colored or close to darkness. In short, this system of symbolic representations, the material conditions that in part produce and continue to legitimate it, and the existential dynamics that occur therein (which are also at the same time derivative and constitutive of such a context) are part of a process that naturalizes the non-ethics or death ethics of war. Sub-ontological difference is the result of such naturalization and is legitimized through the idea of race. In such a world, ontology collapses into a Manicheanism, as Fanon suggested.[72]

Fanon offered the first phenomenology of the Manichean colonial world, understood properly as Manichean and not as ontological reality.[73] In this analysis, he investigated not only the relations between whites and blacks, but also those between black males and black females. Much can be added to his discussion, but to do so is not my purpose here. What I wish to do is firstly to provide a way to understand the Fanonian breakthrough in light of the articulation of sub-ontological difference and the idea of the naturalization of the non-ethics of war. This is important because, among other things, we can now see that when Fanon called for a war against colonialism, what he was doing was politicizing social relations that were already premised upon war. Fanon was not only fighting against anti-black racism in Martinique, or against French colonialism in Algeria. He was simultaneously countering the force and legitimacy of a historical system (European modernity) that utilized racism and colonialism to naturalize the non-ethics of war. He was engaging in a war against war, oriented by "love," which is understood here as the desire to restore ethics to its place and to locate properly trans-ontological and ontological differences.[74] The de-colonial attitude is thus a simultaneously ethical, theoretical, and political form of consciousness. It stands behind efforts to restore the ethical through theoretical and political means, leading Fanon to pursue opposition to racism and colonization as a citizen, a doctor, and, finally, a revolutionary. From here the philosopher appears in Fanon's work not so much as a "functionary of mankind" in the service of a Eurocentrically defined conception of reason and communication (Husserl), but as someone who fights with the condemned against the forces of dehumanization and colonization in the modern world—in short, an epistemological and social revolutionary. This conception of intellectual activity is also different from the analyst in psychoanalysis, with which Fanon was also acquainted but which he ultimately left aside as well.[75]

For Fanon, in the colonial context, sub-ontological difference profoundly marks day-to-day reality.

> There is, first of all, the fact that the colonized person, who in this respect is like the men in underdeveloped countries or the disinherited in all parts of the world, perceives life not as a flowering or a development of an essential productiveness, but as a permanent struggle against an omnipresent death. This ever-menacing death is experienced as endemic famine, unemployment, a high death rate, and inferiority complex and the absence of any hope for the future.
>
> All this gnawing at the existence of the colonized tends to make of life something resembling an incomplete death. Acts of refusal or rejection of medical treatment are not a refusal of life, but a greater passivity before that close and contagious death.[76]

If the most basic ontological question is "why are there things rather than nothing," the question that emerges in this context and that opens up reflection on the coloniality of Being is: "Why go on?" As Lewis Gordon has put it, "why go on?" is a fundamental question for the existential philosophy of the African Diaspora, and it illuminates the plight of the *condemned of the earth*.[77] "Why go on?" is preceded by only one expression, that is, the *cry*.[78] The cry—not a word but an interjection—is a calling of attention to one's own existence. The cry is the pre-theoretical expression of the question—Why go on?—which drives most theoretical reflections by the peoples of the African Diaspora. It is the cry that animates the birth of theory and critical thought and points to a peculiar existential condition: that of the condemned. The *damné* or condemned is not a "being there" but a non-being, or rather, as Ralph Ellison so eloquently elaborated, a sort of invisible entity.[79] What is invisible about the person of color is his or her very humanity, and it is in fact to this that the cry attempts to draw attention. I elaborated a phenomenology of the cry in chapter 4, and my intention here is to make clear that there is a connection between the phenomenology of the racialized self already provided in that chapter and the phenomenology of the "I conquer" offered here. Together they provide a genealogical and phenomenological alternative to Hegel's, Husserl's, Koselleck's, Habermas's, or Taylor's conceptualizations of modernity. I would like briefly to make this more explicit with reference to Levinas, who introduced the idea of modernity's master morality in relation to war, with which this book opened.

Dussel's phenomenology of the "I conquer" contributes certain revelations about modernity and its affiliation with a paradigm of war. As we have seen already, of the three central figures in this book it was Emmanuel Levinas who suggested, after the end of the Second World War, that the priorities of hegemonic views of modernity are shaped by a paradigm of war. Levinas perceived a relationship between the suspension of ethics in war and the ideals that derive from epistemology and ontology as first philosophy. For Levinas, the danger with epistemology and ontology as first philosophies is that they can become complicit with a situation in which war becomes the norm, rather than the exception. The continuity of anti-Semitism in Europe represented for him a continuous state of exception in which ethics was suspended in favor of power or knowledge. Dussel's phenomenology of the "I conquer" complements, corrects, and deepens Levinas's assertions, as Dussel demonstrates that the suspension of ethics in modernity, along with the primacy of the "thinking self," are grounded in experiences of conquest in which war became the norm rather than the exception. In this context, influential philosophical ideas such as Cartesian dualism justified not only a radical split between humans and nature, but also a radical separation between some humans who were considered to represent the climax of reason and others who were considered to be not fully rational and not fully human. Indeed, there exists for Dussel a close relationship between the "I conquer" and the "I think": "The 'I-conquistador' forms the protohistory of Cartesian *ego cogito* and constitutes its own subjectivity as a will-to-power."[80] While others wrote about the dialectic of the

Enlightenment, Dussel offers an account that could be referred to as the dialectic of the Renaissance, which thinkers such as Levinas fail to take into consideration:

> The colonizing ego, subjugating the Other, the woman and the conquered male, in an *alienating erotics* and in a mercantile *capitalist economics*, follows the route of the conquering ego toward the modern *ego cogito*. Modernization initiates an ambiguous course by touting a rationality opposed to *primitive*, mythic explanations, even as it concocts a myth to conceal its own sacrificial violence against the Other.[81]

"Descartes," Dussel comments elsewhere, "studied at La Flèche, a Jesuit college, a religious order with great roots in America, Africa, and Asia at that moment. The 'barbarian' was the obligatory context of all reflection on subjectivity, reason, the *cogito*."[82] Perhaps the genius of Descartes consisted in providing a paradigm that integrated the new conception of reason that began to emerge with the new science and the certainties about European superiority. The *ego cogito* gave philosophical expression to a sense of self that emerged from the first humanist writings, then colonization, and then to the emerging sciences. Science and colonization, as we have seen, have been more aligned or bound up with one another than is often suspected. For instance, the eighteenth-century sciences, legitimated by a Cartesian viewpoint, were highly complicit with new colonial expeditions. Later on in the nineteenth century, Nietzsche would raise questions about the ethics of the scientific vocation, relating the scientific ethos to Christian piety and to a "slave morality" that he traced back to a Jewish revolt in morals. As a response to Nietzsche, Dussel suggests that we should investigate the possible links between philosophy and science on the one hand and a "master morality" of female oppression and racial differentiation on the other. Such "morality" is best explained with reference to Europe's actions in the colonies at the very birth of modernity, and not in the culturalist terms that Nietzsche adopts and that involve a mythical reconstruction of Jewish religiosity. To be sure, Dussel is also responding to another critic of modernity— Sigmund Freud—and to a contemporary successor of the latter—René Girard—both of whom explain the origin of violence in society and its "civilized" responses with reference to an immemorial, repressed original murder.[83] Unlike them, Dussel focuses on one model of civilization rather than speculating about the origins of every single culture from time immemorial, and what he finds at its birth is not the murder of a tribal leader or a father, but rather a warring paradigm. In the *Invention of the Americas*, such a paradigm is no longer articulated in the metaphysical terms that he had used in his *Philosophy of Liberation* (see chapter 5); rather, Dussel uses genealogical terms, which he formulates in light of a phenomenological investigation, as it has been made clear in this chapter. This means that if Dussel supersedes the limits of Levinas's theorizing, it is not so much (as he often claims) in the application of Levinas's categories to politics, but in articulating a genealogical view that helps to explain better the links between modernity and war. Likewise, his contribution to Fanon's project resides not in abandoning phenomenology in favor of the philosophy of liberation, but rather in using phenomenology for the task of elucidating the paradigm of war. The geopolitical focus that I am trying to recover from Dussel's work thus has to do mainly with a combination of phenomenology, history, and genealogy, rather than with applied Levinasian metaphysics and the alleged overcoming of phenomenology by his own liberation philosophy.

In the genealogical and geopolitical view presented here, conquest gave birth to a world in which ideas, ethical codes, and conceptions of the self that defined war became normalized. The expulsion of Jews and Muslims from the Iberian Peninsula in 1492 and, one might add, the Portuguese contacts with Africa earlier in the fifteenth century provided necessary but not sufficient conditions for the reification or naturalization of the ethics of war in the European colonies of the Americas in the late fifteenth century and the sixteenth. The genealogy of the modern paradigm of war cannot be spelled out with reference *only* to the history of anti-Semitism in Europe or the Jewish Holocaust of the Second World War, as Levinas was inclined to do. Recognition of this point helps us to deploy and orient a project of de-colonization forged by the *damnés*, rather than merely inspiring a project that seeks to demonstrate the relevance of Jewish roots or the roots of any particular group to European identity. Levinas's intuition about the links between modernity and the morality or non-morality of war remained undeveloped, as he was unable to make sense of how it related to colonial damnation and modern racism. With Dussel it becomes clear that the "master morality" that Levinas mentioned in his reflections on Hitlerism can be traced back to a paradigm of war that was put in place in colonial adventures and that persists through racial prejudice. Race is largely absent in Dussel's analysis, and this is one of the central limitations of his work. In this sense, my formulation of damnation as a naturalization through the idea of race of the non-ethics of war follows a Fanonian detour or inflection in Dussel's account, which comes into view when one juxtaposes and compares Fanon's phenomenology of the racial self (of the *damnés*) with Dussel's phenomenology of the "I conquer."

Dussel's genealogical account and his phenomenology of the "I conquer" complements Fanon's phenomenology of the racial sub-other as much as it enriches and corrects Levinas's views regarding the links between the suspension of ethics, knowledge, and war. It offers historical depth and helps to explain the mechanisms that sustain and animate the racist gaze that Fanon confronted: "Look a negro!" or "dirty nigger." The gaze identifies the bodies in respect to which ethical behavior is suspended and authorizes the reenactment of the brutal death ethics of war forged in conquest, slavery, and colonization. This is a situation in which the *state of exception* becomes the rule, and this is why racial subjects, as Gordon puts it, make extraordinary efforts to live in ordinary ways. The continued legitimacy of colonization, racialization, and particular ways of understanding gender roles testifies to modernity's fundamental link with the paradigm of war.

I have argued that Fanon's work as well as his revolutionary praxis can be understood in terms of an opposition to the paradigm of war. Dussel's philosophy of liberation joins Fanon's theoretical analyses of modernity as well as the effort to articulate consistent responses to it. Fanon focused on the disalienation of the colonized subject and the process of becoming actional. Dussel, who had a formal training in philosophy and history, targets Hegelian conceptions of history and attempts to provide an account that legitimizes subversive thought and action in opposition to the mythical aspects of modernity. His most consistent response to modernity appears in the Frankfurt lectures themselves under the rubric of transmodernity, and I will conclude this chapter with insights into the meaning and critical potential of such a project.

TRANSMODERNITY AS THE OVERCOMING OF THE PARADIGM OF WAR

The idea of transmodernity belongs to a fourth moment of the decolonial turn. As delineated in the introduction, the first moment begins with an explicit engagement with the dilemmas of emancipated peoples of the African Diaspora at the end of the nineteenth century and the beginning of the twentieth. This engagement leads W. E. B. Du Bois to claim that the problem of the twentieth century is the problem of the color line (*The Souls of Black Folk*, 17). A second drastic moment included the disenchantment with Europe that occurred throughout the two world wars, the rise of Hitlerism and the Jewish Holocaust, and the de-colonization movements that took place soon after the Second World War. Critical philosophies emerged inside Europe and outside Europe within these contexts. Intellectuals of the time witnessed the weakening of Europe alongside the emergence of new world powers such as the United States and the Soviet Union, and the formation of nationalist movements and wars of de-colonization in different parts of the world. For Latin America, which had achieved independence more than one hundred years prior, this period entailed the search for a second de-colonization, this time epistemic and not only political. This search already had a history in Latin America—consider José Martí and Juan Carlos Mariátegui, to name only two consequential figures. But the Second World War and its aftermath—along with the rise of nationalist movements in many parts of the world—gave it a stronger impetus and put it on a global scale. From here, we begin to see Dussel's constant references to the relevance of Africa and Asia within his new account of world history and his philosophy of liberation.

A third moment of the de-colonial turn occurred during the late 1960s. As Dussel writes: "Members of a new generation (of those born after 1930, although it was anticipated by some), began their reflection at the end of the sixties, not without some relation to the events of 1968, with respect to a philosophy of liberation, which was thus linked to Latinamericanist philosophy."[84] The second half of the 1960s saw the almost simultaneous emergence of Latin American social science, Latin American theology of liberation, and Latin American philosophy of liberation. Similar events were occurring in other parts of the world, most notably with the emergence of subaltern studies in India, black theology of liberation, and theories of internal colonialism in the United States. This explosion of radical theories from positions of racialization, gender, and subalterity in the late 1960s and early 1970s is what I refer to as a third moment of the de-colonial turn.

In his *Philosophy of Liberation* of the 1970s, Dussel refers to the newly emerging critical discourses from the periphery—particularly to his own philosophy of liberation—as postmodern. With postmodern philosophy, he referred to a form of philosophical reflection that opened up the awareness of knowledge production beyond the limited realm of modernity, since the latter represented for him a form of discourse that inspired the geopolitics of concealment found in figures such as Hegel and Heidegger. For Dussel, modern philosophy carried with it the weight of the experience of a geopolitical center—Europe—or of nation-states in the semi-peripheral and peripheral worlds, which continued through different means the project of centering some forms of knowledge and concealing others (typically those produced by subaltern peoples and popular classes in the peripheries of power, particularly in the [post]colonial world). For Dussel, modernity was, as it were, a machine of centralization and concealment in the name of development or progress. By postmodernity he was referring to a new horizon where the ethical question of giving to the poor and the ethical modality of listening to those who have been oppressed would become an integral part of emerging philosophical and theoretical positions. The philosophy of liberation was one such movement.

Dussel uses different arguments to legitimize the emergence of postmodern theorizing in the periphery. Some of these arguments are compelling, while others are problematic. Yet, the main thrusts of his arguments remain valid and relevant for critical theorizing today: 1) it is necessary to interrogate the links between philosophical projects and geopolitical positioning; 2) the liberation of formerly colonized subjects has a relevance for philosophy that parallels that of other important moments such as the emancipation of the "people" and the bourgeois elites in the French Revolution; and 3) a critical philosophy takes as its horizon the struggle of the wide majority of people around the globe and seeks to elucidate the challenges that they confront while listening to their demands, supporting their struggle, and aiming to give voice to their aspirations. In short, liberation philosophy insists that philosophy should be decentered and incorporated into the logic of de-colonial unconcealment of being, power, and knowledge.

The philosophy of liberation of the 1970s was an epistemological and philosophical dimension of a larger cultural revival and political upheaval in the region, and Dussel first presented it as being Latin American in character. This designation would remain in Dussel's work, but over time the context for its articulation would change, as would its focus. The increasing globalization of finance capital and the rearticulation of development theories and coloniality through neoliberal policies, along with the increase of poverty and the menace of life (not only human life) around the planet, led Dussel to articulate his ethics of liberation differently. His diagnosis of modernity has been gradually refined, and the concept of postmodernity has been abandoned for the idea of transmodernity.

Dussel uses the concept of transmodernity as a critical response to the Habermasian conception of the unfinished project of the Enlightenment and to the postmodern skepticism of reason and universality. Since he does not fully share the postmodern critique of reason, its increasingly apolitical celebration of difference, and its continuous tendency to conceal non-European questions, concerns, and proposals for change, he decided to abandon the concept of postmodernity as a description of his philosophy of liberation. At the same time, Habermas's conception of finishing the project of modernity appeared to Dussel to be as Eurocentric as that of his intellectual forefathers (Kant and Weber), even though Dussel incorporates elements of Karl-Otto Apel's and Habermas's ethics of discourse into his own work. Dussel's point of departure for his refashioned critique of Eurocentric modernity and postmodern criticism could not be more clear:

> The history of world domination originates with modernity, which thinkers such as Charles Taylor, Stephen Toulmin, or Jürgen Habermas consider as exclusively a European occurrence, having nothing to do with the so-called Third World. The expositions of these thinkers explain modernity by referring *only to classical European and North American authors and events.* My undertaking here differs from theirs, since I argue that while modernity is undoubtedly a European occurrence, it also originates in a dialectical relation with non-Europe. Modernity appears when Europe organizes the initial world-system and places itself at the center of world history over against a periphery equally constitutive of modernity. The forgetting of the periphery, which took place from the end of the fifteenth, Hispanic-Lusitanian century to the beginning of the seventeenth century, has led great thinkers of the center to commit the Eurocentric fallacy in understanding modernity. Because of a partial, regional, and *provincial* grasp of modernity, the postmodern critique and Habermas's defense of modernity are equally unilateral and partially false.[85]

Dussel articulated this position during his visit to Frankfurt in 1992, at a moment when there was a worldwide discussion of the significance of the violent encounter of the Europeans with the indigenous peoples of the Americas. In the previous section, I elaborated on the significance of that moment, in which many intellectuals began to take more seriously than before the plight of indigenous peoples, leading them to produce new analyses of colonial reality and new proposals for change. It is this moment of epistemic change that I refer to as a fourth moment of the de-colonial turn, and it is in this context that the concept of transmodernity is articulated.

Dussel's concept of transmodernity is an alternative to the idea of modernity, which, according to him, is fundamentally ambiguous:

1) For its first and positive conceptual content, modernity signifies rational emancipation. This emancipation involves leaving behind immaturity under the force of reason as a critical process that opens up new possibilities for human development.

2) But, at the same time, in its secondary and negative *mythic* content, modernity justifies an irrational praxis of violence.[86]

For Dussel, both of these ambiguous significations are problematic. The "positive" content of modernity is problematic because it can easily lead to a practice based on superiority and the salvation of others through a civilizing mission. However, it is not altogether vicious, particularly as it concerns the idea of rationality. While Dussel is critical of modernity, he does not share postmodern skepticism of reason as such, and on this point he is closer to Apel and Habermas than to Lyotard, Rorty, or Vattimo, even as he finds Apel's and Habermas's projects deeply problematic as well.[87] As stated before, the association of postmodernism with a radical skepticism of reason is what led him to abandon the concept of "postmodern" as a viable description of his liberation philosophy. At the same time Dussel has never looked with disdain on postmodern critiques, since his method or approach tends to be generous and inclusive, not reactionary and exclusive. As he puts it in his dialogue with Gianni Vattimo: "It is necessary to discern the positive elements in postmodern criticism and modernity, as well as the affirmation of valuable elements in the exteriority of the southern life-world in order to imagine an alternative liberation project which is ethical and necessary for the majority of humankind. It is also necessary to discern the institutional mediations of its effective realization."[88] Transmodernity is an attempt to bring these three perspectives together.

Dussel holds on to the idea of rationality, while he also criticizes an abstract and univocal concept of universality. It is here that the difference between emancipation and liberation is relevant.[89] What emancipation is to modernity and universality, liberation is to transmodernity and the call for a diverse world. For while European emancipation refers to a singular process of coming to maturity, liberation refers to the many attempts, especially by formerly colonized subjects, to affirm their own selves and to create a world *in which many worlds can fit*.[90] Liberation claims liberty, equality, and fraternity, but also solidarity and the embrace of alterity, including epistemic diversity.[91] For Dussel, human beings share a commonality on the basis of which it is possible to discern basic ethical principles (not abstract and purely procedural but material as well; see *Etica de la liberación*). But this very commonality includes the fact of diversity: we are equal in that we are different. This perspective undergirds the ideal of transmodernity. While modernity takes emancipation as its center and elevates reason to an abstract universal or a global design, transmodernity offers the possibility of thinking of commonality diversely.

Dussel's critique of modernity has another side. Modernity's systematic pursuit of the ideal of "rational emancipation" and its view of universality led it to three insurmountable limits. These are the ecological destruction of the planet; "the destruction of humanity itself"; and "the impossibility of the subsumption of the populations, economies, nations, and cultures that it has been attacking since its origin and since it has excluded from its horizon and thus cornered into poverty."[92] Liberation philosophy and the idea of transmodernity are largely oriented by a perception of the limits of modernity, particularly as these are made evident from a global perspective that includes the South as a measuring stick of sorts for the radicalism of critical theories and as a place from which critical perspectives emerge.[93] Indeed, philosophy of liberation is, as it were, a de-colonial philosophy of the limit; that is, it attempts to re-create thinking in light of this kind of failure. Even though the failures are there for all to see, liberation philosophy pays particular attention to the problems that become evident, not so much from the perspective of financial and political centers—whose ideologues and enthusiasts, both at home and abroad, are invested in the "success" of "development" programs—but rather from the perspective of those who often don't count in the calculations of what success means, or whose "development" or lack thereof is ultimately insignificant for those who formulate policy. What is at stake, at least in the focus of liberation philosophy, are the failures and the possibilities for change that can potentially affect or benefit the whole of humanity, particularly the worst off. That is why liberation philosophy calls simultaneously for attention to be paid to the "condemned of the earth" and for the elaboration of a broad perspective that includes consideration of not only regions but the world as a whole. Dussel insisted from early on that a proper response to the geopolitics of concealment demanded a philosophy with a planetary scope elaborated within the general framework of a de-colonial and cosmopolitan geopolitics of knowledge. That view along with the emphasis on the ethico-political question of liberation from oppression define the very core of liberation philosophy.

While Dussel initially focused on Latin American culture and its sources and then went on to pay more attention to the mechanisms of exclusion that fomented poverty and ostracism in Latin America, his most recent work focuses on the modes of oppression in the modern world-system as well as in the possibilities for concrete instantiations of something new. Here, he responds to the increasing inequality of wealth in a world characterized by the increasing globalization of finance capital and modern Western culture. The philosophy of history and the philosophy of culture make themselves relevant in this context once again, since the world appears not as a homogeneous field of cultural production, but as a multiple and varied composite of cultural formations. As Dussel puts it: "This was no longer a matter of 'locating' Latin America. It was a matter of trying to 'situate' *all of the cultures* that today *inevitably* confront each other in all levels of everyday life, from communication, education and research, to the politics of expansion, and cultural or even military resistance."[94] "Situating" the diversity of the world's cultures is Dussel's alternative to the imperial mapping of the world as a battlefield or war zone. It also seeks to undercut the description of our sociocultural and geopolitical condition today as a "clash of civilizations."[95] In the modern world, cultures are not so similar to each other that diversity has disappeared, but difference does not necessarily mean warlike antagonism. Difference means war only through the lenses of the paradigm of war and other similar warring fundamentalisms—the existence of which must be understood, at least in part, in light of the legacies of empire and empire's current workings in the contemporary world, that is, in light of modernity as a paradigm of war.

Dussel's conception of linguistic and "cultural" diversity today is based on the idea that while it may be true that coloniality structures the modern world, neither modernity nor coloniality (or modernity/coloniality) has entirely erased the histories, the memories, and the epistemological and hermeneutical resources of colonized cultures or religious traditions. From here we find that the world, for Dussel, has a reservoir of knowledges and memories that can help undo the devastating and self-destructive effects of modernity's violent tendencies and its naturalization of war. This argument is based on the idea that while modernity emerged in the sixteenth century, it was not until the late eighteenth century and the nineteenth that it began to extend firmly into many regions of the world.[96] There were, in certain cases, centenary and millenary cultures, languages, and knowledges in those regions, and this is the basis for Dussel's depiction of and argument for transmodernity. *Transmodernity involves a double movement: on the one hand the subsumption of "the best of globalized European and North American modernity" from the perspective of liberating reason (not European emancipation), and on the other the critical affirmation of the liberating aspects of the cultures and knowledges excluded from or occluded by modernity.*[97] It is primarily those who belong to the different cultures in question who are in charge of determining the problematic aspects of their cultures and of modernity; they are also responsible for articulating historical projects that can simultaneously help their cultures and help humanity in the process of overcoming the limits of modernity and the legacy of coloniality. But no one can do this alone, and it is here that the relevance of Dussel's proposal for an intercultural dialogue that takes transmodernity as a new horizon for thought resides. In a way, the idea is that instead of a "clash of civilizations" our times demand the creation of transcultural fronts of liberation, that is, of solidarity beyond cultural unity and homogeneity. The presupposition here is that cultures are not closed systems of signification but open doors for communication. Using these doors requires what I have referred to elsewhere as "transgresstopic (or transtopic) hermeneutics and critique," which demand "a fundamental impulse to transgress the space of the other and even one's own space. It involves the notion so well put by Nietzsche of being a traitor even to one's fatherland." In short, what is at stake here is "the denial of epistemic privileged, ultimately, both to colonizer and colonized." Transtopic critical hermeneutics also includes the idea "that spaces are not fixed epistemological grounds, and that transactions between spaces function as enabling conditions for self-understanding and (self)-critique."[98] Instead of inevitable conflict, the idea of transtopic critical hermeneutics suggests that there can be generous transactions of gifts through lines of difference. Opening up the horizon of generosity and receptivity in the face of ideas, concepts, and practices that promote the formation of communities of masters provides the necessary sense of orientation to the struggle for nonsexist human fraternity, better put, following the previous reflections and the work of Chela Sandoval, affiliation through altericity, love, or non-indifference.[99] Dussel believes that it is time for us to imagine, conceive, formulate, and begin to create an alternative historical project to modernity, one in which liberation, not merely emancipation, and radical diversity, not abstract universality, define our goals.

Transmodernity involves recognition of not only cultural but epistemic difference as well. Transmodernity is, among other things, Dussel's response to Eurocentrism and the formation of an epistemic community of masters. It posits that theory does not travel exclusively from Europe to the world, but is rather found in different sites and travels in different directions. In this view, the philosopher is called to be more than a "functionary" (Husserl) or an "interpreter" (Habermas), she is called to be an agent of a de-colonization that furthers critical consciousness, alterity, and the teleological suspension of identity through different epistemologies.[100] The works of Levinas, Fanon, and Dussel provide examples of the complex itinerary of philosophers whose work intersects in Europe but can hardly be reduced to European premises, experiences, histories, or epistemologies. Their theoretical formulations cannot be understood without the irreducible presence of Judaism, the close attention to anti-black racism, and the dynamics of colonialism in the modern world. At their best moments the philosophies of Levinas, Fanon, and Dussel propose creative solutions to problems partly created by Europe, but hardly understood with European lenses alone.

The four moments of the de-colonial turn listed above offer another example of how consciousness acquires new theoretical horizons through events and ideas that can't be traced back exclusively to Europe. They involve crises and initiatives among whose protagonists are those whom Fanon referred to as the condemned of the earth. The very concept of transmodernity emerges in an important moment in the expression of the de-colonial turn, when indigenous peoples firmly protested the celebration of five hundred years of the invasion and invention of the Americas by Europeans. The significance of this moment cannot be underestimated. In Mexico, the mainly indigenous Ejercito Zapatista de Liberación Nacional decided to go to war after demonstrations in 1992 and a number of abuses that it perceived as part of an ongoing process of colonization and dispossession that has lasted for over five hundred years.[101] Dussel recognizes the relevance of the Zapatista struggle in his work, and he takes seriously the question of indigeneity for his articulation of transmodernity, yet at the same time indigenous voices do not figure among Dussel's main interlocutors. His phenomenology of the *ego conquiro* from Moctezuma's perspective is an important contribution to critical theory, but, like any phenomenology, it is incomplete without a necessary dialogical project. For the de-colonial phenomenology that I have been articulating here, the dialogue in question breaks through Eurocentric prejudices and seeks to expand the horizon of interlocutors beyond colonial and imperial differences. The de-colonial attitude seeks to be able to listen to what has been silenced. Such a task cannot be accomplished by the continued centering of European and North American authors in reflections about every important philosophical topic, as Dussel himself tends to do in most of his work. It is for this very reason that figures such as Fanon and many others have remained in the margins of Dussel's thought for so long even though their work intersects so strongly with his. In this sense it is possible to say that Dussel's idea of transmodernity promises more than what he himself delivers—or at least has delivered so far. The same could also be said of Levinas and Fanon—they too promised more than they delivered. While it is true that a proper understanding of their work necessitates going beyond pure European horizons, Levinas hardly conceived of dialogical relations beyond ideas represented by Athens and Jerusalem, and Fanon remained for the most part immune to different strains of Caribbean philosophy and to Islamic philosophical ideas.[102] Levinas, Fanon, and Dussel take us only so far in the task of elaborating de-colonizing epistemologies. Transmodernity serves as an orienting idea in furthering this project—not the unfinished project of the Enlightenment but the unfinished project of de-colonization.[103]

CODA

In addition to transmodernity, Dussel offered in the late 1990s a renewed ethics of liberation as an alternative to the ethical ideas that drive globalization. *Etica de la liberación en la edad de la globalización y la exclusión* [Ethics of liberation in the age of globalization and exclusion] combines Dussel's Levinasian-inspired ethics of liberation with basic concepts and ideas drawn from an intense reading of Marx in the 1980s and a series of dialogues with Karl-Otto Apel in the late 1980s and early 1990s.[104] The task of commenting on this work is more difficult than usual as Dussel has continued expanding, elaborating, and changing ideas that appear in it. The revisions form part of a new work in progress on the politics of liberation, which already comprises two volumes and a projected third. A critical revision of Dussel's newly formulated ethics and politics will be best done when such volumes are completed. Nonetheless, it is possible to raise a few questions on the basis of the arguments presented here.

In this work, I have focused on Dussel's interpretation and appropriation of Levinas, his alternative view of history, and his phenomenology of the *ego conquiro*. There are no major innovations or changes about these topics in *Etica de la liberación*. Perhaps the main difference resides in the combination of Marx and Levinas in his philosophical anthropology. While Marx was absent from the early liberation ethics, now Marx (along with Hinkelammert) provides a basis to articulate a material principle in ethics.[105] Dussel wishes to combine ethics as first philosophy with a materialist conception that posits the preservation of life as the driving idea of his ethics. What remains a mystery is how to reconcile the principle of the preservation of life (primarily one's own) with the primacy of the responsibility for the other person. If Dussel's early philosophy of liberation encountered problems in the application of Levinasian categories to geopolitical reality, it faces similar problems in his *Etica de la liberación* regarding the conciliation between basic material and ethical elements. In order to answer this problem Dussel has formulated an intelligent account of the relation between fact and value (the "is" and the "ought").[106] But such account is elaborated mainly independently of Levinas's ideas, which points to the possible incompatibility between Levinasian categories and his material ethics in the first place. This problem points to another important consideration: since Dussel still relies on his early interpretation and appropriation of Levinas, the Levinasian critique of Dussel's early ethics of liberation that I offer in chapter 5 is still relevant for a discussion of his *Etica de la liberación*. One could also argue that the absence of figures such as Fanon and his perhaps overreliance on Apel in his *Etica de la liberación* lead Dussel to lose track once more of the relevance of phenomenology, but also of the idea of an intrinsic link between the ethical and the political.

I have developed here basic ideas for an ethics and a politics of liberation. I try to bring together the ethical and the political, the practical and the theoretical, as well as the genetic, the existential, and the genealogical/historical through the critical reading and creative expansion of Levinas's ethical metaphysics and genetic phenomenological approach, Fanon's existential phenomenology and sociogeny, and Dussel's genealogy of modernity and phenomenology of the *ego conquiro*. Dussel's *Etica de la liberación* begins with his genealogy of modernity and the formulation of alternative views of history. But he then takes different routes from the ones that I pursue here concerning the primacy of ethics and its relation with de-colonization. I propose this work as a parallel and complementary project to Dussel's liberation philosophy, largely inspired by his own efforts.

CONCLUSION

BEYOND THE PARADIGM OF WAR

Man is motion toward the world and toward his like. A movement of aggression, which leads to enslavement or to conquest; a movement of love, a gift of self, the ultimate stage of what by common accord is called ethical orientation. Every consciousness seems to have the capacity to demonstrate these two components, simultaneously or alternatively.
—FRANTZ FANON[1]

The ontological difference is preceded by the difference between good and evil. —EMMANUEL LEVINAS[2]

In this work I have attempted to make explicit the subtle complicities between dominant epistemological and anthropological ideals and the exercise of violence. The works of Levinas, Fanon, and Dussel oppose what I have called a paradigm of violence and war. This dominant paradigm is characterized by making invisible or insignificant the constitutive force of interhuman contact for the formation of subjectivity, of knowledge, and of human reality in general. The relation with objects, whether practical or theoretical, takes primacy over the relation between human beings. The first motivation for this way of thinking is to attain knowledge, truth, comprehension, or adequate understanding. The self is thereby taken to be primarily a monad, a transcendental ego, or an autonomous and free human being for whom the relation with the Other tends to represent only an undesirable detour in the project of adequately representing the world. The self becomes allergic to the Other, and the intersubjective contact is then accounted for either in epistemological categories or in concepts tied to a theoretical approach. This philosophical anthropology ends up legitimating the superiority of theory over praxis and contemplation over liberation. One of my central points is that once a civilization begins to conceive the humanity of the human in these terms it will either commit violence with good conscience, find itself incapable of opposing violence, or legitimize ideals of peace that are complicit with violence.

I trace dominant themes surrounding the discussion of the crisis or so-called malaise of Europe back to the allegiance of Western civilization to practices that obey the logics opened up by a skewed vision of the human. Such a vision combines claims for autonomy and freedom with the production of the color line or the systematic differentiation between groups taken as the norm of the human and others seen as the exception to it. The so-called discovery of the New World became a crucial point in the establishment of this vision: it oriented Western humanism in a radically dehumanizing direction. From then on, Western humanism argued for the glory of Man and the misery of particular groups of human beings simultaneously. Indeed, Man became the most glorious as he was able to claim relative independence from God and superiority over the supposedly less than human others at the same time. The relationship between (imperial) Man and God has been ambiguous for the most part, but not so the relation between Man and his inferior sub-others. It is as if the production of the "less than human" functioned as the anchor of a process of autonomy and self-assertion. The paradigm of war, at first reconciled to and to some extent promoted by imperial Christendom, legitimates war against God, nature, and, particularly, the less than human others. The relationship with God and nature, however, can vary. What typically remains constant for the warring paradigm is the assertion of the color line. The distinction between God, Man, and the non-human precedes the reduction of subjectivity to a totality or its naturalization. And it was the colonized and the modern slave who experienced the systematic negation of her and his subjectivity, long before positivism, naturalism, or philosophies of history subsumed subjectivity in larger frameworks or anonymous mechanisms. In modernity, the racialized others take the place of enemies in a perpetual war out of which modern ideals of freedom and autonomy get their proper sense. This is the foundation of modernity as a paradigm of war and the source of many of its pathologies, crises, and evils.

The more positive side of this work, that is more constructive and less critical, resides in the effort to formulate an alternative vision of the human and a different conception of peace. I do not deny that many thinkers in the Western tradition had this concern in mind when they developed their ideas. Yet, as we have seen, a commitment to the centrality of Europe and Western man, a more or less open or surreptitious dependence on epistemologically centered ideals and categories, or, as most often happens, both things at the same time, have seriously hindered the success of these efforts. We are looking, then, for a different and more radical point of departure that opens new venues for thinking. To locate this point of departure I focused on the relation between the self and the Other. The relation with the Other is accounted for, following the work primarily of Levinas and Fanon, in ethical and not epistemological terms. The relation with the Other-qua-Other is described here as *goodness*.

Goodness designates the character of the difference between self and Other, or, what I have called following Dussel, trans-ontological difference. It refers, not to the need for things, but to a desire for the Other that emerges beyond any complacency. Goodness means, in this sense, the gift of the self to the Other. By definition, evil refers, in contrast, to the emergence of a concerted effort to put an end to the paradox of the gift and to render ethics unrealizable. Following Fanon, I have referred to this condition as colonialism. As I use it here, colonialism does not refer so much to the presence of imperialism or colonial administrations, but to a modality of being as well as to power relations that sustain a fundamental social and geopolitical divide between masters and slaves. Colonialism, or better put, coloniality (of power, knowledge, and being) is the spinal cord, as it were, of the modern paradigm of war.[3] In colonialism the contours of the relation between good and evil change drastically. While the masters attempt to possess the monopoly of goodness, the slave is rendered as evil. Since the masters also identify or see themselves as servants or shepherds of the true source of signification, the colonized come to represent non-beings. The colonized become then alternatively for the masters extremely visible as representatives of evil and entirely invisible as subhumans. That is why at one point the master can express hate, at another—fascinated by the prohibited—sexual desire, while at other points he can be completely indifferent to the situation of the slave. The neurosis of the master goes hand in hand with the so-called dependency complex of the colonized—both of which are sociogenically produced.

I argued that colonialism is characterized by a situation in which the trans-ontological difference collapses into the sub-ontological difference. The colonized subject is not an alter or an alter ego, but someone who is less than an other. It is what I call the sub-alter. While alterity or the Other-qua-Other introduces the possibility of goodness, the emergence of the sub-alter represents radical evil. The production of evil is related to the unethical excess of signification or Being, or, in other words, to the coloniality of Being. In the unethical excess of Being the Other does not simply become an alter ego, but a sub-alter. The unethical excess of signification is, therefore, tied to the project of creating a world to the measure of a "community of masters." The emergence of sub-alterity is a most fundamental and necessary moment of this effort. In a racist/imperial world the synchrony of signification turns excessively violent: it does not only domesticate the particular to the universal or to the concept, but also turns against the very existence of another subject. In modernity, this fundamentally anti-ethical and genocidal modality has become naturalized through racisms of various kinds. In a racist world, the one-for-the-Other is gradually replaced at the concrete level by the-one-against-the-Other or by the one-without-the-Other, both of which amount to the same thing: the death ethics of war. Being thus turns impersonal, if not homicidal, as it hides the faces and mutes the voices of people. But this task can never be accomplished in its totality. A denunciation, a protest, a "cry" of ethical revolt emerges behind the masks that hide the faces. Suddenly an apparent truth appears as an ideology, and the limits of Being are clearly shown. It is from here that thinking from the limits appears in this work as a radical insurgent act.

At the limits of Being we do not find so much a being-in-the-world who can elevate himself to an extraordinary level in the anticipation of death, but a being whose very existence is questioned and whose ordinary experience is marked by the always threatening act of becoming the victim of murder. Recipients of an evil without measure, the "damned," for whom the problem of projecting their ownmost possibilities of existence represents a travesty of their condition, paradoxically turn to those who are worse than them and give themselves *to the point of substitution*. It is as if the experience of evil, as Levinas points out, has the potential of awakening the soul to the horror of evil.[4] The horror of evil can then turn into an expectation of the good, and, ultimately, into goodness itself. The excess of love is called, at the limits of Being, to oppose the excess of evil. We find then that, in their response to the horror of evil, the "damned" are not so much characterized by "care" as by love.

Love is just another name here for the paradox of the gift and for what I have called before *altericity*. Altericity advances a distinct conception of peace, of interhuman contact, and of the very meaning of the human. The gift of the self represents, beyond the solipsistic achievement of truth and knowledge, the point of entry of the existent into the human. The self is only able to *see* (*theoros*) and *grasp* (comprehend), because it first *hears* and *gives*. Hearing the "cry" of the wounded and the afflicted becomes, in this sense, the enlightening act *par excellence*. At this point the neutralizing and impersonal trend of the process of signification is reoriented by its reference to the interhuman realm, and more particularly, to the one-for-the-Other. The suspension of the priority of the universal by (de-colonial) love represents in this way the effective exorcism from the hypnotic glare of Being.[5]

If we follow Levinas, the presuppositions and implications of alterity lead us away from the modernity of Descartes and seem to introduce us to the modernity of Don Quixote.[6] In contrast to the ego cogito, Don Quixote not only knows that he is enchanted, but also values the knowledge of his enchantment. Such knowledge is, he says, "enough for the firmness of my consciousness, which would grow too big if I thought that I was not enchanted. I would then, lazy and fearful, allow myself to remain in this cage and disappoint all of those in need who have, at the moment, the extreme need for my assistance and protection."[7] Don Quixote knows that giving priority to disenchantment or the search for certainty can make him deaf to the cry of those who are in need of his assistance. Knowing that one is enchanted, reconciling oneself with the fundamental incompleteness of knowledge, and, thus, with the permanent possibility of skepticism, perhaps represents the most effective cure against the enchantment with the absolute priority of disenchantment and its perverse effects. In defying the strictures of the split between enchantment and disenchantment the humanity of the human is articulated here in terms of the attention and response to those who suffer.

In *Totality and Infinity* Levinas provides an alternative reading of Descartes that puts him closer to Don Quixote. In his alternative reading, Levinas emphasizes the idea that even though Descartes claimed the "cogito ergo sum" as the first evidence, there was an even prior moment when the *cogito* must have had access to the idea of the infinite, whose source cannot be the *cogito* itself. The idea of infinity in the *cogito* serves Descartes to argue for the existence of God. For Levinas, it becomes a way to articulate the priority of witnessing the Other (the divine or the human other) in respect to "being" or "reason." From there comes his idea that the birth of reason depends on something like an interpersonal relation at the early moments of the constitution of subjectivity. In short, Levinas wants to make Descartes appear as a proponent of the idea that ethics precedes ontology and epistemology. With this Judaic interpretation of Descartes, Levinas clearly aims to make the point that it is not only possible but indeed desirable for modern Europeans to claim the Jewish roots of Western civilization. Or rather, his point is that a legitimate affirmation of Western roots in the twentieth century has to abandon its problematic and no longer credible theodicy and claim the relevance of its disavowed Jewish roots. In that way Plato, Descartes, and other seminal thinkers of the West could be reclaimed, even after Heideggerian *des-truktion* of the Western philosophical tradition. For Levinas, the important point was not so much the destruction or deconstruction of Western philosophy, but finding another meaning for it and introducing new possibilities for thinking—particularly Judaic. Levinas sought the multifold articulation of the idea of non-indifference or the one-for-the-Other as well as the reinterpretation and critical evaluation of the Western intellectual legacy in light of that purpose.

However viable Levinas's reinterpretation of Descartes may be he did not deny the way in which Cartesian philosophy inspired ideas about the primacy of epistemological problems, the mind-body split, and the relationship between self and other, among other ideas that many, including Levinas himself, considered to be extremely problematic elements in European modernity. That is why he offers Don Quixote as a counterexample to Cartesianism and to the privilege of epistemology in Western philosophy in his preface to the Spanish translation of *Totality and Infinity*, which he wrote more than two decades after the book originally appeared in French. In the preface, he interprets Don Quixote's madness in terms of the idea of skepticism and non-indifference that he articulated in *Otherwise Than Being* a few years before. Don Quixote's madness is consistent with the ethical reduction that Levinas articulated in response to the Cartesian-inspired Husserlian conception of the phenomenological reduction. However, Levinas fails short of articulating the more precise idea of the de-colonial reduction as a response to the modern paradigm of war. The de-colonial reduction is based on the idea that European modernity is intrinsically linked with the realities of racialization and colonization. As a result, there is a need to uncover the ways in which the *saying* of responsibility collapses into the *said* of colonialism and race or the exception from the realm of humanity. The de-colonial reduction is inspired by the skepticism toward modernity as a paradigm of war, which brings out the problem of the self-deception of Europe. The first figure who brought up this point in relation to Descartes was the Martiniquean Aimé Césaire. When Césaire writes in *Discourse on Colonialism* that "a civilization that uses its principles for trickery and deceit is a dying civilization," he was pointing out that the crisis of

Europe is a result of its behavior as an "evil demon" of sorts that deceived humanity and even itself.[8] The irony that Césaire points out is that of a civilization whose philosophy is based on avoiding deception and self-deception and yet ends up becoming a massive deceiver and criminal. At the heart of such a deceptive spirit hides a profound principle that Césaire links to Hitlerism. But Hitlerism, in his view, cannot be understood well without reference to colonialism. In this sense, Hitlerism appears to Césaire as an older principle or commitment: Europe believed itself to be Cartesian when it rather was Hitlerian. Césaire comments:

> Yes, it would be worthwhile to study clinically, in detail, the steps taken by Hitler and Hitlerism and to reveal to the very distinguished, very humanistic, very Christian bourgeois of the twentieth century that without his being aware of it, he has a Hitler inside him, that Hitler *inhabits* him, that Hitler is his *demon*, that if he rails against [it] he is being inconsistent and that, at bottom, what he cannot forgive Hitler for is not *crime* in itself, *the crime against man*, it is not *the humiliation of man as such*, it is the crime against the white man, the humiliation of the white man, and the fact that he applied to Europe colonialist procedures which until then had been reserved exclusively for the Arabs of Algeria, the coolies of India, and the blacks of Africa.

That Hitler is Europe's demon points to Dussel's idea regarding the proto-history of the ego cogito. Before Descartes and Hitler, there was Cortés. Before Cartesianism and Hitlerism, there was racial slavery and colonialism. A de-colonial reduction of Western thought brings out these connections and reveals hidden dimensions in European modernity: from Césaire's link between Hitlerism and colonialism to Dussel's phenomenology of the *ego conquiro*, to Fanon's explorations of the lived experience of the colonized, in respect to which he tested the limits of dominant ontological and psychoanalytical conceptions. The European Cartesian-inspired sciences give way here to de-colonial Césaireian-inspired sciences and forms of critique according to which the truth and the good are only found, if not instantiated, by the preferential option for the *damnés*, the suspicion of master morality, the epistemic priority of the color line, and the ethical suspension of identity and the telos of empire.

Cartesianism introduces a highly abstract conception of subjectivity that renders embodiment unimportant or problematic for the task of knowledge; Hitlerism, in contrast, emphasizes embodiment to the point where it becomes an essence. Levinas posed the alternative of erotic and reproductive embodied subjectivity in response to Hitlerism and liberalism. Fanon proposed the idea of the body as the "open door of every consciousness" (BSWM 123), that is, as a site of hospitality and generous interhuman contact, as his response to the anthropology of colonialism and racism. Recognition of the body does not lead in this account to racial politics but rather to de-colonial engagement defined as the creation of the world of the *You*, which, in a racist and colonial order, demands no less than "the end of the world"—from here the relevance of politics and revolutionary action to Fanon. The embodied self for Fanon is primarily a site of generous interaction. Agency is defined primordially in ethical terms. Fraternity in this context no longer refers to blood relations but rather to the primacy of intersubjective contact. Once the embodied self is recognized as the point of departure, and the body is conceived as the "open door" of consciousness, then nonsexist human fraternity does not take a secondary role to liberty or equality. The demands of a consistent struggle for nonsexist human fraternity, perhaps better put as affiliation, points to the need for a suspension of the ultimate value of the affirmation of identity and to the need of altericity or the suspension of the universal through the preferential option for the *damnés*. Affiliation, which is defined by the Chicana theorist Chela Sandoval as "attraction, combination, and relation carved out of and in spite of difference," goes together here with non-indifference and responsibility, both of which presuppose listening to the cry of the condemned.[9] To be sure, both listening and responsible action are only possible through embodiment. Action is in this sense no longer defined by the hand-that-takes but rather by receptive generosity and what Sandoval has aptly rendered as de-colonial love.[10] In short, in new de-colonial sciences the search for truth and knowledge, the accomplishment of liberty and equality, and the satisfaction of demands for the recognition of identity respond to something greater than themselves: to the humanizing task of building a world in which genuine ethical relations become the norm and not the exception—the very subversion of the paradigm of war.

The creation of the world of the *You* needs to be mediated by the exercise of critique. Philosophy is called to identify and denounce the moments in which structures of meaning respond to the *interest* of Being and betray the *for-the-Other* of signification. Philosophy performs a *reduction* of what has been "said" by showing the many ways in which the said turns against, rather than in favor of, the flourishing of ethics in the interhuman realm. Philosophy is called to show when certain formations of meaning create or are complicit with a context marked by the relation between a master and a slave. This relation is sometimes located at a basic intersubjective level, but its most frightful expression appears when it defines general modes of perception and behavior in communities, social bodies, and growing civilizations. At its highest level, the relation between master and slave takes on the control and division of the whole world and becomes empire. The critique of the imperial formation of the said evokes the de-colonial reduction. The de-colonial reduction attempts to bring out the pathologies of existence in contexts marked by the geopolitical extension of the relation between master and slave. By introducing coloniality as an axis of reflection in the examination of the lived worlds of communities, the de-colonial reduction makes clear how different sorts of pathologies can be traced back to the betrayal of the human in an imperial project of existence. The de-colonial reduction also opens up the mental space to enquire imaginatively into new possibilities of existence and the subversive power of loving or alterical acts.

The critique of the imperial expression of the said or de-colonial reduction is ultimately performed by both the philosopher and the activist. The destabilization of the imperial order of things occurs in thought as well as in praxis. At the end, Don Quixote, in his eccentric reflections, was a sort of philosopher himself. So was Frantz Fanon, who, with a rifle in one hand and a pen in the other, fought against dehumanizing and condescending ways of being and behaving. Expressions of anger and practices of violence represent the last recourse of the "damned." But activism has manifold ways to express itself, and to express itself continually it must, if it ever wants to see some change in the way that institutions work and in the manner in which we behave toward each other.

The de-colonial reduction is, therefore, performed in praxis and not only in theory. It can become then both a way of thinking and a way of life. In both of these ways, the de-colonial reduction gives expression to a peculiar utopian ideal: the end of empire and of imperial man. It becomes a constant alert against the temptation of ever trying to form "a community of masters." This alert and the related utopian ideal pose a challenge to Western civilization. Vanquishing Eurocentrism in its many forms becomes one of the most urgent tasks of the de-colonial reduction. Unfortunately, neither philosophers of the right nor critics of the left yet perceive the importance of this task. On the one hand we find Eurocentric discussions of liberalism, communitarianism, or cosmopolitanism; on the other hand we find equally Eurocentric discussions of radical political action.[11] We even find either open retrievals of Eurocentrism or

Eurocentric critiques of Eurocentrism. These philosophers and critics have not realized that the first and most basic gesture of the critique of Eurocentrism lies in listening to what the peoples on the periphery have to say about truth, justice, love, critique, community life, and so forth. They have to hear the people on the periphery, learn from them, and fight with them for the attainment of a condition in which such people are able to reproduce their lives and contribute fully in discussions about the future of humanity. This does not mean that the learning process is unidirectional. This is rather a matter of enacting a receptive de-colonial attitude by virtue of which true communication can be achieved. The de-colonial attitude highlights the *epistemic priority* of the problem of the color line, which, following Lewis Gordon, could be understood as the line between the allegedly normative and abnormal identities and forms of life.[12] The de-colonial attitude also gives a preferential option for the condemned of the earth, meaning that it takes centrally the questions, concerns, and proposals for de-colonization that emerge in the underside of the modern world. This does not mean that European responses must be rejected in toto since they have contributed and still contribute much to critical thinking; rather, they need to be opened up radically and transformed in light of the challenges posed by colonization and the paradigm of war. Resistance to such opening, dialogue, and transformation is a sad testimony to the persistence of Eurocentrism and the master morality of imperial man. De-colonization is waiting to occur not only in regard to material and cultural levels but also vis-à-vis epistemic levels.

We have, in this study, traveled distances and crossed barriers of time. The initial point of reference was the French Revolution of 1789. Levinas, a Lithuanian Jew who later became a French citizen, assessed the implications and limits of modern French liberalism. He believed that liberalism did not possess the conceptual elements to oppose the emergent Hitlerism of the 1930s in a consistent way. He argued that this conceptual deficiency was partly accounted for by its reliance on problematic articulations of human freedom. The liberal account of freedom is, for Levinas, strongly related to an ideal of a solipsistic and heroic search for and the attainment of truth. This way of accounting for the values of freedom and truth ultimately collapse for Levinas in the forgetfulness of the constitutive dimension of ethical intersubjective contact. This "forgetfulness" accounts clearly for the subtle continuities between liberalism and Hitlerism, as well as for the limits of liberalism in its opposition to Hitlerism.

For Levinas, the forgetfulness of an ethical intersubjective moment in the account of freedom in the West points to a limited appropriation, if not disavowal, of Judaism and of Jewish thought in dominant Western philosophy and religion. Levinas traces the emergence of the Western idea of freedom to a Judaic conception of "pardon." The pardoned subject is freed from previous faults and previous commitments. This conception of freedom, as we have seen, reappears in Levinas's subsequent writings. A crucial part of Levinas's project is thus to go back to Judaic sources and to demonstrate their pertinence for the proper articulation of a more humane Western thought. In this sense Levinas, as Fanon, elevates a "cry" of self-affirmation: "Is Judaism necessary to the world? Isn't Aeschylus enough?" "Where, then, is the difference between Delphi and Jerusalem?"[13] Very much opposed to the spirit of Hitlerian racism, Levinas responds to this question:

> The privilege of Israel resides not in its race but in the *mitzvot* which educate it. The effect of the *mitzvot* lasts beyond their practice, that is true. But, as I have already said, not indefinitely.
>
> What Judaism brings to the world, therefore, is not the easy generosity of the heart, or new and immense metaphysical visions, but a mode of existence guided by the practice of the *mitzvot*.[14]

The education of Israel by the *mitzvot* is directly reflected in its teaching to the world: "Israel would teach that the greatest intimacy of me to myself consists in being at every moment responsible for the others, the hostage of others. *I can be responsible for that which I did not do and take upon myself a distress which is not mine....*"[15]

This point leads Levinas to argue that

> in the world, we are not free in the presence of others and simply their witnesses. We are their hostages. A notion through which, beyond freedom, the self is defined. Rav Zera is responsible for those who are not Hitler. That may be something that we would not find in Aeschylus.
>
> The man who is hostage to all others is needed by men, for without him morality would have no place to start. The little bit of generosity that occurs in the world requires no less. The Jewish tradition has taught this.[16]

The teaching of the *mitzvot* is realized at the point in which, confronting Hitler, Rav Zera responds responsibly to those who are not Hitler. Hitler and his followers have another destiny: like evil itself they have a place reserved in hell.[17]

Levinas's "cry" of self-affirmation is in strange harmony with the preferential option for the oppressed and with the ethical suspension of identity. Being a Jew for Levinas means precisely being aware that our humanity is characterized by a responsibility beyond measure. As he puts it,

> The Jew is perhaps the one who—because of the inhuman history he has undergone—understands the suprahuman demand of morality, the necessity of finding within oneself the source of one's moral certainties. He knows that only a hedge of roses separates him from his own fall. He always suspects thorns beneath those roses: One had to find within oneself the certainty that this barrier was a real obstacle.[18]

Being a Jew is explained here for Levinas not so much in terms of biological relation or adherence to a doctrine, but in terms of an awareness of the "suprahuman demand of morality" gained by an exposure to suffering. This passage is consistent with Levinas's idea that the experience of evil can turn into the horror of evil, and thus, into the fight against evil itself. But this means that, ultimately, we can all become Jews, particularly those who suffer. As cosmopolitan and anti-racist as this formulation may appear to be it is strongly problematic. It is problematic because, first, being a Jew clearly involves more than achieving a particular awareness of the meaning of morality, and second, because it can easily lead to the idea that one defends victimized humanity simply by defending Jews and Judaism.[19] The identification of a particular identity with the ethical suspension of identity itself can, therefore, turn problematic. In this sense, the limits of Levinas's "cry" of self-affirmation are found, precisely, in the formulation of the question that orients his thought in terms of a divide between the Greek and the Jew. To be sure, there is no problem at all in that Levinas, a Jew, aims to reassert the value of Judaism. Questions of identity are a central part of the struggle for de-colonization and humanization. We must not confuse the question of identity with the excesses of identity politics or imply that inquiry into one's identity commits oneself to a divide between recognition and redistribution, or similar dichotomies. The problem resides in that his formulation hides the complexity of the task of "restoration" or de-colonization. Levinas opens a narrow door through which either Judaism or an improved formulation of Western thought through a return to Judaic sources can enter. Levinas fights against Hitlerism, but it is not entirely clear if he is successful in responding responsibly for those who are not Hitler, much less for those who are not European. His approach to Hispanic culture in his interpretation of Don Quixote represents an important step, albeit an initial but limited one, in the task of responding to those who are not Hitler and to those who are not European.

At the point in which the limitations in Levinas's effort to overcome the paradigm of violence and war became obvious we turned to the work of Frantz Fanon. With Fanon we moved from metropolitan France to its colonies. Even though the connections between Levinas's metaphysics of the hither side and Fanon's existential phenomenology are striking, it was noted that the examination of the lived experience of the oppressed allowed Fanon to uncover more adequate and general categories for the articulation of a position that recognizes the relevance of politics and postcolonial thought. What was discussed in the first chapter in terms of Levinas's conception of the "community of masters" was developed in the second part of this work in the context of a discussion of the implications of the Fanonian conception of the relation between master and slave. First, I discussed the ways in which the master is able to sustain his position as master, and then I turned to the slave, who is characterized by Fanon as the "damned." The "damned" is, using now Levinasian terms, the one who confronts evil and who translates suffering into the horror of evil. The "damned" is the paradigmatic alterical subject. Fanon to some extent embodies this existential mode as his life is invested in writing and fighting for the "damned." As Fanon struggles for non-sexist human fraternity, the "damned" become his brothers and sisters. Unfortunately, Fanon puts the emphasis on brotherhood, which gives more emphasis to male dynamics of interaction. Yet, as some feminists of color have noted, his reflections are not uniquely male centered and there are important points of contact between some of the ideas that he articulated and feminist ones.[20] By calling the "poor black," the "Jew," and the "Arab" his "brothers," with all the limits attached to this recognition, Fanon seems to enact a sort of cosmopolitan fraternal ideal that finds expression primarily in the liberating acts orchestrated by the oppressed for the oppressed. In short, Fanon commits himself to fight evil wherever he finds it. The cosmopolitan ideal, however, seems to find limits as Fanon not only declares other peoples as brothers, but as he struggles with them in their own particular battles—including those of both his brothers and sisters. The spirit of cosmopolitan fraternity, or global de-colonial affiliation, is best captured by the active participation in the struggle for the liberation of particular communities or sectors.

The idea of the struggle for nonsexist human fraternity or affiliation as a struggle for the liberation of the damned represents the climax of the effort to articulate a position that opposes the paradigm of war and its expressions in both Hitlerism and in the ambiguities of liberalism. We began our search in the year 1789, but then we traveled to occupied France and its colonies in the twentieth century. The year 1968 was also an important moment, but the events surrounding the date had a different meaning according to the territories in which they took place. While in France we find a critique of obsolete forms of Marxism along with a discourse on the death of man and a liberation of sexuality, in Latin America we have an increasing awareness of dependency along with the formulation of theologies and philosophies of liberation.[21] Empire shows different faces in different places and thus precipitates different forms of critique. But while the critique that emerges in the periphery takes into consideration the philosophies that emerge in the center, the philosophers of the center hardly pay attention to the people of the periphery, not only in terms of their intellectual production but also in terms of the very problem of a geopolitical division that reproduces the relation between master and slaves, that is, in relation to colonialism. As a consequence, philosophers of the center also tend to ignore the role of their own intellectual production in the imperial system of subordination. They want to oppose violence, but they do not care to examine the manifold implications of violence. There is much talk about the Other, but not too much effort in hearing others and in understanding what they have to say. Violence is committed in the very delimitation of scholarship to the languages of the dominant countries. This myopic perspective explains why Dussel went so far as to characterize the philosophies from the center as intrinsically dogmatic. However, what we have here is not so much an essential limitation as the very stultification of a thought that has grown accustomed to represent, with its limited perspective, the rest of the world. This encroachment explains why Fanon calls the "damned" to leave Europe alone and to forge by themselves the beginnings of a more humane world.

These considerations indicate that one of the most urgent tasks in the project of overcoming the paradigm of violence and war is the articulation of a new geography of knowledge.[22] The formulation of this geography entails, first and foremost, elaborating a non-Eurocentric view of world history. As we have seen this is an important part of Dussel's project. The attempt to establish the particularity of Latin America in world history led him to propose an innovative account of global population, of the movement of civilizations, and of the role of imperialism in shaping the contours of the globe. In his account, Dussel also shows how the intellectual production that appears in different locations responds not only to a tradition and a culture but also to the project of imprinting the relation between master and slave at a geopolitical level. At the same time, Dussel demonstrates how the perspective of the conquered is important for the articulation of a radical critique of the civilizing ideals and philosophical presuppositions of the conquerors. For Dussel, the voices of the South must be heard, and this is not because we presume or have "faith" in the equal value of other cultures, as Charles Taylor claims, but because the centuries-old experience of colonialism and dehumanization provides colonized subjects with important perspectives.[23] It is true that this affirmation may collapse, as Dussel's early reflections on knowledge and geopolitics themselves indicate, into an essentialist divide between the perspective of the intellectual of the center and the people of the periphery.[24] Yet, Dussel's own hermeneutic practice points to something entirely different. At the end, he is a Latin American of German descent and not an Indian. When he articulates a critique of European modernity out of the view of the Aztecs he performs an act of altericity and not only an act of self-affirmation. In practice he demonstrates that criticism must transgress the boundaries of geopolitical space and class formation, and, in the spirit of altericity, it must reach the one who is below to hear him or her as well as fight with him or her in the process of liberation. Criticism must be, in short, interspatial.[25] It involves a transgression of the perspectives provided by one's tradition and by one's limited geopolitical location.

The impetus for war and the continuous reproduction of the coloniality of power, being, and knowledge in our contemporary world point to the persistence of the paradigm of war and the need to oppose it frontally. The consistent evasion of the paradigm of violence and war requires a constant learning from the stories, mythical narratives, and intellectual views that emerge in locations whose subjects have experienced the evils of empire. We must be particularly attentive to the points in which the confrontation of evil turns into the horror of evil and the search for goodness. Goodness and love, indeed, become, in the account that I have articulated through the work of Levinas, Fanon, and Dussel, the highest expressions of our humanity. This account has many contacts with proposals by women of color, as I have indicated throughout the text. Appeals to love in the face of colonialism and slavery appear more as consistent responses to systems of dehumanization than as natural expressions of gender difference. Love, once again, appears as a response to war. In that regard, this book is a variation of a classical theme. But love is interpreted here as a de-colonizing activity and war as a paradigm. De-colonization will hardly occur without the understanding of the gravity of the problem that humanity faces and without the courage to put our diverse identities at risk in order to accomplish the ideal of de-colonial justice. Both de-colonial love and justice commence in the attention paid to the "cries" of ethical revolt that emerge at the very limits of Being. Thinking from the limits of Being, thus, becomes a fundamental act of altericity through which a subject struggles for the liberation of the "*damnés.*" May the world never find itself short of these paradoxical acts!

Unfortunately, our age witnesses a reaffirmation of provincial points of view and perspectives. It is true that the decay of Europe in the two world wars led to criticism of Eurocentrism, but it also paved the way for the strengthening of another imperial discourse, Americanism. Americanism was deployed in the first decades of the twentieth century as an assimilationist ideology with respect to European migration. Today it has come to life again in a reinvigorated form as it takes on duties that had belonged to the old-fashioned Eurocentrism. Although Eurocentrism and Americanism are both part and parcel of the master morality that I describe in this book, they are different. Unlike Eurocentrism, which pursues expansion through the idea of the universal, Americanism puts more emphasis on the particularity of culture. I have pursued a comparison of these two concepts elsewhere.[26] Crucial here is to note the way in which Americanism fulfills a twofold role in the age of the war against terror: it resists "barbarians" from the inside and the outside simultaneously. These are Arab Muslims and Hispanics, particularly Mexicans. Americanism is the soul of the war against terror as well as the force behind the militarization of the border zone between the United States and Mexico. While the Muslim is viewed as extremely violent, the Hispanic is rendered as a cultural terrorist of sorts who menaces the cultural integrity of the nation. No matter how postmodern our times may be, this way of conceiving non-European others continues the legacy of the paradigm of war and its characteristic Manicheism. It renders non-European others as evil ("axis of evil"), while the United States appears as an inexhaustible source of freedom and goodness. As I have presented it in this book, de-colonization is an attempt to undo this logic and to promote different ethical and political coordinates.

The reassertion of Americanism has provoked varied responses. Unfortunately, European critiques of Americanism seem to be more concerned with the U.S. declaration of independence from European roots than with the continuation of racist perspectives and imperial policies.[27]

Others, such as Jürgen Habermas and the late Jacques Derrida, made a plea for a common European foreign policy in the face of U.S. unilateralism.[28] What they fail to do is to decisively break with Manicheism by entering into a serious dialogue with communities affected by Western and non-Western violence. That such a dialogue could make a difference is clearly testified to by the situation in which Muslim communities and Muslim scholars find themselves today in Europe. The condition of Muslim communities and African migrants in France became altogether clear in the riots of October and November 2005. The position of intellectuals is evinced by the debate about the European Muslim philosopher and theologian Tariq Ramadan.[29] Ramadan has been publicly accused without concrete evidence in both France and the United States of being a terrorist or a terrorist sympathizer.[30] His strong critiques of terrorism and violence and his large body of work exploring new ideas of conviviality in Islam have been for the most part ignored.

In a sense one could say that Ramadan's struggle today is not much different from that of Levinas decades before: both seek to affirm a non-reducible European Muslim or Judaic consciousness. Ironically, the strongest critiques of Ramadan have come from Levinas's followers in France—so-called *nouveaux philosophes* such as Bernard Henri-Levy, among others. They have arguably exploited the worst aspects of Levinas's thought: not its de-colonial potential but its more strictly identitarian and provincial elements. What they tend to forget, along with Levinas, is that "Musselman," and not only Jew, has been a category of damnation in modernity, just as Primo Levi reminds us in his reflections about the concentration camps.[31] For Levi, the Musselmans "have no distinguished acquaintance in camp. . . . They suffer and drag themselves along in an opaque intimate solitude, and in solitude they die or disappear, without leaving a trace in anyone's memory." Levi also describes them as "non-men who march and labor in silence, the divine spark dead within them, already too empty to really suffer. One hesitates to call their death death, in the face of which they have no fear, as they are too tired to understand."[32] The Musselman, along with the black, the Jew, and other subjects today and through modernity, is the privileged target of the paradigm of war.

If philosophy (as the "wisdom of love") and critical theory, as I have argued here, acquire their exact meanings in the responsible response to "the condemned" beyond self-interests, abstract conceptions of universality, and the demands of identity, then our times call for serious engagements with bodies of work and experience that have remained ignored and disavowed in modernity. Fortunately, good examples exist today. Among them is the work of Enrique Dussel, who has met publicly with Tariq Ramadan and supported him, and who has also kept the lines of communication opened with Latinos and Latinas in the United States. He has also become part of the project of the recently formed Caribbean Philosophical Association where Fanon's work is central. The Association's motto is "shifting the geography of reason." Another good example is the continuing struggle of women of color, such as Cherríe Moraga and the late Gloria Anzaldúa, to forge cross-theoretical enrichment through lines of difference.[33] Much is to be done and to be learned in these transgressive dialogical engagements. But continue they must as they are fundamental for the emergence of new ideas that help to provide alternatives to modernity and undermine the paradigm of war. Hopefully, this work contributes in at least a small part to such efforts.

NOTES

PREFACE

1. I am in conversation here with Walter Mignolo's fascinating account of the colonial experience as the "darker side of the Renaissance." See Mignolo, *The Darker Side of the Renaissance*, 2nd ed.
2. Martinot used the term "death ethic of war" in a draft of an essay entitled "Movement Consciousness as Border Thinking: An Andaluzan Meditation on Democracy." In an exchange of June 26, 2007, he informed me that he dropped the concept for a more conceptual elaboration of what he wished to elaborate. My elaboration of the theory of modernity as a paradigm of war preceded my reading of Martinot's draft. What I found in it was the term "death ethic of war," which complemented the notion of nonethics of war that I was already using. Martinot's ideas about a warring ethic in the society of the United States and its link with white supremacy and coloniality complement in some ways the ideas that I develop in this book. For Martinot's formation of the idea see Martinot, "Patriotism and Its Double" and "Pro-democracy and the Ethics of Refusal."
3. Todorov, *The Conquest of America*; Fanon, *Black Skin, White Masks*; and Wyschogrod, *Spirit in Ashes*.
4. Conversation with Sylvia Wynter, December 2006. The full development of the idea will appear in her book, which is in preparation, but many of the essays that she has already published give an indication of its complex meaning.
5. For some of the discussions that ensued in this group, see the dossier coordinated by Berger, "The Poetics of the Sacred and the Politics of Scholarship."

INTRODUCTION

1. Levinas, *Difficult Freedom*, 152–53.
2. Fanon, *Black Skin, White Masks*, 109.
3. Cited in Lequan, *La paix*, 77, translation mine.
4. For a discussion of the topic of war in Rosenzweig and Levinas, see Mosès, "Rosenzweig et Lévinas," 137–59; and Reyes Mate, *Memoria de Auschwitz*, 13, 66–69.
5. Todorov, *The Conquest of America*, 145. I elaborate this idea in chapter 6.
6. See Gilroy, *Postcolonial Melancholia*, 39.
7. See Sandoval, *Methodology of the Oppressed*.
8. The de-colonizing ethico-political turn, or de-colonial turn, may be seen as the postcolonial variation of the better-known ethical turn in philosophy, cultural studies, and literary theory. On the ethical turn, see Garber, Hanssen, and Walkowitz, *The Turn to Ethics*; and Davis and Womack, *Mapping the Ethical Turn*.
9. Levinas, "Useless Suffering," 97.
10. For a discussion of the apartheid of theoretical domains, see Sandoval, *Methodology of the Oppressed*. I owe the recognition of the relevance of creolization to Lewis R. Gordon.
11. On the concepts of the people and the multitude, see Hardt and Negri, *Empire*; and Hardt and Negri, *Multitude*. For an elaboration of the concept of the "condemned" in relation to these two ideas, see Maldonado-Torres, "On the Coloniality of Being," 253–63.
12. For reflections on the de-colonial attitude, see Maldonado-Torres, "Decolonization and the New Identitarian Logics after September 11," 35–67; Maldonado-Torres, "Intervenciones filosóficas al proyecto incompleto de la descolonizacion"; and Maldonado-Torres, "Reconciliation as a Contested Future."
13. See, among others, Maldonado-Torres, "Decolonization and the New Identitarian Logics," 35–67; Maldonado-Torres, "Searching for Caliban in the Hispanic Caribbean," 106–22; and Maldonado-Torres, "Toward a Critique of Continental Reason." I continue this line of work in a book-length study in progress entitled *Fanonian Meditations*.
14. Dussel himself once pointed this out to me in conversation.
15. Martin Jay refers to an "intense fascination with Judaism" and to certain philo-Semitism in France after the Second World War. Jay, *Downcast Eyes*, 546.
16. This is particularly evident in the recent work of Slavoj Žižek. See Žižek, *The Fragile Absolute or, Why Is the Christian Legacy Worth Fighting For?*; Žižek, *On Belief*; and Žižek, *The Puppet and the Dwarf*. For a critique of

Žižek's romance with Christian radical orthodoxies, see Maldonado-Torres, "Liberation Theology and the Search for the Lost Paradigm," 39–61. Other important critiques of his work include Mignolo, "The Geopolitics of Knowledge and the Colonial Difference," 57–96; Hart, "Slavoj Žižek and the Imperial/Colonial Model of Religion," 553–78; and Maldonado-Torres, "The Regressive Kernel of Orthodoxy."

17. For discussions on transmodernity, see Dussel, "Modernity, Eurocentrism, and Trans-Modernity," 129–59; and Dussel, "World System and 'Trans'-Modernity," 221–44. For a concise articulation of critical cosmopolitanism, see Mignolo, "The Many Faces of Cosmo-polis," 721–48.

18. Important here are King, *Orientalism and Religion*; and Majid, *Unveiling Traditions*. I have explored this point more in depth elsewhere. See Maldonado-Torres, "Secularism and Religion in the Modern/Colonial World System."

19. Transversality is a sort of weak universality that includes its own suspension in relation to a higher good.

20. For a related idea, see Walter Mignolo's discussions of epistemic diversality in Mignolo, *Local Histories/Global Designs*. He has also introduced the notion of a pluri-verse, which can be related to similar efforts by other scholars to think through the idea of polycentrality. See Gilroy, *Postcolonial Melancholia*; King, *Orientalism and Religion*; and Majid, *Unveiling Traditions*. Two of these four scholars, namely Gilroy and Mignolo, do cite favorably Dussel's formulation of transmodernity and his critical engagement with Eurocentric accounts of modernity.

21. One could say that these are spurious reasons, but Kant has similar kinds of reasons when he defends the Enlightenment. They were concerned with emancipation from religion and with the protection of the emerging bourgeois order in Germany. Here we refer to different concerns. In a sense, this work positions itself in relation to transmodernity in a similar way to how Kant's critique of pure reason related to the Enlightenment. While Kant was solving problems in the tradition of modern European philosophy from Descartes to Hume, I try to solve problems in the tradition of subaltern thinkers from Fanon to Dussel. While Kant was primarily concerned with the emancipation of the bourgeoisie, my focus here is rather liberation and the coloniality of power.

22. For a discussion of the concept of double critique, see Cooke, "Multiple Critique," 91–110. For a discussion of the concept of transmodernity in relation to questions of religious discourse and secularity, see Maldonado-Torres, "Secularism and Religion."

23. A succinct account of the phenomenological concept of reduction appears

in Husserl, *Ideas Pertaining to a Pure Phenomenology and to a Phenomenological Philosophy*, 131–46.

24. See, for example, Turner, "On the Difference between the Hegelian and the Fanonian Dialectic of Lordship and Bondage," 134–51.

25. Hannah Arendt, for instance, portrays Fanon as a sort of irrational Sorelian. See Arendt, *On Violence*, 71. For a critical discussion of similar judgments, see Gendzier, *Frantz Fanon*, especially 195–205.

26. I refer to the group of young Argentinean intellectuals who reflected on Levinas's work in the early 1970s. This group included, in addition to Dussel, the influential Jesuit Juan Carlos Scannone and Daniel Guillot, responsible for the Spanish translation of *Totality and Infinity* in 1977.

27. Dussel, *The Invention of the Americas*.

1. FROM LIBERALISM TO HITLERISM

1. Levinas, "Useless Suffering," 97.
2. Levinas, "Signature," 291.
3. Heidegger's explicit argument for the subordination of ethics to fundamental ontology may have been present in Levinas's reflections on this theme. See Heidegger, "Letter on Humanism," 231–36.
4. A similar point is developed by Zygmunt Bauman:
   > We need to take stock of the evidence that the civilizing process is, among other things, a process of divesting the use and deployment of violence from moral calculus, and of emancipating desiderata of rationality from interference of ethical norms or moral inhibitions. As the promotion of rationality to the exclusion of alternative criteria of action, and in particular the tendency to subordinate the use of violence to rational calculus, has been long ago acknowledged as a constitutive feature of modern civilization—the Holocaust-style phenomena must be recognized as legitimate outcomes of civilizing tendency, and its constant potential. (Bauman, *Modernity and the Holocaust*, 28).

   The only difference between Bauman and Levinas on this point is that Levinas avoids the risk of talking about civilization in general. He rather refers to Western civilization and to the ways in which the ideal of the unconditional search for knowledge has been expressed within it. His project is therefore defined by the effort to find alternative ways of conceiving the search for knowledge and the idea of civilization.
5. Levinas, "Transcendence and Height," 30. Original French in Levinas, "Transcendance et hauteur," 117.
6. Levinas, "Meaning and Sense," 91.

7. Levinas, "Reflections on the Philosophy of Hitlerism," 63–71. Some of Heidegger's speeches in 1933 and 1934, including the famous "The Self-Assertion of the German University" (1933), appear translated in Wolin, *The Heidegger Controversy*.
8. Reyes Mate, *Memoria de Auschwitz*, 48.
9. Nietzsche, *On the Genealogy of Morals and Ecce Homo*.
10. See, among others, Nietzsche, *Beyond Good and Evil*; the fifth book of Nietzsche, *The Gay Science*; and the third part of Nietzsche, *On the Genealogy of Morals*, 97–163.
11. See Nietzsche, *The Will to Power* § 5, 10.
12. For a critical account of the relation between asceticism, slavery, and the Jews in Hegel and Nietzsche, see Yovel, *Dark Riddle*.
13. Nietzsche, *On the Genealogy of Morals*, 34.
14. Ibid., 43, § 11.
15. Ibid., 36, §10.
16. This point is elaborated in Levinas, *Time and the Other*.
17. See Nietzsche, *Beyond Good and Evil*, § 259, 03. For a discussion of death and the will-to-power in Nietzsche, see Dollimore, *Death, Desire and Loss in Western Culture*.
18. Camus, *The Rebel*, 77.
19. Ibid.
20. Quoted in ibid.
21. Quoted in Lequan, *La paix*, 77, translation mine.
22. Ibid., 80, 81–82.
23. See especially Husserl, "Philosophy as Rigorous Science," 168, 95.
24. Husserl, *Ideas Pertaining to a Pure Phenomenology and to a Phenomenological Philosophy*, §33, 63. Hereafter quoted as *Ideas I*.
25. It should be noted that there are various reductions, and that what is known as the phenomenological reduction is but the first and most basic one. For the purpose of this discussion, however, I do not think that such differentiations are necessary. See part 2, chapter 4 of *Ideas I* on "The Phenomenological Reductions" for a more precise account.
26. Ibid., § 50, 113, 55, 30.
27. Ibid., § 34, 68–69.
28. Husserl, "Philosophy as Rigorous Science," 168.
29. Ibid., 195.
30. Levinas, *The Theory of Intuition in Husserl's Phenomenology*, 24–25, italics mine. Following Levinas, Sartre will put it as follows:

> Against the digestive philosophy of empirico-criticism, of neo-Kantianism, against all "psychologism," Husserl persistently af-

firmed that one cannot dissolve things in consciousness. You see this tree, to be sure. But you see it just where it is: at the side of the road, in the midst of the dust, alone and writhing in the heat, eight miles from the Mediterranean coast. It could not enter your consciousness, for it is not of the same nature as consciousness. One is perhaps reminded of Bergson and the first chapter of Matter and Memory. But Husserl is not a realist: this tree on its bit of parched earth is not an absolute which would subsequently enter into communication with us. Consciousness and the world are given at one stroke: essentially external to consciousness, the world is nevertheless essentially relative to consciousness. (Sartre, "Intentionality," 4)

31. See, Levinas, *Theory of Intuition*, 146.
32. Levinas, *Discovering Existence with Husserl*, 48.
33. Levinas, *Theory of Intuition*, 150.
34. Levinas, *Discovering Existence with Husserl*, 74.
35. Ibid.
36. For an analysis of Husserl's conception of Hegelianism, see Rockmore, *On Hegel's Epistemology and Contemporary Philosophy*. Also see Heidegger, *Hegel's Phenomenology of Spirit*.
37. Sartre, "Intentionality," 5. The affinity between the early Levinas and Sartre's views on Husserlian phenomenology is adequately formulated by Richard Cohen in his foreword to Levinas's *Theory of Intuition* (xxviii): "What Levinas does not question—because, like Sartre, it pleases him—is that Husserl has succeeded in opening the door to the concrete, to meaning as lived, including practical significations such as 'goal,' 'end,' 'purpose,' and 'value.' Purpose is not a gloss that can be stripped off reality in the name of science but is of a piece with the constitution of the real as meaningful."
38. Levinas, *Theory of Intuition*, 53.
39. For a discussion of Levinas's adherence to a Lithuanian Judaism with a rather strong rationalist vein, see Lescourret, *Emmanuel Levinas*, 26–29.
40. A few paragraphs in this section also appear in Maldonado-Torres, "Postimperial Reflections on Crisis, Knowledge, and Utopia," 277–84. In that article, I compare and contrast Husserl's diagnoses and responses to the crisis of Europe with Immanuel Wallerstein's and Walter Mignolo's reflections on the crisis of the modern world-system.

For the relation between Husserl's reflections on the crisis and the political environment in Germany during the early 1930s, see Husserl, *The Crisis of European Sciences and Transcendental Phenomenology*, xvi–xvii.

41. Buckley, *Husserl, Heidegger and the Crisis of Philosophical Responsibility*, 9.
42. Husserl, *The Crisis of European Sciences and Transcendental Phenomenology*, 6–7.
43. See Husserl, "Philosophy and the Crisis of European Man," 149–92; and Gómez Romero, *Husserl y la crisis de la razón*, 84.
44. Gómez Romero, *Husserl y la crisis de la razón*, 73.
45. Husserl, "Philosophy and the Crisis of European Man," 157, italics mine.
46. References to ancient Greece and to the European Renaissance by German intellectuals during the last two to three centuries cannot be completely understood without considering the urgent concern for a mythical identity that would offer unity and historical depth, and, as Gayatri Spivak puts it, for the "fabrication of new representations of self and world that would provide alibis for the domination, exploitation, and epistemic violation entailed by the establishment of colony and empire." Spivak, *A Critique of Postcolonial Reason*, 7.
47. Husserl, *The Crisis of European Sciences and Transcendental Phenomenology*, 8.
48. Ibid., 12.
49. Husserl's conception of phenomenology, his reflections on the "possibility of philosophy as a task," and the related idea of the vocation of philosophers (as "functionaries of mankind") are, as we have seen, deeply related to his conception of both the crisis and the greatness of Europe (ibid., 16–18). A similar configuration of themes is found in the work of Max Weber, whose reflections on politics and science as vocations were originally published in 1919 and 1922 respectively and can be found in Weber, *From Max Weber*, 77–128, 129–56. Weber's reflections presuppose a particularly Eurocentric account of rationalization and "disenchantment." Weber's attempt to account for the "universal significance and value" of Western civilization in a time when there was as much imperialism as "disenchantment" remains exemplary of paradigmatically Eurocentric social scientific conceptions. For a discussion of this point, see Mignolo, *Local Histories/Global Designs*, 3–6.
50. This point complements Joan-Charles Mèlich's discussion on the Husserlian conception of barbarism and his indebtedness to the Greek concept of disinterested *theoria*. See Mèlich, *Totalitarismo y fecundidad*, 42–53.
51. According to Walter Mignolo, "space" in the sixteenth century and then "time" (history) toward the end of the eighteenth century and the beginning of the nineteenth became the privileged tools to proclaim differentiation with non-Europeans and the superiority of European forms of knowledge. Space and time merged when people living in different non-

European territories were considered to have no history. Mignolo refers to Max Weber as a figure in the beginning of the twentieth century who "transformed this lack [of alphabetic writing] into a celebration of true knowledge, an Occidental achievement of universal value." Mignolo, *Local Histories/Global Designs*, 3. The conceptual links between Husserl's and Weber's approaches are most interesting, though there are, as it has been suggested above, some notable differences in their conceptions of the relation of time and space to the subordination of non-European forms of knowledge.

52. Mèlich, *Totalitarismo*, 46, translation mine.
53. Husserl, *The Crisis of European Sciences and Transcendental Phenomenology*, 16.
54. Ibid., 17.
55. Buckley, *Husserl*, 137.
56. See Dussel, "Europe, Modernity, and Eurocentrism," 465–78; and Quijano, "Coloniality of Power, Eurocentrism, and Latin America," 539–80.
57. Césaire makes a similar point when he argues that Nazi Germany did to Europe something similar to what Europe had been doing to its colonies for centuries. See Césaire, *Discourse on Colonialism*.
58. I have further developed this critical analysis of Eurocentrism in Maldonado-Torres, "Decolonization and the New Identitarian Logics after September 11," 35–67.
59. Reyes Mate, *Memoria*, 13.

2. FROM FRATERNITY TO ALTERICITY

1. Glover, *Humanity*, 1, italics mine.
2. Levinas's "Reflections on the Philosophy of Hitlerism," which was originally published in 1934, was preceded a year before by an essay written in Lithuanian in which Levinas describes the French and German conceptions of spirituality (Levinas, "The Understanding of Spirituality in French and German Culture," 1–10). About this essay the translator comments:

> It is written by a young philosopher who is looking at what is, for him, two relatively new cultures, two new worlds. . . . The proof that Levinas is an outsider to these two cultures lies not only in the fact that the article is written in Lithuanian, but also in that he does not actively identify himself with either one and talks about them as only an outsider can. Thus, perhaps we now have a key to Levinas's acute criticism of Western philosophy which has garnered him so much popularity and respect for its perceptiveness. Perhaps he was able to

be so perceptive of the Western philosophical tradition because he came into it from the outside. (Valevicius, "Afterword," 13)

Although Valevicius's depiction of Levinas as an outsider of Western culture may be exaggerated, his description of the essay rightly points to the peculiarity of his intellectual concerns in comparison with European thought.

3. I refer mainly to those who, after the wake of deconstruction and poststructuralism, and after the subsequent enchantment with Heidegger in the United States, have almost exclusively examined Levinas's thought in terms of poststructuralist dilemmas. Another tendency is to reduce the pertinence of his reflections to the problems raised by interpersonal relations in contrast to strictly social problems. The discussion later on in chapter 5 gives a more precise idea regarding these approaches.

4. For a succinct account of the importance of the theme of war in Levinas's work, see Moses, "Rosenzweig et Lévinas," 137–59.

5. Levinas, "As If Consenting to Horror," 487–88. For references to *Sein und Zeit*, see Heidegger, *Being and Time*, trans. John Macquarrie and Edward Robinson. For a different translation, see Heidegger, *Being and Time*, trans. Joan Stambaugh.

6. I will make the genealogy alluded to here more evident in my discussion of the work of Enrique Dussel in part 3 of this book.

7. There are many accounts of Heidegger's involvement with Nazism. Among them, see Wolin, *The Heidegger Controversy*; Farias, *Heidegger and Nazism*; Wolin, *The Politics of Being*; Caputo, *Demythologizing Heidegger*; and Sluga, *Heidegger's Crisis*. For an examination of other philosophers' relations with Nazism, see, in addition, Losurdo, *Heidegger et l'idéologie de la guerre*; and Glover, *Humanity*, 367–76. For an unambiguous defense of Heidegger that sets out to "de-Nazify" Heidegger's thought, see Young, *Heidegger, Philosophy, Nazism*. A more moderate critical reconstruction appears in McCumber, *Metaphysics and Oppression*.

8. Levinas remarks that he may have learned of Heidegger's sympathy with National Socialism even before 1933. See Levinas, "As If Consenting to Horror," 485.

9. Ibid.

10. Consider Levinas's testimony of his encounter with Heidegger in his sojourn in Freiburg:

"La grande chose que j'ai trouvée fut la manière dont la voie de Husserl était prolongée et transfigurée par Heidegger. Pour parler un langage de touriste, j'ai eu l'impression que je suis allé chez Husserl et que j'ai trouvé Heidegger. Je n'oublierai certes jamais

Heidegger dans ses rapports à Hitler. Même si ces rapports ne furent que de brève durée. . . . Mais les ouvres de Heidegger, la manière dont il pratiquait la phénoménologie dans *Sein und Zeit*—j'ai su aussitôt que c'est l'un des plus grands philosophes de l'histoire. Comme Platon, comme Kant, comme Hegel, comme Bergson.
[The great thing I found was the way in which Heidegger extended and transfigured Husserl's path. To use the language of a tourist, I had the impression that I went to visit Husserl and found Heidegger instead. I will certainly never forget Heidegger in his relations with Hitler. Even though these relations were only brief, they are forever. But Heidegger's works, the way in which he practiced phenomenology in *Sein und Zeit*—I knew immediately that he is one of the greatest philosophers in history. Like Plato, Kant, Hegel, Bergson.] (The interview in which this passage appears is found in Poirié, *Emmanuel Lévinas*, 78. The interview took place in the spring of 1986.)

11. See Levinas, *The Theory of Intuition in Husserl's Phenomenology*.
12. Levinas makes this point in Levinas, *Time and the Other*, 40.
13. Particularly relevant in this regard is Levinas, "Is Ontology Fundamental?," 1–10. This essay was originally published in 1951.
14. Levinas went so far as to comment that "such a powerful and original philosophy as Heidegger's, even though it is in many respects different from Husserlian phenomenology, is to some extent only its continuation." Levinas, *The Theory of Intuition in Husserl's Phenomenology*, lvi.
15. See Losurdo, *Heidegger et l'idéologie de la guerre*, 11–15.
16. Ibid., 13.
17. Caputo, *Demythologizing Heidegger*, 40.
18. Ibid., 50.
19. Ibid., 44–45.
20. There are important differences, however, between Nietzsche's philosophy of the Overman and Heidegger's account of authenticity. See Thiele, *Timely Meditations*, 56–57.
21. See Caputo, *Demythologizing Heidegger*, 50.
22. Ibid., 56.
23. Levinas studied in Freiburg during the academic year of 1928–29. Heidegger offered his lecture course "The Fundamental Concepts of Metaphysics" in the year 1929–30.
24. See Wolin, *The Politics of Being*, 73.
25. See ibid., 107; Buckley, *Husserl, Heidegger and the Crisis of Philosophical Responsibility*, 219.

26. Wolin, *The Politics of Being*, 107.
27. See Caputo, *Demythologizing Heidegger*, 57; Buckley, *Husserl, Heidegger and the Crisis of Philosophical Responsibility*, 220.
28. Quoted in Buckley, *Husserl, Heidegger and the Crisis of Philosophical Responsibility*, 220.
29. Ibid., 222–23.
30. Ibid., 223.
31. Fritzsche, *Germans into Nazis*, 6.
32. Ibid., 7.
33. Heidegger, "'Only a God Can Save Us,'" 113. It was as early as 1935 that Heidegger was already commenting on the superiority of the Greek language over Latin and over traditions that were spread through Latin. See Heidegger, *An Introduction to Metaphysics*, 13.
34. Wolin, *The Politics of Being*, 24.
35. Wolin elaborates on the conservative anti-democratic abhorrence of "publicity" in Heidegger's work. See ibid., 36. This notion of publicity is behind Heidegger's concept of the fall, his conception of *Mitsein* (being-with), and his notion of inauthenticity.
36. Faye, *Heidegger*.
37. In his interview with *Der Spiegel* Heidegger indicates that his strong advocacy of the Führer in 1933 only reflected the recognition that he would not have been able to complete his position as rector without some compromises. He also remarks that he would no longer write sentences like "The Führer himself and he alone *is* the present and future German reality and its rule." Heidegger, "'Only a God Can Save Us,'" 96. For Levinas Heidegger's silences were more significant than his effort at clarification. As I aim to demonstrate above, I believe that, even when one leaves aside the question of the uncertainty of some data concerning Heidegger's involvement with Nazism, his responses to the questions in the interview themselves reflect an extremely problematic and dangerous position.
38. See Levinas, "As If Consenting to Horror," 487. For other views on the implications of Heidegger's silence about the Shoah, see Milchman and Rosenberg, *Martin Heidegger and the Holocaust*.
39. Levinas, "As If Consenting to Horror," 487.
40. Levinas, *God, Death, and Time*, 93.
41. See especially, Heidegger, "Letter on Humanism," 189–242; Heidegger, "On the Essence of Truth," 113–41; Heidegger, *The Question Concerning Technology and Other Essays*.
42. On this point see Manning, "The Cries of Others and Heidegger's Ear," 19–38.

43. Levinas, *De l'évasion*, 93, translation mine. This book version is a reprint of the essay with the same title originally published in the journal *Recherches Philosophiques* in 1935. The reprint version is introduced and annotated by Jacques Rolland. This text, in which Levinas explicitly declares war against all forms of "ontologism," is also marked, as is all his work, by the presentiment of Hitlerism. As he will put it years later,

> Dans le texte original, écrit en 1935, on peut distinguer les angoisses de la guerre qui approchait, et toute la "fatigue d'être," l'état d'âme de cette période. Méfiance à l'égard de l'être, qui, sous une autre forme, s'est continuée dans ce que j'ai pu faire après cette date, à une époque qui, tout entière, était le pressentiment de l'hitlérisme imminent partout. Ma vie se serait-elle passée entre l'hitlérisme incessamment pressenti et l'hitlérisme se refusant à tout oubli?
> (Poirié, *Emmanuel Lévinas*, 90)

44. Levinas, *De l'évasion*, 127, translation mine.
45. Levinas uses the neologism "besoin d'*excendance*" to express this idea of evasion. See ibid., 22.
46. In this sense, Levinas's efforts may be considered to be *trans-ontological*.
47. The following statement by Heidegger indicates the nature of the discourse that Levinas was opposing so fiercely:

> To philosophize is to inquire into the *extra*-ordinary. But because, as we have just suggested, this questioning recoils upon itself, not only what is asked after is extraordinary but also the asking itself. In other words: this questioning does not lie along the way so that we bump into it one day unexpectedly. Nor is it part of everyday life. . . . The questioning itself is "out of order." It is entirely voluntary, based wholly and uniquely on the mystery of freedom, on what we have called the leap. The same Nietzsche said: "Philosophy . . . is a voluntary living amid ice and mountain heights." . . . To philosophize, we may now say, is an extra-ordinary inquiry into the extraordinary.
> (Heidegger, *An Introduction to Metaphysics*, 12–13)

Later on we will see how Levinas goes beyond the attempt to redeem ordinary life to a rearticulation of the very meaning of philosophy in ways different from Nietzsche and Heidegger.

48. As I have attempted to make clear so far, the links between these positions indicate that they continue the general lines of a dominant paradigm of thought and are not purely identical. The point is, then, that their oppositions are more superficial than often thought. The positions are also internally ambiguous. This will be made more evident later when we

consider the internal tension in the liberal ideas of liberty, equality, and fraternity.

49. I refer to the series of lectures, essays, and monographs that begin with Levinas, *De l'existence à l'existant*. *De l'existence à l'existant* was originally published in 1947. The research and the writing for the study, however, began before the war and was continued under captivity. This study was immediately followed by the publication in 1948 of four lectures that Levinas offered in 1946 and 1947. These lectures were published under the title of *Time and the Other*. *Totality and Infinity* was originally published in 1961.

50. Aryanism, to be sure, is connected with other forms of racism. The difference is that in typical formulations of racism blacks or Jews, for example, have been regarded and defined in biological terms. White liberal Europeans tended to conceive themselves in terms of *res cogitans* or thinking substance, while they saw non-European peoples as biological entities. It is possible, therefore, to be anti-Semitic without being Aryan, just as it is possible to be liberal and racist.

51. Consider Lawrence Birken's argument that "it is, of course, a great mistake to see anti-Semitism as a rejection of Enlightenment values. On the contrary, the Enlightenment simply secularized rather than destroyed traditional Judeophobia. Indeed, there was a sense in which the notion of fraternity was implicitly more dangerous to the Jews as Jews than was the older idea of estate society. While the latter tolerated the Jewish religion, the former demanded assimilation as the price of tolerance." Birken, *Hitler as Philosophe*, 29.

52. See ibid.

53. The Levinasian protest against Hitlerian racism is clear in *Totality and Infinity*:
> There does indeed exist a human race as a biological genus, and the common function of men may exercise in the world as a totality permits the applying to them of a common concept. But the human community instituted by language, where the interlocutors remain absolutely separated, does not constitute the unity of genus. . . . The very status of the human implies fraternity and the idea of the human race. Fraternity is radically opposed to the conception of a humanity united by resemblance, a multiplicity of diverse families arisen from the stones cast behind by Deucalion, and which, across the struggle of egoisms, results in a human city. (TI 213–14)

54. For this point, see Levinas, *De l'existence à l'existant*, 163.

55. To be sure, Levinas was decisively opposed to the Heideggerian idea that the traditional picture of the world was "metaphysical." The opposition between their points of view on this matter is clearly dramatized in a letter Levinas wrote a few months after the publication of *Totality and Infinity*:

> The idea of being is not the most ancient; and thought, history, and humanity do not begin with the understanding of being.... Must Being, which transcends beings, that is to say, an impersonal and faceless power, give a meaning to the real like some *fatum*? Impious questions! They will tell us that we have understood nothing of Heidegger.... To which it is necessary to reply that respect for the person—infinite responsibility for the Other (*Autrui*)—imposes itself on thought with the power of primordial coordinates; that to seek the condition for the personal and the human is already to undermine them. Sartre, in his article "Merleau-Ponty vivant," writes about Heidegger: "when he first speaks of the *opening onto being*, I smell (*flaire*) alienation." Sartre's flair does not deceive him. The poetry of the peaceful path that runs through the fields does not simply reflect the splendor of Being beyond beings. That splendor brings with it more somber and pitiless images. The declaration of the end of metaphysics is premature. This end is not at all certain. Besides, metaphysics—the relation with the being (*étant*) which is accomplished in ethics—precedes the understanding of being and survives ontology. (Levinas, "Transcendence and Height," 31. The French original appears in Levinas, "Transcendance et hauteur," 122–23.)

56. Levinas, *De l'existence à l'existant*, 164, translation mine.
57. See ibid., 162, translation mine.
58. Ibid.
59. Ibid.
60. "Autrui, en tant qu'autrui, n'est pas seulement un alter ego. Il est ce que moi je ne suis pas: il est le faible alors que moi je suis le fort; il est le pauvre, il est 'le veuve et l'orphelin.'" [The Other as Other is not only an alter ego. He is that which I am not; he is the weak one whereas I am the strong one; he is the poor one, he is "the widower and the orphan."] Ibid.
61. The "difference" in question here is not the difference between Being and beings, or ontological difference, but the difference between myself and Other, or, in my terms, trans-ontological difference.
62. Levinas, "Transcendance et hauteur," 90–91, translation mine. This essay was originally published in 1962, just a year after *Totality and Infinity*. The text was presented for discussion in a meeting of the French Society of

Philosophy at the Sorbonne. The current bibliographic source contains the original lecture, the discussion, and a brief exchange by mail between Levinas and José Etcheveria.

63. Levinas, *Time and the Other*, 88, cf. 76.
64. Ibid., 86.
65. Levinas is very strong on this point: "C'est dans l'eros que la transcendance peut être pensée d'une manière radicale, apporter au moi pris dans l'être, retournant fatalement à soi, autre chose que ce retour, le débarrasser de son ombre." [It is in Eros that transcendence can be thought of in a radical manner, to bring to the self caught in its being, fatally returning to itself, something other than this return, to rid it of its shadows.] Levinas, *De l'existence à l'existant*, 164.
66. Ibid.
67. Consider also that for Levinas eros takes place on a ground where the embodied *existant* is susceptible to suffering and confronts death. See Levinas, *Time and the Other*, 76.
68. Ibid., 78.
69. Ibid., 74.
70. Ibid., 76. The idea of originary solitude will change considerably from *Time and the Other* to *Totality and Infinity* and then to *Otherwise Than Being*. The existent will go from originary solitude to a solitude (as "atheism") needed for the Infinite to be possible to the obsession with the Other at a pre-originary anarchical moment of subjectivity.
71. Levinas, *Time and the Other*, 79.
72. Ibid., 91. In *Totality and Infinity* this passage is read differently: "The son is not only my work, like a poem or an object, nor is he my property. Neither the categories of power nor those of knowledge describe my relation with the child. The fecundity of the I is neither a cause nor a domination. I do not have my child; I am my child." Notice here that Levinas substitutes "having" in *Time and the Other* with "knowledge" in *Totality and Infinity*.
73. It is important to consider the explicit reference to the Bible in this passage. This reference makes the obvious explicit, that is, that in his confrontation with Western philosophy and civilization Levinas is to a great extent thinking *from* Judaic sources.
74. Uniqueness and election serve here as philosophical categories to articulate the generation of human subjectivity and temporality. In the human realm, Levinas argues, we do not find causes and effects. We need to overcome the vocabulary of causality. See TI 278–79.
75. Logic here must be understood in terms of a process of unfolding that does not necessarily follow the laws of Aristotelian logic.

76. This idea appears in TI 247, 281. Levinas is clearly working here in terms of the Kantian critique of justifying morality in terms of the possibility of achieving happiness. Levinas feels that he needs to account for the possibility of an "infinite time of triumph without which goodness would be subjectivity and folly" (TI 181). This problem ultimately justifies the transition to the discussion of eros and fecundity. In *Totality and Infinity* the main motivation for grounding fraternity in eros and fecundity is tied to the problem of the time when goodness can be fulfilled. This theme is associated with Levinas's effort to oppose the ontology of war with an eschatology of peace. Levinas believes that in order for morality to be real—that is, more than illusory—he needs to account for the possibility of the triumph or the always possible emergence of goodness. As will become evident further on, I think that Levinas is deluded on this point. I will argue that we need a teleology of peace rather than an eschatology, not a teleology *within the totality* to be sure, of which Levinas is rightly afraid (see TI 22). We must comply with the requirements of morality—to the point of extending them to the political realm—even though we do not envision a plausible desired end. We must certainly hope, but hope does not need an assurance because it can survive only as a possibility. What we need is a purpose, or telos, and a utopia. Nobody gives better expression to this idea than Frantz Fanon: "The explosion will not happen today. It is too soon . . . or too late. I do not come with timeless truths. My consciousness is not illuminated with ultimate radiances. Nevertheless, in complete composure, I think it would be good if certain things were said." Fanon, *Black Skin, White Masks*, 7. I think that Fanon's awareness and reconciliation with the fragility of the time of goodness is what accounts for his political turn. Levinas's concerns with legitimating the possibility of goodness, in contrast, lead him to develop the notion of eros and fecundity. Paradoxically, these notions, as we will see, introduce regressive and unethical considerations. Levinas will be thus forced to change his argumentative strategy. It will be at this point that his work will come closest to Fanon's.
77. The insistence on the fundamental role of fraternity complements accounts that interpret Levinas's early work primarily in terms of eros and fecundity. See among others, Thayse, *Eros et fécondité chez le jeune Levinas*; and Mèlich, *Totalitarismo y fecundidad*.
78. Wallerstein, *Unthinking Social Science*, 205.
79. For a similar perspective, see also the more recent Attali, *Fraternités*.
80. Wallerstein's "The French Revolution as a World-Historical Event" is the

first essay of *Unthinking Social Science*. It was originally published in *Social Research* 56, no. 1 (spring 1989).

81. Wallerstein, *Unthinking Social Science*, 22.
82. Arrighi, Hopkins, and Wallerstein, "1968," 97–115; Watts, "1968 and All That," 157–88.
83. Kurlansky, *1968*.
84. Watts, "1968 and All That," 167.
85. Maldonado-Torres, "Notes on the Current Status of Liminal Categories and the Search for a New Humanism," 192–208.
86. For a sociological and a philosophical point of view, see respectively Arrighi, Hopkins, and Wallerstein, "1968," 97–115; and Ferry and Renaut, *French Philosophy of the Sixties*.
87. Consider Levinas's views on the woman in Judaism:
    > "The house is woman," the Talmud tells us. Beyond the psychological and sociological obviousness of such an affirmation, the rabbinic tradition experiences this affirmation as a primordial truth. The last chapter of Proverbs, in which woman, without regard for "beauty and grace," appears as the genius of the hearth and, precisely as such, makes the public life of man possible, can, if necessary, be read as a moral paradigm. But in Judaism the moral always has the weight of an ontological basis: the feminine figures among the categories of Being. (Levinas, "Judaism and the Feminine," 31–32)

    The relation between the feminine and the household and the related idea of their role in the possibility of publicity appears in section 2 of *Totality and Infinity*, entitled "Interiority and Economy." More particularly, see what Levinas says on habitation and the feminine in the section on "The Dwelling," TI 152–54. Consider also Luce Irigaray's related critical point: "What Levinas does not see is that the locus of paternity, to which he accords the privilege of ethical alterity, has already assumed the place of the genealogy of the feminine, has already covered over the relationships between mothers and daughters, in which formerly transmission of the divine word was located." Irigaray, "Questions to Emmanuel Levinas," 112.
88. For a fine exposition of this point in relation to Heidegger, see P. Huntington, "Heidegger, Irigaray, and the Masculine Ethos of National Socialism or, How to Tame the Feminine," 33–75.
89. One only has to read the painful story of the gay poet Reinaldo Arenas in Cuba after the Cuban Revolution of 1959. See Arenas, *Antes que anochezca*.

90. See P. Huntington, "Heidegger, Irigaray, and the Masculine Ethos of National Socialism or, How to Tame the Feminine," 33–75.
91. This concern has found expression nowadays in a variety of ways. Consider Judith Butler's statement:, "I've worried that the return to ethics has constituted an escape from politics, and I've also worried that it has meant a certain heightening of moralism and this has made me cry out, as Nietzsche cried out about Hegel, 'Bad air! Bad air!'" Butler, "Ethical Ambivalence," 15. Butler's justified fears are clearly behind the effort of the present work to overcome the turn to ethics by an ethico-political turn to which the work of Levinas has much to contribute.
92. See particularly the final section "Truth and Justice" in TI 82–101.
93. Consider also that Levinas relates dogmatism with ontology and critique with metaphysics. See TI 43.
94. See Amnesty International USA, *The Universal Declaration of Human Rights 1948–1988*.
95. Consider that the first article of the Universal Declaration of Human Rights reads, "All human beings are born free and equal in dignity and rights. They are endowed with reason and should act towards one another in a spirit of brotherhood." Ibid., 112.
96. "The Prohibition against Representation and 'The Rights of Man,'" originally published in 1981, and "The Rights of the Other Man," originally published in 1989, appear in translation in Levinas, *Alterity and Transcendence*, 121–30, 45–50. "The Rights of Man and Good Will," originally published in 1985, appears in Levinas, *Entre Nous*, 155–59.
97. In truth, the two narratives correspond, in Levinas's perspective, to two aspects of fraternity. In *Totality and Infinity* he argues that "human fraternity then has two aspects: it involves individualities whose logical status is not reducible to the status of ultimate differences in a genus, for their singularity consists in each referring to itself. . . . On the other hand, it involves the commonness of a father, as though the commonness of race would not bring together enough" (TI 214). My argument here is that while these two aspects of fraternity have been present throughout most of Levinas's work, it was the latter that received a more careful elaboration, at least in Levinas's early work. His work after *Totality and Infinity* will exploit the possibilities of the first aspect. The conception of singularity as responsibility, that is, the idea that "it is my responsibility before a face looking at me as absolutely foreign . . . that constitutes the original fact of fraternity" (TI 214), becomes central for Levinas's intellectual production after *Totality and Infinity*. This idea is captured by the notion of proximity, which, though it is only central in *Otherwise than Being*, appears in *Totality*

and Infinity as well. "Society must be a fraternal community to be commensurate with the straightforwardness, the *primary proximity*, in which the face presents itself to my welcome. Monotheism signifies this human kinship, this idea of a human race that refers back to the approach of the Other in the face, in dimension of height, in responsibility for oneself and for the Other" (TI 214, italics mine). As must be now evident, the effort to clarify Levinas's reflections on fraternity may be interpreted as a way of articulating clearly certain fundamental contributions and limitations of Levinas's ethical monotheism to social and political philosophy in the modern West, in particular, to a centuries-old dominant liberalism and to a more recent, though no less rampant, neoliberalism.

98. Here the fatherly concern with the survival of the self and with descent begins to give way to a motherly ethics anchored in the idea of maternity. Maternity would be tied here to the notion of the priority of the Other over the self. For a discussion of the virtues and limitations in Levinas's shifting conception of the ontological function of the feminine, see Chalier, "Ethics and the Feminine," 119–29; and Vasey, "Faceless Women and Serious Others," 317–30. The idea of the primacy of the death of the Other over my own death appears already in *Totality and Infinity* (see TI 236, 244–47). As demonstrated by Levinas's lectures in 1975–76 at the Sorbonne, these ideas form an important part of Levinas's reflections later on. These lectures are published in Levinas, *God, Death, and Time*.

99. In his introduction to the Spanish translation of *Time and the Other* Felix Duque correctly points out the transition from *eros* to an "*amour sans eros: ágape, caritas,*" but he attributes the motivation for the transition only to Levinas's fear of the possibility of the conversion of *eros* into pure enjoyment. Like many others, Duque leaves aside the questions of the challenges that Levinas confronted to articulate a consistent view of fraternity that overcame the paradigm of violence and war. See Duque, Introduction, 47–48.

100. Levinas's conception of the difference between fear and anguish will be made evident later on in the chapter. The implications of the subversion are obvious: it only suffices that angst be taken in the Heideggerian sense of a confrontation with one's own death to promote certain insensibility toward evil. It appears that Heidegger participates actively in the concerted effort of a civilization to turn upside down the ethical meaning of human reality and to advance ideals of existence that promote a deafness so intense that no cry of suffering or demand for justice would be able to penetrate.

101. The theme of commerce appeared before in TI 226–32.

102. Levinas will adopt a genetic phenomenological approach to articulate a conception of subjectivity that makes clear the ethical birth of the subject. He will thus explain language and cognition in terms of sensibility, passivity, and givenness. I will discuss these themes in the fifth chapter.

103. The idea that justice "straddles the moral and the political realm" is central to recent efforts to articulate a conception of justice *beyond fairness* oriented by the concept of love and its requirements. See Gaita, *A Common Humanity*. This project, like that of Levinas, emphasizes the ideas of fraternity over liberty and rights:

> Persons, rights, obligation—they are concepts at the center of one way of thinking about morality. Human being, human fellowship, love and its requirements are concepts at the center of another. While I favor the latter, nothing I say finally proves that I am right to do so, and nothing prevents a determined translation of the latter into the former. But if I am right about the place love plays in the constitution of our moral concepts, in my claim that talk of inalienable rights and so on is dependent on the language of love, and if love is dependent on our responses to the human form and its expressive possibilities, then my case at least seems plausible, and perhaps even convincing. (OB 14–15)

Consider also Levinas's reflections on love:

> We must ask ourselves whether peace, instead of consisting in the absorption or the disappearance of alterity, would not on the contrary be the *fraternal* way of a proximity to the other, which would not be simply the failure of coincidence with the other, but which would signify precisely the *excess* of sociality over all solitude—excess of sociality and love. I do not pronounce this often misused word lightly. (Levinas, "Peace and Proximity," 137)

Continuing his reflections on peace and love Levinas adds: "But the uniqueness of the unique is the uniqueness of the beloved. The uniqueness of the unique signifies in love. Hence peace as love. Not that the uniqueness of alterity is conceived of as some subjective illusion of a lover. Quite to the contrary, the *subjective* as such is precisely the penetration . . . toward the unique, the absolutely other, by love, proximity and peace" (ibid., 138). Although it does not seem that Gaita is aware of the work of Levinas, I am sure that Levinas would have been intrigued by Gaita's work and that Gaita would find much to learn from Levinas—particularly on the question regarding the appropriate demarcation between philosophy and religion. See Gaita, *A Common Humanity*, xx.

104. Levinas, *Time and the Other*, 84.

105. For instance, the need of restraining self-interest is clearly one of the motivations behind the need to conceive justice in terms of a procedure that posits all subjects behind a "veil of ignorance." See Rawls, *A Theory of Justice*.
106. Levinas, "Peace and Proximity," 131–32.
107. In connection with this point, see the chapters "Goodness beyond Virtue," "Evil beyond Vice," and "Justice beyond Fairness: Mabo and Social Justice" in Gaita, *A Common Humanity*, 17–28, 29–56, 73–86. The classical statement of justice as fairness is found in Rawls, *A Theory of Justice*. The most recent formulation appears in Rawls, *Justice as Fairness*.
108. Levinas, *Entre Nous*, 104, 200.
109. For a discussion of Levinas's conception of skepticism, this time in connection with Derrida's critiques of Levinas, see De Greef, "Skepticism and Reason,," 159–79; and Bernasconi, "Skepticism in the Face of Philosophy," 149–61.
110. For an ample discussion of this point, see Maldonado-Torres, "Decolonization and the New Identitarian Logics after September 11," 40–48.
111. Levinas, "No Identity," 150, note 9. Cited from the reprinted edition.
112. Ibid., 150–51.
113. Ibid., 150ff.
114. This is evinced in Levinas, "Signature."
115. I take the notion of a darker side of the Renaissance from a book with the same title. See Mignolo, *The Darker Side of the Renaissance*, 2nd ed.
116. Levinas began to reflect on the implications of de-colonization as early as the early 1960s, just after the publication of *Totality and Infinity*. The essay that appears in the first part of *Humanisme de l'autre homme*, "La signification et le sens," is based on a series of lectures that Levinas offered in Brussels from 1961 to 1963. See Levinas, "La signification et le sens," especially 58ff. The English translation appears in Levinas, "Meaning and Sense," 75–107.
117. Levinas, "Peace and Proximity," 133. "Peace and Proximity" was originally published in 1984. Note that in "Meaning and Sense," written some twenty years before (the text was based on a series of lectures offered from 1961 to 1963), Levinas rejects the historicist turn and the relativism implied by the European recognition of other cultures and advocates a return to Greek wisdom through a refashioned Platonism (Levinas, "Meaning and Sense," 100–102). Note also that in the passage quoted above he condemns Aristotle and not Plato. Levinas's Plato, defender of the idea of the good beyond Being, is not precisely the traditional Plato of European scholarship. Moreover, it is clear that in his defense of Plato, Levinas con-

tinues a dispute with Heidegger on the meaning and significance of metaphysics. Heidegger locates the birth of metaphysics in Plato. Thus, Plato inaugurates the process of the forgetfulness of Being. In contrast, it is Aristotle, along with Franz Brentano, who first inspires Heidegger in his incessant questioning of Being. Jacques Derrida noted early on the selective appropriation and critique of Greek thought by Levinas. The recovery of metaphysics indicates a turn to Plato and an opposition "to the entire tradition derived from Aristotle." Derrida, "Violence and Metaphysics," 83. John McCumber, a Heidegger scholar, has recently published a study in which he argues that Heidegger was wrong to assign Plato all the perversity that he sees in metaphysics. McCumber traces the beginnings of the metaphysics of oppression to Aristotle. See McCumber, *Metaphysics and Oppression*, 97–101.

118. Levinas, "Peace and Proximity," 133. The allusion to a "Europe that is not just Hellenic" is the other part of Levinas's critical appropriation of the meaning of Greek wisdom in the light of "the development of contemporary philosophy." Levinas, "Meaning and Sense," 101. Levinas makes these two assertions in the context of a discussion on the implications of colonialism for dominant Western thought. Although Levinas's internal critique of Europe is ingenious, it is unfortunate that he focuses exclusively on the conscience of the European and that he does not explore the ways in which those colonized by Europe thought about the project of colonization or about the conscience of the European. In what may be described as an anti-Levinasian move, the colonized remain silenced in Levinas's reflections on colonialism. Wisdom is only Greek, and if Europe is not just Hellenic it is only for Levinas because it is also Hebraic. The wisdom of traditions and ways of thinking born in colonized territories remain invisible. For an alternative to these seemingly Levinasian anti-Levinasianisms consult, among others, Walter Mignolo's elaborations of "border gnosis" and "border thinking" in Mignolo, *Local Histories/Global Designs*, 13–16.

119. Levinas, "Peace and Proximity," 134.
120. Ibid., 135.
121. Fanon, *The Wretched of the Earth*, 236.
122. *Les damnés de la terre* was originally published in 1961.
123. Consider that Fanon is one of the major influences behind Edward Said's *Orientalism*, the study with which the postcolonial studies boom commences. See Said, *Orientalism*.
124. For pertinent biographical information about Fanon's participation in

the war, consult the chapters "War from Within, War from Without," and "Motherland" in Ehlen, *Frantz Fanon*.

125. It was none other than Jean-Paul Sartre who in the midst of the war dared to write an analysis of French anti-Semitism and of the ways in which the French were accomplices of German genocide. See Sartre, *Réflexions sur la question juive*.

126. For an examination of the notion of ethics as the limit of the political in Levinas, see Herzog, *Penser autrement la politique*, 316–18.

127. The themes of hypocrisy and self-deception are central in Césaire, *Discourse on Colonialism*. This text was originally published in France in 1955. I am currently working on an elaboration of this theme for another book project tentatively entitled *Fanonian Meditations*.

3. GOD AND THE OTHER

1. For an influential and recent view of Fanon as an existential philosopher, see Gordon, "The Black and the Body Politic," 74–84.

2. Consider Fanon's argument that "a normal Negro child, having grown up within a normal family, will become abnormal on the slightest contact with the white world" (BSWM 143). Further ahead in the text Fanon adds: "A drama is enacted *every day* in colonized countries. How is one to explain, for example, that a Negro who has passed his baccalaureate and has gone to the Sorbonne to study to become a teacher of philosophy is already on guard before any conflictual elements have coalesced round him?" (BSWM 145, italics mine).

3. For an account of this conception of the extraordinary and of its relation with the ordinary, see Gordon, *Her Majesty's Other Children*, 13, 36–37. See also BSWM 116.

4. On this point consider, for instance, Fanon's idea that "the Negro's inferiority or superiority complex or his feeling of equality is *conscious*. These feelings forever chill him. They make his drama. In him there is none of the affective amnesia characteristic of the typical neurotic" (BSWM 150). Fanon adds to this that in an anti-black world the Negro is phobogenic, which means that he generates, rather than simply symbolizes, fear (BSWM 154–55).

5. "Modern/colonial" replaces the concepts of early and late modernity. For this point, see Mignolo, "José de Acosta's *Historia natural y moral de las Indias*," 451–518.

6. I am adopting and adapting here the notion of the "preferential option for the poor," which is so central to the Latin American theology of liberation.

The first decisive articulations of this position were made in the Second Conference of the Latin American Episcopal Council in Medellín, Colombia, in (among all dates!) 1968. For a concise account of the significance of this event for Latin American theology and spirituality, see Gutiérrez, "The Meaning and Scope of Medellín," 59–101. The notion of the "preferential option for the poor" has been recently expanded and explained in Sueiro, "Opción preferencial por los pobres," 135–47. For recent accounts of liberation theology in English, see Rowland, *The Cambridge Companion to Liberation Theology*.

7. The most elaborated and sophisticated articulation of this theme appears in Hadot, *Philosophy as a Way of Life*. Hadot's insistence on the links between philosophy and life provides a good antidote to the dominant analytical mindset in the discipline of philosophy nowadays. As commendable as this effort may be, Hadot, however, appears to be more interested in demonstrating the therapeutic power of philosophy than in showing its link with the political. That is, in his work, the care of the self seems to take precedence over the care for justice—a topic only made explicit in the last two pages of his study. Given the nature of this work it is necessary to question the extent to which Hadot's conception of philosophy as practice gives appropriate expression to the Levinasian conception of philosophy as the wisdom of love, or if it still remains within the confines of the idea of philosophy as the love of wisdom. An adequate answer to this question, however, is clearly beyond the limits of this work.

8. Hegel, *Hegel's Philosophy of Right*, 21-1.

9. BSWM 12–13.

10. Gordon, "The Black and the Body Politic," 76.

11. In using the term intentionality I refer to the implicit but ultimate purpose or goal (the telos) of a certain configuration of meaning and systems. Fanon suggested, for instance, that colonialism not only intends but *is* itself violence (WE 61). Colonialism gives expression to a fundamental hatred of the other human being. And if, as Levinas argues, hatred finds its most consistent expression in suffering (even more than in death), then it is clear why Fanon says that "torture is inherent in the whole colonialist configuration" (see Levinas, TI 239; and Fanon, *Toward the African Revolution*, 64). The creation of a world animated (via force) by these goals is bound to make pathologies normal. Consider Fanon's diagnosis of the true sources behind the so-called North African syndrome:

> "Threatened in his affectivity, threatened in his social activity, threatened in his membership in the community—the North Afri-

can combines all the conditions that make a sick man. Without a family, without love, without human relations, without communion with the group, the first encounter with himself will occur in a neurotic mode, in a pathological mode; he will feel himself emptied, without life, in a bodily struggle with death, a death on this side of death, a death in life—and what is more pathetic than this man with robust muscles who tells us in his truly broken voice, 'Doctor, I'm going to die'?" (Fanon, *Toward the African Revolution*, 13)

Of course, not everything is purely negative in the colonial death-world—I take the notion of the "death-world" from Wyschogrod, *Spirit in Ashes*. As Foucault has persuasively demonstrated, "It would not be possible for power relations to exist without points of insubordination which, by definition, are means of escape" (Foucault, "The Subject and Power," 225). But consider that Foucault also comments: "Every power relationship implies, at least *in potentia*, a strategy of struggle, in which the two forces are not superimposed, do not lose their specific nature, or do not finally become confused. Each constitute for the other a kind of permanent limit, a point of possible reversal" (ibid.). Fanon's main concern resides in thinking from the limit, finding the most consistent way to subvert the dominant structure of power. That is why even though it is true that there are exhibitions of life in the midst of the "death-world," as there are marks that testify to the *"besoin d'évasion"* that Levinas talked about in his youth, from a Fanonian perspective these moments of affirmation remain limited if they do not ultimately aim at overcoming the dominion of the binary master/slave over ordinary life. For critical expositions of this point, see Hall, "The After-life of Frantz Fanon," 13–37; and Lazarus, "Disavowing Decolonization," 68–143.

12. It is in this sense that we should understand Fanon's claim that "in most cases, the black man lacks the advantage of being able to accomplish a descent into the hell where an authentic upheaval can be born" (BSWM 8). Consider also the Fanonian diagnosis of the status of the colonized in Algeria:

> There is, first of all, the fact that the colonized person, who in this respect is like men in underdeveloped countries or the disinherited in all parts of the world, perceives life not as a flowering or a development of an essential productiveness, but as a permanent struggle against an omnipresent death. This ever-menacing death is experienced as endemic famine, unemployment, a high death rate, an inferiority complex and the absence of any hope for the future. All

this gnawing at the existence of the colonized tends to make of life something resembling an incomplete death. (Fanon, *A Dying Colonialism*, 128; see also Fanon, *Toward the African Revolution*, 13–14)

According to this description the anticipation of death in the colonial context represents not so much a possibility as a reality. As a reality, the anticipation of death doesn't have the same connotation or meaning as it does in a context where life is taken for granted—compare Fanon's view to the discussion on nihilism and "black angst" in West, *Race Matters*, especially 22–28. The anxiety of the white man when he anticipates death, however, hardly puts him in a better position than the black—compare Fanon to de Beauvoir, *The Second Sex*, 720. This anxiety is often bought at the expense of a forgetfulness of the Other who suffers by one's own hand or by virtue of a system that gives life to some only by making life a misery or an impossibility for others. The white man's anxiety is also marred by a more terrible fear: the fear of mixing with the Other, of corrupting purity by getting in contact with the colonized other, or more terrible even, by one day becoming that hated other himself. This is exactly the reason why Fanon writes that the Negro is a phobogenic object (BSWM 155). After our twentieth century I believe that no one will doubt the idea that some would confront death happily instead of becoming *one of them*. This arguably finds expression today in the collapse of the multiculturalist's tendency to love and defend the culture of the oppressed into the implicit hate of the producer of the culture. Consider on this point, among other writings by the same author, Žižek, "Multiculturalism, or the Cultural Logic of Multinational Capitalism," 28–51. In another more recent essay Žižek notes how racism tends to occupy the space left by the suspension of the political in postmodern multiculturalism. See the unfortunately titled and conceived Žižek, "A Leftist Plea for 'Eurocentrism,'" especially 997–98; on a similar vindicating vein, see also Žižek, *The Fragile Absolute or, Why Is the Christian Legacy Worth Fighting For?* I hope that the discussion in the next chapter will make evident at least part of Žižek's ignorant, regressive, and irresponsible (not to say racist) "plea" for Eurocentrism. I will come back to this point in the conclusion.

13. The death-world may be defined, following Edith Wyschogrod, as a system of multiple and contradictory meanings whose telos is the destruction of meaning itself and the negation of life. See Wyschogrod, *Spirit in Ashes*, 33.

14. I owe this felicitous term to Walter Mignolo, who has developed it in a different context and with different connotations in Mignolo, *Local Histories/Global Designs*.

15. Maldonado-Torres, "Post-imperial Reflections on Crisis, Knowledge, and Utopia," 277–315.
16. Hegel, *Phenomenology of Spirit*, 115–16, §190.
17. Ibid., 115, § 189.
18. Ibid., 118, §196.
19. Fanon, *Toward the African Revolution*, 18. For a different but related account of the links between Fanon's focus on contingency and his existential phenomenological approach, see Gordon, *Fanon and the Crisis of European Man*, 34–35.
20. For the ruminations on the idea that "language is the house of Being," see Heidegger, "Letter on Humanism," 193.
21. Ronald A. T. Judy submits the related idea that "the unrealizability of ontology in the bifurcated colonial society is not a call for the abandonment of ontology," but that it rather represents the "need to realize ontology by returning it to existence" (Judy, "Fanon's Body of Black Experience," 60). I believe, in contrast, that the challenge to ontology is part of a more general critique of Hegel's philosophy of Spirit that Judy seems to ignore when he then argues that Fanon's "critique of ontology is that in setting aside existence, it [ontology] excludes whatever form of consciousness attends the black in the becoming of absolute spirit" (ibid.). This statement indicates that, for Judy, Fanon still subscribes to the general agenda of finding a space in the becoming of Spirit. While my treatment of Fanon's work takes a different direction, I nonetheless believe that it is possible to illuminate dimensions of Fanon's work with reference to modes of argumentation related to the general outlines of Hegel's philosophy of Spirit. Sekyi-Otu provides an outstanding example of this. See Sekyi-Otu, *Fanon's Dialectic of Experience*.
22. Fanon clearly becomes the paradigmatic philosopher of what I call the sub-ontological difference, an ontological dimension "forgotten" by Heidegger in his many explorations on being and the ontological difference. I will spell out the meaning of this term more clearly in chapter 5 and in the conclusion.
23. The spatial configuration of empire is a central component of the Manichean form of valuation and reality produced by imperialism. This condition penetrates and divides settler colonies accordingly. About these Fanon writes, "A world divided into compartments, a motionless, Manicheistic world, a world of status: the statue of the general who carried out the conquest, the statue of the engineer who built the bridge; a world which is sure of itself, which crushes with its stones the backs flayed by whips: this is the colonial world" (WE 65–66).

24. I coin the term "sub-alter" to highlight the condition of someone whose alterity is made to play a significant role in contexts of subjugation. The colonial Other is not so much an Other, as a sub-alterized or sub-alterical Other, that is, a subject whose being and meaning have been altered to such an extent that his alterity only works in the function of a system of subordination. This idea is not exactly the same as the one conveyed by the recognized and most used term, sub-altern, which refers mainly to questions of class and status. Sub-alter, rather, focuses on the existential and ontological dimensions of subordination, as well as on the very conditions of possibility for there to be sub-alternity in the first place.
25. For a recent analysis on the relation between Hegel's and Fanon's accounts of the "dialectic" between master and slave, see Turner, "On the Difference between the Hegelian and the Fanonian Dialectic of Lordship and Bondage," 134–51. Perhaps the most fundamental divergence between Turner's approach and my own consists in Turner's view that Fanonian dialectics represents only a variant of Hegel's, while in my view there are important points wherein Fanon's existential phenomenology clearly challenges basic methodological premises of Hegelian dialectics and philosophy of Spirit. The de-colonial reduction is certainly one of these points.
26. That the master/slave dialectic remains valid as an explicative factor for contexts dominated by imperial and colonial features is not so strange if we consider Susan Buck-Morss's argument that the Hegelian account of the dialectic in the *Phenomenology of Spirit* was largely inspired by the Haitian Revolution. See Buck-Morss, "Hegel and Haiti," 821–63. If Buck-Morss's argument is correct, Fanon's critique of Hegel may be interpreted as a response from a black colonized Caribbean to Hegel's interpretation of the condition of slavery and the struggle for freedom.
27. Sabbagh, "Going Against the West from Within," 29–30.
28. Ibid., 30.
29. Ibid.
30. Ibid.
31. See, for instance, Judy, "Fanon's Body of Black Experience"; and Turner, "On the Difference between the Hegelian and the Fanonian Dialectic of Lordship and Bondage."
32. Alighieri, *Monarchy and Three Political Letters*, 13.
33. As William Hart has persuasively shown, it is not possible to understand the anti-religious trend in contemporary critical voices such as Edward Said's without considering the strong influence of Marx's view on religion in the secular world of the academy. See Hart, *Edward Said and the*

Religious Effects of Culture. Marx's view on religion, as on other important matters, was at the same time strongly influenced by Ludwig Feuerbach's revolutionary *The Essence of Christianity*. See Feuerbach, *The Essence of Christianity*. The translation cited here was first published in 1854.

34. Feuerbach, *The Essence of Christianity*, 20.
35. Ibid., 12.
36. I refer to Harvey, *Feuerbach and the Interpretation of Religion*.
37. Ibid., 229.
38. Ibid., 36.
39. Ibid.
40. See ibid., 37.
41. Ibid., 230.
42. Quoted in ibid., 180.
43. The eradication of the religions of the slave most often occurs only, if at all, when the master ends up killing the slave. In such cases, though not merely in them, the religion in question becomes an object of archaeological *research*, and religious artifacts are decoratively *organized* and *exhibited* in museums. The position of the master is, indeed, partly defined by the monopoly of *research, organization,* and *exhibition,* which become, in such monopolized form, trademarks of the imperial world.
44. The logic of the process of recognition of lordship ends up creating a Manichean context wherein the native of colonial territories, or slave, is rendered as evil. Fanon develops this point in relation to his phenomenological description of the colonial world:

    > The colonial world is a Manichean world. It is not enough for the settler to delimit physically, that is to say with the help of the army and the police force, the place of the native. As if to show the totalitarian character of colonial exploitation the settler paints the native as a sort of quintessence of evil. Native society is not simply described as a society lacking in values. It is not enough for the colonist to affirm that those values have disappeared from, or still better never existed in, the colonial world. The native is declared insensible to ethics; he represents not only the absence of values, but the negation of values. He is, let us dare to admit, the enemy of values, and in this sense he is the absolute evil. (WE 41)

45. Dussel argues that European subjectivity is formed by the similar principle, "I conquer, therefore I am" (Dussel, "Modernity, Eurocentrism, and Trans-Modernity," 133). The notion of homicide is also central to Dussel's work. "The designs of the ruling system are imposed univocally on

everybody.... Whoever resists is kidnapped, jailed, tortured, expelled, or killed." And, he concludes, "The dialectic of master and slave is no longer possible: the slave disappears from the horizon—by death" (PL 51).

46. The contrast between communication and imposition is central to Fanon's work. Conquest for him implies a combination of imposition and murder:

> Expropriation, spoliation, raids, objective murder, are matched by the sacking of cultural patterns, or at least condition such sacking. The social panorama is destructed; values are flaunted, crushed, emptied. The lines of force, having crumbled, no longer give direction. In their stead a new system of values is imposed, not proposed, but affirmed, by the heavy weight of cannons and sabers. (Fanon, *Toward the African Revolution*, 33–34)

For a related but different account of these themes, see Todorov, *The Conquest of America*.

47. Fanon offers several descriptions of these failures of assimilation in the first chapters of *Black Skin, White Masks*. "The Negro and Language," the first chapter of the book, is a striking analysis of how the attempt to erase certain inflections from the accent never allows the colonized to become or be recognized as something other than what his skin indicates.

48. In relation to this, see Fanon's reflections on the epidermal schema (BSWM 111–12), and Gordon's phenomenological examination of the body in bad faith (Gordon, *Bad Faith and Antiblack Racism*, 97–103).

49. Empire, indeed, appears in many ways to obey the impulses of a return to a primordial condition of a total anonymity that allows no escape. Something similar to this is what Levinas understands by "il y a." See Levinas, *Time and the Other*, 44–51.

50. Levinas, "Beyond Intentionality," 112.

51. In this light it is no coincidence that in an anti-black world "the black body lives as Absence," while "the white body is presumed to live itself as Presence" (Gordon, *Bad Faith and Antiblack Racism*, 100).

52. The very mapping of the world testifies to the geopolitical dimensions of coloniality. See Mignolo, *Local Histories/Global Designs*, 18–38.

53. Edward Said and Walter Mignolo provide extraordinary accounts of the relation between violence, classification, and the conception of space from a postcolonial and a post-Occidental perspective respectively. See Said, *Orientalism*; and Mignolo, *Local Histories/Global Designs*.

54. Fanon offers persuasive arguments to sustain the thesis that "torture is inherent in the whole colonialist configuration" (Fanon, *Toward the African Revolution*, 64).

55. Gordon calls attention to this in his phenomenology of an anti-black world: "From the standpoint of the black in an antiblack world, God is a desire that can never truly be satisfied—the desire to be white" (Gordon, *Bad Faith and Antiblack Racism*, 149).
56. Imperial man aspires to be God, and structurally takes the place of God—that is, he becomes normative—but he *cannot* be God and must remain conscious of that impossibility. This idea is crucial in Gordon's existential analysis of the role of God in an anti-black world: "If the black *is* human, and whiteness is above blackness, then to be white is tantamount to being a god. The white is aware of this ideal. But every white is simultaneously aware of not being this ideal. To *be* white requires the choice of whiteness as a project" (ibid., 147). The internal tensions in the process of recognition give rise to unexpected developments that will be considered in the second section of the essay.
57. Sartre's ideas on God and human reality appear in succinct form in Sartre, *Being and Nothingness*, 138–40.
58. Gordon, *Bad Faith and Antiblack Racism*, 149.
59. Ibid., 156.
60. It is not fortuitous that Michael Hardt and Antonio Negri use the term "empire" to refer to the new form of sovereignty that emerged with the new global order. Their work makes patently clear the important idea that our world is not only "postmodern" but imperial as well, and that it is time to analyze carefully the manifold structure of the imperiality of power in the old, modern, and contemporary worlds. Hardt and Negri, *Empire*.
61. Sylvia Wynter provides sophisticated analyses on the projection of man as the ideal to which all humans should aspire and its relations with race and the nation. See Wynter, "On Disenchanting Discourse," 432–69.
62. We must not ignore that for Hegel the development of Spirit culminates in the appearance of speculative philosophy on the one hand, and of the nation-state on the other.
63. For an analysis of the ways in which scientific knowledge and the scientific discipline are historically marked by a profound relation with empire, see Said, *Orientalism*. Immanuel Wallerstein offers a similar account but in relation to nationalism. See Wallerstein, *Unthinking Social Science*.
64. Dussel refers to the theological dimensions of the system when he writes: "The truth is that there comes a time when every system becomes a totality, it becomes structurally auto-sufficient. Religion, as a group of symbolic mediations and ritual gestures, as an explicative doctrine of the world and in reference to the absolute . . . , comes to be an essential moment of this 'self-closure' of the system. The totalization of the system is

a process of divinization" (Dussel, *Filosofía ética latinoamericana*, 5:105, §§ 2.3.1–2.3.2, my translation). See also Dussel, *Las metáforas teológicas de Marx*. Franz Hinkelammert, the German economist and philosopher of liberation, has pursued, along with a group of theologians in the Ecumenic Department of Investigations in Costa Rica, a critique of the links of the market with a sacrificial idolatrous religiosity. See, especially, the proceedings of a conference with René Girard, edited by the theologian Hugo Assmann, in Assmann, *Sobre ídolos y sacrificios*.

65. On the notion of conservatism and liberalism as ideologies of the modern world-system, see Wallerstein, *After Liberalism*, 72–92. For an account of the sacrificial logic in Western thought, particularly as it shows itself in neoliberal economics, see Hinkelammert, *Sacrificios humanos y sociedad occidental*; Hinkelammert, *Solidaridad o suicidio colectivo*.

66. See Gordon's illuminating remarks on the secularization of theodicy in light of the challenge found by Du Bois in his scientific descriptions of black folk (Gordon, *Existentia Africana*, 67–68).

67. For an account of the basic principles and fundamental ideas of world-system theory, see Wallerstein, *The Capitalist World-Economy*; and Wallerstein, *The Modern World-System*.

68. For the definition and development of Mignolo, *Local Histories/Global Designs*.

69. Examples of this go from the "crisis theology" of the young Karl Barth to Stanley Hauwerwas. For references on this topic, see Hauerwas and Willimon, *Resident Aliens*; Kereszty, *God Seekers for a New Age*; Tanner, *The Politics of God*; Yoder, *The Christian Witness to the State*; Yoder, *Discipleship as Political Responsibility*; Yoder, *For the Nations*; and Yoder, *Karl Barth and the Problem of War*.

70. Although the formulation of the idea of the "death of God" is typically assigned to Nietzsche, Hegel called attention to it before him. Hegel, *Phenomenology of Spirit*, 455, § 752. For Nietzsche's articulation of the idea, see among others the fifth book of Nietzsche, *The Gay Science*.

71. For an example of more recent expressions of empire, see Hardt and Negri, *Empire*. See also the chapters "Mercado total y democracia: La democracia y la nueva derecha en América Latina," and "Frente a la cultura de la post-modernidad: Proyecto político y utopía" in Hinkelammert, *La fe de Abraham y el edipo occidental*, 63–102.

72. For the notion of "unlearning privilege," see Spivak, *The Post-Colonial Critic*, 30.

4. RECOGNITION FROM BELOW

1. Guevara, *Che Guevara Reader*, 225.
2. See, particularly, the essays collected in Habermas, *The Inclusion of the Other*.
3. See Rawls, *Political Liberalism*.
4. The civil rights movement took place during the 1950s and the 1960s. The connection with 1968 is significant, since Martin Luther King Jr. was assassinated that year.
5. C. Taylor, "The Politics of Recognition," 3–24.
6. See C. Taylor, *Hegel*.
7. C. Taylor, "The Politics of Recognition," 50.
8. See Fraser, "From Redistribution to Recognition?," 19–49; and Blum, "Recognition, Value, and Equality," 73–99.
9. Honneth, *The Struggle for Recognition*, 1.
10. Ibid., 29–30.
11. Ibid., 60.
12. Ibid., 59.
13. For an extended consideration of this theme, see Honneth, *Critique of Power*. Also pertinent to understanding the nature of the tensions between Habermas and Foucault is Kelly, *Critique and Power*.
14. Honneth, *The Struggle for Recognition*, 168.
15. See ibid., 129.
16. Fanon makes explicit his conception of the limits of psychoanalysis, and the advantages of his own approach in the introduction to *Black Skin, White Masks*:

    > Reacting against the constitutionalist tendency of the late nineteenth century, Freud insisted that the individual factor be taken into account through psychoanalysis. He substituted for a phylogenetic theory the ontogenetic perspective. It will be seen that the black man's alienation is not an individual question. Beside phylogeny and ontogeny stands sociogeny. In one sense, conforming to the view of Leconte and Damey, let us say that this is a question of a sociodiagnostic. (BSWM 11)

    Fanon's conception of sociogenesis was clearly indebted to the views of his teacher, thesis director, and partner François Tosquelles. For an account of the extent of Tosquelles's influence on Fanon and of the ways in which his own practice as a doctor shaped his views on psychotherapy and on the nature of revolutionary struggle, see the second part of Gendzier, *Frantz Fanon*, 61–116.

17. See Gordon, *Her Majesty's Other Children*, 23.
18. Disrespect emerges in relation to something that is taken from oneself—for example, in theft. See Honneth, *The Struggle for Recognition*, 21. But the slave does not own anything. He himself becomes the object of possession. What emerges in this context, or so I will argue, is a "cry" of ethical revolt. This "cry" is also different from bourgeois anguish, meaninglessness, and nihilism. The next section focuses on the clarification of the meaning of this "cry."
19. What emerges in this context, to repeat, is not a feeling of disrespect (a notion that presupposes a bourgeois and liberal conception of the subject), but a "cry" of ethical revolt.
20. For a related critique see Oliver, *Witnessing*, 48–49. Oliver criticizes Honneth for making respect depend on struggles that create disrespect. In a sense, I articulate the other side of Oliver's complaint, which is that respect must take precedence over disrespect.
21. This claim stands at the basis of black existentialism and the Africana philosophy of existence. See Gordon, *Existentia Africana*; and Gordon, ed., *Existence in Black*. Gordon's elaboration of an Africana philosophy of existence provides a strong antidote against formulations of existentialism modeled exclusively in terms of the experience of Western man. In this tradition we find Albert Camus arguing that "the problem of rebellion seems to assume a precise meaning only within the confines of Western thought" (Camus, *The Rebel*, 20). Camus disqualifies non-Western cultures because, according to him, they are still enmeshed in the authority of religion and in the power of the sacred. In this, Camus simply restates the typical Eurocentric rationalistic and developmentalist conception that posits Western atheism as the most advanced expression of critical rationality. I will revise this point critically further ahead in relation to Honneth and Habermas. Gordon's explorations into Africana philosophy of existence also enter in tension with the claim that subaltern subjects are for the most part seduced by the spirit of seriousness, and that, as a result, their work lacks "metaphysical resonances and also anger" (de Beauvoir, *The Second Sex*, 720). What de Beauvoir fails to consider in her study is the extent to which the "metaphysics" and the "anger" of the dominant subjects tend to lose from view the main problem, which is, to put it in Fanonian terms, to fight against dehumanization. The recognition of this limitation is what leads Fanon to consider carefully the meaning of the cries that emerge from subaltern subjectivities. In this sense, the "cry" itself represents the limit of the human; it is the point in which the absolute negation of the subject and the community turns into the possibility

of the absolute affirmation and liberation of the self, of a culture, and of a more humane political system. For similar reasons to the ones articulated above Camus's call for a recognition of the limits of rebellion and his call for moderation—even at the points in which he makes reference to the "cries" for justice that emerge in a totalitarian world—are deeply problematic (Camus, *The Rebel*, 294ff.). The limits of Camus's propositions are evinced in his position concerning the Algerian war. On this point, see the discussion on the debate between Sartre and Camus over the Algerian Revolution in Hart, *Edward Said and the Religious Effects of Culture*, 176–86.

22. The relation between power and law is spelled out in Foucault, *Discipline and Punish*.
23. For a similar reason Buck-Morss includes Honneth in the list of those philosophers who have tended "to turn away from social contextualization completely" (Buck-Morss, "Hegel and Haiti," 851).
24. See on this point ibid., 843. In contrast to the dominant Eurocentric and region-centered approach, Buck-Morss points out, "If we have become accustomed to different narratives, ones that place colonial events on the margins of European history, we have been seriously misled. Events in Saint-Domingue were central to contemporary attempts to make sense out of the reality of the French Revolution and its aftermath. We need to be aware of the facts from this perspective" (ibid., 836).
25. This difference in perspective accounts for Walter Mignolo's articulation of what he calls the "colonial difference." See Mignolo, *Local Histories/Global Designs*. I will submit this concept to a detailed examination in the next chapter.
26. For an account of Husserl's conception of "evidence," see Husserl, *Cartesian Meditations*; and Levin, *Reason and Evidence in Husserl's Phenomenology*. To be sure, I only use evidence in order to show the limits of the Husserlian reliance on the term. What appears as "evidence" in the de-colonial reduction transforms itself into skepticism in regard to the imperial order of things. Moreover, since the imperial order seems to be an always already present form of temptation—in which the human becomes inhuman—then it is clear that the de-colonial reduction cannot rely on any idea of complete or full evidence. In short, the tasks of the de-colonial reduction never end.
27. This section and the next appear in Maldonado-Torres, "The Cry of the Self as a Call from the Other," 46–60.
28. In like manner Levinas points out that ultimately "war like peace presupposes beings structured otherwise than as parts of a totality" (TI 222).

War, for Levinas, gives testimony to a fundamental refusal of totality (TI 223).

29. For accounts of Kierkegaard's depiction of the different "stages" in the emergence of authentic subjectivity and of his pedagogical style, see M. Taylor, *Journeys to Selfhood*. Fanon makes his pedagogical goals explicit: "This book is a clinical study. Those who recognize themselves in it, I think, will have made a step forward. I seriously hope to persuade my brother, whether black or white, to tear off with all his strength the shameful livery put together by centuries of incomprehension" (BSWM 12). For Fanon de-colonization represents a fundamental step in the process of the formation of a mature humanity. For an account of Fanon's views on de-colonization as learning and of his contributions to education theory, see Mostern, "Decolonization as Learning," 253–71. See also Maldonado-Torres, "Frantz Fanon and C. L. R. James on Intellectualism and Enlightened Rationality," 151–68.

30. Consult *The American Heritage Dictionary*, 3rd ed. (Boston: Houghton Mifflin Co., 1993) for these and related senses.

31. This interpretation of the cry is developed in Hinkelammert, *El grito del sujeto*, 197, 210. In English, the title is "The Cry of the Subject." A similar interpretation appears in Dussel, *Teología de la liberación*, 10–18. For Dussel,

> La noción de ideología se descubre por su contrario: la revelación no-ideológica. Si hay una expresión que permite irrumpir la exterioridad a todo sistema ideológico constituido es la proto-palabra, la exclamación o interjección de dolor, consecuencia inmediata del traumatismo sentido. El "¡Ay!" del grito de dolor producido por un golpe, una herida, un accidente, indica de manera inmediata no algo sino a alguien. [The notion of ideology is discovered by its contrary: the non-ideological revelation. If there is an expression that allows the irruption of the exteriority of any ideologically constituted system it is the proto-word, the exclamation or interjection of pain, which arises as a consequence of the trauma. The "Ouch!," result of the cry of pain produced by a shock, a wound, an accident, indicates immediately not *something* but *someone*.] (10, translation mine)

These reflections clearly stand behind Dussel's interpretation of the content of the "speech acts" that emanate from the victims of a system—or "interpellation of the poor." See Dussel, "The Reason of the Other," 19–48. Dussel extends his reflections further in the context of a discussion with the German philosopher Karl-Otto Apel; see Dussel, ed., *Debate en torno a la ética del discurso de Ape*. For a more systematic treatment of these themes in Dussel's oeuvre, see Dussel, *Etica de la liberación en la edad de la globalización y de la exclusión*.

32. The link between crying and these varieties of feelings is made particularly evident in black music such as spirituals and the blues. In his classical work on these two musical expressions, James Cone shows how joy and sorrow, love and hate, hope and despair are united in the "cry" elevated by black people in spirituals and the blues; see Cone, *The Spirituals and the Blues: An Interpretation*. Cone argues that the unity of these strong feelings and emotions in music "moves the people toward the direction of total liberation. It shapes and defines black being and creates cultural structures of black expression" (ibid., 5). With this enigmatic link between the reconciliation of the contradictory and the possibility of action Cone points to the intrinsic paradoxical nature of the "cry," which is going to be made more clear as our phenomenological exploration unfolds.

33. I follow Gordon in taking the literal translation of the title as a key to the reading of the chapter. See Gordon, *Existentia Africana*, 33. It is not difficult to see the philosophical and the political problems raised by Markmann's translation. "The Fact of Blackness" erases the reference to the interiority of the subject and ultimately adds support to the idea that "blackness" is something merely "out there," like a stone. By doing this Markmann not only obscures the existential-phenomenological approach adopted by Fanon but confirms the objectifying look that is at the origin of the perverse politics of racial discrimination.

34. Ibid., 33.

35. Ibid.

36. I am indebted here to Hinkelammert's depiction of the story of Abraham and Isaac. For him, Jesus occupies a position similar to that of Isaac. Opposing murder and violence, Jesus rebels against the homicidal tendencies of a reified law. He represents the "living subject" who protests against a divinized system of laws. See Hinkelammert, *El grito del sujeto*, 38–46.

37. Négritude is the name of a literary movement founded in Paris by black intellectuals who came from different French colonies in Africa and in the West Indies. The poets included, among others, the Martiniquean Aimé Césaire and the Senegalian Leopold Senghor.

38. The source of Fanon's query is the preface written by Sartre in 1948 to an important anthology of Négritude poetry. See Sartre, preface to *Anthologie de la nouvelle poésie nègre e malgache*.

39. On substitution, see Levinas, OB 113–18.

40. This paradoxical discourse is qualitatively different in character from the

rational discourse through which Fanon initially attempted to analyze his situation and to communicate with white people (see BSWM 117ff.). The "composure" with which Fanon begins *Black Skin, White Masks* comes into being as a result of a series of paradoxes and is far from reflecting the "enthusiasm" with which he begins "cataloguing and probing" his surroundings previous to the cry (BSWM 119).

41. For Heidegger's conception of the "They," see particularly Heidegger, *Being and Time*, 146–68.

42. For this reason we find Hinkelammert arguing that *"el sujeto es el otro. Por eso no es el individuo"* [The subject is the Other. For this reason it is not the individual] (Hinkelammert, *El grito del sujeto*, 197).

43. I revise here again Markmann's unfortunate one-sided translation of the second sentence of this passage in which he translates the French *"don"* as "master," instead of "gift" or "generosity." This way of rendering the meaning of *"don"* makes invisible the paradoxical character of Fanon's subjectivity. The paradoxical event of substitution and the transubstantiation of the self are betrayed by this attempt to integrate Fanon's words to the logic of a powerful and self-centered self. To be sure the translation of *"don"* as master is not completely misleading since the root *do-* makes reference both to "take" and to "give"; see Benveniste, "Gift and Exchange in the Indo-European Vocabulary," 34. Yet, if we put the term in context it is clear that the "taking" plays a role in Fanon's narrative only, if at all, in the sense of "taking hold of something in order to give" (see ibid., 24). The paradox thus remains intact. This paradoxical conception of the formation of the ethical self clearly differs from the Hegelian conception of possession, struggle to death, and war found in Hegel, *Phenomenology of Spirit*; and in Hegel, *Hegel's Philosophy of Right*. The translation of *"don"* as "gift" in this passage is backed up by the Spanish translation of *Black Skin, White Masks*, which translates "Je suis don" as "Soy gracia, donación, presente," and by other passages in the book in which Fanon explicitly defines the self in terms of generosity—for example, "I said in my introduction that man is a *yes*. I will never stop reiterating that. *Yes* to life. *Yes* to love. *Yes* to generosity" (BSWM 222). For the Spanish translation that I cite here see Fanon, *Piel negra, máscaras blancas*, 116.

44. For a complementary view, see Gordon's reflections on the Fanonian prayer and the openness of the body in Gordon, *Existentia Africana*, 35, 132.

45. Benveniste, "Gift and Exchange in the Indo-European Vocabulary," 34.

46. Ibid., 40.

47. It must be noted here that for Levinas God is never present. His conception of divinity is also at odds with the God of traditional theology and with the imperial God that I analyzed in the previous chapter. See Levinas OB 149–52; and Lévinas, "God and Philosophy."
48. Fanon, in fact, criticizes Karl Jaspers for believing that the obligation of responsibility stems from God. Fanon, nonetheless, admits that his thoughts on responsibility are in part indebted to Jaspers (BSWM 89). There are other points in which Jaspers's ideas could have been crucial to Fanon's thought. Consider that for Jaspers "men do leap out of immanence, in two ways at once: from the *world* to *deity* and from the *existence* of the conscious spirit to *Existenz*. *Existenz* is the self-being that relates to itself and thereby also to transcendence from which it knows that it has been *given* to itself and upon which it is grounded" (Jaspers, *Philosophy of Existence*, 21, italics mine). Fanon's conception of subjectivity as a gift seems to give expression to the Jaspersian idea of *Existenz*, but without making that from which the subject is given into a ground. In this sense Fanon's thought may be more compatible with an idea of divinity as a G-d that only shows itself in a trace. Fanon's interpretation of the colonized as damned or condemned would seemingly mark a contribution to religious thought: if the damned are the colonized, then salvation has to entail in one way or another de-colonization.
49. Hegel, *Elements of the Philosophy of Right*, 86, §57. Hereafter in this chapter this title will be cited parenthetically in the text.
50. Honneth, *The Struggle for Recognition*, 168.
51. Ibid., 158.
52. Habermas, *Between Facts and Norms*, 507.
53. As with many others with a developmentalist conception of rationality Habermas locates significant epistemological changes only in the history of Europe. Modernity is understood as secularization, and secularization is interpreted as a process of de-Christianization. See the first part of Habermas, *The Theory of Communicative Action*.
54. See Locke, *The Second Treatise of Civil Government and a Letter Concerning Toleration*, 14ff. For a critical discussion of this point, see Chakrabarty, "Family, Fraternity, and Salaried Labor," 229–36.
55. See Honneth, *The Struggle for Recognition*, 21. It is indeed from theft, as I mentioned above, that disrespect emerges. Now it becomes clear that the focus on respect presupposes a philosophical anthropology centered on the notion of property and possession. Honneth's vindication of the bourgeois liberalism of the French Revolution reflects his insensitivity to

this issue. In contrast to Honneth, Fanon focuses not on theft but in the "damné," and not in disrespect but in the "cry" of the subject who *wants* to give and who is unable to do it.

56. Ibid., 21–24.
57. For an explicit engagement with Hegel, see Marx, "Critique of the Hegelian Dialectic and Philosophy as a Whole," 170–93. Marx's influential reflections on the creation of surplus value appear in Marx, *Capital*; see especially parts 3 through 5.
58. From here we get the alliance between political and economic liberalism and neoliberalism. It is from here also that Western liberalism joins hands with the market economy and with its ultimate expression in the deterritorialization of the economy, that is, in globalization. For an account of the close ties between twentieth-century consumerism and the predominance of the values of liberty and equality, see Birken, *Consuming Desire*.
59. See, among others, Fraser, "From Redistribution to Recognition?," 19–49.
60. Coles, *Rethinking Generosity*, 203.
61. Derrida's explorations on the gift are oriented by the idea that the gift can also be poisonous, for example, when it puts the other in debt. See Derrida, *Given Time*, 12–13. For a more productive and provocative treatment of the theme of giving and receiving that ties the problems in the constitution of subjectivity with the political sphere, see Coles, *Rethinking Generosity*.
62. Gordon, *Her Majesty's Other Children*, 15.
63. Consider Fanon's blunt statement: "The black man wants to be white. The white man slaves to reach a human level" (BSWM 9).
64. The dangers of unilateral forms of giving that resist receptivity are spelled out in Coles, *Rethinking Generosity*, 2ff. It is important to note that Coles relates unilateral forms of giving with dominant forms of Christianity and with modern rational discourse. In both cases, Coles persuasively demonstrates, we find the idea of a transcendental ground that may be able to give but that cannot receive anything radically other (ibid., 2). Coles's complaint is clearly compatible with Levinas's critique of the anthropology of Christianity and liberalism in his early essay on Hitlerism (see chapter 1 of this work for a thorough discussion of this point). It also provides additional considerations to sustain the phenomenological description that shows intrinsic ties between the positionality of and the basic features of dominant conceptions of God.
65. See Gustavo Gutiérrez on charity in his *Liberation Theology*.
66. Roger Burggraeve makes an interesting contribution to this point:

The true gift is not primarily some cheap feeling of "sympathy," that can be given so easily, but rather "my morsel of bread" taken from my mouth, i.e. that from which I myself must live. This implies that a genuine "gift" always will be a "gift of self." My gift is the "being-reserved-for-the-Other" of my own "materiality," of my own skin and body.... Only as an enjoying economic can I give myself in the gift of my bread (and by extension, in the gift of my home and my work) to the Other. I must enjoy it in advance, not in order to have the merit of giving, but in order to put my "heart"—my "self"—in it, in order, in giving, to give myself. (Burggraeve, *From Self-Development to Solidarity*, 97)

"Having" has a similar place in the logic of the gift as enjoying.

67. The neologism "altericity" names the paradoxical act of love whereby the death of the Other, and not one's own death, becomes the source of one's concern and angst. Following Levinas's usage of the term, I use sanctity as a synonym. Consider that for Levinas "le côté matériel de l'homme, la vie matérielle m'important en autrui, prennent en autrui pour moi une signification élevée, concernent ma 'sainteté.' ... Cette sainteté n'est peut-être que la sainteté du problème social. Tous les problèmes du manger et du boire, en tant qu'ils concernent autrui, se font sacrés" [the material side of man, the material life that matters to me in the Other, takes on (in the Other) a higher significance for me concerning my "sanctity." ... This sanctity is perhaps only the sanctity of the social problem. All the problems related to eating and drinking, insofar as they have to do with the Other, are sacred.] (Poirié, *Emmanuel Lévinas*, 114). Levinas made this statement in an interview with Poirié in 1986. The reinterpretation and adoption of the concept of sanctity assumes the suspension of a strong modern secularizing anxiety over the possible contributions of religious thought. This anxiety is even present in conceptions of the human and of morality that take love, and not the secular notion of inalienable rights, as the core of moral experience. For an example of this, see Gaita, *A Common Humanity*, 4–5.

68. Charles Taylor commits a horrendous mistake when he argues that for Fanon the struggle for liberation entails a blind and uncompromising view of the equal worthiness and value of all cultures. See C. Taylor, "The Politics of Recognition," 3–34.

69. Has not our entire critique of Western culture been mounted on this possibility? Consider Levinas's judgment that "before culture and aesthetics, meaning is situated in the ethical, presupposed by all culture and all meaning. Morality does not belong to culture: it enables one to judge

it; it discovers the dimension of height. Height ordains being" (Levinas, "Meaning and Sense," 100). Levinas distances himself from an emergent relativistic historicism that leaves behind problematic forms of universalism—such as the ones analyzed in the first chapter of this work in the context of the examination of Levinas's critique of liberalism and Hitlerism. By 1961 to 1963 Levinas had noticed a change in the Western conception of universality: "No direct or privileged contact with the world of Ideas is possible. Such a conception of universality would express the radical opposition, so characteristic of our epoch, to the expansion of culture by colonization. To cultivate and colonize should be completely separated" (ibid.). That is, whereas universality tends to legitimate in Western philosophy the creation of a "community of masters," an opposition to colonization would necessarily entail an altogether different conception of universality. But, while Levinas is surely against the formation of a "community of masters," he is equally against the comfortable relativism into which Western assertions of the alleged de-occidentalization of the world collapse. Levinas demonstrates here his acute critical perception of the ambiguous advances of Western thought, yet he clearly failed in locating more consistent efforts in the articulation of more radical post-imperial forms of thinking. I recall again that Levinas worked on the ideas that led up to the publication of "Meaning and Sense" from 1961 to 1963. By that time every Frenchman knew about Algeria's struggle for de-colonization. Algeria gained independence in 1962 after tens of thousands of Algerians had been killed. In 1961 Fanon published *The Wretched of the Earth*. The grievous question is this: why is it that Fanon, a black Martiniquean, fought and wrote for "his brothers" the Jew and the Algerian, while Levinas only commented about the ambiguities of Western thought without showing an interest in the struggles for liberation and de-colonization? Was Levinas's interest in criticizing the West in relation to its departure from Judaic sources so strong and exclusive that he was not able to stand up positively in favor of non-European and non-Judaic cultures? And why is it that while Levinas expects Sartre to defend the State of Israel he does not talk in favor of the process of de-colonization in Algeria? See Levinas, *Les imprévus de l'histoire*, 155–56. These are grave questions, but they are very important and pertinent ones—particularly if we consider Levinas's judgment of Heidegger's statements in the *Der Spiegel* interview; that is, Heidegger's silence concerning the Shoah. Putting it in the gravest terms, the question is this: To what extent does Levinas's *silence* on the Algerian struggle denote a certain complicity with the politics of invisibility and aggression that defined French colonialism? Levinas, to be sure, is not alone in confronting these questions. Already in 1957 Fanon had criticized French intellectuals in a short piece titled "French Intellectuals and Democrats and the Algerian Revolution." See Fanon, *Toward the African Revolution*, 76–90. A more detailed and thorough discussion of the topic appears in Sorum, *Intellectuals and Decolonization in France*.

70. This is the main argument of Fanon, *A Dying Colonialism*.
71. For a similar argument, see Oliver, *Witnessing*. Oliver does an outstanding job in articulating the limitations of the struggle for recognition and in showing how Fanon advocates a conception of love beyond the logics of recognition (see especially ibid., 42–43). She also makes clear how love involves a process of social and political transformation. Consider also her treatment of what she refers to as Levinas's touch-based ethics and its connection with a form of relationship beyond recognition (ibid., 206ff.). There are many other points of contact between this book and Oliver's work. Perhaps the main difference between the two works is that while Oliver tends to portray the struggle for recognition of identity as an inadequate endeavor, I see it rather as an insufficient but necessary activity. That is why I introduce later the notion of the teleological suspension of identity, instead of simply advocating the cessation or perversity of the struggle for the recognition of identity.
72. Fanon took his answerability in all seriousness, as his participation in the Second World War clearly shows.
73. Fanon, *Toward the African Revolution*, 16.
74. Ibid.
75. See the section "Is There a Teleological Suspension of the Ethical?" in Kierkegaard, *Fear and Trembling and Repetition*, 54–67. In this text Kierkegaard identifies the ethical with the universal. For Fanon, in contrast, the ethical, understood as the upsurge or excess of the loving subjectivity, itself presents, as we have seen before, the possibility of elevating existence beyond the demands of propositional and dialectical logic. As a result, Fanon's conception of the ethical resembles more the Kierkegaardian conception of the religious than that of the ethical proper. Yet, while Kierkegaard (at least through some of his pseudonymous works) links the religious with solitude, secrecy, and hiddenness (the extraordinary in the ordinary), for Fanon the impetus of love ultimately transforms itself in solidarity with the oppressed and in explicit political action. Levinas develops a critique of Kierkegaard that follows a similar logic. He disavows the identification of the ethical with the universal and the exclusive links

between the religious and intimate experience. Levinas's view is summed up in his own interpretation of the story of Abraham and Isaac in Mount Moriah. Levinas suggests that the highest point in the drama of Abraham and Isaac may very well have been located not in the preparation of the sacrifice of Isaac, as Kierkegaard assumes, but in the very moment when Abraham hears the command to spare the life of his son. Levinas adds that Kierkegaard never mentions the moment when Abraham enters into dialogue with God and intercedes for Sodom and Gomorrah. "In that passage," Levinas mentions, "Abraham is fully aware of his nothingness and mortality. . . . But death is powerless, for life receives meaning from an infinite responsibility" (Levinas, *Proper Names*, 74). Fanon, in turn, expands the meaning of this infinite responsibility by examining contexts shaped by the relation between master and slaves. In these contexts it becomes obvious that a subversion of the system of lordship and bondage demands explicit political activity. There have been, to be sure, attempts to introduce Kierkegaard as a sort of sociopolitical philosopher. Among the strongest and more radical positions are Matuštík, *Postnational Identity*; and the more theologically focused Bellinger, *The Genealogy of Violence*.

76. Levinas, *God, Death, and Time*, 11.
77. Ibid., 9.
78. Quoted in Zahar, *Frantz Fanon*, xx.
79. Aimé Césaire captured the thrust of Fanon's humanism when he declared in a tribute to Fanon:
> If the word "commitment" has any meaning, it was with Fanon that it acquired significance. A violent one, they said. . . . But his violence, and this is not paradoxical, was that of the non-violent. By this I mean the violence of justice, of purity and intransigence. This must be understood about him: his revolt was ethical and his endeavor generous. He did not simply adhere to a cause. He gave himself to it. Completely, without reserve. Wholeheartedly. In him resided the absoluteness of passion. . . . (Quoted in Hansen, "Frantz Fanon, 81)
80. Referring to Levinas's work, Guy Petitdemange differentiates between two kinds of "slavery" associated with the notion of the Other:
> Autrui fait apercevoir en nous deux figures non pas du maître, mais de l'esclave: d'un cote, l'esclavage de la convoitise qui vise à la domination . . . de l'autre, l'esclave par amour, l'esclave *pour*; ce *pour* deviendra une catégorie essentielle chez Lévinas. Esclave est sans doute un mot excessif, mais Lévinas durcit les termes pour

faire apparaître en toute clarté que l'homme n'est pas d'abord maître et seigneur, position de soi, mais pris dans un mouvement qui l'emporte, soit en l'enfermant (la nature), soit en le libérant (autrui). [The Other makes us perceive two figures in ourselves, not the figure of the master, but of the slave: on the one hand, the slave of covetousness that aims for domination, the slave from the point of view of the self; and on the other, the slave by love, the slave *for*. The *for* will become an essential category in Lévinas's work. Slave is without any doubt an excessive word, but Lévinas makes the terms stronger in order to make it appear in all its clarity that man is not above all a master and lord, a self positioned being, but caught in a movement that takes him away (from himself), either by imprisoning him (nature), or liberating him (the Other).] (Petitdemange, "La notion paradoxale d'histoire," 28)

81. Alterictiy may be described, in the words of a Levinasian scholar, as follows:
    The truly ethical living subject can be recognized from the fact that it is less afraid to die than it is afraid to be the Other's murderer. At the same time this implies that life finds meaning in ethical goodness in spite of death. . . . True goodness is only possible as *patience*. . . . In goodness, I situate my behaviour in the Other's time or future, without, in so doing, wanting to guarantee my own future beyond the grave. This "being-for-what-reaches-beyond-my-death" therefore, does not yet imply per se a denial of immortality, but rather implies its ethical irrelevance insofar as it has an egocentric meaning. It does provide the possibility to draw the "offering" to its extreme consequences, namely, to the point of giving one's own life for the Other. . . . (Burggraeve, *From Self-Development to Solidarity*, 86–87)

82. In Poirié, *Emmanuel Lévinas*, 115, translation mine. In the original it reads: "le fait d'être affecté pour la mort d'autrui est l'événement remarquable et essentiel de mon psychisme en tant que psychisme humain."

83. Levinas, "Meaning and Sense," 94.

84. It is in this way that both Levinas and Fanon are opposed to the Hegelian conception of subjectivity and desire. Kelly Oliver has made a similar move in her account of the logics of identity and difference. For her, "Hegel was right that the subject is desire. But desire is not as he describes it. Desire is not the urge to overcome the otherness in the self and to recuperate oneself from the other. Subjectivity does not attempt to close in on itself

and fortify itself against the other. Rather, subjectivity opens itself onto the other.... Desire is the urge to move out into otherness" (Oliver, *Witnessing*, 171).

85. Sandoval, *Methodology of the Oppressed*. Much of what is discussed here could be related to Sandoval's magnificent effort in articulating a "methodology of the oppressed." I will pursue a systematic comparison of her view with the main arguments in this chapter in a book-length project preliminary entitled *Fanonian Meditations*.

5. DUSSEL'S ETHICS AND PHILOSOPHY

1. Dussel, "En búsqueda del sentido," 17, translation mine. The Spanish original reads:

    Contándole la historia latinoamericana una de esas noches frescas en nuestra pobre barraca de la cooperativa de construcción hecha para trabajadores árabes que construían sus propias casas en Nazaret, me entusiasmé con un Pizarro que conquistaba el imperio inca con pocos hombres. Gauthier mirándome a los ojos preguntó: "¿Quiénes eran en aquella ocasión los pobres, Pizarro o los indios?" Aquella noche, con una vela por toda iluminación, escribí a mi amigo historiador mendocino Esteban Fontana: "¡Algún día deberemos escribir la Historia de América Latina del otro lado, desde abajo, desde los oprimidos, desde los pobres!"

2. Mignolo, "Dussel's Philosophy of Liberation," 39.
3. See Dussel, "En búsqueda del sentido," 18.
4. See Barber, *Rationality in Enrique Dussel's Philosophy of Liberation*.
5. See Dussel, *Philosophy of Liberation*, 13. This is a translation of the second edition of *Filosofía de la liberación*, which was published in 1980. The first edition was published in 1977.
6. Gordon, *Existentia Africana*; Gordon, *Fanon and the Crisis of European Man*.
7. Husserl, *Cartesian Meditations*, 85.
8. Levinas, *Totality and Infinity*, 28.
9. Sartre, *Being and Nothingness*, 23.
10. Husserl, *Ideas Pertaining to a Pure Phenomenology and to a Phenomenological Philosophy*, 216.
11. Sartre, *Being and Nothingness*, 318.
12. These descriptions and analyses appear in the first and third chapters of the third part of Sartre's *Being and Nothingness*.
13. Hintikka, "The Phenomenological Dimension," 88, 92. These criticisms are directed by Hintikka to scholars who interpret the noema as meaning

(such as Føllesdal and his disciples David Woodruff Smith and Ronald McIntyre). I believe, however, that they apply to Husserl's argument of the *Ideas* as well. This opinion will be substantiated through a consideration of Robert Sokolowski's analysis of the concept of constitution in Husserl.

14. Sokolowski, *The Formation of Husserl's Concept of Constitution*, 159.
15. See, for instance, Føllesdal's interpretation, in which *hyletic* data appear as "boundary conditions which limit the range of noemata that we can have in a given case of perception" (Føllesdal, "Brentano and Husserl on Intentional Objects and Perception," 41).
16. Sokolowski, *The Formation of Husserl's Concept of Constitution*, 210–11.
17. In this, perhaps, consists Hintikka's main mistake. His attempt to find a solution to the problems dealt with here is skewed by the acritical use of the matter-form schema. The use of the matter-form schema does not allow him to offer a satisfactory explanation of the relationship between sensuous data and the formation of the noema (see, for instance, Hintikka, "The Phenomenological Dimension," 93). This is the main reason why I do not follow him into his more positive considerations. Like other interpretations, Hintikka's also repeat the problems raised in Husserl's *Ideas*.
18. See Sokolowski, *The Formation of Husserl's Concept of Constitution*, 206.
19. Ibid., 164.
20. Husserl, *Cartesian Meditations*, 90.
21. Ibid., 77–78.
22. Sokolowski, *The Formation of Husserl's Concept of Constitution*, 207.
23. Ibid., 209.
24. Ibid., 218.
25. To some extent, indeed, the turn toward genetic phenomenology can be explained in relation to the limits of static descriptions in accounting for the constitution of the Other. See Ricoeur, *From Text to Action*, 51.
26. Levinas, *Unforeseen History*, 92.
27. Recall that, for Fanon, "Man is not merely a possibility of recapture or of negation. If it is true that consciousness is a process of transcendence, we have to see too that this transcendence is haunted by the problems of love and understanding. Man is a *yes* that vibrates to cosmic harmonies" (BSWM 8).
28. See the discussion of "The Body-for-Others" in Sartre, *Being and Nothingness*, 445ff. For a discussion of the idea of the call in Fanon, see the analysis in chapter 4 of this work on the cry of the self as a call from the Other.
29. Cohen, introduction to *Time and the Other*, 1.

30. Note here the play of words. *Maintenant* means "now" in French. "*Maintenant*" would mean something like "the act of having something at hand, or taking something by the hand." Presence, the spatial and the temporal presence in the *now*, is achieved by the *hand that takes*. The achievement of re-presentation ultimately entails, at least when it takes the status of a first principle, physical possession and violence.
31. Levinas, "Beyond Intentionality," 102.
32. Levinas, *Time and the Other*, 83.
33. Dussel, *Philosophy of Liberation*, 8.
34. Among these see, especially, Cerutti Guldberg, *Filosofía de la liberación latinoamericana*; and Schutte, *Cultural Identity and Social Liberation in Latin American Thought*.
35. See Barber, *Rationality in Enrique Dussel's Philosophy of Liberation*.
36. For this and other related points, see Castro-Gómez, *Crítica de la razón latinoamericana*.
37. Dussel, *Filosofía ética de la liberación*, vol. 1, *Presupuestos de una filosofía de la liberación*, 12, translation mine. The first edition of this volume was published in 1973 with the title *Para una ética de la liberación latinoamericana*.
38. See for this point Dussel, *Filosofía ética de la liberación*, vol. 1, *Presupuestos de una filosofía de la liberación*, 130.
39. See Gordon, *Existentia Africana*, 35, 47.
40. See Dussel, *20 tesis de política*.

6. THE DE-COLONIAL TURN

1. Chalier, "L'histoire sainte"; Levinas, "The Meaning of History," 226–27; Levinas, *Unforeseen History*; and Schroeder, *Altared Ground*. See also the issue of *Cahiers d'Etudes Lévinassiennes* dedicated to the concept of the messianic in Levinas and Jewish philosophy (2005, no. 4).
2. For this point, Gordon, *Existentia Africana*. The tension between liberation and identity questions often appears today in the guise of the analytic divide between either distribution or recognition, or political economy or culture. Often missing in the discussion regarding these terms is a serious engagement with the work of radical theorists of color such as Du Bois, Césaire, and Fanon, who are often ignored or lumped together as defending one side of the dichotomy. Also missing in these discussions is the relevance of a third term in the equation: knowledge. As my analysis of Levinas, Fanon, and Dussel shows, radical theorists of color are deeply interested in questions of identity, liberation, and the transformation and expansion of knowledge, which informs their efforts to rearticulate their

identity and to make proposals for social, economical, and/or political change.
3. Dussel, "Transmodernity and Interculturality," 1. Pagination refers to the single-spaced translated manuscript. The essay is twenty-five pages long.
4. Ibid.
5. Dussel's studies on Marx were originally published in Spanish between 1985 and 1990. An English translation of the second volume, *Hacia un Marx desconocido* (1988), was published by Routledge in 2001. *Etica de la liberación en la edad de la globalización y de la exclusión* was published in 1998. See Dussel, *El ultimo Marx (1863–1882) y la liberación latinoamericana*; Dussel, *Etica de la liberación en la edad de la globalización y de la exclusión*; Dussel, *Hacia un Marx desconocido*; Dussel, *La producción teórica de Marx*; and Dussel, *Towards an Unknown Marx*.
6. Dussel, *El humanismo semita*, xi–xii. This work was completed in the Institut für europäische Geschichte in Germany in 1964. The original is in Spanish. The English translation is mine.
7. Dussel, "En búsqueda del sentido," 17. Translation mine.
8. Dussel, *El humanismo helénico*, xii. This text was completed in Paris in 1963. The original is in Spanish. The English translation and emphasis in italics are mine.
9. Examples of "continentalism" are found in Bagú, "La identidad continental"; and Husserl, *The Crisis of European Sciences and Transcendental Phenomenology*. Continentalism arguably appears as well in conceptions of the United States as the entire New World or the climax of New World forms of life and civilization. For a critique of this posture, see Maldonado-Torres, "Decolonization and the New Identitarian Logics after September 11"; and Maldonado-Torres, "Toward a Critique of Continental Reason.
10. Husserl, *The Crisis of European Sciences and Transcendental Phenomenology* 274.
11. Ibid., 275.
12. Ibid., 290–91.
13. Koselleck, *Critique and Crisis*, 1.
14. Ibid., 184.
15. Ibid., 185.
16. Ibid., 2.
17. Ibid., 1.
18. Ibid., 5.
19. See Raynal, *Philosophical and Political History of the Settlement and Trade of the Europeans in the East and West Indies*.
20. Ibid., 181.

21. James, *The Black Jacobins*, 82.
22. See Trouillot, *Silencing the Past*. See also Scott, "Conscripts of Modernity," 98–101, 246 n. 6; and Fischer, *Modernity Disavowed*, 210–11.
23. Pratt, *Imperial Eyes*.
24. For a brief history of the emergence and development of the social sciences, see Gulbenkian Commission on the Restructuring of the Social Sciences, *Open the Social Sciences*. See also Wallerstein, "The Unintended Consequences of Cold War Area Studies," 195–232.
25. Kant, "An Answer to the Question," 58. Italics mine.
26. Dussel, *The Invention of the Americas*, 20.
27. Dussel, "World System and 'Trans'-Modernity," 222.
28. Césaire, *Discourse on Colonialism*, 9.
29. Ibid., Italics mine.
30. Dussel, *The Invention of the Americas*, 74.
31. Ibid., 74–75.
32. Ibid., 116.
33. For critiques of Husserl that go in this direction, see Gordon, *Fanon and the Crisis of European Man*; Knies, "On the Idea of Post-European Science"; and Maldonado-Torres, "Post-imperial Reflections on Crisis, Knowledge, and Utopia." See also the section on Husserl in chapter 1.
34. See Du Bois, *The Souls of Black Folk*.
35. Husserl, *The Crisis of European Sciences and Transcendental Phenomenology*, 197.
36. Ibid., 115.
37. Dussel, "World System and 'Trans'-Modernity," 231–32.
38. Ibid., 232.
39. See, among others, Césaire, *Toussaint Louverture*.
40. Pagden, "Europe," 50.
41. Dussel, "Modernity, Eurocentrism, and Trans-Modernity," 132.
42. Ibid., 131.
43. Ibid., 132.
44. For this auto-critical reflection and rectification, see Dussel, "World System and 'Trans'-Modernity," 221–44.
45. Dussel, *The Invention of the Americas*, 32.
46. Ibid., 38.
47. Dussel, *Etica de la liberación en la edad de la globalización y de la exclusión*, 60. Translation mine.
48. Dussel, *The Invention of the Americas*, 40.
49. Quoted in ibid., 40.
50. Ibid., 42.

51. Ibid., 43.
52. Todorov, *The Conquest of America*, 145.
53. Dussel writes,
    > Although the conquistador participated in the king's lordship, he surpassed even the king, because he had the opportunity to face another lord and lord it over him. The conquistador exerted his power by denying the Other his dignity, by reducing the Indian to the Same, and by compelling the Indian to become his docile, oppressed instrument. The conquest practically affirms the conquering ego and negates the Other as Other. (Dussel, *The Invention of the Americas*, 44)

    Here I only differ with Dussel in the idea that the conqueror reduces the Indian to the Same. In truth, the conqueror reduces the Indian to a level below the Same. Fanon metaphorically refers to it as hell. For an expanded discussion, see the analysis of the relation between God, man, and the racially condemned modern subjects in chapter 3 of this book.
54. This point is elaborated in chapter 3 of this book.
55. Colón, *Los cuatro viajes*, 63. For a fuller development of this point, see Maldonado-Torres, "Imperio, raza y religión." A briefer account appears in Maldonado-Torres, "Reconciliation as a Contested Future."
56. On the early Christian conception of slavery and Christians' relationship with the Roman empire, see Horsley, *Paul and Empire*.
57. I articulate this point in Maldonado-Torres, "Imperio, raza y religión."
58. See Hanke, *All Mankind Is One*.
59. The poetics of the *propter nos* refers to a macro-narrative that reveals the world as "for our sake," where "our" referred to the kingdoms and emerging European nations in the sixteenth century. See Wynter, "1492"; Wynter, "Columbus and the Poetics of the Propter Nos," 251–86.
60. Quijano, "Coloniality of Power, Eurocentrism, and Latin America," 533.
61. See, especially, Agamben, *Homo Sacer*; and Agamben, *Means without End*.
62. Gordon, *Her Majesty's Other Children*, 13–14.
63. Parts of the next four paragraphs also appear in Maldonado-Torres, "On the Coloniality of Being." This essay marks a transition between this book and a different book project entitled *Fanonian Meditations*.
64. In this respect, Dussel writes: "El *sujeto* europeo que comienza por ser un 'yo conquisto' y culmina en la 'voluntad de poder' es un sujeto *masculino*. El *ego cogito* es el *ego* de un varón." [The European *subject* who begins in the mode of "I conquer" and reaches its climax in the "will to power" is a *masculine* subject. The *ego cogito* is the *ego* of a male.] Dussel, *Filosofía*

ética de la liberación, 3: 50. Dussel also comments in this text on the ways in which the colonized male subject repeats the same behavior toward colonized women.
65. Dussel, Filosofía ética de la liberación, 3: 99.
66. Sharpley-Whiting and White, Spoils of War, xiv–xv.
67. Goldstein, War and Gender, 332.
68. Many examples of these elements also appear in Cooke and Woollacott, Gendering War Talk.
69. This analysis is informed by Lewis Gordon's description of sexual and racial dynamics. See Gordon, Her Majesty's Other Children, 73–88. Gordon writes: "For, in an antiblack world, a black penis, whatever its size, represents a threat. Given our discussion of the black signifying the feminine, the underlying nature of the threat should be obvious: the black penis is feared for the same reason that a woman with a penis is feared. She represents a form of revenge" (ibid., 83).
70. Consider in this light Bill Bennett's statement in his radio show: "If you wanted to reduce crime, you could—if that were your sole purpose—you could abort every black baby in this country and your crime rate would go down. That would be an impossibly ridiculous and morally reprehensible thing to do, but your crime rate would go down." Problematic in the statement is the presumption that blacks are more conducive to crime than other social groups. Bennett also adds that if ends were to justify the means, then it would be logical to reduce crime by aborting black babies. The irony of Bennett's comments is that, while he considers such a measure morally reprehensible, his statement could be taken as a description of the challenge that black people confront in the United States and modernity at large. The modern world is one in which ethics is constantly trumped by arguments for efficiency. The kind of measure that Bennett describes is less a hypothetical situation and more a variation of the kinds of actions systematically perpetrated upon blacks and people of color ordinarily. Morality is more the exception than the rule in this context. And when the moral racist speaks he often reflects the *desire* to do what he knows must be done to resolve a situation, while his morality allegedly holds him back. This leads the moral racist to celebrate such morality (and typically Christian values), while also partially justifying the actions of other racists—because, after all, eliminating blacks is the logical thing to do if one wants to reduce crime. The moral racist is condescending toward blacks, who also appear as irrevocably linked to crime, which makes their actions subject to excessive penalization, while the racist white is only condemned for not sharing the same morality with other racists. For

a summary of Bennett's comments and a discussion about them, see "Bennett Under Fire for Remarks about Blacks, Crime," http://www.cnn.com/2005/POLITICS/09/30/bennett.comments (consulted July 8, 2007).
71. The argument here is that race plays a peculiar role in modernity and that this role is connected to the naturalization of the non-ethics of war, not that there may not have been racial categories in the past.
72. See Fanon, *The Wretched of the Earth*.
73. I am referring to Fanon, *Black Skin, White Masks*.
74. The idea of "love" appears in several parts of *Black Skin, White Masks*, particularly in the conclusion. For a discussion of the relevance of the idea of love in Fanon, see chapter 4. Consider also the importance of the concept in de-colonial theoretical interventions, especially Sandoval, *Methodology of the Oppressed*.
75. For reflections on the different elements that intervened in Fanon's transition from analyst to revolutionary, see Gendzier, *Frantz Fanon*. Gendzier shows that there was an internal dynamic at stake by which Fanon was led to political activism and revolution. I argue that such internal dynamic can be ultimately defined as the de-colonial attitude, which was at work from the moment that Fanon left Martinique to fight in the Second World War.
76. Fanon, *A Dying Colonialism*, 128.
77. Gordon, *Existentia Africana*, 13–15.
78. For an analysis of the meaning of the "cry" from the perspective of the coloniality of being and de-colonization, see Maldonado-Torres, "The Cry of the Self as a Call from the Other," 46–60. This article appears in an expanded form in chapter 4.
79. Ellison, *Invisible Man*.
80. Dussel, *The Invention of the Americas*, 43.
81. Ibid., 48.
82. Dussel, "Modernity, Eurocentrism, and Trans-Modernity," 133.
83. See, among others, Freud, *Totem and Taboo*; Girard, *Things Hidden since the Foundation of the World*; and Girard, *Violence and the Sacred*.
84. Dussel, "Philosophy in Latin America in the Twentieth Century," 30.
85. Dussel, *The Invention of the Americas*, 9–10.
86. Ibid., 136.
87. See Dussel, *Etica de la liberación en la edad de la globalización y de la exclusión*; and Dussel, *The Invention of the Americas*, 26.
88. "Es necesario saber discernir lo positivo de la crítica de los posmodernos, lo positivo de la modernidad, y la afirmación de lo valioso de la exterioridad del mundo de la vida del Sur, para imaginar un proyecto de liberación,

alternativo, ético y necesario para la mayoría de la humanidad, y las mediaciones institucionales de su efectiva realización" (Dussel, *Posmodernidad y transmodernidad*).

89. Dussel, *The Invention of the Americas*, 138.
90. Subcomandante Marcos relates the Zapatista view with the struggle of subjects considered different and marginalized by their societies: "O sea que cuando los zapatistas dicen 'queremos un mundo donde quepan muchos mundos' no están descubriendo nada nuevo, simplemente están diciendo lo que ya dicen los "otros" y "diferentes" que caminan los mundos de abajo." [That is to say, that when the Zapatistas state "we want a world where many worlds fit" they are not making any new discovery, they are simply saying what the "others" and the "different" who walk in the underworlds say.] See http://www.ezln.org/documentos/1999/19991026.es.htm (consulted July 8, 2007). Dussel would agree with this statement. His philosophy of liberation and idea of transmodernity can be seen as an effort to articulate criteria that could serve to orient the construction of such a new world.
91. Dussel, *The Invention of the Americas*, 138.
92. Ibid., 69; and Dussel, "The 'World-System,'" 70.
93. The South here is ultimately a metaphorical concept that includes reference to the south in the north.
94. Dussel, "Transmodernity and Interculturality," 9.
95. The description of post-cold-war dynamics in terms of the "clash of civilizations" is advanced in S. Huntington, *The Clash of Civilizations and the Remaking of World Order*.
96. See Dussel, "World System and 'Trans'-Modernity," 221–44.
97. Dussel, "World System and 'Trans'-Modernity," 223–24.
98. Maldonado-Torres, "Post-Imperial Reflections on Crisis, Knowledge, and Utopia," 301.
99. See Sandoval, *Methodology of the Oppressed*, 169–70, and the conclusion of this book.
100. See Husserl, "Philosophy and the Crisis of European Man," 149–92; and Habermas, "Philosophy as Stand-In and Interpreter," 1–20.
101. The Zapatistas prepared for approximately two years and launched an attack in several Mexican cities on January 1, 2004. For a brief account of the origins of the rebellion, see Carrigan, "Afterword," 419–20. There are more relevant documents in the official website of the EZLN, at http://www.ezln.org.mx (consulted July 8, 2007).
102. For a critique of Fanon that goes in this direction, see Henry, "Frantz

Fanon, African, and Afro-Caribbean Philosophy," 68–89. For a critique of Levinas, see Maldonado-Torres, "The Topology of Being and the Geopolitics of Knowledge," 29–56.

103. On the idea of the unfinished project of de-colonization, see Grosfoguel, "Subaltern Epistemologies, Decolonial Imaginaries and the Redefinition of Global Capitalism"; Grosfoguel, Maldonado-Torres, and Saldívar, "Latin@s and the 'Euro-American' Menace"; and Maldonado-Torres, "Intervenciones filosóficas al proyecto inacabado de la descolonizacion."

104. See Dussel, *Etica de la liberación en la edad de la globalización y de la exclusión*. Dussel's writings on Marx include three volumes of commentaries to the fourth drafts of Marx's *Capital*. See Dussel, *El ultimo Marx (1863–1882) y la liberación latinoamericana*; Dussel, *Hacia un Marx desconocido*; and Dussel, *La producción teórica de Marx*. The second volume has appeared in English (see Dussel, *Towards an Unknown Marx*). On Marx, see also Dussel, *Las metáforas teológicas de Marx*. For the complete texts of the discussions of Dussel and Apel, see Apel and Dussel, *Etica del discurso y ética de la liberación*.

105. From Hinkelammert, see Hinkelammert, *El grito del sujeto*; Hinkelammert, *Sacrificios humanos y sociedad occidental*; Hinkelammert, *Solidaridad o suicidio colectivo*; and Hinkelammert, ed., *El huracán de la globalización*.

106. Dussel, "Algunas reflexiones sobre la 'falacia naturalista,'" 87–102.

CONCLUSION

1. Fanon, *Black Skin, White Masks*, 41.
2. Levinas, "Transcendence and Evil," 182.
3. For elaborations of the concept of coloniality of power, see Quijano, "Coloniality of Power, Eurocentrism, and Latin America," 533–80. For reflections on the coloniality of knowledge, see Lander, *La colonialidad del saber*. And for considerations of the coloniality of being in relation to the coloniality of power and knowledge, see Maldonado-Torres, "On the Coloniality of Being"; Maldonado-Torres, "The Topology of Being and the Geopolitics of Knowledge," 29–56; Mignolo, "Decires fuera de lugar," 9–32; Mignolo, "Os esplendores e as misérias da 'ciência,'" 667–709; and Wynter, "Unsettling the Coloniality of Being/Power/Truth/Freedom," 257–337.
4. See Levinas, "Transcendence and Evil," 183–85.
5. On de-colonial love, see Sandoval, *Methodology of the Oppressed*, 144–46.
6. My analysis of Don Quixote in this paragraph only aims to make explicit Levinas's discussion of this character in the preface to the Spanish trans-

lation of *Totality and Infinity*. See Levinas, preface to *Totalidad e infinito*, 9–11. This is the second edition of the translation. The first Spanish edition was published in 1977. Levinas wrote the preface in 1976.
7. Quoted in Levinas, preface to *Totalidad e infinito*, 11, translation mine.
8. Césaire, *Discourse on Colonialism*, 9.
9. Sandoval, *Methodology of the Oppressed*, 169–70.
10. See ibid., 144–46.
11. For typically rightist approaches, see Cohen, *For Love of Country*; for the views of a self-declared leftist, see Žižek, "A Leftist Plea for 'Eurocentrism,'" 988–1009.
12. See Gordon, *Existentia Africana*, 63.
13. Levinas, "'As Old as the World?'" 77–78.
14. Ibid, 84.
15. Ibid., 85.
16. Ibid., 87.
17. Ibid.
18. Ibid., 82.
19. There is also the risk of turning victimization into the declaration of a permanent innocence that serves as a license to commit violence and that ultimately creates new victims. See on this point Bruckner, *La tentation de l'innocence*.
20. To be sure, it is clear that Fanon's work must be complemented, further enriched, and criticized in light of feminist work and queer theory. On this point, see Sandoval, *Methodology of the Oppressed*; and Sharpley-Whiting, *Frantz Fanon*.
21. Compare the discussion at the beginning of chapter 5 with the analysis of French thought in relation to the events of May 1968 in Ferry and Renaut, *French Philosophy of the Sixties*.
22. The most notable recent works in this direction are Dussel, *Etica de la liberación en la edad de la globalización y de la exclusión*; Gordon, *Existentia Africana*; and Mignolo, *Local Histories/Global Designs*. Important also in this context is Mall, *Intercultural Philosophy*.
23. Charles Taylor's discussion of these issues appears in C. Taylor, "The Politics of Recognition," 65ff.
24. As I noted before, the essentialist overtones in Dussel's early work are very much related to a direct application of Levinas's conception of the relation between ontology and metaphysics, and between self and the Other, to the realm of geopolitics and concrete social life.
25. I refer to this as "transgresstopic critical hermeneutics." See Maldonado-

Torres, "Post-imperial Reflections on Crisis, Knowledge, and Utopia," 277–315.
26. See Maldonado-Torres, "Decolonization and the New Identitarian Logics after September 11," 35–67.
27. See, for instance, Hutton, *A Declaration of Interdependence*.
28. See Habermas and Derrida, "February 15, or What Binds Europeans Together," 291–97.
29. See, among others, Ramadan, *Être musulman européen*; Ramadan, *Islam, le face à face des civilisations*; and Ramadan, *Western Muslims and the Future of Islam*.
30. I discuss the case of Ramadan in Maldonado-Torres, "Decolonization and the New Identitarian Logics after September 11," 35–67.
31. I have commented on this point elsewhere. See Maldonado-Torres, "Topology of Being and the Geopolitics of Knowledge," 47–48.
32. Levi, *Survival in Auschwitz*, 89–90.
33. See, among others, Anzaldúa, ed., *Making Face, Making Soul*; Anzaldúa and Keating, *This Bridge We Call Home*; and Moraga and Anzaldúa, *This Bridge Called My Back*.

BIBLIOGRAPHY

Agamben, Giorgio. *Homo Sacer*. Translated by Daniel Heller-Roazen. Stanford, Calif.: Stanford University Press, 1998.

———. *Means without End*. Translated by Vincenzo Binetti and Cesare Casarino. Minneapolis: University of Minnesota Press, 2000.

Alighieri, Dante. *Monarchy and Three Political Letters*. Translated by Donald Nicholl and Colin Hardie. London: Weidenfeld and Nicholson, 1954.

Amnesty International USA. *The Universal Declaration of Human Rights 1948–1988: Human Rights, the United Nations and Amnesty International*. New York: Amnesty International USA Legal Support Network, 1988.

Anzaldúa, Gloria, ed. *Making Face, Making Soul=Haciendo caras: Creative and Critical Perspectives by Feminists of Color*. San Francisco: Aunt Lute Foundation Books, 1990.

Anzaldúa, Gloria E., and AnaLouise Keating, eds. *This Bridge We Call Home: Radical Visions for Transformation*. New York: Routledge, 2002.

Apel, Karl-Otto, and Enrique Dussel. *Etica del discurso y ética de la liberación*. Madrid: Editorial Trotta, 2005.

Arenas, Reinaldo. *Antes que anochezca*. 2nd ed. Barcelona: Tusquets, Fábula, 1998.

Arendt, Hannah. *On Violence*. New York: Harcourt, Brace and World, 1969.

Arrighi, Giovanni, Terrence K. Hopkins, and Immanuel Wallerstein. "1968: The Great Rehearsal." In *Antisystemic Movements*, 97–115. London: Verso, 1989.

Assmann, Hugo, ed. *Sobre ídolos y sacrificios: René Girard con teólogos de la liberación*. San José, Costa Rica: Editorial Departamento Ecuménico de Investigaciones, 1991.

Attali, Jacques. *Fraternités: Une nouvelle utopie*. Paris: Fayard, 1999.

Bagú, Sergio. "La identidad continental." In *La identidad continental: Indige-

nismo y diversidad cultural, by Sergio Bagú and Hector Díaz Polanco, 13–31. Mexico, D.F.: Universidad de la Ciudad de México, 2003.

Barber, Michael. *Rationality in Enrique Dussel's Philosophy of Liberation*. New York: Fordham University Press, 1998.

Bauman, Zygmunt. *Modernity and the Holocaust*. Ithaca, N.Y.: Cornell University Press, 1989.

Bellinger, Charles K. *The Genealogy of Violence: Reflections on Creation, Freedom, and Evil*. Oxford: Oxford University Press, 2001.

Benveniste, Émile. "Gift and Exchange in the Indo-European Vocabulary." In *The Logic of the Gift: Toward an Ethic of Generosity*, edited by Alan D. Schrift, 33–42. New York: Routledge, 1997.

Bernasconi, Robert. "Skepticism in the Face of Philosophy." In *Re-Reading Levinas*, edited by Robert Bernasconi and Simon Critchley, 149–61. Bloomington: Indiana University Press, 1991.

Berger, Teresa. "The Poetics of the Sacred and the Politics of Scholarship." In *Worlds and Knowledges Otherwise*, vol. 1, dossier 2. http://www.jhfc.duke.edu/wko/.

Birken, Lawrence. *Consuming Desire: Sexual Science and the Emergence of Abundance, 1871–1914*. Ithaca, N.Y.: Cornell University Press, 1988.

———. *Hitler as Philosophe: Remnants of the Enlightenment in National Socialism*. Westport, Conn.: Praeger, 1995.

Blum, Lawrence. "Recognition, Value, and Equality: A Critique of Charles Taylor's and Nancy Fraser's Accounts of Multiculturalism." In *Theorizing Multiculturalism: A Guide to the Current Debate*, edited by Cynthia Willett, 73–99. Malden, Mass.: Blackwell, 1998.

Bruckner, Pascal. *La tentation de l'innocence*. Paris: Éditions Grasset and Fasquelle, 1995.

Buckley, R. Philip. *Husserl, Heidegger and the Crisis of Philosophical Responsibility*. Dordrecht: Kluwer Academic Publishers, 1992.

Buck-Morss, Susan. "Hegel and Haiti." *Critical Inquiry* 26 (2000): 821–63.

Burggraeve, Roger. *From Self-Development to Solidarity: An Ethical Reading of Human Desire in Its Socio-Political Relevance According to Emmanuel Levinas*. Translated by Catherine Vanhove-Romanik. Leuven: Center for Metaphysics and Philosophy of God in association with Peeters, 1985.

Butler, Judith. "Ethical Ambivalence." In *The Turn to Ethics*, edited by Marjorie Garber, Beatrice Hanssen, and Rebecca L. Walkowitz, 15–28. New York: Routledge, 2000.

Camus, Albert. *The Rebel: An Essay on Man in Revolt*. Translated by Anthony Bower. New York: Vintage Books, 1991.

Caputo, John D. *Demythologizing Heidegger.* Bloomington: Indiana University Press, 1993.

Carrigan, Ana. "Afterword: Chiapas, the First Postmodern Revolution." In *Our World Is Our Weapon*, edited by Juana Ponce de León, 417–44. New York: Seven Stories Press, 2001.

Castro-Gómez, Santiago. *Crítica de la razón latinoamericana.* Barcelona: Puvill Libros, 1996.

Cerutti Guldberg, Horacio. *Filosofía de la liberación latinoamericana.* 2nd ed. Mexico, D.F.: Fondo de Cultura Económica, 1992.

Césaire, Aimé. *Discourse on Colonialism.* Translated by Joan Pinkham. New York: Monthly Review Press, 1972.

———. *Toussaint Louverture: La Révolution française et le problème colonial.* Paris: Présence Africaine, 1981.

Chakrabarty, Dipesh. "Family, Fraternity, and Salaried Labor." In *Provincializing Europe: Postcolonial Thought and Historical Difference*, 214–36. Princeton, N.J.: Princeton University Press, 2000.

Chalier, Catherine. "Ethics and the Feminine." In *Re-Reading Levinas*, edited by Robert Bernasconi and Simon Critchley, 119–29. Bloomington: Indiana University Press, 1991.

———. "L'histoire sainte." In *Emmanuel Lévinas et l'histoire*, edited by Nathalie Frogneux and Françoise Mies, 235–57. Paris: Les Éditions du Cerf, 1998.

Cohen, Joshua, ed. *For Love of Country: Debating the Limits of Patriotism; Martha C. Nussbaum with Respondents.* Boston: Beacon Press, 1996.

Cohen, Richard A. "Translator's Introduction." in *Time and the Other*, by Emmanuel Levinas. Pittsburgh: Duquesne University Press, 1987: 1–28.

Coles, Romand. *Rethinking Generosity: Critical Theory and the Politics of Caritas.* Ithaca, N.Y.: Cornell University Press, 1997.

Colón, Cristóbal. *Los cuatro viajes: Testamento.* Madrid: Alianza Editorial, 1986.

Cone, James H. *The Spirituals and the Blues: An Interpretation.* New York: Seabury Press, 1972.

Cooke, Miriam. "Multiple Critique: Islamic Feminist Rhetorical Strategies." *Nepantla: Views from South* 1, no. 1 (2000): 91–110.

Cooke, Miriam, and Angela Woollacott, eds. *Gendering War Talk.* Princeton, N.J.: Princeton University Press, 1993.

Davis, Todd F., and Kenneth Womack, eds. *Mapping the Ethical Turn: A Reader in Ethics, Culture, and Literary Theory.* Charlottesville, Va.: University Press of Virginia, 2001.

de Beauvoir, Simone. *The Second Sex.* Translated by H. M. Parshley. Middlesex, Eng.: Penguin Books, 1972.

De Greef, Jan. "Skepticism and Reason." In *Face to Face with Levinas*, edited by Richard A. Cohen, 159–79. Albany: State University of New York Press, 1986.

Derrida, Jacques. *Given Time*. Vol. 1, *Counterfeit Money*. Translated by Peggy Kamuf. Chicago: University of Chicago Press, 1992.

———. "Violence and Metaphysics: An Essay on the Thought of Emmanuel Levinas." In *Writing and Difference*, edited by Alan Bass, 79–153. Chicago: University of Chicago Press, 1978.

Dollimore, Jonathan. *Death, Desire and Loss in Western Culture*. New York: Routledge, 1998.

Du Bois, W. E. B. *The Souls of Black Folk*. Edited by Henry Louis Gates Jr. and Terri Hume Oliver. New York: W. W. Norton, 1999.

Duque, Félix. "Introducción." In *Tiempo y el otro*, by Emmanuel Levinas. Barcelona: Ediciones Paidós, 1993: 9–64.

Dussel, Enrique. "Algunas reflexiones sobre la 'falacia naturalista.'" In *Hacia una filosofía política crítica*, 87–102. Bilbao: Desclée de Brouwer, 2001.

———. "En búsqueda del sentido. (Origen y desarrollo de una Filosofía de la Liberación)." *Anthropos* (Spain) 180 (1998): 13–37.

———. *Etica de la liberación en la edad de la globalización y de la exclusión*. Madrid: Editorial Trotta, 1998.

———. "Europe, Modernity, and Eurocentrism." Translated by Javier Krauel and Virginia C. Tuma. *Nepantla: Views from South* 1, no. 3 (2000): 465–78.

———. *Filosofía ética de la liberación*. Vol. 1, *Presupuestos de una filosofía de la liberación*. 3rd ed. Buenos Aires: Ediciones la Aurora, 1987.

———. *Filosofía ética de la liberación*. Vol. 3, *Niveles concretos de la ética latinoamericana*. 3rd ed. Buenos Aires: Ediciones Megápolis, 1977.

———. *Filosofía ética latinoamericana*. Vol. 5, *Arqueológica latinoamericana: Una filosofía de la religión antifetichista*. Bogotá: Universidad Santo Tomás, 1980.

———. *Hacia un Marx desconocido: Un comentario de los Manuscritos del 61–63*. Mexico, D.F.: Siglo Veintiuno Editores y Universidad Autónoma Metropolitana, Iztapalapa, 1988.

———. *El humanismo helénico*. Buenos Aires: Editorial Universitaria de Buenos Aires, 1975.

———. *El humanismo semita: Estructuras intencionales radicales del pueblo de Israel y otros semitas*. Buenos Aires: Editorial Universitaria de Buenos Aires, 1969.

———. *The Invention of the Americas: Eclipse of "the Other" and the Myth of Modernity*. Translated by Michael D. Barber. New York: Continuum, 1995.

———. *Las metáforas teológicas de Marx*. Estella, Sp.: Verbo Divino, 1993.

———. "Modernity, Eurocentrism, and Trans-Modernity: In Dialogue with Charles Taylor." In *The Underside of Modernity: Apel, Ricoeur, Rorty, Taylor, and the Philosophy of Liberation*, edited by Eduardo Mendieta, 129–59. Atlantic Highlands, N.J.: Humanities Press, 1996.

———. "Philosophy in Latin America in the Twentieth Century: Problems and Currents." In *Latin American Philosophy: Currents, Issues, Debates*, edited by Eduardo Mendieta, 11–53. Bloomington: Indiana University Press, 2003.

———. *Philosophy of Liberation*. Translated by Aquilina Martinez and Christine Morkovsky. Maryknoll, N.Y.: Orbis Books, 1985.

———. *Posmodernidad y transmodernidad: Diálogos con la filosofía de Gianni Vattimo*. Puebla, Mex.: Universidad Iberoamericana, Golfo Centro; Instituto Tecnológico y de Estudios Superiores de Occidente; Universidad Iberoamericana, Plantel Laguna, 1999.

———. *La producción teórica de Marx: Un comentario a los Grundrisse*. 3rd ed. Mexico, D.F.: Siglo Veintiuno Editores, 1998.

———. "The Reason of the Other: 'Interpellation' as Speech-Act." In *The Underside of Modernity: Apel, Ricoeur, Rorty, Taylor, and the Philosophy of Liberation*, edited by Eduardo Mendieta, 19–48. Atlantic Highlands, N.J.: Humanities Press, 1996.

———. *Teología de la liberación: Un panorama de su desarrollo*. Mexico, D.F.: Potrerillos Editores, 1995.

———. *Towards an Unknown Marx: A Commentary on the "Manuscripts of 1861–63."* Translated by Yolanda Angulo. New York: Routledge, 2001.

———. "Transmodernity and Interculturality: An Interpretation from the Perspective of Philosophy of Liberation." In *Unsettling Postcolonial Studies: Coloniality, Transmodernity, and Border Thinking*, edited by Ramón Grosfoguel, Nelson Maldonado-Torres, and José David Saldívar; translated by Kirstie Dorr and George Ciccariello Maher, in preparation.

———. *El ultimo Marx (1863–1882) y la liberación latinoamericana: Un comentario a la tercera y a la cuarta redacción de "El Capital."* Mexico, D.F.: Siglo Veintiuno Editores y Universidad Autónoma Metropolitana, Iztapalapa, 1990.

———. *20 tesis de politica*. Mexico, D.F.: Siglo XXI: Centro de Cooperación Regional para la Educación de Adultos en América latina y el Caribe, 2006.

———. "The 'World-System': Europe as 'Center' and Its 'Periphery' beyond Eurocentrism." In *Beyond Philosophy: Ethics, History, Marxism, and Liberation Theology*, edited and translated by Eduardo Mendieta, 53–84. Lanham, Md.: Rowman and Littlefield, 2003.

———. "World System and 'Trans'-Modernity." Translated by Alessandro Fornazzari. *Nepantla: Views from South* 3, no. 2 (2002): 221–44.

———, ed. *Debate en torno a la ética del discurso de Apel: Diálogo filosófico norte-sur desde América Latina.* Mexico, D.F.: Siglo Veintinuno Editores, and Universidad Autónoma Metropolitana, Iztapalapa, 1994.

Ehlen, Patrick. *Frantz Fanon: A Spiritual Biography.* New York: Crossroad Publishing Company, 2000.

Ellison, Ralph. *Invisible Man.* Philadelphia: Chelsea House Publishers, 1999.

Fanon, Frantz. *Black Skin, White Masks.* Translated by Charles Lam Markmann. New York: Grove Press, 1968.

———. *A Dying Colonialism.* Translated by Haakon Chevalier. New York: Grove Press, 1965.

———. *Piel negra, máscaras blancas.* Buenos Aires: Editorial Abraxas, 1973.

———. *Toward the African Revolution: Political Essays.* Translated by Haakon Chevalier. New York: Grove Press, 1988.

———. *The Wretched of the Earth.* Translated by Constance Farrington. New York: Grove Press, 1991.

———. *The Wretched of the Earth.* Translated by Richard Philcox. New York: Grove Press, 2004.

Farias, Victor. *Heidegger and Nazism.* Translated by Paul Burrell and Gabriel Ricci. Philadelphia: Temple University Press, 1989.

Faye, Emmanuel. *Heidegger: L'introduction du nazisme dans la philosophie.* Paris: Albin Michel, 2005.

Ferry, Luc, and Alain Renaut. *French Philosophy of the Sixties: An Essay on Antihumanism.* Translated by Mary H. S. Cattani. Amherst: University of Massachusetts Press, 1990.

Feuerbach, Ludwig. *The Essence of Christianity.* Translated by George Eliot. Buffalo, N.Y.: Prometheus Books, 1989.

Fischer, Sibylle. *Modernity Disavowed: Haiti and the Cultures of Slavery in the Age of Revolution.* Durham, N.C.: Duke University Press, 2004.

Føllesdal, Dagfinn. "Brentano and Husserl on Intentional Objects and Perception." In *Husserl: Intentionality and Cognitive Science,* edited by Hubert L. Dreyfus. Cambridge, Mass.: MIT Press, 1982.

Foucault, Michel. *Discipline and Punish: The Birth of the Prison.* Translated by Alan Sheridan. New York: Pantheon Books, 1978.

———. "The Subject and Power." Afterword to *Michel Foucault: Beyond Structuralism and Hermeneutics,* by Hubert L. Dreyfus and Paul Rabinow. 2nd ed. Chicago: University of Chicago Press, 1983.

Fraser, Nancy. "From Redistribution to Recognition? Dilemmas of Justice in a 'Post-Socialist' Age." In *Theorizing Multiculturalism: A Guide to the Current Debate,* edited by Cynthia Willett, 19–49. Malden, Mass.: Blackwell, 1998.

Freud, Sigmund. *Totem and Taboo: Some Points of Agreement Between the Men-*

tal *Lives of Savages and Neurotics*. Translated by James Strachey. New York: W. W. Norton, 1989.

Fritzsche, Peter. *Germans into Nazis*. Cambridge, Mass.: Harvard University Press, 1998.

Gaita, Raimond. *A Common Humanity: Thinking about Love and Truth and Justice*. London: Routledge, 2000.

Garber, Marjorie, Beatrice Hanssen, and Rebecca L. Walkowitz, eds. *The Turn to Ethics*. New York: Routledge, 2000.

Gendzier, Irene L. *Frantz Fanon: A Critical Study*. New York: Pantheon Books, 1973.

Gilroy, Paul. *Postcolonial Melancholia*. New York: Columbia University Press, 2004.

Girard, René. *Things Hidden since the Foundation of the World*. Translated by Stephen Bann and Michael Metteer. Stanford, Calif.: Stanford University Press, 1987.

———. *Violence and the Sacred*. Translated by Patrick Gregory. Baltimore: Johns Hopkins University Press, 1977.

Glover, Jonathan. *Humanity: A Moral History of the Twentieth Century*. New Haven, Conn.: Yale University Press, 2000.

Goldstein, Joshua S. *War and Gender: How Gender Shapes the War System and Vice Versa*. Cambridge: Cambridge University Press, 2001.

Gómez Romero, Isidro. *Husserl y la crisis de la razón*. Madrid: Ediciones Pedagógicas, 1995.

Gordon, Lewis R. *Bad Faith and Antiblack Racism*. Atlantic Highlands, N.J.: Humanities Press, 1995.

———. "The Black and the Body Politic: Fanon's Existential Phenomenological Critique of Psychoanalysis." In *Fanon: A Critical Reader*, edited by Lewis R. Gordon, T. Denean Sharpley-Whiting, and Renée T. White, 74–84. Oxford: Blackwell, 1996.

———. *Existentia Africana: Understanding Africana Existential Thought*. New York: Routledge, 2000.

———. *Fanon and the Crisis of European Man: An Essay on Philosophy and the Human Sciences*. New York: Routledge, 1995.

———. *Her Majesty's Other Children: Sketches of Racism from a Neocolonial Age*. Lanham, Md.: Rowman and Littlefield, 1997.

———, ed. *Existence in Black: An Anthology of Black Existential Philosophy*. New York: Routledge, 1997.

Grosfoguel, Ramón. "World-Systems Analysis in the Context of Transmodernity, Border Thinking, and Global Coloniality." *Review* 29, no. 2 (2006): 167–88.

Grosfoguel, Ramón, Nelson Maldonado-Torres, and José David Saldívar. "Latin@s and the 'Euro-American' Menace: The Decolonization of the U.S. Empire in the 21st Century." In *Latin@s in the World-System*, edited by Ramón Grosfoguel, Nelson Maldonado-Torres, and José David Saldívar. Boulder, Colo.: Paradigm Press, 2005.

Guevara, Ernesto. *Che Guevara Reader*. 2nd ed. New York: Ocean Press, 2003.

Gulbenkian Commission on the Restructuring of the Social Sciences. *Open the Social Sciences: Report of the Gulbenkian Commission on the Restructuring of the Social Sciences*. Stanford, Calif.: Stanford University Press, 1996.

Gutiérrez, Gustavo. "The Meaning and Scope of Medellín." In *The Density of the Present: Selected Writings*, 59–101. Maryknoll, N.Y.: Orbis Books, 1999.

———. *A Theology of Liberation: History, Politics and Salvation*. Translated by Sister Caridad Inda and John Eagleson. Maryknoll, N.Y.: Orbis Books, 1973.

Habermas, Jürgen. *Between Facts and Norms: Contributions to a Discourse Theory of Law and Democracy*. Translated by William Rehg. Cambridge, Mass.: MIT Press, 1998.

———. *The Inclusion of the Other: Studies in Political Theory*. Translated by Ciaran Cronin and Pablo De Greiff. Cambridge, Mass.: MIT Press, 1998.

———. "Philosophy as Stand-In and Interpreter." In *Moral Consciousness and Communicative Action*, translated by Christian Lenhardt and Shierry Weber Nicholsen, 1–20. Cambridge, Mass.: MIT Press, 1990.

———. *The Theory of Communicative Action*. Vol. 1, *Reason and the Rationalization of Society*. Translated by Thomas McCarthy. Boston: Beacon Press, 1983.

Habermas, Jürgen, and Jacques Derrida. "February 15, or What Binds Europeans Together: A Plea for a Common Foreign Policy, Beginning in the Core of Europe." *Constellations* 10, no. 3 (2003): 291–97.

Hadot, Pierre. *Philosophy as a Way of Life*. Translated by Michael Chase. Edited by Arnold I. Davidson. Oxford: Blackwell, 1995.

Hall, Stuart. "The After-life of Frantz Fanon: Why Fanon? Why Now? Why *Black Skin, White Masks?*" In *The Fact of Blackness: Frantz Fanon and Visual Representation*, edited by Alan Read, 13–37. London: Institute of Contemporary Arts, 1996.

Hanke, Lewis. *All Mankind Is One: A Study of the Disputation between Bartolome de Las Casas and Juan Gines de Sepulveda in 1550 on the Intellectual and Religious Capacity of the American Indians*. DeKalb: Northern Illinois University Press, 1974.

Hansen, Emmanuel. "Frantz Fanon: Portrait of a Revolutionary." In *Rethinking Fanon: The Continuing Dialogue*, edited by Nigel C. Gibson, 49–82. Amherst, N.Y.: Humanity Books, 1999.

Hardt, Michael, and Antonio Negri. *Empire*. Cambridge, Mass.: Harvard University Press, 2000.

———. *Multitude: War and Democracy in the Age of Empire*. New York: Penguin Press, 2004.

Hart, William D. *Edward Said and the Religious Effects of Culture*. Cambridge: Cambridge University Press, 2000.

———. "Slavoj Žižek and the Imperial/Colonial Model of Religion." *Nepantla: Views from South* 3, no. 3 (2002): 553–78.

Harvey, Van A. *Feuerbach and the Interpretation of Religion*. Cambridge: Cambridge University Press, 1995.

Hauerwas, Stanley, and William H. Willimon. *Resident Aliens: Life in the Christian Colony*. Nashville: Abingdon Press, 1989.

Hegel, G. W. F. *Elements of the Philosophy of Right*. Translated by H. G. Nisbet. Edited by Allen W. Wood. Cambridge: Cambridge University Press, 1991.

———. *Hegel's Philosophy of Right*. Translated by H. B. Nisbet. Edited by Allen Wood. Cambridge: Cambridge University Press, 1991.

———. *Phenomenology of Spirit*. Translated by A. V. Miller. Oxford: Oxford University Press, 1977.

Heidegger, Martin. *Being and Time*. Translated by John Macquarrie and Edward Robinson. San Francisco: HarperCollins, 1962.

———. *Being and Time: A Translation of Sein und Zeit*. Translated by Joan Stambaugh. Albany: State University of New York Press, 1996.

———. *Hegel's Phenomenology of Spirit*. Translated by Parvis Emad and Kenneth Maly. Bloomington: Indiana University Press, 1988.

———. *An Introduction to Metaphysics*. Translated by Ralph Manheim. New Haven, Conn.: Yale University Press, 1959.

———. "Letter on Humanism." In *Martin Heidegger: Basic Writings*, edited by David Farrell Krell, 189–242. San Francisco: HarperCollins, 1977.

———. "'Only a God Can Save Us:' Der Spiegel's Interview with Martin Heidegger (1966)." In *The Heidegger Controversy: A Critical Reader*, edited by Richard Wolin, 91–116. Cambridge, Mass.: MIT Press, 1993.

———. "On the Essence of Truth." In *Martin Heidegger: Basic Writings*, edited by David Farrell Krell, 113–41. San Francisco: HarperCollins, 1977.

———. *The Question Concerning Technology and Other Essays*. Translated by William Lovitt. New York: Harper and Row, 1977.

Henry, Paget. "Frantz Fanon, African, and Afro-Caribbean Philosophy." In *Caliban's Reason: Introducing Afro-Caribbean Philosophy*, 68–89. New York: Routledge, 2000.

Herzog, Annabel. *Penser autrement la politique: Éléments pour une critique de la philosophie politique*. Paris: Éditions Kimé, 1997.

Hinkelammert, Franz J. *La fe de Abraham y el edipo occidental*. 2nd ed. San José, Costa Rica: Editorial Departamento Ecuménico de Investigaciones, 1991.

———. *El grito del sujeto: Del teatro-mundo del evangelio de Juan al perro-mundo de la globalización*. San José, Costa Rica: Editorial Departamento Ecuménico de Investigaciones, 1998.

———. *Sacrificios humanos y sociedad occidental: Lucifer y la bestia*. 3rd ed. San José, Costa Rica: Editorial Departamento Ecuménico de Investigaciones, 1998.

———. *Solidaridad o suicidio colectivo*. Heredia, Costa Rica: Ambientico Ediciones, 2003.

———, ed. *El huracán de la globalización*. San José, Costa Rica: Editorial Departamento Ecuménico de Investigaciones, 1999.

Hintikka, Jaakko. "The Phenomenological Dimension." In *The Cambridge Companion to Husserl*, edited by Barry Smith and David Woodruff Smith, 78–105. Cambridge: Cambridge University Press, 1995.

Honneth, Axel. *Critique of Power: Reflective Stages in a Critical Social Theory*. Translated by Kenneth Baynes. Cambridge, Mass.: MIT Press, 1991.

———. *The Struggle for Recognition: The Moral Grammar of Social Conflicts*. Translated by Joel Anderson. Cambridge, Mass.: MIT Press, 1996.

Horsley, Richard A., ed. *Paul and Empire: Religion and Power in Roman Imperial Society*. Harrisburg, Pa.: Trinity Press International, 1997.

Huntington, Patricia J. "Heidegger, Irigaray, and the Masculine Ethos of National Socialism or, How to Tame the Feminine." In *Ecstatic Subjects, Utopia, and Recognition: Kristeva, Heidegger, Irigaray*, 33–75. Albany: State University of New York Press, 1998.

Huntington, Samuel P. *The Clash of Civilizations and the Remaking of World Order*. New York: Simon and Schuster, 1996.

Husserl, Edmund. *Cartesian Meditations: An Introduction to Phenomenology*. Translated by Dorion Cairns. Dordrecht: Kluwer Academic Publishers, 1960.

———. *The Crisis of European Sciences and Transcendental Phenomenology*. Translated by David Carr. Evanston, Ill.: Northwestern University Press, 1970.

———. *Ideas Pertaining to a Pure Phenomenology and to a Phenomenological Philosophy: First Book*. Translated by F. Kersten. Dordrecht: Kluwer Academic Publishers, 1982.

———. "Philosophy and the Crisis of European Man." In *Phenomenology and the Crisis of Philosophy*, 149–92. New York: Harper and Row, 1965.

———. "Philosophy as Rigorous Science." In *Husserl: Shorter Works*, edited by Peter McCormick and Frederick A. Elliston, 166–97. Notre Dame, Ind.: University of Notre Dame Press, 1981.

Hutton, Will. *A Declaration of Interdependence: Why America Should Join the World.* New York: W. W. Norton, 2003.

Irigaray, Luce. "Questions to Emmanuel Levinas: On the Divinity of Love." In *Re-Reading Levinas*, edited by Robert Bernasconi and Simon Critchley, 109–18. Bloomington: Indiana University Press, 1991.

James, C. L. R. *The Black Jacobins: Toussaint L'Ouverture and the San Domingo Revolution.* 2nd ed. New York: Vintage Books, 1989.

Jaspers, Karl. *Philosophy of Existence.* Translated by Richard R. Grabau. Philadelphia: University of Pennsylvania Press, 1971.

Jay, Martin. *Downcast Eyes: The Denigration of Vision in Twentieth-Century French Thought.* Berkeley: University of California Press, 1993.

Judy, Ronald A. T. "Fanon's Body of Black Experience." In *Fanon: A Critical Reader*, edited by Lewis R. Gordon, T. Denean Sharpley-Whiting, and Renée T. White, 53–73. Oxford: Blackwell, 1996.

Kant, Immanuel. "An Answer to the Question: What Is Enlightenment?" In *What Is Enlightenment?: Eighteenth-Century Answers and Twentieth-Century Questions*, edited by James Schmidt, 58–64. Berkeley: University of California Press, 1996.

Kelly, Michael, ed. *Critique and Power: Recasting the Foucault/Habermas Debate.* Cambridge, Mass.: MIT Press, 1994.

Kereszty, Roch A. *God Seekers for a New Age: From Crisis Theology to Christian Atheism.* Dayton: Pflaum Press, 1970.

Kierkegaard, Søren. *Fear and Trembling and Repetition.* Translated by Howard V. Hong and Edna H. Hong. Princeton, N.J.: Princeton University Press, 1982.

King, Richard. *Orientalism and Religion: Postcolonial Theory, India, and "The Mystic East."* London: Routledge, 1999.

Knies, Kenneth. "On the Idea of Post-European Science." In *Not Only the Master's Tools: Theoretical Explorations in African American Studies*, edited by Lewis Gordon and Jane Anna Gordon, 85–106. Boulder, Colo.: Paradigm Press, 2006.

Koselleck, Reinhart. *Critique and Crisis: Enlightenment and the Pathogenesis of Modern Society.* Cambridge, Mass.: MIT Press, 1988.

Kurlansky, Mark. *1968: The Year That Rocked the World.* New York: Random House, 2003.

Lander, Edgardo, ed. *La colonialidad del saber: Eurocentrismo y ciencias sociales; Perspectivas latinoamericanas.* Caracas: Facultad de Ciencias Económicas y

Sociales (FACES-UCV) and Instituto Internacional de la UNESCO para la Educación Superior en América Latina y el Caribe (IESALC), 2000.

Lazarus, Neil. "Disavowing Decolonization: Nationalism, Intellectuals, and the Question of Representation in Postcolonial Theory." In *Nationalism and Cultural Practice in the Postcolonial World*, 68–143. Cambridge: Cambridge University Press, 1999.

Lequan, Mai, ed. *La paix*. Paris: Flammarion, 1998.

Lescourret, Marie-Anne. *Emmanuel Levinas*. N.p.: Flammarion, 1994.

Levi, Primo. *Survival in Auschwitz: The Nazi Assault on Humanity*. Translated by Giulio Einaudi. New York: Touchstone Books, 1996.

Levin, David Michael. *Reason and Evidence in Husserl's Phenomenology*. Evanston, Ill.: Northwestern University Press, 1970.

Levinas, Emmanuel. *Alterity and Transcendence*. Translated by Michael B. Smith. New York: Columbia University Press, 1999.

———. "As If Consenting to Horror." Translated by Paula Wissing. *Critical Inquiry* 15 (1989): 485–88.

———. "'As Old as the World?'" In *Nine Talmudic Readings by Emmanuel Lévinas*, 70–88. Bloomington: Indiana University Press, 1990.

———. "Beyond Intentionality." In *Philosophy in France Today*, edited by Alan Montefiore, 100–115. Cambridge: Cambridge University Press, 1983.

———. *De l'évasion*. N.p.: Fata Morgana, 1982.

———. *De l'existence à l'existant*. 2nd ed. Paris: Librairie Philosophique J. Vrin, 1993.

———. *Difficult Freedom: Essays in Judaism*. Translated by Seán Hand. Baltimore: Johns Hopkins University Press, 1990.

———. *Discovering Existence with Husserl*. Translated by Richard A. Cohen and Michael B. Smith. Evanston, Ill.: Northwestern University Press, 1998.

———. *Entre Nous: On Thinking-of-the-Other*. Translated by Michael B. Smith and Barbara Harshav. New York: Columbia University Press, 1998.

———. "God and Philosophy." In *The Levinas Reader*, edited by Seán Hand, 166–89. Oxford: Blackwell, 1989.

———. *God, Death, and Time*. Translated by Bettina Bergo. Stanford, Calif.: Stanford University Press, 2000.

———. *Les imprévus de l'histoire*. N.p.: Fata Morgana, 1994.

———. "Is Ontology Fundamental?" In *Emmanuel Levinas: Basic Philosophical Writings*, edited by Adriaan T. Peperzak, Simon Critchley, and Robert Bernasconi, 1–10. Bloomington: Indiana University Press, 1996.

———. "Judaism and the Feminine." In *Difficult Freedom: Essays in Judaism*, 30–38. Baltimore: Johns Hopkins University Press, 1990.

———. "Meaning and Sense." In *Collected Philosophical Papers*, 75–107. Dordrecht: M. Nijhoff, 1987. Reprint, Pittsburgh: Duquesne University Press, 1998.

———. "The Meaning of History." In *Difficult Freedom: Essays in Judaism*, translated by Seán Hand, xiv, 306. Baltimore: Johns Hopkins University Press, 1990.

———. "No Identity." In *Collected Philosophical Papers*, edited by Alphonso Lingis, 141–51. Dordrecht: M. Nijhoff, 1987. Reprint, Pittsburgh: Duquesne University Press, 1998.

———. *Otherwise Than Being or, Beyond Essence*. Translated by Alphonso Lingis. Pittsburgh: Duquesne University Press, 1998.

———. "Peace and Proximity." In *Alterity and Transcendence*, 131–44. New York: Columbia University Press, 1999.

———. *Proper Names*. Translated by Michael B. Smith. Stanford, Calif.: Stanford University Press, 1996.

———. "Reflections on the Philosophy of Hitlerism." In *Critical Inquiry*, 17, no. 1 (1990): 63–71.

———. "Signature." In *Difficult Freedom: Essays in Judaism*, 291–95. Baltimore: Johns Hopkins University Press, 1990.

———. "La signification et le sens." In *Humanisme de l'autre homme*, 15–70. N.p.: Fata Morgana, 1972.

———. *The Theory of Intuition in Husserl's Phenomenology*. Translated by André Orianne. 2nd ed. Evanston, Ill.: Northwestern University Press, 1995.

———. *Time and the Other*. Translated by Richard A. Cohen. Pittsburgh: Duquesne University Press, 1987.

———. *Totality and Infinity: An Essay on Exteriority*. Translated by Alphonso Lingis. Pittsburgh: Duquesne University Press, 1969.

———. Preface to *Totalidad e infinito: Ensayo sobre la exterioridad*. Translated by Daniel E. Guillot. 2nd ed. Salamanca: Ediciones Sígueme, 1987.

———. "Transcendance et hauteur." In *Liberté et commandement*, 49–100. N.p.: Fata Morgana, 1994.

———. "Transcendence and Evil." In *Collected Philosophical Papers*, edited by Alphonso Lingis, 175–86. Dordrecht: M. Nijhoff, 1987. Reprint, Pittsburgh: Duquesne University Press, 1998.

———. "Transcendence and Height." In *Emmanuel Levinas: Basic Philosophical Writings*, edited by Adriaan T. Peperzak, Simon Critchley, and Robert Bernasconi; translated by Simon Critchley, Tina Chanter, and Nicholas Walker, 11–32. Bloomington: Indiana University Press, 1996.

———. "The Understanding of Spirituality in French and German Culture." In *Continental Philosophy Review* 31, no. 1 (1998): 1–10.

———. *Unforeseen History*. Translated by Nidra Poller. Urbana: University of Illinois Press, 2004.
———. "Useless Suffering." In *Entre Nous: On Thinking-of-the-Other*, 91–101. New York: Columbia University Press, 1998.
Locke, John. *The Second Treatise of Civil Government and a Letter Concerning Toleration*. Oxford: Basil Blackwell, 1946.
Losurdo, Domenico. *Heidegger et l'idéologie de la guerre*. Translated by Jean-Michel Buée. Paris: Presses Universitaires de France, 1998.
Majid, Anouar. *Unveiling Traditions: Postcolonial Islam in a Polycentric World*. Durham, N.C.: Duke University Press, 2000.
Maldonado-Torres, Nelson. "The Cry of the Self as a Call from the Other: The Paradoxical Loving Subjectivity of Frantz Fanon." *Listening: Journal of Religion and Culture* 36, no. 1 (2001): 46–60.
———. "Decolonization and the New Identitarian Logics after September 11: Eurocentrism and Americanism against the Barbarian Threats." *Radical Philosophy Review* 8, no. 1 (2005): 35–67.
———. "Frantz Fanon and C.L.R. James on Intellectualism and Enlightened Rationality." *Caribbean Studies* 33, no. 2 (2005): 149–94.
———. "Imperio, raza y religión." In *Enciclopedia iberoamericana de las religiones: Religion e imperio*, edited by Eduardo Mendieta. Madrid: Trotta, forthcoming.
———. "Intervenciones filosóficas al proyecto incompleto de la descolonizacion." In *Filosofía y liberación: Homenaje a Enrique Dussel*, edited by Juan Manuel Contreras Colín and Mario Rojas, n.p. Mexico, D.F.: Universidad de la Ciudad de México, forthcoming.
———. "Liberation Theology and the Search for the Lost Paradigm: From Radical Orthodoxy to Radical Diversality." In *Latin American Liberation Theology: The Next Generation*, edited by Ivan Petrella, 39–61. Maryknoll, N.Y.: Orbis Books, 2005.
———. "Notes on the Current Status of Liminal Categories and the Search for a New Humanism." In *After Man, the Human: Critical Essays on the Thought of Sylvia Wynter*, edited by Anthony Bogues, 190–208. Kingston, Jamaica: Ian Randle Publishers, 2006.
———. "On the Coloniality of Being: Contributions to the Development of a Concept." In *Cultural Studies*, 21, no. 2–3 (2007): 240–70.
———. "Post-imperial Reflections on Crisis, Knowledge, and Utopia: Transgresstopic Critical Hermeneutics and the 'Death of European Man.'" *Review: A Journal of the Fernand Braudel Center for the Study of Economies, Historical Systems, and Civilizations* 25, no. 3 (2002): 277–315.
———. "Reconciliation as a Contested Future: Decolonization as Project or

Beyond the Paradigm of War." In *Reconciliation: Nations and Churches in Latin America*, edited by Iain S. Maclean, n.p. London: Ashgate, 2006.

———. "The Regressive Kernel of Orthodoxy." Review of *The Puppet and the Dwarf: The Perverse Core of Christianity*, by Slavoj Žižek. *Radical Philosophy Review* 6, no. 1 (2003): 59–70.

———. "Searching for Caliban in the Hispanic Caribbean." *C.L.R. James Journal* 10, no. 1 (2004): 106–22.

———. "Secularism and Religion in the Modern/Colonial World System: From Secular Postcoloniality to Postsecular Transmodernity." In *Coloniality at Large: Latin America and the Postcolonial Debate*, edited by Mabel Moraña, Enrique Dussel, and Carlos Jauregui, in preparation.

———. "The Topology of Being and the Geopolitics of Knowledge: Modernity, Empire, Coloniality." *City* 8, no. 1 (2004): 29–56.

———. "Toward a Critique of Continental Reason: Africana Studies and the Decolonization of Imperial Cartographies in the Americas." In *Not Only the Master's Tools: Theoretical Explorations in African-American Studies*, edited by Lewis Gordon and Jane Anna Gordon, 51–84. Boulder, Colo.: Paradigm Press, 2006.

Mall, Ram Adhar. *Intercultural Philosophy*. Lanham, Md.: Rowman and Littlefield Publishers, 2000.

Manning, Robert J. S. "The Cries of Others and Heidegger's Ear: Remarks on the Agriculture Remark." In *Martin Heidegger and the Holocaust*, edited by Alan Milchman and Alan Rosenberg, 19–38. Atlantic Highlands, N.J.: Humanities Press, 1996.

Martinot, Steve. "Patriotism and Its Double." *Peace Review* 15, no. 4 (2003): 405–410.

———. "Pro-democracy and the Ethics of Refusal." *Socialism and Democracy* 19, no. 2 (2005): 106–15.

Marx, Karl. *Capital: A Critique of Political Economy*. Translated by Ben Fowkes. Vol. 1. London: Penguin Books in association with *New Left Review*, 1976.

———. "Critique of the Hegelian Dialectic and Philosophy as a Whole." In *The Economic and Philosophical Manuscripts of 1844*, edited by Dirk J. Struik, 170–93. New York: International Publishers, 1964.

Matuštík, Martin J. *Postnational Identity: Critical Theory and Existential Philosophy in Habermas, Kierkegaard, and Havel*. New York: Guilford Press, 1993.

McCumber, John. *Metaphysics and Oppression: Heidegger's Challenge to Western Philosophy*. Bloomington: Indiana University Press, 1999.

Mèlich, Joan-Charles. *Totalitarismo y fecundidad: La filosofía frente a Auschwitz*. Barcelona: Anthropos, 1998.

Mignolo, Walter. *The Darker Side of the Renaissance: Literacy, Territoriality, and Colonization.* Ann Arbor: University of Michigan Press, 1995.

———. *The Darker Side of the Renaissance: Literacy, Territoriality, and Colonization.* 2nd ed. Ann Arbor: University of Michigan Press, 2003.

———. "Decires fuera de lugar: Sujetos dicentes, roles sociales y formas de inscripción." *Revista de crítica literaria latinoamericana* 11 (1995): 9–32.

———. "Dussel's Philosophy of Liberation: Ethics and the Geopolitics of Knowledge." In *Thinking from the Underside of History: Enrique Dussel's Philosophy of Liberation,* edited by Linda Martín Alcoff and Eduardo Mendieta, 27–50. Lanham, Md.: Rowman and Littlefield, 2000.

———. "The Geopolitics of Knowledge and the Colonial Difference." *South Atlantic Quarterly* 101, no. 1 (2002): 57–96.

———. "José de Acosta's *Historia natural y moral de las Indias*: Occidentalism, the Modern/Colonial World, and the Colonial Difference." In *Natural and Moral History of the Indies by José de Acosta,* 451–518. Durham, N.C.: Duke University Press, 2002.

———. *Local Histories/Global Designs: Coloniality, Subaltern Knowledges, and Border Thinking.* Princeton, N.J.: Princeton University Press, 2000.

———. "The Many Faces of Cosmo-polis: Border Thinking and Critical Cosmopolitanism." *Public Culture* 12, no. 3 (2000): 721–48.

———. "Os esplendores e as misérias da 'ciência': Colonialidade, geopolítica do conhecimento e pluri-versalidade epistémica." In *Conhecimento Prudente para uma Vida Decente: Um Discurso sobre as Ciências' revistado,* edited by Boaventura de Sousa Santos, 667–709. Porto, Portugal: Edições Afrontamento, 2003.

Milchman, Alan, and Alan Rosenberg, eds. *Martin Heidegger and the Holocaust.* Atlantic Highlands, N.J.: Humanities Press, 1996.

Moraga, Cherríe, and Gloria Anzaldúa, eds. *This Bridge Called My Back: Writings by Radical Women of Color.* Watertown, Mass.: Persephone Press, 1981.

Mosès, Stéphane. "Rosenzweig et Lévinas: Au-delà de la guerre." In *Emmanuel Lévinas et l'histoire,* edited by Nathalie Frogneux and Françoise Mies, 137–59. Paris: Les Éditions du Cerf, 1998.

Mostern, Kenneth. "Decolonization as Learning: Practice and Pedagogy in Frantz Fanon's Revolutionary Narrative." In *Between Borders: Pedagogy and the Politics of Cultural Studies,* edited by Henry A. Giroux and Peter McLaren, 253–71. New York: Routledge, 1994.

Nietzsche, Friedrich. *Beyond Good and Evil: Prelude to a Philosophy of the Future.* Translated by Walter Kaufmann. New York: Vintage Books, 1966.

———. *The Gay Science.* Translated by Walter Kaufmann. New York: Random House, 1974.

———. *On the Genealogy of Morals and Ecce Homo*. Translated by Walter Kaufmann and R. J. Hollingdale. New York: Vintage Books, 1989.

———. *The Will to Power*. Translated by Walter Kaufmann and R. J. Hollingdale. New York: Random House, 1968.

Oliver, Kelly. *Witnessing: Beyond Recognition*. Minneapolis: University of Minnesota Press, 2001.

Pagden, Anthony. "Europe: Conceptualizing a Continent." In *The Idea of Europe: From Antiquity to the European Union*, edited by Anthony Pagden, 33–54. Washington, D.C.: Woodrow Wilson Center Press, 2002.

Petitdemange, Guy. "La notion paradoxale d'histoire." In *Emmanuel Lévinas et l'histoire*, edited by Nathalie Frogneux and Françoise Mies, 17–44. Paris: Les Éditions du Cerf, 1998.

Poirié, François. *Emmanuel Lévinas: Essai et entretiens*. N.p.: Babel, 1996.

Pratt, Mary Louise. *Imperial Eyes: Travel Writing and Transculturation*. New York: Routledge, 1992.

Quijano, Aníbal. "Coloniality of Power, Eurocentrism, and Latin America." Translated by Michael Ennis. *Nepantla: Views from South* 1, no. 3 (2000): 533–80.

Ramadan, Tariq. *Être musulman européen: Étude des sources islamiques à la lumière du contexte européen*. Lyon: Éditions Tawhid, 1999.

———. *Islam, le face à face des civilisations: Quel projet pour quelle modernité?* Lyon: Éditions Tawhid, 2001.

———. *Western Muslims and the Future of Islam*. Oxford: Oxford University Press, 2004.

Rawls, John. *Justice as Fairness: A Restatement*. Cambridge, Mass.: Harvard University Press, 2001.

———. *Political Liberalism*. New York: Columbia University Press, 1993.

———. *A Theory of Justice*. Cambridge, Mass.: Harvard University Press, 1971.

Raynal, Abbé. *Philosophical and Political History of the Settlement and Trade of the Europeans in the East and West Indies*. 3 vols. 1770. Reprint, Glasgow: D. McKenzie, 1812.

Reyes Mate, Manuel. *Memoria de Auschwitz: Actualidad moral y política*. Madrid: Editorial Trotta, 2003.

Ricoeur, Paul. *From Text to Action: Essays in Hermeneutics, II*. Translated by Kathleen Blamey and John B. Thompson. Evanston, Ill.: Northwestern University Press, 1991.

Rockmore, Tom. *On Hegel's Epistemology and Contemporary Philosophy*. Atlantic Highlands, N.J.: Humanities Press, 1996.

Rowland, Christopher, ed. *The Cambridge Companion to Liberation Theology*. Cambridge: Cambridge University Press, 1999.

Sabbagh, Suha. "Going Against the West from Within: The Emergence of the West as an Other in Frantz Fanon's Work." Ph.D. diss., University of Wisconsin, Madison, 1982.

Said, Edward. *Orientalism*. New York: Pantheon Books, 1978.

Sandoval, Chela. *Methodology of the Oppressed*. Minneapolis: University of Minnesota Press, 2000.

Sartre, Jean-Paul. *Being and Nothingness: A Phenomenological Essay on Ontology*. Translated by Hazel E. Barnes. New York: Washington Square Press / Pocket Books, 1966.

———. "Intentionality: A Fundamental Idea of Husserl's Phenomenology." *Journal of the British Society for Phenomenology* 1, no. 2 (1970): 4–5.

———. Preface to *Anthologie de la nouvelle poésie nègre e malgache*. Paris: Presses Universitaires de France, 1948.

———. *Réflexions sur la question juive*. 1944. Reprint, Paris: Gallimard, 1954.

Schroeder, Brian. *Altared Ground: Levinas, History, and Violence*. New York: Routledge, 1996.

Schutte, Ofelia. *Cultural Identity and Social Liberation in Latin American Thought*. Albany: State University of New York Press, 1993.

Scott, David. "Conscripts of Modernity." In *Conscripts of Modernity: The Tragedy of Colonial Enlightenment*, 98–131. Durham, N.C.: Duke University Press, 2004.

Sekyi-Otu, Ato. *Fanon's Dialectic of Experience*. Cambridge, Mass.: Harvard University Press, 1996.

Sharpley-Whiting, T. Denean. *Frantz Fanon: Conflicts and Feminisms*. Lanham, Md.: Rowman and Littlefield, 1997.

Sharpley-Whiting, T. Denean, and Renée T. White, eds. *Spoils of War: Women of Color, Cultures, and Revolutions*. Lanham, Md.: Rowman and Littlefield, 1997.

Sluga, Hans D. *Heidegger's Crisis: Philosophy and Politics in Nazi Germany*. Cambridge, Mass.: Harvard University Press, 1993.

Sokolowski, Robert. *The Formation of Husserl's Concept of Constitution*. The Hague: Martinus Nijhoff, 1964.

Sorum, Paul Clay. *Intellectuals and Decolonization in France*. Chapel Hill: University of North Carolina Press, 1977.

Spivak, Gayatri Chakravorty. *A Critique of Postcolonial Reason: Toward a History of the Vanishing Present*. Cambridge, Mass.: Harvard University Press, 1999.

———. *The Post-Colonial Critic: Interviews, Strategies, Dialogues*. Edited by Sarah Harasym. New York: Routledge, 1990.

Sueiro, Adelaida. "Opción preferencial por los pobres." In *Globalizar la esperanza: Reflexiones desde América Latina y el Caribe en la aurora del tercer mile-*

nio, edited by Fundación Amerindia, 135–47. Mexico, D.F.: Ediciones Dabar, 1998.

Tanner, Kathryn. *The Politics of God: Christian Theologies and Social Justice*. Minneapolis: Fortress Press, 1992.

Taylor, Charles. *Hegel*. Cambridge: Cambridge University Press, 1975.

———. "The Politics of Recognition." In *Multiculturalism: Examining the Politics of Recognition*, edited by Amy Gutman, 3–24. Princeton, N.J.: Princeton University Press, 1994.

Taylor, Mark C. *Journeys to Selfhood: Hegel and Kierkegaard*. Berkeley: University of California Press, 1980.

Thayse, Jean-Luc. *Eros et fécondité chez le jeune Levinas*. Paris: L'Harmattan, 1998.

Thiele, Leslie Paul. *Timely Meditations: Martin Heidegger and Postmodern Politics*. Princeton, N.J.: Princeton University Press, 1995.

Todorov, Tzvetan. *The Conquest of America: The Question of the Other*. Translated by Richard Howard. New York: HarperCollins / HarperPerennial, 1992.

Trouillot, Michel-Rolph. *Silencing the Past: Power and the Production of History*. Boston: Beacon Press, 1995.

Turner, Lou. "On the Difference between the Hegelian and the Fanonian Dialectic of Lordship and Bondage." In *Fanon: A Critical Reader*, edited by Lewis R. Gordon, T. Denean Sharpley-Whiting, and Renée T. White, 134–51. Oxford: Blackwell, 1996.

Valevicius, Andrius. "Afterword: Emmanuel Levinas, the Multicultural Philosopher." In *Continental Philosophy Review*, 31, no. 1 (1998): 11–14.

Vasey, Craig R. "Faceless Women and Serious Others: Levinas, Misogyny, and Feminism." In *Ethics and Danger: Essays on Heidegger and Continental Thought*, edited by Arleen B. Dallery and Charles E. Scott with P. Holley Roberts, 317–30. Albany: State University of New York Press, 1992.

Wallerstein, Immanuel. *After Liberalism*. New York: New Press, 1995.

———. *The Capitalist World-Economy: Studies in Modern Capitalism*. Cambridge: Cambridge University Press, 1979.

———. *The Modern World-System: Capitalist Agriculture and the Origins of the European World Economy in the Sixteenth Century*. New York: Academic Press, 1974.

———. "The Unintended Consequences of Cold War Area Studies." In *The Cold War and the University: Toward an Intellectual History of the Postwar Years*, edited by Noam Chomsky et al., 195–232. New York: New Press, 1997.

———. *Unthinking Social Science: The Limits of Nineteenth-Century Paradigms*. Cambridge: Polity Press, 1991.

Watts, Michael. "1968 and All That." *Progress in Human Geography* 25, no. 2 (2001): 157–88.

Weber, Max. *From Max Weber: Essays in Sociology*. Edited and translated by H. H. Gerth and C. Wright. New York: Oxford University Press, 1946.

West, Cornel. *Race Matters*. New York: Vintage Books, 1994.

Wolin, Richard. *The Politics of Being: The Political Thought of Martin Heidegger*. New York: Columbia University Press, 1990.

———, ed. *The Heidegger Controversy: A Critical Reader*. New York: Columbia University Press, 1991.

Wynter, Sylvia. "Columbus and the Poetics of the Propter Nos." *Annals of Scholarship* 8, no. 2 (1991): 251–86.

———. "1492: A New World View." In *Race, Discourse, and the Origin of the Americas: A New World View*, edited by Vera Lawrence Hyatt and Rex Nettleford, 5–57. Washington, D.C.: Smithsonian Institution Press, 1995.

———. "On Disenchanting Discourse: 'Minority' Literary Criticism and Beyond." In *The Nature and Context of Minority Discourse*, 432–69. New York: Oxford University Press, 1990.

———. "Unsettling the Coloniality of Being/Power/Truth/Freedom: Towards the Human, after Man, Its Overrepresentation—An Argument." *The New Centennial Review* 3, no. 3 (2003): 257–337.

Wyschogrod, Edith. *Spirit in Ashes: Hegel, Heidegger, and Man-made Mass Death*. New Haven, Conn.: Yale University Press, 1985.

Yoder, John Howard. *The Christian Witness to the State*. Scottdale, Pa.: Herald Press, 2002.

———. *Discipleship as Political Responsibility*. Scottdale, Pa.: Herald Press, 2003.

———. *For the Nations: Essays Evangelical and Public*. Grand Rapids, Mich.: W. B. Eerdmans, 1997.

———. *Karl Barth and the Problem of War*. Nashville: Abingdon Press, 1970.

Young, Julian. *Heidegger, Philosophy, Nazism*. Cambridge: Cambridge University Press, 1997.

Yovel, Yirmiyahu. *Dark Riddle: Hegel, Nietzsche, and the Jews*. University Park: Pennsylvania State University Press, 1998.

Zahar, Renate. *Frantz Fanon: Colonialism and Alienation; Concerning Frantz Fanon's Political Theory*. Translated by Willfried F. Feuser. New York: Monthly Review Press, 1974.

Žižek, Slavoj. *The Fragile Absolute or, Why Is the Christian Legacy Worth Fighting For?* London: Verso, 2000.

———. "A Leftist Plea for 'Eurocentrism.'" *Critical Inquiry* 24 (1998): 988–1009.

―――. "Multiculturalism, or the Cultural Logic of Multinational Capitalism." *New Left Review* 225 (1997): 28–51.

―――. *On Belief*. London: Routledge, 2001.

―――. *The Puppet and the Dwarf: The Perverse Core of Christianity*. Cambridge, Mass.: MIT Press, 2003.

INDEX

Active geneses, 171
Africana philosophy, 288 n. 21
African Diaspora, 197, 222
Agamben, Giorgio, 217
Altericity, 15, 152, 157–58
An-other politics, 96
Anthropology, 199
Anti-Semitism: Aryanism and, 267 n. 50; in liberal France, 31, 64; Nazi, 64
Anzaldúa, Gloria, 7, 254
Arendt, Hannah, 5
Asceticism, 118
Assimilation, 191
Authenticity, 52, 55–57, 60–61
Autonomy, 26, 69
Aztecs, 205, 214

Bad conscience, 86–87, 88, 89
Bad faith, 168, 174, 284 n. 48
Barbarianism, 46, 62, 181, 224
Bauman, Zygmunt, 258 n. 4
Being and Nothingness (Sartre), 167
Being and Time (Heidegger), 56–57
Being/being, 18, 64, 80, 172, 180–82, 240, 268 n. 55. *See also* Non-being
Benveniste, Émile, 142
Birken, Lawrence, 267 n. 51

Black Jacobins (James), 197
Blackness, 102, 104, 127, 130–42, 152, 220–21
Black Skin, White Masks (Fanon), 97, 98, 102, 105–6, 127, 131–32, 134, 136, 137–42, 207
Buckley, Philip, 56
Buck-Morss, Susan, 282 n. 26, 289 n. 24
Burggraeve, Roger, 294–95 n. 66
Butler, Judith, 272 n. 91

Camus, Albert, 32, 288–89 n. 21
Caputo, John, 55–56
Care, 55
Cartesian Meditations (Husserl), 171, 172
Castro-Gómez, Santiago, 183–84
Césaire, Aimé, 7, 201–2, 208–9, 242–43, 298 n. 79
Christianity: freedom and, 26–27, 29; liberation and, 9–10; others and, 216
Citizenship, 54, 64
Cohen, Richard, 174–75, 260 n. 37
Coles, Romand, 294 n. 64
Colonialism: modernity and, 3–4; racism and, 3, 5–6, 95–97, 99–102, 130, 203–26, 221–22

Coloniality, 239. *See also* De-colonial turn
Colonization by Spain, 3, 4, 5
Color line, 7–8, 206, 218, 226, 238, 243, 246
Columbus, Christopher, 215–16
Community of masters, 13–14, 42–43, 47–50, 53, 64, 66, 249. *See also* Morality
Community vs. individuality, 64
Concentration camps, 1, 6
Cone, James, 291 n. 32
Conquest vs. colonization, 108, 213
Conquistadores, 3, 4, 5
Consciousness: intentional, 37, 40; philosophy of, 125; transcendental, 35–36, 67, 167–69
Continentalist vision, 194–95, 209
Cortés, Hernán, 212, 213, 214, 215
Critical reactivation, 11
Critique: ethical, 15, 95–96, 97, 99–101; philosophy as, 52–53
Cry: enlightenment and, 241; ethical dimension of, 137–42; giving and, 142; love and, 140–41; phenomenology of, 122, 133–37; of self-affirmation, 247–48
Cultural hermeneutics, 164, 191

Damnation, 18, 217
Damnés, 151–52, 159, 218, 223, 245
Darker Side of the Renaissance (Mignolo), 203
Death, 67, 100, 295 n. 67
Death ethics of war, 4, 218, 221, 226, 240
Death-world, 100, 279 n. 11
Decadence, 29, 32, 36
Declaration of the Rights of Man, 14, 26, 28, 30
De-colonial attitude, 8, 89, 105, 158, 186, 206, 222, 234, 246
De-colonial love, 244, 245, 252–53

De-colonial reduction, 15, 89, 98–102, 188
De-colonial turn, 6–7, 187–236
Derrida, Jacques, 253
Descartes, René, 211, 224, 241–43
Desire, 157–58
Determinism, natural, 28
Discourse on Colonialism (Césaire), 201–2
Discovery of Americas, 203–4, 212, 215, 238
Dreyfus Affair, 25, 31, 33, 49–50, 64
Dualism in the Anthropology of Christendom (Dussel), 193
Du Bois, W. E. B., 5, 6–7, 206–7, 226
Dussel, Enrique: on colonialism and racism, 5, 203–26; on Eurocentrism, 194, 200–201; Fanon, Levinas, and, 3, 9, 187–89; Frankfurt lectures of, 203–26; history reconstructed by, 204–5; on humanism, 191; I conquer concept and, 204–5, 216, 223, 226; on identity, 10–11, 188, 189–92, 201, 202; Levinas appropriated by, 164–66, 179, 187, 189, 235–36; liberation theology of, 9–10, 179–86, 188, 225, 229, 235–36; on modernity, 202, 228; on Other, 183; as racialized subject, 4; on transmodernity, 229–30, 308 n. 90

Elitism, 42, 75
Ellison, Ralph, 223
Enlightenment, 14, 195–203
Equality, 29, 63–64, 71
Eros, 66–67, 177, 270 n. 76
Essence of Christianity (Feuerbach), 109–13
Ethico-political praxis, 74–76, 79, 89, 94–97, 152, 188
Ethics: orientation of, 237; primacy of, 6, 62–63, 76, 77, 176–78; revolt

and, 137–42. *See also* Non-ethics of war
Ética de la liberación en la edad de la globalización y de la exclusión (Dussel), 191
Eurocentrism, 5–6, 18, 24, 43–49, 58–59, 86, 99, 189, 200–201, 208, 217, 245–46
Evidence, 28, 129–30, 241
Evil, 18, 23, 239–40, 252
Exclusion, 43–49
Existence, 135
Expansionism, 42, 48

Fanon, Frantz, 93–121; on colonialism and racism, 5, 6, 95–97, 99–101, 130, 221–22; on consciousness, 237; on cry, 133–37; on death, 156–57; on de-colonial reduction, 98–102; on de-colonial turn, 7; on denial of man, 87; Dussel, Levinas, and, 3, 9, 187–89; on ethico-political movement, 152; on existential phenomenology, 12–13; on freedom, 128, 150; on humanism, 158–59; on humanization, 153; on master/slave, 103–8, 129–31, 249; on ontology, 104–5; on the oppressed, 96; as philosopher of love, 93; on recognition, 122–23; on reduction, 15, 93–94, 97, 98–102
Fear and Trembling (Kierkegaard), 135
Fecundity, 67–70, 270 n. 76
Feminine, 177, 273 n. 98
Feuerbach, Ludwig, 108, 109–13
Filosofía de la liberación (Dussel), 179–85, 191, 225, 227
Filosofía ética de la liberación (Dussel), 184
Forgiveness, 34. *See also* Pardon
Formal and Transcendental Logic (Husserl), 171
Fraternity, 14–15, 63–89, 244; Being and, 66; civilization and, 64–65; Hitlerism and, 64; solidarity and, 72–73, 74
Freedom: as American mission, 6; Christianity and, 26–27, 29; as gift, 128, 144; heroic, 33; individualism and, 34, 148–49; liberty and, 63; love and, 173–74; others and, 173; as state, 144–45; truth and, 26–27, 39–40; violence and, 13
French Revolution, 30, 54, 63, 70–72, 208, 246
Freud, Sigmund, 224

Gaita, Raimond, 82
Gautier, Paul, 192
Gift, giving, 123, 240; alterity and, 15; cry and, 142; recognition and, 143–59; self as, 16, 155; subjectivity and, 142–43; time as, 67
Gilroy, Paul, 5
Girard, René, 224
Globalization, 228
Glover, Jonathan, 51
God: death of, 118–21; Other and, 108–17
Goldstein, Joshua, 219
Goodness, 18, 69, 239, 270 n. 76
Gordon, Lewis, 7, 98, 116–17, 127, 134, 150, 189, 222, 246, 306 n. 69
Grace and liberation, 26
Gramsci, Antonio, 48
Guevara, Ché, 122

Habermas, Jürgen, 123, 126–27, 147, 229, 253
Hadot, Pierre, 278 n. 7
Hardt, Michael, 285 n. 60
Hart, William, 282 n. 33
Harvey, Van A., 109–10
Hegel, G. W. F.: on consciousness, 110–11; on idea, 98; on I/Thou, 111; on master/slave, 94, 106; on

Hegel, G. W. F. (*continued*)
self-possession, 144, 145; on Spirit, 125–26
Heidegger, Martin: on authenticity, 52, 60–61; on community of masters, 13–14; on Hitler, 25; on ideology of war, 52–63; interview with, 58–59; on metaphysics, 276 n. 117; Nazism and, 14, 53–54, 56, 58–60; on philosophy, 266 n. 47
Hellenistic Humanism (Dussel), 192–93
Henri-Levy, Bernard, 253
Hintikka, Jaako, 169
Histoire philosophique (Raynal), 197
Hitler, Adolf, 57
Hitlerism, 23–50; Cartesianism vs., 243; as community of masters, 13–14, 47–48; detachment from morality of, 24; fraternity and, 64; liberalism and, 26–28, 64, 246; nationalism and, 58–59; philosophy of, 25–29, 62, 63, 196; will to power and, 42
Holocaust, 10, 59
Homosexuality, 184–85
Honneth, Axel, 124–29, 146–48
Hospitality, 138, 244
Humanity (Glover), 51
Humanization, 153
Humanness/non-humanness, 7–8, 238
Huntington, Patricia, 73
Husserl, Edmund: on community of masters, 13; on Eurocentrism, 43–49; on exclusion/inclusion, 43–49; on phenomenology, 25, 35–49, 167–72, 206–7, 210–11; on psychologism, 46; on reality, 172; on sense, 171; on transcendental subjectivity, 166
Hyletic data, 169–70
Hypotheses for the Study of Latin America in Universal History (Dussel), 193–94

I conquer concept, 189, 204–5, 215–16, 223, 226
Ideals of war, 2–3, 24, 52, 54–55, 87, 89
Identity, 10–11, 188, 189–92, 201, 202, 248
Ideology of war, 53–63, 73–76, 95
Imperial Eyes (Pratt), 203
Imperialism, 5, 47, 61, 107, 146, 238
Imperial Man, 114–19
Inclusion, 43–49
Individuality: authentic, 54, 57; community vs., 64; freedom and, 34, 148–49; heroic, 34, 67; restriction of, 41
Intentionality, 39, 55
Intuition, 40
Invention of the Americas (Dussel), 17–18, 188–89, 203, 207, 212, 224–25

James, C. L. R., 197
Jaspers, Karl, 293 n. 48
Judaism: Levinas on, 9–10; Nietzsche on, 29–30
Judy, Ronald A. T., 281 n. 21
Justice, 61, 75, 78–89

Kierkegaard, Søren, 132, 135, 297–98 n. 75
knowledge: geopolitics of, 183, 231; theory of, 37–38
Koselleck, Reinhart, 188, 195–98, 201–2, 207–9

Language, 137
Las Casas, Bartolomé de, 204, 212
Levi, Primo, 253
Levinas, Emmanuel: on colonialism and racism, 5; on death of Other, 157; on the diabolical, 53; Dussel, Fanon, and, 3, 9, 187–89; on eros,

66–67, 177; on fecundity, 67–70; on fraternity, 62–89; on freedom, 13, 34, 173, 247; on Hitlerism, 1, 23–50, 52, 68–69, 246; on Judaic spirituality, 9–10; on morality, 51, 237; on ontology of war, 60–61; on Other, 174–75, 177–78; on phenomenology, 37–38; on philosophy, 84, 93; as racialized subject, 5; on reduction, 93–94; on self-affirmation, 247–48; on subalterity, 6; on subjectivity and human experience, 8, 24, 80–81; on theodicy and evil, 23; theory of knowledge of, 37–38; on violence, 13, 24, 25, 62, 77

Liberalism: equality and, 29–30, 63; fraternity and, 63, 65; Hitlerism and, 26–28, 63; liberty and, 63, 64

Liberation theology, 9–10, 179–86, 188, 235, 250

Liberty, 63–64, 71, 151

Losurdo, Domenico, 54

L'Ouverture, Toussaint, 197

Love: cry and, 140–41; de-colonial, 244, 245, 252–53; freedom and, 173–74; gift and, 123, 240; recognition and, 16, 156; reign of, 117; of wisdom, 84; wisdom of, 82, 83, 93, 121, 253

Lucidity, 24, 51

Malcolm X, 5
Man vs. nature, 110–11
Marx, Karl, 235–36
Master morality, 2–3, 5, 13–14, 35, 53–54, 60, 94, 223–25, 246, 252
Master-slave relationship, 15–17, 102–8, 112, 120, 129–31, 142–43, 150, 153, 187, 245, 249
May 1968 demonstrations, 14, 86, 89
Mèlich, Joan-Charles, 46–47
Methods, 98

Mignolo, Walter, 203, 261–62 n. 51
Moctezuma, 212, 214
Modernity: Christianity and, 11; colonialism and, 3–4; crisis in, 28; de-colonial turn and, 3–4, 228; emergence of, 202; myth of, 200, 212; paradigm of war and, 187, 189, 213, 218, 223, 225–26, 232, 238, 242; roots of, 210, 214; subalterity in, 6; violence and, 2; war as central feature of, 4, 232. *See also* Transmodernity
Moraga, Cherríe, 254
Morality: master, 2–3, 5, 13–14, 35, 53–54, 60, 94, 223–25, 246, 252; of slaves, 30, 32, 41; suspension of, 24, 51

Nationalism, 58–59, 64
National Socialism. *See* Hitlerism
Naturalization of war: death ethic and, 4; Nietzsche on, 2, 32–33
Nature vs. man, 110–11
Nazism. *See* Hitlerism
Negri, Antonio, 285 n. 60
Nietzsche, Friedrich: on community of masters, 13; on Jews, 29–30; on liberalism, 31; on nihilism, 29–35; on phenomenology, 25; on power, 32–33, 42, 52; on slave morality, 224; on war as normal, 2, 32–33
Nihilism, 29–35, 85
Noema, 167–70
Non-being, 104–5, 107, 181–82, 223
Non-ethics of war, 217–21, 225
Non-humanness, 7–8, 238

Oliver, Kelly, 297 n. 71, 299–300 n. 84
Ontology of war, 60–61, 73, 104–5, 144, 180
Orientalism, 199
Other: Being and, 15, 61, 65, 181–83, 240–42, 244; death and, 67, 77,

Other (*continued*)
  140, 156–57; desire and, 157–58; of Europe, 184; freedom and, 173–74; genetic phenomenology and, 175–76; giving and, 15, 79, 81, 83, 151; God and, 108–17; humanism of, 6; infinity of, 84; master and, 102, 106, 150, 154; self and, 6, 17–18, 60, 66, 176, 185, 237, 239; subjectivity and, 75, 80
Otherwise Than Being (Levinas), 14, 78–89, 242

Pagden, Anthony, 209–10
Paradigm of war: defined, 3; modernity and, 187, 189, 218, 223, 225–26, 232, 238, 242; origins of, 4
Pardon, 34, 69, 86, 247
Passive geneses, 171
Paternity, 68
Peace, eschatology of, 62, 270 n. 76
Persuasion, 47
Petitdemange, Guy, 298–99 n. 80
Phenomenology: of colonization, 207; of cry, 133–37; of eros, 66; of Fanon, 12–13, 93–94; genetic, 175, 183; Hitlerism and, 25; of Husserl, 25, 35–49, 167–72, 206–7, 210–11; reduction and, 35, 36, 38–39, 93–94, 166
Phenomenology of Spirit (Hegel), 123–24, 129, 148
Philosopher vocation, 47–48
Philosophy: as critique, 52–53; as love of wisdom, 84; as wisdom of love, 82, 83, 93, 121, 253
Philosophy of history, 195–203, 208
Philosophy of Liberation (Dussel), 179–85, 191, 225, 227
Plato, 275–76 n. 117
Politics, 74–76, 79, 89, 94–97, 152, 188
Positivism, 36

Power: coloniality of, 217–18; Nietzsche on, 32–33, 42, 52; philosophy of, 62
Pratt, Mary Louise, 198, 201, 203, 209
Presence, 115

Quijano, Anibal, 217
Quixote, Don, 241, 242, 245, 248–49

Race: determinism and, 28; idea of, 220; naturalization of war and, 218, 220–21, 225
Racism: colonialism and, 3, 5–6, 95–97, 99–101, 130, 218–19, 221–22, 243–44; Fanon on, 1, 5, 88, 137–42, 184–85; ideals of war and, 2–3, 87; Nietzsche on, 33; roots in *reconquista* of, 3; science and, 198–99; search for truth and, 41; slavery and, 217, 221
Ramadan, Tariq, 253
Rape, 220–21
Rawls, John, 123
Raynal, Buillaume-Thomas-François, 196–97
Reason, 78
Recognition, 117–21; slaves and, 16, 122–23; struggle for, 122, 123–30, 143–50, 151
Reduction: de-colonial, 15, 89, 98–102, 188; ethical, 83–84, 93; phenomenological, 35, 36, 38–39, 93–94
"Reflections on the Philosophy of Hitlerism" (Levinas), 25–26
Relativism, 43–44, 99
Religions, 12
Revolt, ethical, 137–42
Reyes Mate, Martin, 25
Ricoeur, Paul, 191
Rights of Man, 14, 26, 28, 30
Rosenzweig, Franz, 49

Sacrifice, 54
Sandoval, Chela, 5, 7, 233, 244
Sartre, Jean-Paul, 101, 152, 167–70, 172–74, 258–59 n. 30, 277 n. 125
Science, 198–99
Secular-religious divide, 12
Self-possession, 144, 145
Semitic Humanism (Dussel), 191–92, 193
Senses, 171–72
Sexism, 73, 219
Sexual revolution, 74
Sharpley-Whiting, T. Denean, 219
"Signature" (Levinas), 23
Skepticism, 35–37, 41, 82, 96, 99, 118–19
Slaves: freedom and, 144; morality of, 30, 32, 41, 224; racism and, 217; recognition and, 16, 122–23; religion and, 283 n. 43. *See also* Master-slave relationship
Smith, Linda Tuhiwai, 7
Sokolowski, Robert, 169–72
Solidarity, 72–73
Sons, 68–69
Spanish *reconquista*, 3, 4, 5
Spirit, 125–26, 146, 188, 194, 199
Spivak, Gayatri, 261 n. 46
Spoils of War (Sharpley-Whiting and White), 219
Struggle, 55, 73; for recognition, 122, 123–30, 143–50, 151
Struggle for Recognition (Honneth), 124–25
Subalterity, 6, 11, 127, 239, 240
Subjectivity: authenticity and, 55; consciousness and, 40; ethical critique and, 15; freedom and, 155; giving and, 142–43; human experience and, 8, 24, 49, 80–81, 187; transcendental, 166
Substitution, 154–55

Taylor, Charles, 123–24, 125, 211, 251
Temporality, 67, 69
Theodicy, Western, 7, 23
Theory of Intuition (Levinas), 39–40
Theory uprising, 5
Time: discontinuity of, 70; as gift, 67; human beings and, 98; present, 115
Time and the Other (Levinas), 174–75, 177
Todorov, Tzvetan, 4, 214–15
Torquemada, Juan de, 214
Tosquelles, François, 287 n. 16
Totality and Infinity (Levinas), 23–24, 51, 52, 62–63, 68–69, 74–75, 179, 241
Transmodernity, 11–12, 226–35, 257 n. 21, 308 n. 90
Truth: freedom and, 27, 39–40; justice and, 75; possibility of war and, 51; search for, 28, 29, 41

"Understanding of Spirituality in French and German Culture" (Levinas), 262–63 n. 2
Universal Declaration of Human Rights, 76
Universality, 41–42, 44–50, 152, 296 n. 69

Vattimo, Gianni, 230
Victimization, 78
Violence: freedom and, 13, 174; ideals of war and, 2–3, 24, 52, 62, 78, 87, 89, 249; modernity and, 2; sexuality and, 73; sources of, 24, 224

Wallerstein, Immanuel, 71–72
War: death ethics of, 4, 218, 221, 226, 240; ideals of, 2–3, 24, 52, 54–55, 87, 89; ideology of, 53–63, 73–76, 95; modernity and, 4, 187, 189, 213, 218, 223, 225–26, 232, 238, 242; naturalization of, 2, 4, 32–33; non-

War (continued)
  ethics of, 217–21, 225; as normal, 2, 32–33; ontology of, 60–61, 73, 104–5, 144, 180; paradigm of, 3, 4, 187, 189, 218, 223, 225–26, 232, 238, 242; race and, 218, 220–21, 225; as regenerative, 57; truth and, 51; violence and, 2–3, 24, 52, 62, 78, 87, 89, 249

Weber, Max, 261 n. 49, 262 n. 51
White, Renée T., 219
Wisdom of love, 82, 83, 93, 121, 253
Women, 72, 219–20, 224, 271 n. 87
Wretched of the Earth (Fanon), 142
Wynter, Sylvia, 216–17, 285 n. 61

Zapatista, Ejercito, 234, 308 n. 90, 308 n. 101
Zera, Rav, 247

NELSON MALDONADO-TORRES is an assistant professor of ethnic studies at the University of California, Berkeley.

Library of Congress Cataloging-in-Publication Data
Maldonado Torres, Nelson.
Against war : views from the underside of modernity / Nelson Maldonado-Torres.
p. cm. — (Latin America otherwise)
Includes bibliographical references and index.
ISBN 978-0-8223-4146-8 (cloth)
ISBN 978-0-8223-4170-3 (pbk.)
1. War (Philosophy) 2. Postcolonialism. 3. Civilization, Modern. 4. Postmodernism. 5. Political science—Philosophy. I. Title.
B105.W3M35 2008   172'.42—dc22
2007039436

www.ingramcontent.com/pod-product-compliance
Lightning Source LLC
Chambersburg PA
CBHW070745020526
44116CB00032B/1974